Geotourism:
The Tourism of Geology and Landscape

Edited by

David Newsome
Murdoch University, Australia

and

Ross K. Dowling
Edith Cowan University, Australia

 Goodfellow Publishers Ltd

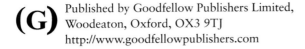

(G) Published by Goodfellow Publishers Limited,
Woodeaton, Oxford, OX3 9TJ
http://www.goodfellowpublishers.com

British Library Cataloguing in Publication Data: a catalogue record
for this title is available from the British Library.

Library of Congress Catalog Card Number: on file.

ISBN: 978-1-906884-09-3

Design and typesetting by P.K. McBride, www.macbride.org.uk

Printed by Marston Book Services, www.marston.co.uk

Cover design by Cylinder, www.cylindermedia.com

Cover photo: Uluru (Ayers Rock) is a 340 m high inselberg comprised of feslpathic
sandstone. It is one of the world's iconic landforms located in the heart of the continent
and visited by approximately 450,000 people every year. The rock's original sedimentary
layers have been tilted almost to the vertical as a result of mountain building which
occurred some 300–400 million years ago. Together 'The Rock', as it is universally
known, and some nearby rock domes (Kata Tjuta) located west of Uluru, combine to
form spectacular geological formations that dominate the vast plains of central Australia.
For these values, the area was inscribed on the World Heritage List in 1987.

Source: Jane Newsome.

Contents

Dedication

To our wives and families

Jane, Benjamin and Rachel Newsome

and

Wendy Dowling and Jayne, Trevor, Shenee & Paige Belstead (England);
Simon, Lynette, Amelie & Exan MacLennan (Australia); Mark, Jess & Nessa
Dowling (Australia); Tobias & HyeHyang Dowling (China), Aurora, Mike,
Helena & Nina Gibbs (New Zealand) and Francis Dowling (New Zealand)

About the editors

David Newsome

David Newsome is an Associate Professor in the School of Environmental Science at Murdoch University, Perth, Western Australia. His principal research interests are geotourism and the biophysical impacts of recreation and tourism in protected areas. Professor Newsome's research and teaching focus on the sustainable recreational use of landscapes and the assessment and management of tourism activity in protected areas. He is the lead author of two books *Natural Area Tourism: Ecology, Impacts and Management* and *Wildlife Tourism* and co-editor of *Geotourism*, a book which has helped set the scene for the emergence of geotourism as a distinct discipline within the area of natural area tourism.

Ross K. Dowling

Ross Dowling is Foundation Professor of Tourism in the School of Marketing, Tourism and Leisure, Faculty of Business and Law, at Edith Cowan University in Western Australia. Internationally he is an Advisor, UNESCO Global Network of National Geoparks, Executive Board Member of the Indian Ocean Tourism Organization, and Co-founder, International Cruise Research Society. In Australia he is Co-founder and Executive Director of Ecotourism Australia as well as an Advisor to Cruise Down Under. In Western Australia he is Chair of the Forum Advocating Cultural and Eco Tourism (FACET) as well as a Council Member of the Royal Automobile Club and the Minister of Tourism's appointee to the Council of the National Trust.

Professor Dowling conducts international research in the fields of geotourism, cruise ship tourism and ecotourism and has 200 publications. In recent years he has co-authored or co-edited eight books on tourism. They are *Ecotourism, Tourism in Destination Communities, Natural Area Tourism, Ecotourism Policy and Planning, Wildlife Tourism, Geotourism, Cruise Ship Tourism* and *Coastal Tourism Development*. Two have been translated into Chinese, one into Persian and others published in India.

In 2008 he convened the Inaugural Global Geotourism Conference in Australia and was Advisor to the Sarawak Tourism Board for the Second Global Geotourism Conference held in Mulu. Malaysian Borneo in 2010.

Together with his wife Wendy, Ross Dowling is a director of the tourism consultancy Ideology which carries out international tourism planning, training and development (www.ideology.net.au).

Contributors

Ari Brozinski is a geologist currently working on his geotourism PhD in Turku, Finland. His research combines modern ICTs with geology and also presents a framework for geotourism development. Besides his research, Brozinski has worked in many geopopularisation projects covering various computer-centered technologies such as touchscreen interfaces in geological multimedia kiosks and semantic design on geoscience websites. His great passion is to find new ways tell the world how our planet operates and deliberately document them to be used again in various situations where geotourism is to be realised. Contact: ari.brozinski@utu.fi

Roy Ballantyne is the Head of the School of Tourism, University of Queensland, Australia. He has a well established international reputation for his work in environmental education, interpretation, and free-choice learning, wildlife tourism and ecotourism research. He has 86 papers in refereed journals, over 60 other publications and has a substantial record of competitive research grants including six Australian Research Council grants. He is the co-editor of the international journal *Visitor Studies*. Contact: r.ballantyne@uq.edu.au

Richard Edmonds is Earth Science Manager for the Jurassic Coast Project in Dorchester, England. Here he works in conservation, education and marketing through the promotion of geotourism. He has previously worked in the North Sea oil industry, the National Trust for Scotland, and the Charmouth Heritage Coast Centre. Contact: r.edmonds@dorsetcc.gov.uk

Anjana Ford is Education Coordinator, Jurassic Coast World Heritage Site, Dorchester, England. She is an Earth Scientist specialising in communicating ideas about geology, geomorphology and processes that form natural landscapes to a wide range of audiences. After gaining a PhD in glacial geology at the University of Southampton she moved to the USA to continue a postdoctoral research career, during which she was most inspired by time spent working with the US National Park Service. Contact: A.K.Ford@dorsetcc.gov.uk

Wesley Hill is the International Secretariat of The Geological Society of America (GSA). Ms. Hill managed the geotourism program at GSA for many years and currently manages GSA's international affairs and is very involved with bringing the USA into the Global Geoparks Network. Ms. Hill is on the UNESCO Geoparks Advisory Board, Member of the IUCN World Commission on Protected Areas, Member of the Executive Committee of the International Union of Geological Sciences (IUGS), and Member of the US National Committee for the International Year of Planet Earth. Contact: whill@geosociety.org

Tom Hose is a Principal Lecturer in tourism at Buckinghamshire New University, previously working as a biologist and geologist in UK museums and schools. His long-standing commitment to geoconservation, presently for GeoconservationUK, the British Institute of Geological Conservation and ProGEO underpins his expertise as a field naturalist and geologist – crucial in his recognising, defining and developing the geotourism concept for his groundbreaking doctoral thesis on geotourism. Over the past 20 years he has authored numerous geotourism book chapters, journal articles, conference papers and consultancy reports. Contact: Tom.Hose@bucks.ac.uk

Karen Hughes is a Senior Research Officer in the School of Tourism, University of Queensland, Australia. She has worked as a tourism researcher and lecturer for many years and has a particular interest in environmental interpretation, interpretive signage, free-choice environmental learning and visitor research. Karen has recently completed a PhD exploring the impacts of post-visit support on families' conservation learning at wildlife tourism sites. She is a co-author of the book *Designing Effective Interpretive Signs – Principles in Practice*, published by Fulcrum Press, Colorado (USA) in 2007. Contact: k.hughes2@uq.edu.au

Min Huh is Professor of Paleontology in the Faculty of Earth Systems and Environmental Sciences, Chonnam National University, South Korea, and Director of the Korea Dinosaur Research Center. During the past decade he has undertaken several projects on dinosaur excavation and contributed to develop many dinosaur geotourism sites in Korea. He is currently Vice-president of Korean Committee for inscription of UNESCO World Heritage on Korean Cretaceous Dinosaur Coast, Korea. Contact: minhuh@chonnam.ac.kr

John Hull is a Senior Lecturer at the New Zealand Tourism Research Institute at AUT University, Auckland, New Zealand. His present research addresses tourism development issues in peripheral regions. John is a guest professor at the Icelandic Tourism Research Centre and has been Project Director for Northeast Iceland's strategic tourism plan and geotourism workshop. His past clients include the UNWTO, UNCBD, UNEP, UNESCO, World Bank, Nordic Council, European Tourism Research Institute, Commission on Environmental Cooperation, Canadian Tourism Commission, and Parks Canada. Contact: jhull@aut.ac.nz

Edmund Bernard Joyce is Honorary Principal Fellow at the School of Earth Sciences of The University of Melbourne, Australia. He is the former Chair of the Australian Heritage Commission Natural Evaluation Panel (Victoria), and for more than 20 years the Convener of the Standing Committee for Geological Heritage of the Geological Society of Australia. There he convened heritage workshops, produced the first report on Australian sites of National and International significance, and a volume on geological heritage methodology. He is currently studying volcanic landforms and how best to look after the landscape heritage of the new Kanawinka Global Geopark. Contact: ebj@unimelb.edu.au

Jonathan Karkut is a specialist in project development, design and management for London Metropolitan University, England. Foci have included research around intangible heritage and its application within tourism, tourism in conflict and post-conflict regions, and geotourism with reference to sites of active vulcanicity. He is now studying for his PhD by combining experience in exploration geology and in the anthropology of tourism to provide a critical analysis of the geoparks global network. Contact: j.karkut@londonmet.ac.uk

Hyun Joo Kim is a Doctoral candidate in Sedimentary Geology, Department of Earth Environmental Sciences, Pukyong National University, Korea. She has participated in several researches on the interpretation of the Cretaceous paleoenvironments of Korea and excavation and reconstruction of various fossils including dinosaur. She has previously worked with the Program of Natural History Experience, where she guided children through Korean Cretaceous dinosaur and bird track sites and museums. Contact: sunstay@pknu.ac.kr

Sook Ju Kim is Master of Science and a Research Assistant in the Department of Earth Environmental Sciences, Pukyong National Universtiy, Korea. She studied Geotourism and wrote the thesis for the degree of M.S., 'Cretaceous geological records along the rocky coast of Busan, Korea as a Geotourism site'. She has also participated in the excavation and reconstruction of dinosaur fossils. She has previously worked as a guide for the Program of Natural History Experience for children. Contact: namul486@pknu.ac.kr

Lisa King is a PhD student in Tourism at James Cook University, Cairns, Australia. She is a third generation field geologist who holds degrees in science, ecotourism, and education. Lisa's research interests include visitor monitoring and management within World Heritage geosites, branding and marketing geosites, and geosite 'collecting' behaviour by geotourists. Currently she is conducting research in the Hawaiian Islands; Queensland, Australia and southeast Asia. She has published book chapters on lava tube tourism and geotourism in the Hawaiian Islands and on Jeju Island, S. Korea. Contact: volcanolisa@hotmail.com

Sally King is the Visitor Manager for the Jurassic Coast World Heritage Site in Dorset and East Devon, UK. Sally's success in managing the inherent conflict between attracting visitors to the Jurassic Coast whilst protecting one of the world's most important geological sites was recognised through the Jurassic Coast winning the international Tourism for Tomorrow Award. Sally has also spent time involved in conservation tourism in Namibia. Contact: s.a.king@dorsetcc.gov.uk

Yu-Fai Leung is an associate professor in the Department of Park, Recreation and Tourism Management at North Carolina State University, USA. His interests focus on recreation ecology and sustainable visitor management in protected areas. His research supports the development of visitor impact indicators and monitoring programs in national parks in the U.S. and East Asia. He has published papers in various peer-reviewed journals and as chapters in edited books. He is a founding member of the Recreation Ecology Research Network and a member of IUCN's World Commission on Protected Areas. Contact: Leung@ncsu.edu.

Wojciech Mayer is a geologist and Assistant Professor at the AGH-University of Science and Technology in Kraków, Poland. He is working in geology, mineralogy and geochemistry of ore deposits, and in geotourism. He was the co-organizer of education in Geotourism and in Tourism & Recreation at the AGH-UST. He was one of the founders of the International Association for Geotourism (IAGt) and is its current Secretary. He is the co-editor of the *Geotourism Quarterly*. Contact: wmayer@geol.agh.edu.pl

Patrick McKeever is Principal Geologist, Geological Survey of Northern Ireland. He has run the Survey's Landscape Heritage/Geotourism sector since 1995. He has pub lished over 70 geological walking routes, 13 geotourism driving routes and numerous other popular-style books and guides to the geology of the north of Ireland. Since 2000, he has been actively involved in the geoparks movement and is currently one of the two elected coordinators of the European Geoparks Network and a member of the Global Geoparks Network Bureau. In 2009 he was the official delegate for the Republic of Ireland to the Natural Science discussions at the UNESCO General Conference. Contact: patrickgsni@yahoo.ie

Andreas Megerle is lecturer and researcher at the Institute for Regional Science of the Karlsruhe Institute of Technology, Germany. He was a member of the German Expert Board for National Geoparks and is an advisor for different geoparks and geotouristic initiatives. As initiator and manager of the Geotouristic Network History of the Earth he was one of the foundation members of the UNESCO Geopark Swabian Alb. His research mainly concerns the role of geotourism and geoparks for regional development and its management, focussed on the learning effects within heterogenous cooperation networks. Contact: megerle@kit.edu

In Sung Paik is Professor of Sedimentary Geology at Department of Earth Environmental Sciences of Pukyong National University, South Korea, and Vice-President of the Geological Society of Korea. During the past decade he has undertaken several projects on paleoenvironmental reconstruction of the Age of Dinosaurs in the Korean Peninsula, and provided a number of geological and paleobiological records in geotourism. Contact: paikis@pknu.ac.kr

Sarah Palmer is a researcher in Social Sciences and Environmental Science, at Murdoch University, Australia. She is currently researching on various projects related to ecotourism, conservation biodiversity, regional community development and natural resource management. Her main interest is in the socio-cultural aspects of science communication, public understanding of science and behaviour change. Contact: sarahpalmer14@gmail.com

Margarete Patzak is the Programme Specialist for the International Geoscience Programme and Global Geoparks Network initiative, UNESCO, France. She has completed studies in Geology and Mineralogy at the University of Würzburg, Germany and her doctorate in the mineralogy on metamorphic rocks, was completed in 1991. She is the Coordinator of European projects on the protection and conservation of cultural heritage, EUROCARE, based at the University of Karlsruhe. Contact: m.patzak@unesco.org

Sally Pearce is the director of the Scenic and Historic Byways Program for the Colorado Department of Transportation, USA. She is a nationally recognized expert on scenic byways and is a board member of the National Scenic Byways Foundation. Ms. Pearce holds an MA in History from Colorado State University and has published several books on historic mining communities. Contact: sjpearce@comcast.net

Christof Pforr is Course Coordinator (Tourism & Event Management) and Research Director in the School of Management, Curtin Business School, Curtin University, Australia. His main research interests include geotourism and regional development, tourism policy and planning, sustainable (tourism) development and coastal tourism, all fields he has frequently published in. He has contributed to more than 100 publications and numerous international research collaborations, in addition to national projects under the umbrella of the Sustainable Tourism Cooperative Research Centre and the Desert Knowledge Cooperative Research Centre. Contact: c.pforr@curtin.edu.au

Catherine Pickering conducts research at the International Centre for Ecotourism, Griffith University, Australia. She has undertaken a wide range of research relating to ecology and tourism, including research in recreation ecology, mountain tourism, nature-based tourism, protected area management, alpine ecology and the effects of climate change on tourism destinations. She has over 140 publications, including over 60 papers published in international referred academic journals. Contact: c.pickering@griffith.edu.au

Pascal Scherrer is a Research Fellow in Sustainable Tourism, School of Natural Sciences, Edith Cowan University, Australia. His main research interest is in sustainable tourism and visitor management in natural areas, addressing environmental and social impacts and their relationship. His research and publications span the areas of sustainable tourism, alpine ecology, visitor management and environmental and socio-cultural tourism impacts. He has a PhD in Environmental Science from Griffith University and a Bachelor of Science (Hons) with majors in Environmental Science and Ecotourism. Contact: p.scherrer@ecu.edu.au

Tadeusz Słomka is a professor of sedimentology, general geology, mathematical geology and geotourism at the AGH-University of Science and Technology in Kraków, Poland, and was the founder and the chief organizer of education in Geotourism and in Tourism and Recreation there. He is currently the Vice-Rector at that University. He was the Chief Editor of the 'Catalogue of Geotouristic Sites in Poland', and the Chief Editor of the Geotourism quarterly. He was the founder of the International Association for Geotourism (IAGt) and is recently its Vice-president. Contact: slomka@geol.agh.edu.pl

Kevin Stewart is a professor of Geological Sciences at the University of North Carolina at Chapel Hill, USA. His research is focused on the structural geology and tectonics of mountain belts. He has worked in the southern Appalachian Mountains of North Carolina, the Rocky Mountains of Montana, Wyoming, and New Mexico, and the Apennine Mountains of Italy. Contact: kgstewar@email.unc.edu

Stacy Supak is a PhD student in the Department of Parks, Recreation and Tourism, North Carolina State University, USA. She holds a B.S. in Civil Environmental Engineering from Columbia University and an M.S. in Geophysics from the University of California at Santa Barbara. Her current interests relate to quantifying and understanding trends in nature-based tourism. Contact: sksupak@ncsu.edu

Judy Walden is the president of Walden Mills Group, Denver, Colorado, USA, a consultancy that specializes in economic development for rural communities, many serving as gateways to public lands with significant geologic features. She has worked to help designate Scenic and Historic Byways across North America, and has developed tourism training materials that teach local residents and tourism business owners the concepts of interpretation, resource protection and tourism ethics. Prior to her work in tourism, she was the Vice President of Educational Services for Colorado Mountain College. Contact: walden.judy@q.com

Jutta Weber is Geoscience and Public Relations Manager of the Global and European Geopark Bergstrasse-Odenwald, Germany. She is member of the European Geoparks Network (EGN) and of the Global Geoparks expert group and on the Editorial Board of the EGN. During the last decade, she has contributed to the Geoparks issue with papers, presentations and workshops at EGN and GGN conferences. Contact: j.weber@geo-naturpark.de.

Christian Wittlich is a PhD student who researches in the field of environmental education and interpretation. A 2007 research project brought him to New Zealand where he studied Geography and Environmental Science and investigated geotourism on Rangitoto Island. He currently contributes as a research assistant and tutor to the Geography Didactics team at Mainz University. Contact: C.Wittlich@geo.uni-mainz.de

Nickolas Zouros is a Professor in Physical Geography, Department of Geography, University of the Aegean, Greece. He has been the Director of the Natural History Museum of the Lesvos Petrified Forest since its foundation in 1995. He is one of the founders of the European Geoparks Network in 2000 and is a member of the UNESCO Global Geoparks Bureau. He was co-convenor of several Geopark Conferences and is the author of several articles and books on Geoparks, geoconservation and geotourism. Contact: nzour@aegean.gr

Preface

Geotourism is an exciting subject that has arisen out of the nexus between geology and tourism. While interest in both subjects has been around since time immemorial, it is only in relatively recent times that tourism specifically to see geological features has been put in the spotlight.

The 'Grand Tour' of the 19th century was primarily for tourists to see and experience the natural and cultural features of Europe and of course the establishment of the National Parks System in the USA over 100 years ago was mainly to protect America's wild lands and landscapes from forestry, mining and other exploitative activities as a form of conservation through tourism. In the latter part of the last century, environmental tourism emerged as a separate discipline within tourism, largely through the growth of ecotourism, with its focus on tourism in natural areas which is sustainable, conservation supporting, educative and locally beneficial.

Then in the early part of the 2000s, geotourism emerged as an area of interest with research and conference initiatives and the establishment of geoparks. The editors of this volume contributed through their earlier book on *Geotourism* (Dowling and Newsome eds, Butterworth Heinemann, UK, 2006) and their hosting of the Inaugural Global Geotourism Conference 'Discover the Earth Beneath our Feet'. This was held in Perth, Western Australia from 17-20 August 2008. Over 220 delegates from 36 countries participated in the conference which was held to broaden our knowledge of geotourism and introduce the concept of geoparks to Australia. Major supporters of the conference were Tourism Western Australia and the Department of Environment and Conservation; as well as Tourism Australia, Edith Cowan University, the Geological Survey of Western Australia and the National Trust of Western Australia. The conference was held during the International Year of Planet Earth and was endorsed by UNESCO.

For the conference a 478 page book was produced, *Geotourism – Inaugural Global Geotourism Conference Proceedings* (Dowling and Newsome, eds, Promaco Conventions, Australia, 2008). It comprised over 100 abstracts and papers and quickly became sold out due to strong demand for information on the subject.

Arising from this interest we decided to publish a new book to update the subject we first visited in 2006. Interest in our project grew and so this volume represents the first of two new books on the topic. This volume is specifically designed to set the scene and provide a clear definition of geotourism as well as provide information on its characteristics. Thus it contains content on landscape appreciation, geoheritage, management, interpretation, education and the future of geotourism.

Our second publication *Global Geotourism Perspectives* (Dowling and Newsome, eds, Goodfellow Publishers, 2010) brings together in the second volume a range of case studies of geotourism from a number of countries including Australia, Brazil, China, Greece, Malaysia, Mauritius, Oman, South Africa and the USA. Taken together the two books propel the subject to another level and provide an informed platform on which to build the future of geotourism.

Naturally these two books form only part of the picture. There are other books and journals, emerging research and of course now many conferences on geotourism. Recent books have included *GeoTourism in Ethiopia* (Asrat, Demissie, and Mogessie, eds, Shama Books, Ethiopia, 2009) and *Geotourism and Local Development* (de Carvalho and Rodrigues, eds, Câmara Municipal de Idanha-a-Nova and Geopark Naturtejo da Meseta Meridional, Portugal, 2009).

Journals include *GeoTurystyka* [*Geotourism*], published by the International Association of Geotourism in Poland (www.geoturystyka.pl) and *Geoheritage* published by ProGeo, the European Association for the Conservation of the Geological Heritage, Portugal (www.springer.com). Another useful publication is *Earth Heritage*, 'The Geological and Landscape Conservation Magazine', published by the Joint Nature Conservation Committee, Natural England, the Scottish Natural Heritage and the Countryside Council for Wales (www.seaburysalmon.com/earth.html).

Research is being conducted in a range of countries as evidenced by the chapters in this book and its companion. Conferences abound on the subject with the World Heritage and Geotourism Conference hosted by the Geological Society of South Africa, held in Pretoria from 4–5 June 2009; the 8th European Geoparks Conference focusing on Geotourism, held from 12–14 September 2009 at Geopark Naturtejo, Portugal and the Second Global Geotourism Conference held from 17–20 April 2010 at Gunung Mulu World Heritage Region, Sarawak, Borneo, Malaysia.

Thus the subject of geotourism is growing rapidly. This book is a research volume which aims to add knowledge to the many facets of this emerging subject. It has been compiled for a broad audience including natural area tourism professionals, planners and managers; government and business decision-makers; and students from a wide range of disciplines seeking general information on geotourism development in one volume. We hope that you enjoy it as well as its companion volume of case studies, *Global Geotourism Perspectives*.

David Newsome and Ross Dowling

Perth, Australia

February 2010

Acknowledgements

The editors would like to thank a number of people who contributed to this book. They include the authors and publishing staff. First we would like to thank the contributors, all 33 of them. Some we have known for many years and have worked with before, others were unknown to us before this project. Some are emerging new or young researchers whereas others are icon academics and well established authors. All we have got to know better through the many iterations of the text during the evolution of the book and we salute each and every one of you for having the faith in this project and the fortitude to deal with our demands over a long period of time. This book is yours and we know that it has been immeasurably enriched by your contributions.

We particularly wish to thank the staff of Goodfellow Publishers, Oxford, England, especially Tim Goodfellow (Co-Director) and our old friend Sally North (Publisher), who worked with us on our first book on Geotourism back in 2006.

Individually as editors we wish to thank some people.

David Newsome

I would like to express my thanks to Professor Nick Costa (former Dean of the School of Environmental Science) and Professor Stuart Bradley (Dean of the Faculty of Sustainability, Environmental and Life Sciences) who facilitated the completion of this project through an approved Outside Studies Programme at Murdoch University.

In addition I would like to thank my wife Jane for her support in managing the household when we have hosted international visitors and during the times that I have been away on fieldwork. I am particularly grateful to Steve Martin for assistance during a visit to the Grand Canyon National Park and to Tom Hose for helpful discussions on the definition of geotourism. Thanks also go to Associate Professor Yu-Fai Leung and Professor In Sung Paik who are recent collaborators in geotourism research.

As always I would like to give thanks to the Newsome family in the UK who have, and continue to, provide support for fieldwork in England and Wales. Appreciation goes to Ken and Paul Newsome and to my sister Linda for continuing the great family tradition of cooking the best liver and onion casserole in England. Sadly, my mother, who brought me into this world, is not here to share in the success of previous book writing endeavours. Finally I would like to thank the unknown midwife who said to my mother upon my arrival on this planet 'this boy will travel'.

Ross Dowling

I would like to thank my co-editor David Newsome. We have worked well together over the years authoring and editing a number of books. As always the experience in co-editing this book has been extremely productive and very enjoyable.

My love of geology began through the interest of a friend, Donald Lumsdon, from Nelson, New Zealand. He started my lifetime fascination with the subject. My interests were further enhanced by the comprehensive knowledge of an early lecturer and mentor, Professor Paul Williams, Professor of Geography and globally recognised Karst Geomorphologist, whilst I studied under his direction at the University of Auckland, New Zealand. In recent years I acknowledge my renewed interest comes from working with my co-editor David Newsome, a passionate advocate of exploring and understanding the world through the appreciation of landforms.

As with all previous books, I wish to acknowledge the support of my employer, Edith Cowan University, one of Australia's leading new generation universities that is committed to excellence in teaching and research. It is a truly great university.

Initial thanks goes to Professor Kerry Cox (Vice Chancellor) who continues to inspire me and encourage me to achieve great things, A/Professor David Clark-Murphy (Head, School of Marketing, Tourism and Leisure), and Tourism Program Staff Dr Dale Sanders and Dr Iris Mao. In addition Julie Connolly, Anna Johansson and Leishele Pearce (Administration Officers, School of Marketing, Tourism and Leisure) have also contributed to my work through their excellence as efficient administrators and superb colleagues.

I also wish to thank my many Australian and international students from around the world who have participated in my undergraduate and postgraduate geotourism classes. We have had a lot of fun and I have learned a lot about the industry from your research assignments and oral presentations.

Finally I wish to thank my wife Wendy for her unfailing love and support through this my ninth book in the last nine years. I could not have achieved this without her. I also wish to thank my children and grandchildren for the contributions they have made, and continue to make, to my life. This book is part of my legacy for you all.

1 Setting an agenda for geotourism

David Newsome and Ross Dowling

Introduction

Travel to and appreciation of natural landscapes and geological phenomena continues to grow as a niche area of tourism. Despite economic recessions, political problems, the increasing price of oil and even the risk of natural disasters, such as volcanic eruptions, people still yearn for new experiences and need to fulfil that deep aspect our humanity, which is having a sense of wonder about the planet we live on. It is our belief that geotourism will continue to rise as an important tourism activity as our planet becomes increasingly overcrowded, as wild places continue to be diminished and people strive for sustainable lifestyles and authentic natural experiences.

Geotourism, as a distinct subsector of natural area tourism, has quickly evolved since the rapid expansion of the global geopark movement from 2002 onwards and the publication of Dowling and Newsome (2006). Accordingly, this is the second book that comprehensively explores the nexus between landscape, geological phenomena and tourism. As with its predecessor, in this book various researchers, specialists, practitioners and protected area managers from different countries have been invited to contribute their thoughts and experience of geotourism. This book therefore contains examples of geotourism concepts, development and practice from around the world. These accounts of geotourism provide insight and scope for further discussion as to what geotourism is, how it might be promoted, on how to present geotourism to the visitor, views on the management of geotourism and collectively they build and help to set an agenda for the future.

A question of definition

Hose (2008) fully explores the history surrounding the definition of geotourism and points out that a definition was not published until 1995 (see Hose, 1995). He also examines (Chapter 2 in this book) where geotourism has come from and further considers the importance of the historical perspective in helping to define what geotourism is today. However, the definition of geotourism remains contentious due to the promotion of a broad meaning as advanced by *National Geographic* (undated). Nonetheless, the extent to which a particular definition of geotourism will be accepted will depend on individual interpretation as to how someone wishes to develop geotourism and associated tourism activity in a particular country and/or location.

It is clear that as a consequence of the confusion surrounding the definition of geotourism there is a need for clarity. Moreover in order to set a widey accepted definition, and in an attempt to avoid confusion, the discussion here follows on from the first published definitions by Hose (1995; 2000) and expands on the argument raised by Dowling and Newsome (2006).

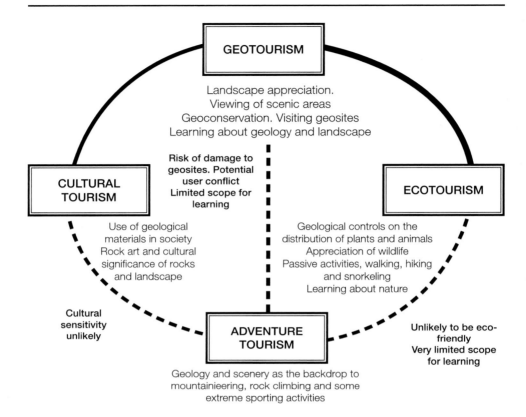

Figure 1.1: The relationship of geotourism with other forms of tourism. Solid and dashed lines represent interconnecting pathways. The connection between ecotourism and geotourism is represented as a particularly strong relationship

Figure 1.1 indicates the context of geotourism in relation to other forms of tourism. The *National Geographic* (undated) perspective includes cultural tourism and ecotourism and, possibly, because of its broad meaning, some examples of soft adventure tourism. While clearly there are strong links between geotourism and ecotourism as represented by the bold line connecting geotourism with ecotourism in Figure 1.1 and to a lesser extent with cultural tourism; the dashed lines connecting geo, cultural and ecotourism with adventure tourism (especially hard forms that overlap into extreme sporting activities) are more tenuous in regard to concepts of sustainability and an appropriate learning environment, both of which are essential aspects of natural area tourism. As indicated by Dowling and Newsome (2006) many forms of adventure tourism take place in geological settings which may be incidental to 'geotourism' as in the case of a mountain biking event taking place in a scenic setting. Alternatively geology may be the focus of the activity as with mountaineering, rock climbing, abseiling, large scale running events/challenges (e.g. Mount Kinabalu and other readily accessible and prominent mountains around the world), snowmobiling, quad biking in glacial environments and geo-caching. Activities such as these have limited capacity for a sensitive approach to environmental issues and may indeed be environmentally damaging (e.g. Cater *et al*. 2008; Newsome and Davies, 2009). With some sporting events, such as mountain bike challenges, participants and some managers informally claim there is potential for education and learning about geology but there is no evidence to support this. Geo-caching, however, has the capacity to contain a substantive educational component. Arguably the most important issue with regard to using geology as a backdrop or centrepiece for adventure tourism and physical endurance events is the message given to the wider public is that it is apparently acceptable to use the natural environment in a way that is risky in terms of environmental degradation. This is an approach that is counter to the appropriate use of natural areas in terms of conservation of geoheritage, preservation of wild places, having places for contemplation and that are inspiring to the visitor and where there is minimal disturbance to the environment. The message we wish to convey here is that in the case of adventure tourism and competitive sporting activities, there is a need for assessment of appropriate use of protected areas and a call for only those areas that are not important for conservation, ecotourism and geotourism to be available for such uses.

The National Geographic Geotourism Charter (National Geographic, 2005) emphasises sustainable aspects of tourism such as appropriate planning, destination protection, conservation of resources, interactive interpretation, tourist satisfaction and community benefit, and these are aspects of the Charter that have received widespread support. But in terms of geotourism as a particular tourism activity National Geographic stands alone in its definition (Table 1).

Table 1.1: Definitions of geotourism

Source	Definition
National Geographic (undated)	Geotourism is defined as tourism that sustains or enhances the geographical character of a place — its environment, culture, aesthetics, heritage, and the well-being of its residents.
Hose (1995)	The provision of interpretive and service facilities to enable tourists to acquire knowledge and understanding of the geology and geomorphology of a site (including its contribution to the development of the Earth sciences) beyond the level of mere aesthetic appreciation
Hose (2000)	The provision of interpretive facilities and services to promote the values and societal benefit of geologic(al) and geomorphologic(al) sites and their materials, and to ensure their conservation for the use of students, tourists and casual recreationalists
Slomka & Kicinska-Swiderska (2004)	Geotourism is an offshoot of cognitive tourism and/or adventure tourism based upon visits to geological objects (geosites) and recognition of geological processes integrated with aesthetic experiences gained by the contact with a geosite
Joyce (2006)	People going to a place to look at and learn about one or more aspects of geology and geomorphology
Dowling and Newsome (2006)	Tourism relating specifically to geology and geomorphology and the natural resources of landscape, landforms, fossil beds, rocks and minerals, with an emphasis on appreciating the processes that are creating and created such features
Newsome and Dowling (this book)	A form of natural area tourism that specifically focuses on landscape and geology. It promotes tourism to geosites and the conservation of geo-diversity and an understanding of Earth sciences through appreciation and learning. This is achieved through independent visits to geological features, use of geo-trails and view points, guided tours, geo-activities and patronage of geosite visitor centres.

The awkwardness surrounding the approach taken by *National Geographic* is reiterated in this book by Brozinski (Chapter 4). So why not use a broad definition and take from it what you need? An advantage of the National Geographic approach is the focus on sustainability but the main disadvantage is that it is so broad that it also encompasses other major forms of tourism. Karkut (Chapter 7) raises the before-mentioned issue by pointing out that a more holistic approach would expand the profile of geotourism by engaging a wider range of tourists. This is certainly our objective and considering that geotourism takes place in a range of settings in which other forms of related tourism activity are present (Figure 1.1), this combined aspect of geotourism is already taking place.

Why then is it important to pin down the definition of geotourism to something more specific? The reasoning for this is that because such an approach sets the direction as to where we need to focus our attention. Examples of this include geosite marketing, geo-interpretation and geosite management and geo-conservation. In such cases a mix of specific geological and tourism knowledge is required in order to conduct the activity with accuracy and effectiveness. A more specific definition is also important because the prime attractions at many sites around the world are primarily geological in nature, such as at Wave Rock in Western Australia, highlighting the benefits that a local community can derive from a geosite. Perhaps the most important reason of all is that without a specific definition of geotourism, a knowledge of geology and landscapes, as could be delivered through various geo-interpretive strategies, will remain poor as compared to what is presented to the public in regard to many ecosystems, plants and wild animals. Mao *et al.* (2009) indicate that geo-tourists who already know about geology like to increase their knowledge of geological sites via satisfying curiosity, intellectual stimulation and gaining memorable experiences. These aspects of learning do not only apply to people with prior knowledge of geology but also extend across many professional groups and other individuals interested in natural areas with unique features. As in the case of ecotourism, education and particularly interpretation fosters the protection of geo-diversity and appreciation and learning about geology and landscape and are fundamental components of geotourism.

To clarify the situation, we propose the following definition which builds upon those forwarded by Hose (1995; 2000; 2008), Joyce (2006) and Dowling and Newsome (2006).

> *Geotourism is a form of natural area tourism that specifically focuses on geology and landscape. It promotes tourism to geosites and the conservation of geo-diversity and an understanding of earth sciences through appreciation and learning. This is achieved through in dependent visits to geological features, use of geo-trails and view points, guided tours, geo-activities and patronage of geosite visitor centres.*

Such a definition also embraces the wider aspects of tourism activity in that visitation to geotourism destinations requires transport, access, accommodation and services, trained staff, planning and management.

The scope and content of geotourism

According to Dowling (2001) there are five key principles that define ecotourism as follows: it is nature based, ecologically sustainable, environmentally educative, locally beneficial and generates tourist satisfaction. A set of geotourism principles can also be developed in a similar fashion comprising: being geologically based, environmentally educative, generating tourist satisfaction, sustainable and being locally beneficial. The details of each principle of geotourism are considered in turn.

Geologically based

The recognition and identification of geosites is essential in order to draw up an inventory of geotourism resources. It is important to note that geotourism can take place in a range of settings that include urban environments (Figure 1.2), peri-urban locations, quarries and mine sites, agricultural land, remote natural areas and protected areas such as national parks, nature reserves and national monuments.

Figure 1.2: Graveyard at Whitby, England with headstones made of local sandstone. The source of rock and its susceptibility to weathering in a coastal environment provide content for an urban geotour.

Environmentally educative

This will comprise the specific interpretive aspects of geotourism consisting of the development of specific pre-visit and on-site pamphlets; viewpoint and geosite panel design and location; self-guiding trails (supported by books, printed guides, marked points and panels); geological gardens; guided tours (e.g. cave tours, guided fossil collecting); interpretive/visitor centres (audio-visual content, interactive displays, collections of rocks, lectures and film shows). A key aspect will be the availability and expertise of geo-guides something that it dependent upon funding and training opportunities.

Tourist satisfaction

How a tourist perceives their geotourism experience will depend on good access to geosites, and if in a remote location a safe environment in which to conduct their geotourism activities (Figure 1.3). A central part of geotourism is the interpretive component and visitors will always rate their experiences higher if they have also learned something about the landscape and geology they are visiting. Suitably attractive and detailed information at geosites and good tour guiding is therefore essential. Not all people require the same approach to tourism and managers need to cater for independent travellers as well as organised tour groups. Finally, and especially if located away from centres of population, a suitable range of accommodation must be available so that visitors can stay and maximise their opportunities to experience, enjoy and learn about a geological asset.

Figure 1.3: Viewpoint with interpretive sign at Kalbarri National Park, Western Australia. The hardened site with barrier affords safety and contains impacts that would otherwise develop at such a popular viewing location. The interpretive panel offers explanation of local geology and enhances visitor understanding of the view.

Sustainable

Geotourism is tourism that fosters the protection of geoheritage. This is frequently achieved via promotion and communication of knowledge about geology and geomorphology. The latter point again serves to illustrate the vital importance of education and interpretation in geotourism. Increased awareness raised through geotourism can play a significant role in gaining support from various sectors to initiate and continue to work on geoconservation projects. Conserving geosites especially when subject to high levels of tourism is dependent upon informed management pertaining to site access (roads, trails), managing visitor numbers, site development (site hardening, viewing areas, signage and interpretive panels) and monitoring for signs of degradation. Sustainability is also framed in economic terms and the sustainability of tourism businesses is dependent on well-protected and managed sites that yield high levels of visitor satisfaction.

Locally beneficial

Such benefits include the employment of local people as guides and staff to service geotourism activities and facilities. The accommodation sector has the potential to contribute to local communities through employment opportunities, events, retail and the provision of services. Geotourism development may, however, depend on outsiders for approvals and expertise. Dowling (2009) notes that stakeholders in geotourism can include investors, government planners, environmental groups and universities.

Structure and contents of this book

This book comprises 18 chapters written by 34 authors from a host of countries around the world. It covers a range of topics, includes numerous examples and case studies, and essentially adds to our knowledge of geotourism as an emerging distinct form of tourism which is rapidly growing globally.

Chapter 2 (Thomas Hose) examines the significance of landscape appreciation from renaissance times through the eyes of European travellers. Whether viewed as natural features of cultural creations, landscape in fact comprises both elements. An in depth historical account of tourism in England's Lake District is complemented by an account of early guide books and geotourism as well as travellers' writings and modern geotourism. Hose finishes by suggesting that the lessons learnt from the knowledge and understanding of the aesthetic landscape and conservation movements will be of considerable benefit to the stakeholders involved in modern geotourism initiatives, especially the rapidly emerging geopark community.

In Chapter 3 Bernard Joyce describes Australia's geological heritage through the pioneering work of the Geological Society of Australia and the Australian Government initiatives. This work carried out over many years has established a national inventory for future geoparks and geotourism. From Australia to Finland where Ari Brozinski (Chapter 4) discusses the relevance of Centralised Data Management (CDM) to the management and promotion of geology and geotourism. He presents a case study on geologica.fi established by the Finnish National Commission of Geology in 2006 to interpret the geology of the country. Case studies are presented on a limestone quarry in the Parainen Area as well as to the small island of Björkö. The CDM system presents a framework which allows geotourism to be developed and integrated into the existing tourism infrastructure.

Further development and promotion of geotourism is outlined by John Hull in a case study from Northeast Iceland (Chapter 5). The chapter highlights a number of planning and management efforts to promote the development of a sustainable tourism industry by integrating geotourism into its overall destination development strategy based on a United Nations Development Program (UNDP) framework. The five-year tourism development plan is being viewed as a tool of social and economic development and as a method of protecting the region's cultural and natural heritage.

In Chapter 6 Pascal Scherrer and Catherine Pickering outline the opportunities and challenges for geotourism in the Australian Alps through a case study of Mt Kosciuszko, Australia's highest mountain. They argue that as the area's land use has shifted from grazing to tourism, conservation and water catchment, management approaches to the area have had to develop, respond and adapt. They suggest that the geology of the area provides a common element for interpretation of the region's history and its natural and cultural features to visitors.

Moving from Australia to Italy, Jonathan Karkut in Chapter 7 considers the boundaries and applications of geotourism through a study of Mount Vesuvius. Karkut states that little has been written with respect to how destinations near to active volcanic sites may balance sustainable tourism development with the demands required for effective risk management. He redresses this through his case of the Vesuvian region and outlines the National Emergency Plan for the Area before placing this in the context of the region's growing number of tourists. He argues that little consideration has been given as to where tourism fits into volcanic risk management plans and strategies and suggests that input from a tourism perspective has to be woven into any emergency policy and planning, otherwise a significant sector of those at risk will be overlooked.

From risk management to the management of geotourism stakeholders, Christof Pforr and Andreas Megerle share their experiences with Germany's Network History of the Earth (Chapter 8). The Network was founded in 1997 as a framework for cooperation amongst a range of stakeholders to develop sustainable geotourism based on the geological resources of South-West Germany. The management team of the network not only acts as its engine by coordinating activities and disseminating information, but it also plays a important role in initiating local geotourism projects.

Geotourism development in the islands of Hawaii, USA is the focus of Chapter 9 by Lisa King. Tourists are drawn to the islands to witness their past volcanic history and experience the current eruption activity of Kilauea on Hawaii Island. King suggests that most visitors to the islands are geotourists as the majority participate in at least one geotourism related activity during their visit. She presents three case studies of geotourism management issues. The first looks at how Hawaii Volcanoes National Park minimizes the risk to visitors in an active volcanic landscape. The second reports on the Sulphur Banks attraction and how the Park transformed this from a congested visitor area to a natural volcanic area where visitors learn about the active volcanic processes being experienced. The final case study examines a small business working within Kazumura lava tube, finding a balance that works for both the visitor and the resource. The risk management issues addressed by Karkut (Chapter 7) are again visited by King who concludes that it plays a pivotal role within Hawaii's geosites and that managing visitor risk in such dynamic landscapes requires constant assessment by park staff.

The links between geosites, science and geotourism are outlined in a case study of the Cretaceous fossil sites of South Korea (Chapter 10, In Sung Paik, Min Huh, Hyun Joo Kim, Ju Kim and David Newsome). The authors argue that it is the 'scientific value' of a geosite that is an essential feature for it to be presented for geotourism and that this can be ranked according to various degrees or levels, from local to international. Through a number of case studies the authors note that the Korean Cretaceous geosites have many attributes in terms of accessibility, unique and significant attractions, and low tour expenses, compared with many other geotourism destinations. Here local authorities have constructed geological museums and exhibition halls which are being marketed and promoted as geotourism attractions and are now attracting an increasing number of domestic tourists.

Geotourism and geotourist education in Poland is the focus of Chapter 11 by Tadeusz Slomka and Wojciech Mayer. The authors provide an overview of the geology of Poland followed by the description of a number of geological attractions. Of much interest to readers will be the account of the Wieliczka Mine and Saltwork Museum, both of which are world-class geotourism attractions visited by over 1 million tourists annually. The underground trail is about 3.5 kilometers long and includes shafts, chambers, and galleries, and an underground pond. The main attraction is the St. Kinga Chapel located at a depth of 100 metres. The museum offers a unique exhibition from historical documents and maps through rock-salt sculptures, minerals and rocks to original mining equipment.

Another key development is the formation of The International Association for Geotourism (IAGT) which was established in 2007. It organizes conferences, symposia, workshops and professional training as well as prepares databases related to geologic and mining heritage sites. Allied to this has been the production of the new academic journal Geoturystyka (Geotourism). The Journal is published quarterly and there are already 15 volumes with over 70 papers. Finally, the development of a new Masters degree with a specialist stream in geotourism has produced 300 graduates in the last decade, all of whom have secured jobs in tourism industry in Poland and Europe. Indeed there is a much geotourism development in Poland which is helping to lead the way in this subject.

The interpretation of geotourism product is outlined for the volcanic Rangitoto Island in Auckland, New Zealand by Christian Wittlich and Sarah Palmer (Chapter 12). Dominating the skyline of New Zealand's largest city, Rangitoto erupted from the sea 600 years ago, the youngest in a region of 48 volcanoes that have erupted in the past 150 000 years. Already a well established popular tourism attraction, the volcano is a mature tourist destination with a range of established activities. The authors of this chapter seek to assess the effectiveness of on-site interpretive media, such as information signs, posters, an information shelter and guided tours. Their findings are interesting and they come up with a number of suggested improvements.

In Chapter 13 Stacy Supak, Yu-Fai Leung and Kevin Stewart examine the Geotourism Potential of North Carolina, USA from the perspective of interpretation in State Parks. The state is embracing geotourism as a form of sustainable tourism development, in order to foster its geoheritage and geoconservation. The chapter investigates the current status and potential of geotourism in North Carolina from an interpretive perspective using the example of state parks. The focus is to find the extent to which North Carolina's geoheritage is communicated to state park visitors and in what ways. One of the central findings is that there is a self-identified lack of geologic knowledge of park mangers. This discrepancy needs to be overcome and so state park staff are now being exposed to geologically based educational activities and a number of geologic guides have been trained.

This theme of the value of interpretation is continued in Chapter 14 by Karen Hughes and Roy Ballantyne through a study using Australian examples. The chapter describes the process of developing interpretive plans and signage for geotourism attractions focussing on the principles and procedures underlying the development of interpretive materials, as well as the importance of appealing to target markets. Their central suggestion is the need to have an interpretive plan which is used to guide and support the process. Such a plan encompasses the three steps of defining the objectives of interpretation, turning objectives into themes, and electing the best interpretive medium. A key concept is ensuring that the interpretive medium is the appropriate vehicle to 'connect' the information with the visitors that encounter it. Thus using analogies, metaphors and humour is suggested along with sharing stories and encouraging visitor participation. Additional key points are outlined making this an extremely useful summary of modern and effective interpretive practices for geotourism sites, with application for a range of media.

Chapter 15 presents a case study on the Jurassic Coast World Heritage site in the United Kingdom (Sally King, Anjana Ford and Richard Edmonds). The Jurassic Coast stretches for 155 km across the southern English coastline, encompassing one of the most spectacular geological sequences in the world. The internationally renowned coastal exposures of the Jurassic Coast have a near complete sequence of Mesozoic rocks, which record evidence and development of early reptiles through to the age of the dinosaurs. In the chapter the authors examine ways in which the region's geological stories can be interpreted in such a way as to engage the audience on a variety of levels. This is carried out through visitor centres, interpretation panels, publications, and guided walks.

Complementing the account of interpretation methods are informative accounts of several issues facing the region's mangers. They include the issue of fossil collecting, which has been an important part of the culture of the Jurassic Coast for well over 200 years, and that of ensuring the natural erosional processes are allowed to continue, whereas often in the past a popular view was that natural processes such as coastal erosion, should be stopped. How these issues are addressed makes interesting reading. For example, the misunderstanding about the role of erosion in coastal environments is addressed in the Jurassic coastline case study, where erosion (Figure 1.4) is seen as an integral part of preserving the geotourism experience. This of course does not mean that all geosites fit into this category, and while some sites may be an optimum geotourism resource due to active erosional processes the natural values of others may be degraded due to erosion especially if it is a result of human access and activities such as specimen collecting.

Figure 1.4: Jurassic Coastline, Lyme Regis, UK. The coastline is unstable and constantly eroding revealing numerous fossils. The white outlines of ammonites are clearly visible in the wave cut platform in the foreground

The topic of connecting people to places is the topic of Chapter 16 by Judy Walden and Wesley Hill, using the example of the scenic roads in the United States of America. This is carried out through America's Scenic Byways program which presents as attractions 151 scenic roadways and the landscapes that surround them. This program which was established in 1991 was initiated in order to provide high quality visitor experiences, strengthen local economies, and develop ways to manage these tourist corridors. This is carried out through a National Scenic Byway Program which is carried out at the grassroots level by volunteers and is maintained by local leadership. The program has achieved considerable success as it connects visitors to the highway corridors in an educative and experiential manner.

The penultimate chapter (17) is on The UNESCO Global Network of National Geoparks. Here, Patrick Mc Keever, Nickolas Zouros, Margarete Patzak and Jutta Weber, the global leaders of the movement, outline this phenomenal success story of the geoparks initiative. Started in 2000 and with the first geoparks established in 2004, today there are approximately 64 geoparks in 19 countries including 34 in Europe and 20 alone in China. A geopark is a nationally protected area containing a number of geological heritage sites of particular importance, rarity or aesthetic appeal. These Earth heritage sites are part of an integrated concept of protection, education and sustainable development. A Geopark achieves its goals through conservation, education and geotourism. The chapter outlines the success of the network and briefly showcases a number of geoparks in Greece, Ireland and Germany.

In the final chapter (18), the editors synthesize the main themes emerging from this volume. Reviewing the book's many contributions and case studies and introducing some additional case material, we bring together a number of theoretical and practical insights into the development of policies and strategies to plan and manage the growth of geotourism. In doing so, it highlights the book's contribution to a better understanding of geology through tourism and sets an agenda for the future.

References

Cater, C., Buckley, R., Hales, R., Newsome, D., Pickering, C. and Smith, A. J., (2008) *High-impact activities in parks: Best practice management and future research*. Technical Report. Cooperative Research Centre for Sustainable Tourism. The Gold Coast, Queensland, Australia.

Dowling, R. K. (2001) Environmental tourism, in N. Douglas, N. Douglas and R. Derrett (eds) *Special Interest Tourism: Contexts and Cases* (pp. 283-306). Brisbane: John Wiley and Sons.

Dowling, R.K. (2009) Geotourism's contribution to local and regional development, in de Carvalho, C. & Rodrigues, J. eds. *Geotourism and Local Development*. Camara Municipal de Idanha-a-Nova, Portugal, 15-37.

Dowling, R. and Newsome, D. (eds) (2006) *Geotourism*. Elsevier/Heineman, Oxford, UK.

Hose, T.A. (1995) 'Selling the Story of Britain's Stone'. *Environmental Interpretation*, 10, 2, 16-17.

Hose, T.A. (2000) European Geotourism – Geological Interpretation and Geoconservation Promotion for Tourists, in Barretino, D., Wimbledon, W.P. & Gallego, E. (eds.) *Geological Heritage: Its Conservation and Management*. Madrid: Instituto Tecnologico Geominero de Espana. pp.127-146.

Hose, T.A. (2008) Towards a history of Geotourism: definitions, antecedents and the future in Burek, C.V. & Prosser, C.D. (eds.) *The History of Geoconservation*. London: The Geological Society. pp.37-60.

Joyce, E. B. (2006) Geomorphological sites and the new Geotourism in Australia. http://web.earthsci.unimelb.edu.au/Joyce/heritage/geotourosmReviewebj.htm

Mao, I., Robinson, A.M. & Dowling, R.K. (2009) Potential Geotourists: An Australian Case Study. *Journal of Tourism*.

Newsome, D. and Davies, C. (2010) A case study in estimating the area of informal trail development and associated impacts caused by mountain bike activity in John Forrest National Park, Western Australia. *Journal of Ecotourism*, **8**: 237-253.

National Geographic (undated) www.nationalgeographic.com/travel/sustainable/about_geotourism.html (accessed 24/9/09)

National Geographic (2005) Geotourism Charter, http://www.nationalgeographic.com/travel/sustainable/pdf/geotourism_charter_template.pdf (accessed 4/1/2009).

Slomka T. and Kicinska-Swiderska A. (2004) Geotourism – the basic concepts. *Geoturystyka* (Geotourism), **1**: 2-5.

2 The significance of aesthetic landscape appreciation to modern geotourism provision

Thomas A. Hose, Buckinghamshire New University, UK

Introduction

Many of the stakeholders involved in modern geotourism provision lack awareness of how the concept essentially emerged, developed and was defined in Europe. Such stakeholders are unaware of how many of the modern approaches to landscape promotion and interpretation actually have nineteenth century antecedents. Similarly, many of the apparently modern threats to, and issues around, the protection of wild and fragile landscapes and the geoconservation of specific geosites also first emerged in the nineteenth century; the solutions that were developed to address those threats and issues were first applied in the early twentieth century and were subsequently much refined by the opening of the twenty-first century. However, the European engagement with wild and fragile landscapes as places to be appreciated and explored began much earlier than the nineteenth century and can be traced back to Renaissance times. The purpose of this chapter is to provide a summary consideration of this rather neglected aspect of geotourism, initially by considering its modern recognition and definitions and then by examining the English Lake District (with further examples from Britain and Australia available at the website) as a particular case study along with examples.

The contemporary approach to landscape promotion with a geological basis was initially recognised and termed 'geotourism' in the 1990s when it was first defined (Hose, 1995: 17). Geotourism is a form of 'special interest' tourism in which the participants are motivated by their dedication to geological enquiry. Its original definition with some of its associated concepts was included within the *Geoparks Programme Feasibility Study* (UNESCO, 2000) as were the essential elements of a later redefinition to:

> *The provision of interpretative facilities and services to promote the value and societal benefit of geologic[al] and geomorphologic[al] sites and their materials, and ensure their conservation, for the use of students, tourists and other recreationalists.*

> (Hose, 2000: 136)

Thus it encompass geosites' interpretative and promotional media, along with the artefacts, locales, and memorials of their associated Earth scientists. It is a geo-heritage promotional approach with antecedents in aesthetic landscape movements that promoted travel into 'wild' areas, a view which emerged in Britain and Europe and was spread to their colonial territories, from the late seventeenth century onwards. Its modern practitioners generally do not recognise the significance of the aesthetic movements and their associated artistic and literary heritages that have impacted upon the perception of landscapes, even though these underpin much modern geotourism. Landscapes are social and cultural constructs; the perceptions of landscapes and the values ascribed to them are an admixture of direct observation and cultural interpretation (see Figure 2.1).

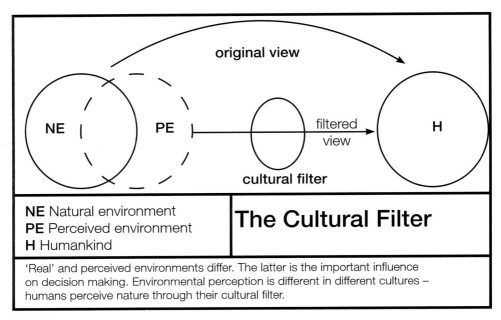

NE Natural environment	The Cultural Filter
PE Perceived environment	
H Humankind	

'Real' and perceived environments differ. The latter is the important influence on decision making. Environmental perception is different in different cultures – humans perceive nature through their cultural filter.

Figure 2.1: The Cultural Filter.

The recognition of aesthetic landscapes

From the Renaissance onwards, the activities of European leisure travellers have been centred upon their search for new and different experiences and places – a quest for the novel, exotic and authentic; their experiences of places and landscapes were a core element of that quest. Landscapes are always viewed through travellers' mindsets which are influenced by what they already know or expect and by their preoccupying interests. Specific expectations about the places and landscapes travellers and tourists plan to go to or actually visit are created and dominated by the images in art galleries and tourism publications rather than their actual physical encounters; they exist as images composed of key reference points woven or mapped together by imagination, experiences and their recollections. Landscapes are essentially jumbles of elements ordered and bounded by travellers' and tourists' knowledge and experiences. Their knowledge is based upon their education and major interests. Landscapes must be experienced to be properly known as they can never be fully described by one individual's experiences because everyone perceives them differently. Travellers, tourists, artists, writers, geographers and Earth scientists define, delineate, describe and depict places and landscapes from different perspectives or mindsets. Landscapes as seen and valued are then a function of the mind, with individuals reacting to specific places and landscapes as defined by their educational and cultural, especially visual art, experiences.

For some individuals, landscapes only consist of natural features whilst for others they are either purely cultural creations or are an admixture of both natural and cultural elements. Edmund Burke in his *A Philosophical Enquiry into the Origin of Our Ideas of the Sublime and Beautiful* published in 1757, equated the Sublime with astonishment, fear, pain, roughness, and obscurity whilst the romantics associated it with the tumultuous chaos of mountains lying beyond rolling foothills, deep valleys and dangerous rocky precipices. Wordsworth suggested in the fifth and final edition of his *A Guide Through the District of The Lakes* that it was: 'the result of Nature's first great dealings with the superficies of the earth' (Wordsworth, 1835: 35); the wildness and ruggedness of the rock masses, hills and lakes solicited observers' awe and wonder. Conversely, within the Picturesque movement the softer effects stemming from nature's subsequent operations produced the variegation and harmony expressed by a river's meandering curve or lake shore, the grouping of their flanking trees, the interplay of light and shade over these features and the subtle colour gradations that bounded the scene were observers' major interest. This topographical approach was adopted from the late-eighteenth century by the pioneering travellers and artists who picture-framed landscapes from scenic 'stations'. The Romantic was an all-embracing movement, from around 1780 to 1850, involving observers' emotional reflections on landscapes and their evocation in visual art and literature. All three pre-twentieth century movements reflected interrelated elements: the travellers' nature and purpose; the meanings ascribed to, and understandings of, natural phenomena; the shift from a rural to an industrial society and the concomitant rise of the middle-classes in numbers, education and influence. Late-twentieth century 'neo-romanticism' has landscapes visualised and employed for leisured and past 'aristocratic' pursuits now partaken by the expanded middle classes.

Britain's geology and landscapes

From the eighteenth century onwards, field observation-based scientific geology was primarily a British development with significant French and German contributions, built upon earlier Italian observations. These observations were mainly by gentlemen of considerable social and economic standing, and sometimes members of the established Church, whose involvement suggests a change in the social climate influencing and encouraging their intellectual employment to venture into 'wild' landscapes. This interest in geology was part of a wider fascination with general natural history in Australia, Europe, and North America seemingly because:

> *With relatively little in the way of accumulated facts and established doctrines to be memorized and digested, they could be quickly and easily comprehended by the beginner even the amateur could hope to make significant contributions and participate in important national, even international scientific endeavours.*
>
> (Bedell, 2000: 4-5)

These fieldworkers generally trod in the footsteps of earlier travellers who guided them though publications focussed on agricultural, industrial and socio-economic reportage. Up to the mid-eighteenth century, the: 'preferred rural landscape was generally a humanised scene of cultivation, evidence of the successful control of nature' (Towner, 1996: 138).

'Wild' areas, such as those later geologically mapped in the Scottish Highlands and Lake District by MacCulloch (1819 and 1836), Otley (1812) and Sedgwick (1820s; see Sedgwick, 1835), were considered waste places of no economic worth. By the late-eighteenth century, interest and pleasure in these often upland areas is evident in naturalists' and travellers' writings. The early leisure travellers were commonly directed by the selections of authors, diarists, poets, and artists promoting the three major landscape aesthetic movements; their application can profitably be studied in key regions in Britain and in Australia (e.g. Figure 2.1).

However, the Peak District is the birthplace of British geotourism (Hose, 2008); Celia Fiennes, a privileged late-seventeenth century horseback traveller, visited Ashbourne's copper mines in 1698 (Morris, 1949: 109). It is also the birthplace of the tourist guidebook; by the late-seventeenth century its major attractions were organised, described and promoted by Thomas Hobbes (in *De Mirabilibis Pecci: Being the Wonders of the Peak in Darby-shire* of 1678) and Charles Cotton (in *The Wonders of the Peake* of 1681), into seven 'wonders' of which five were distinctly geological. However, its subsequent over-commercialisation forced tourists into the wilder uplands of the Lake District and then the Scottish Highlands and Islands.

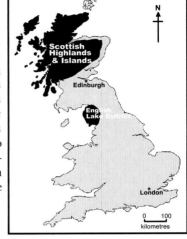

Figure 2.1: Two key regions of early geotourism in Britain

The English Lake District, romanticism and geotourism

The Lake District's extensive industrial and mining sites were ignored when it was promoted by the 'Lake School' of poets (Samuel Taylor Coleridge, Robert Southy and William Wordsworth) who were first recognised as such in the *Edinburgh Review* of August 1817. Celia Fiennes had ridden through the District in 1698 and, believing it as an unprofitable wilderness, recorded only Windermere's potted char and some bread recipes. Daniel Defoe in the 1720s recorded the region as barren and frightful. From the 1750s onwards travellers (popularly called 'lakers') visited the region mainly because of its landscapes, which by then were perceived as of some quality, and also because of their appealing antiquities. The poet Thomas Gray travelled through it in 1767 and 1769, the artist William Gilpin in 1772 and the agrarian writer Arthur Young in 1768. Thomas Gray recorded that the Derwentwater to Borrowdale journey reminded him of Alpine passes where travellers were threatened by avalanches! Such a scene is captured in William Turner's 1804 painting *The Passage of the St Gothard*. William Gilpin wrote, in his *Observations, Relative Chiefly to Picturesque Beauty*, on Borrowdale:

> *the road grew wilder, and more romantic. There is not an idea more tremendous, than that of riding along the edge of a precipice, unguarded by any parapet, under impending rocks, which threaten above.*

(Gilpin, 1786, vol.1: 187)

Thomas Young, focused on agricultural improvement, described Derwentwater as elegant but the surrounding mountains were, he thought, wild with dreadful chasms.

By the end of the eighteenth century, illustrated guidebooks to the Lake District's antiquities were available (e.g. William Hutchinson's two-volume *The History of the County of Cumberland, And some places adjacent*, published in 1794). Whilst travellers had recorded their private impressions which were occasionally published as journals, in 1778 Thomas West ordered the principal sites and sights of the Lake District into its first tourist guidebook, setting the pattern for later tours and guidebooks by establishing 'stations' from which travellers could best view the scenic wonders whilst reading erudite descriptions. Numerous amateur and professional artists recorded its lakes, mountains and curiosities, occasionally publishing sets of engravings which were sometimes accompanied by prose or poetry. John Constable sketched and painted around Kendal, Brathay, Skelwith, Thirlmere, and Windermere on his only visit in Autumn 1806; his watercolours, *Windermere* and *The Castle Rock, Borrowdale*, of that visit indicate a familiarity with geology. He exhibited at least ten Lake District scenes between 1807 and 1809. The young William Turner who made a living as a topographical artist exhibited two Lake District paintings at the Royal Academy in 1798, with *Morning Amongst the Coniston Fells, Cumberland* being noteworthy.

Turner's artistic rival, John Glover, exhibited paintings of the Lake District from 1795 onwards and lived there from around 1818 to 1820. His painting *Thirlmere* of circa 1820 is typical of his faithful detailed depictions. Glover, although rather neglected in the UK today, was a landscape artist of high contemporaneous repute who from 1820 had his own gallery in London's fashionable Old Bond Street. His major influence on landscape painting in Australia, after his emigration there in 1830, is examined in the extended version of this chapter available on the Goodfellow website. Confusingly, he settled in an area of Tasmania in which the topographic features were given Lake District names; however, his circa fine 1831 *Derwentwater* pen and wash drawing is definitely set in the Lake District!

Derwentwater was popular with early tourists and, as Thomas West's late-eighteenth century guidebook (Figure 2.3) noted, its view from the Cockshott Hill 'station' was close to the ideal requirements of the 'picturesque' because in:

> *a spacious amphitheatre, of the most picturesque mountains imaginable, an elegant sheet of water is spread out before you, shining like a mirror, and transparent as chrystal; variegated with islands . . . clothed with forest verdure.*
>
> (West, 1778: 89-90)

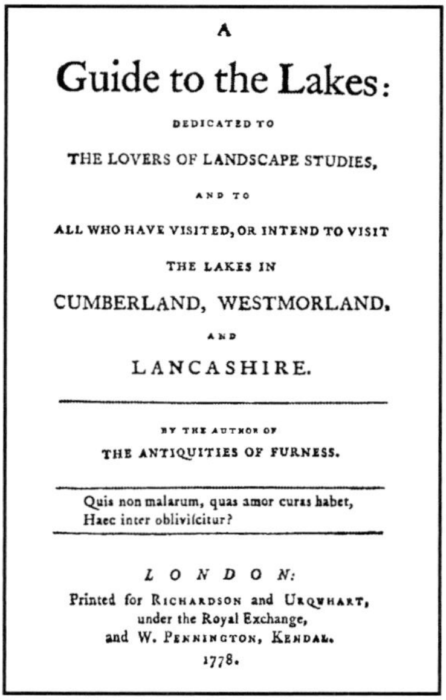
A

Guide to the Lakes:

DEDICATED TO

THE LOVERS OF LANDSCAPE STUDIES,

AND TO

ALL WHO HAVE VISITED, OR INTEND TO VISIT

THE LAKES IN

CUMBERLAND, WESTMORLAND,

AND

LANCASHIRE.

BY THE AUTHOR OF

THE ANTIQUITIES OF FURNESS.

Quis non malarum, quas amor curas habet,
Haec inter obliviscitur?

LONDON:

Printed for RICHARDSON and URQUHART,
under the Royal Exchange,
and W. PENNINGTON, KENDAL.
1778.

Figure 2.3: Title page from Thomas West's guidebook

West's guidebook mainly consists of numbered stations described with the textual precision necessary before detailed maps appeared in the first quarter of the nineteenth century; Coniston's first station was above Nibthwaite where it was found as the lake came into view: ' by observing an ash tree on the west side of the road, and passing that till you are in a line with the peninsula, the rock is then at your feet' (West, 1778: 50-51). Peter Crosthwaite published maps from 1783 showing both his own and West's stations. Crosthwaite improved access to some of his stations; for example, for his two stations above Derwentwater, for which he had produced a fairly detailed map (Crossthwaite, 1783), one had steps cut and a cross marked on the ground and the other, near his museum which he had opened in 1780 at Keswick, was advertised by beating a gong. After Young toured in 1768 he urged that the stations should be made more accessible (much as modern geopark managers would urge) to a greater range of travellers and resting places provided because of the precipitous nature of many paths.

He also wanted maturing trees felled once they obscured stations. The popular stations often had structures provided for travellers but these were not universally welcomed; in 1799 James Plumtree thought Windermere's first station was somewhat lacking in rustic charm.

The employment of rock features as geo-attractions was an early commercial geotourism enterprise. In 1798 Joseph Pocklington turned the Bowder Stone - a 1250 tonne perilously balanced boulder – in Borrowdale into the first such commercial attraction. West had described its location 20 years earlier:

> *The rocky scenes in Borrowdale are most fantastic… Bowdar-stone … a mountain in itself, the road winds round its base. Here rock riots over rock, and mountain intersecting mountain, form one grand sweep of broken pointed crags.*
>
> (West, 1778: 100)

As well as building a cottage for the resident guides, by 1807, Pocklington had also erected a druid stone, small chapel and placed a ladder for visitors to clamber atop of the stone. Rock fragments around its base were cleared away and a hole was dug through which visitors could shake hands. When William Green's 1819 illustrated guidebook was published it had seemingly further declined in natural and contemplative appeal because the guardian presented the visitor with an: 'exordium preparatory to the presentation of a written paper, specifying the weight and dimensions of the stone' (Green, 1819, vol.2: 134).

The Lake District was well promoted to discerning elite tourists by Green's guidebook which was well known to Wordsworth who fulsomely praised it in his own as a: 'complete Magazine of minute and accurate information' (Wordsworth, 1835, p.6). Whilst Green popularised the Lake District in pictures, Wordsworth did so in poetry and prose. The closure of continental Europe to the British from 1789 to 1815, due to the French Revolution and the Napoleonic Wars, was a major impetus to the Lake District's exploration because its landscapes were promoted as imitating Europe's Alps, with which Wordsworth and his literary and artistic contemporaries were familiar. Wordsworth's guidebook was innovative in that alongside describing what could be seen, it linked landscape features to natural history (including geology with which Wordsworth was evidently acquainted as evidenced in his 1814 poem *The Excursion*), history and people. It gave tourists an:

> *alternative to what its author considered the superficial and exploitive approach to the Lakes taken by many other works, which treated landscape and village as aesthetic spectacles offering tourists the chance to display their suitable passionate response.*
>
> (Buzzard, 1993: 29-30)

its opening paragraph articulated Wordsworth's desire to:

> *furnish a Guide or Companion for the Minds of Persons of taste, and feeling for Landscape, who might be inclined to explore..with that degree of attention to which its beauty may fairly lay claim.*
>
> (Wordsworth, 1835: 1)

It had evolved from the anonymous text accompanying the Rev. Joseph Wilkinson's 1810 volume of engravings, *Select Views in Cumberland, Westmoreland and Lancashire*. In 1820 it became an appendix to his River Duddon sonnets in which he recorded that he did not know:

any tract of country in which, within so narrow a compass, may be found an equal variety in the influences of light and shadow upon the sublime or beautiful features of landscape.

(Wordsworth, 1820: 222)

It was a guidebook in its own right by 1822 and, through revision and expansion, it went to several further editions up to the 1840s. Later editions included three geology letters requested from Adam Sedgwick, but this was not a novel or singular inclusion for natural history because the 1842 edition also included notes on botany (Wyatt, 1995: 60).

The later guidebooks were not mere station descriptions but holistic accounts supporting serious landscape study inviting and informing excursionists from the nearby industrial and mill towns – such as the 1865 Manchester Quaker party's visit to Loweswater (Hodgson and Lunt, 1987). Such guidebooks, like Charles Mackay's *The Scenery and Poetry of the English Lakes: A Summer Ramble*, of 1846 were noteworthy for their strong literary content focussing readers' attentions upon site-centred poetry and other literary allusions. The creation of literary landscapes is enduring achievement of these pioneering travel writers; their approach pervades many modern geopark and protected landscape publications.

By the beginning of the nineteenth century the Lake District was readily accessible to the new tourists, with new paths cut to the waterfalls and stations and summer houses provided as resting places. However, this commercialisation and consequent increase in visitor numbers began to threaten the landscape. This was recognised by the best known of the early, but not the earliest, landscape conservationists, Wordsworth, who was attempting to stop mass tourism by the lower middle and working classes from the nearby industrial and mill towns because he wanted only educated elite travellers for whom he and West published. Condemnation of mass tourists was not universal and Harriet Martineau's *A Complete Guide to the English Lakes* of 1855 encouraged such tourists to spend a day in the mountains.

Geology guidebooks were somewhat slow in appearing for the Lake District. The geologist, Johnathan Otley, published the first populist account, *A concise description of the English Lakes... and observations on the mineralogy and geology of the district*, in 1823 (Figure 2.4).

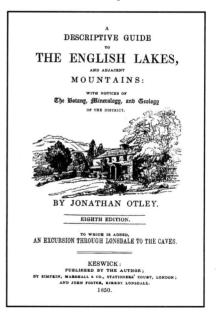

Figure 2.4: Title page from Otley's guidebook.

The noteworthy nineteenth century geologist Adam Sedgwick supplemented John Hudson's 1842 *Complete Guide to the Lakes* with geological notes. Most significantly for modern geotourism, West and his contemporaries in reducing the Lake District's landscape to a series of eruditely described viewpoints established locations and patterns of tourist behaviours observable today, albeit with well-advertised car-parking and digital snapshot opportunities. Significantly for modern geotourism management, Wordsworth and his successors who were opposed to mass tourism were instrumental in establishing the late-nineteenth century conservation movements that ultimately led to the mid-twentieth century establishment of National Parks of which the Lake District is the United Kingdom's second most visited after the Peak District.

Early guidebooks and geotourism

The actual necessity for a geologist to examine artists' landscape visualisations and travellers' literature for accuracy of fact and interpretation when considering geology-based geotourism is evident from the numerous inaccuracies still found within the travel literature and its illustrations' captions. The guidebook in: ' the nineteenth century was, initially, a British and a German invention, people from those countries being the first to have the money and the intellectual curiosity to travel, at least in any numbers' (Sillitoe, 1995: 221). The first guidebooks were for educated elite travellers, but they became a much smaller market than the middle-classes of more modest means by the mid-nineteenth century. However, in both cases any geotourism element within the guidebooks was aimed at 'casual geotourists' (Hose, 2000: 136). Prior to these dedicated 'professional' guidebooks the travel literature abounded with personal reminiscences; as Henry Holland commented in 1811: 'nobody you know, travels now a days without writing a quarto to tell the world where he has been, etcetera, what he has beheld' (in Barton, 1998: 3). This genre is making something of an unwelcome comeback, but the quarto has given way to the (digital) 'photo' album. John Murray's 'handbooks' were written for the educated elite traveller to: 'to point out things peculiar to the spot, or which might be better seen there than elsewhere' (in Buzzard, 1993: 174) rather than mention everything without discrimination, producing a compendium focused on visitors' perspectives of what was important, including where to eat, stay and bank: 'By the 1840s "Murray's Handbooks" were a household name, and no serious traveller would dream of leaving England without one' (Norwich, 1987: 7). Karl Baedeker's *Handbuchlein* (or Handbooks) were the first to employ asterisks as commendations for significant tourist sites and sights. His first England guide, in German, was published in 1862. Many rival publications were produced in the UK and Europe and by the late nineteenth century, the tourist was well provided with affordable guidebooks of which a few included some mention of geology.

Guidebooks were probably slow to emerge in those areas at the extremities of Europe's influence, such as Australia, because demand for them was insufficient to underwrite their production and distribution costs. One of the earliest volumes, although not a tourist guidebook as such, was Sarah Lee's 1851 *Adventures in Australia; or the wanderings of Captain Spencer in the Bush and the Wilds*; although the accuracy of its descriptions were doubted by many critical later readers. Finney Eldershaw's *Australia as it really is, in its life, scenery, and adventure: with the character, habits, and customs of its aboriginal inhabitants, and the prospects and extent of its gold fields*, published in London in 1854, is one of the many books written by those who were tempted to try their hand at prospecting. Louisa Anne Meredith was an established authoress prior to her marriage and initial settlement in Sydney in 1839. From Sydney she made several excursions including one to the Blue Mountains describing the Pass of Mount Victoria as: 'by far the most grand and striking scene in this mountain region' (Meredith, 1844 p. 74) in *Notes and sketches of New South Wales: during a residence in that colony from 1839 to 1844*. After she moved to Tasmania she continued recording her domestic life and travels. The former were published in *My Home in Tasmania During a Residence of Nine Years* of 1852. The latter included an 1860 excursion to Victoria, publishing her observation in *Over the straits: a visit to Victoria* in 1861; this is noteworthy because of its inclusion of her sketches and illustrations from photographs. Hume Nisbet's *The Bushranger's Sweetheart* published in 1893 openly romanticised the wild Australian outback but, given his early upbringing in Scotland before his arrival in 1865 in Australia as a fresh-faced sixteen year old, this is perhaps not unexpected. The artist travelled widely in Australia (1865 to 72, 1886 and 1895). Later he taught art in Edinburgh, exhibited at the Royal Scottish Academy and illustrated many books, including his own, and was commissioned as an illustrator by one of the leading publishers.

One of the most significant publications connected with landscape appreciation in 19th-century Australia was the subscription-only multi-volume *Picturesque Atlas of Australia* (Garran 1886–88). Writers, artists, academics, and politicians combined to prepare volumes of unprecedented grandeur and ambition to describe Australia as it was then known. It had over 1100 engravings, many especially commissioned from the country's leading artists, and 30 maps within its 800 pages. It illustrates not just landscapes and caves but also urbanscapes such as street scenes, monuments, churches, hills, the seaside, farms, horses, scrub, country towns, ships, daily life activities, headstones, bridges, people and aborigines. Its illustrations are set within texts describing landscape, industry and city streets. Something of a pre-occupation for productive landscapes and urban scenes can be deduced from the *Atlas's* many illustrations of agricultural processes, mines and factories. The slag heaps of a mine were then seen to be almost as 'picturesque' as a fern-filled valley. Although photography was invented by the time of its publication, all of the illustrations were engravings, although some of these were based on photographs. Later publications, none of which rivalled the *Atlas* in coverage, relied heavily upon monochrome photographic reproductions.

Geological information only filtered into tourist guidebooks in Britain and Australia as geological information became widely available, initially in specialists' and later in a few populist texts. Two early major specialists' works summarising southern Britain's geology, Phillips's *A Selection of Facts...to Form an Outline of the Geology of England and Wales* published in 1818 and Conybeare's and Phillips's *Outlines of the Geology of England and Wales* published in 1822 provided an outline of the geology observable in the field; they became the standard introduction to southern Britain's geology for several decades. Setting aside the less than comprehensive 1850 *A Sketch of the Physical Structure of Australia* (Jukes, 1850) similar contemporary Australian texts appeared somewhat later and were generally focused on individual states; for example Johnston's officially published 1888 *Systematic Account of the Geology of Tasmania*. Concomitant with these texts, various field manuals were published such as De La Beche's *A Geological Manual* (1832) and *The Geological Observer* (1851); these were available in the United States and Australia within a year or so of their publication in London. Some introductory texts, such as Mantell's *Thoughts on a Pebble* published in 1849, were aimed at children.

Towards the end of the nineteenth century, quite detailed English county-based geology accounts appeared in trade directories; Harrison's 1882 *Geology of the Counties of England and Wales*, bound a series of individual accounts into a single volume. The London-based Geologists' Association's nineteenth-century excursions were published as discrete volumes in 1891 as *A Record of Excursions Made Between 1860 and 1890* and in 1909 as *Geology in the Field 1858–1908*, with both providing invaluable accounts of contemporary field practices and geoconservation attitudes. The development of tourist guidebooks has been quite well charted but that of geology field-guides has been virtually ignored (Hose, 2006). One of the earliest English regional geology accounts is Englefield's *A Description...of the Isle of Wight* published in 1816, but its bulk and weight precluded its use as a field-guide. Gideon Mantell was influential in the development of geology field-guides and his populist and highly portable *Geological Excursion Round the Isle of Wight and Along the Adjacent Coast of Dorsetshire* published in 1847 covered much the same area as Engenfield's text and was ground-breaking in bringing field geology to a wider audience than ever before. However, unlike Engenfield's tome, it was aimed at the burgeoning number of middle class 'dedicated geotourists' (Hose, 2000: 136). Modern field-guides are remarkably similar in format and approach to this mid-nineteenth century illustrated publication.

Travellers' writings and modern geotourism

The development of geotourism required a fundamental shift in the way in which landscapes were and are perceived and exploited for tourism. The recognition that 'wild' landscapes were safe and worth visiting was essential. However, it should be borne in mind that up to the latter part of the nineteenth century travel over any distance for leisure was restricted to the social elite with the available time, financial resources and cultural education. It was only with the arrival of the passenger railways that opportunities for excursions, especially on the coast, opened up the countryside for the majority of the, by then, largely urban-based population. Until then, they had to make do with published second-hand observations and accounts. For much of the early development of landscape appreciation the dominant visual representations were provided by artists principally, even in Australia, trained in the major cultural centres of England and Scotland and working in the main mediums of watercolour and oils. These artworks in their original forms were originally viewed by the educated elite in commercial galleries and then by the middle classes in the public art galleries that opened from the 1840s onwards. For those unable to view the originals by geography or social class, the emergence of lithography in its various forms enabled the production and distribution of fair colour copies. Although photography was increasingly employed as a recording medium from the later mid-nineteenth century it was almost exclusively a monochrome medium. Thus, for those persons unfamiliar with the landscapes their impressions and expectations were markedly influenced by the available artistic visualisations, some of which eventually made their appearance, usually as monochrome engravings, in tourist guidebooks. The curiosity and aesthetic worth that inspired travellers and tourists, before scientific value, as motivators for travel was partly evoked by such visualisations.

Tourist guidebooks were, and still are, written to satisfy the curious and to promote newly recognised attractions. The rise of scientific geology encouraged field excursions and field-guides evolved to support such trips. The field locations and activities included in the nineteenth century field-guides are embedded within much current geotourism provision. The major change has been in the relationship that geotourists enjoy with the landscape. There is a greater emphasis by modern tourists on pleasure and leisure than on the past tourists' intellectual endeavour and religious awareness.

From the mid-twentieth century, a new impetus was given to landscape conservation and scenic tourism with various protected habitats and landscape national legislation. Since 1972 UNESCO international recognition has been available, with the most significant being citation within the World Heritage List. Because not all significant geosites could meet the 'outstanding universal value' criterion required by the World Heritage Convention, an additional and alternative recognition was required. Hence in 2000 the UNESCO geoparks programme was developed to promote landscapes on a holistic, rather than purely geological, basis. Ideally, the geological interest was to be allied with archaeological, cultural, historical or ecological interest. Geoparks are a natural development of the nineteenth century approaches to landscape promotion and are usually developed as a means of regenerating local economies, such as was the case in the mid-nineteenth century with the Lake District's Kendal and Windermere Railway scheme.

The key geoconservation consideration is to apply the early lessons from regions where over-commercialisation damaged the geo-attractions and led to tourists seeking new and alternative locations to visit; such was demonstrably the case with the Peak District in the late eighteenth century. The Lake District's nineteenth-century developments exemplify threats to, and issues around, the conservation and protection of wild and fragile landscapes created by increasing tourists' access by such methods as constructing new paths, trails and structures and with the environmental degradation that higher visitor numbers can inflict on landscapes. The Scottish Highlands and Tasmania exemplify the significance of the opening up of a few safe roads and some tourist accommodation, together with the popularisation of aesthetic landscapes in illustrated accounts, in the development of tourism. As these improved in quality and quantity so the mass appeal of the regions increased. The Lake District, the Scottish Highlands and Tasmania provide good case studies in both regional and local contexts with which to explore the current debate about whether regions and locations should provide for the needs of elite/niche tourists as an alternative to maintaining and/or providing the infrastructure for mass tourism; that is, they address the issues raised by accepting the concept of sustainable tourism. The various new geopark developments will undoubtedly reignite these debates and force to the fore the issues around improved access, increased visitor numbers, and their conservation impact, which began to be recognised in the nineteenth century.

The relevance to modern geotourism provision stakeholders of the history, development and philosophy of landscape promotion to tourists should be evident when the appropriate case studies are examined. For example, the potential impacts of improving future physical access and publishing specialist guidebooks to encourage elite tourists to visit previously somewhat inaccessible locations can be partially gauged from examining the early attempts in the Peak District and the Lake District. Likewise, the impact of promoting landscapes for mass tourism can also be considered by examining the Lake District and Tasmania's lakes area (See the Goodfellow website). Such detailed case studies from Britain and Australia will only emerge when both their academic communities and geotourism practitioners recognise the mutual benefits of undertaking historical studies as useful and applied research into geotourism management (see Figure 2.5). For the academic community an underpinning theoretical framework will be developed and for the geotourism practitoners a better understanding of the needs of geotourists and how they can best be met in a sustainable manner within wild and fragile landscapes will emerge. It is clear from the already albeit limited published case-studies that issues related to increased public awareness of, and access to, wild and fragile areas commonly considered to be new by geotourism practitioners are in reality similar if not fully alike to those that emerged in the nineteenth and earlier centuries in Europe and Australia. Perhaps the major difference between the past and the present is that the employment of modern imaging, mapping and data analysis technologies affords a considerably greater ability to model geotourism provision scenarios and to devise possible solutions. It is therefore unfortunate that many of those stakeholders involved in modern geotourism initiatives, and especially the rapidly emerging geopark community, are unaware of the lessons that could be gleaned from a good knowledge and understanding of the key aesthetic and conservation movements previously summarised in this chapter. In recognising and appreciating the change in artists' visualisations and travellers' writings and their combined perceptions and impacts on geology and geotourism, general trends in

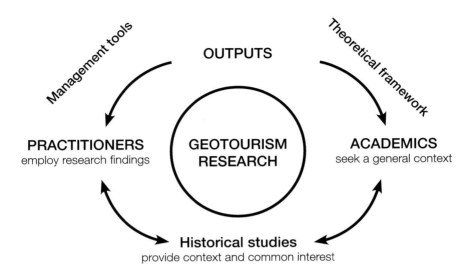

Figure 2.5: A context for geotourism historical studies

landscape recognition and promotion influencing and informing modern provision are discernable. Likewise, past mistakes can be seen as useful learning experiences and their solutions can profitably be employed to ensure that any future geotourism provision is truly sustainable. Sustainability, one of the major tenets of the initial approach to geoturism as defined in Europe, it also should be one of the underpinning rationales of the geopark movement and its significance is best appreciated by stakeholders' awareness of geotourism's past legacy and its significance for any future provision.

References

Barton, H.A. (1998) *Northern Arcadia: Foreign Travellers In Scandinavia, 1765-1815.* Carbondale and Edwardsville: Southern Illinois University Press.

Bedell, R. (2000) *The Anatomy of Nature: Geology and American Landscape Painting, 1825-1875.* Princeton: Princeton University Press.

Buzzard, J. (1993) *The Beaten Track: European Tourism, Literature, and the Ways to Culture 1800-1918.* Oxford: Oxford University Press.

Cotton, C. (1681) *The Wonders of the Peake.* London: Joanna Brome.

Crosthwaite, P. (1783) *An Accurate Map of the Matchless Lake of Derwent (fituate in the most delightful Vale which perhaps Human Eye beheld) near Keswick, Cumberland; with Weffs eight stations,* scale 3 inches to 1 mile, engraved by S Neele, (variously corrected and published 1788, 1794, 1809, 1819; reprinted 1863). Keswick: Peter Crosthwaite.

De La Beche, H.T. (1832) *A Geological Manual.* Philadelphia: Carey and Lea.

De La Beche, H.T. (1851) *The Geological Observer.* Philadelphia: Blanchard and Lea.

Eldershaw, F. (1854) *Australia as it really is, in its life, scenery, and adventure: with the character, habits, and customs of its aboriginal inhabitants, and the prospects and extent of its gold fields.* London: Darton and Company.

Englefield, H.C. (1816) *A description of the principal picturesque beauties, antiquities and geological phenomena of the Isle of Wight. With additional observations on the strata of the Island, and their continuation in the adjacent parts of Dorsetshire by Thomas Webster.* London: T. Webster.

Garran, A. (ed.) (1886-1888) *Picturesque Atlas of Australia.* Sydney: Picturesque Atlas Publishing Company.

Gilpin, W. (1786) *Observations, Relative Chiefly to Picturesque Beauty, Made in the Year 1772, on Several Parts of England: Particularly the Mountains and lakes of Cumberland and Westmorland* (in 2 volumes). London: R. Blamire.

Green, W. (1819) *The Tourist's New Guide, Containing a Description of the Lakes, Mountains, and Scenery in Cumberland, Westmorland, and Lancashire, with Some account of Their Bordering Towns and Villages. Being the Result of Observations Made During a Residence of Eighteen Years in Ambleside and Keswick* (in 2 volumes). Kendal: Lough and Company.

Harrison, W.J. (1882) *Geology of the Counties of England and Wales.* London: Kelly and Company/Simpkin, Marshall and Company.

Hobbs, T. (1678) *De Mirabilibuis Pecci: Being the Wonders of the Peak in Darby-shire, Commonly called The Devil's Arfe of Peak.* London: William Crook.

Hodgson, M. and Lunt, L. (1987) *Excursion to Loweswater: A Lakeland Visit 1865.* London: Macdonald Orbis.

Hose, T.A. (1995) 'Selling the story of Britain's stone', *Environmental Interpretation*, 10 (2), 16-17.

Hose, T.A. (2000) 'European geotourism – geological interpretation and geoconservation promotion for tourists', in Barretino, D., Wimbledon, W.P. and Gallego, E. (eds.) *Geological Heritage: Its Conservation and Management.* Madrid: Instituto Tecnologico Geominero de Espana. pp.127-146.

Hose, T.A. (2008) 'Towards a history of geotourism: definitions, antecedents and the future', in Burek, C.V. and Prosser, C.D. (eds) *The History of Geoconservation.* London: Geological Society. pp.37-60.

Hudson, J. (1842) *Complete Guide to the Lakes.* Kendal: Hudson and Nicholson.

Hutchinson, W. (1794) *The History of the County of Cumberland. And some places adjacent from the Earliest Accounts to the Present Time: comprehending the Local History of the County, its Antiquities, the Origin, Geneology and Present State of the Principal Families with Biographical Notes; its mines, minerals and plants, with other curiosities, either of Nature or of Art* (in 2 volumes). London: F. Jollie.

Johnston, R.M. (1888) *Systematic Account of the Geology of Tasmania.* Hobart: J. Walch and Sons/Government Printer.

Jukes, J.B. (1850) *A Sketch of the Physical Structure of Australia, so far as it is at present known.* London: T. and W. Boone.

Lee, R. (1851) *Adventures in Australia; or, The wanderings of Captain S in Australia; or, The wanderings of Captain Spencer in the bush and wilds; containing accurate descriptions of the habits of the natives, and the natural productions and features of the country by Mrs R. Lee.* London: Grant and Griffith.

MacCulloch, J. (1819) *A Description of the Western Isles of Scotland, including the Isle of Man: Comprising an Account of their Geological Structure, with Remarks on their Agriculture, Scenery and Antiquities.* London: A. Constable & Co.

MacCulloch, J. (1836) *Memoirs to His Majesty's Treasury respecting a Geological Survey of Scotland.* London: Samuel Arrowsmith.

Mackay, C. (1885) *The Scenery and Poetry of the English Lakes: A Summer Ramble*. London: Longman and Company.

Mantell, G. (1847) *Geological Excursion Round the Isle of Wight and Along the Adjacent Coast of Dorsetshire*. London: Henry G. Bohn.

Mantell, G. (1849) *Thoughts on a Pebble*. London: Reeves, Benham and Reeve.

Martineu, H. (1885) *A Complete Guide to the English Lakes*. Windermere: J. Garnett.

Meredith, L.A. (1844) *Notes and sketches of New South Wales: during a residence in that colony from 1839 to 1844*. London: Murray and Company.

Meredith, L.A. *(1852) My Home in Tasmania During a Residence of Nine Years*. London: John Murray.

Meredith, L.A. (1861) *Over the straits : a visit to Victoria*. London: Chapman and Hall.

Morris, C. (ed.) (1949) *The Journeys of Celia Fiennes*. London: Cresset Press.

Nisbett, H. (1893) *The Bushranger's Sweetheart*. London: F.V. White and Company.

Norwich, J.J. (1987) *A Taste for Travel*. New York: Alfred H. Knopf.

Otley, J. (1823) *A concise description of the English lakes and adjacent mountains*. London: Simpkin Marshall and Company.

Phillips, W. (1818) *A Selection of Facts from the Best Authorities, Arranged so as to Form an Outline of the Geology of England and Wales*. London: Phillips.

Sedgwick, A. (1835) Introduction to the general structure of the Cumbrian Mountains; with descriptions of the great dislocations by which they have been separated from the neighbouring Carboniferous chains, *Transactions of the Geological Society of London*, 4, Series 2, 47-68.

Sillitoe, A. (1995) *Leading the Blind: A Century of Guidebook Travel 1815 – 1911*. London: Macmillan.

Towner, J. (1996) *An Historical Geography of Recreation and Tourism in the Western World 1540-1940*. London: Wiley.

UNESCO, 2000, UNESCO *Geoparks Programme Feasibility Study*, August 2000. Paris: UNESCO.

West, T. (1778) *A Guide to the Lakes: Dedicated to the Lovers of Landscape Studies, and to All Who Have Visited, or Intend to Visit the lakes in Cumberland, Westmorland and Lancashire*. London: Richardson and Urqwhart; and Kendal: W. Pennington.

Wordsworth, W. (1820) *The River Duddon, A Series of Sonnets: Vaudravour and Julia and Other Poems to which is Annexed a Topographical Description of the County of the Lakes in the North of England*. London: Longman, Hurst, Rees, Orme and Brown.

Wordsworth, W. (1835) *A Guide Through the District of the Lakes in The North of England, with A Description of the Scenery etc. For the Use of Tourists and Residents* (5th edn.). London: Longman and Company, Moxon, and Whittaker and Company.

Wyatt, J. (1995) *Wordsworth and the Geologists*. Cambridge: Cambridge University Press.

A longer version of this chapter, with additional material on Australia and Britain can be found in the *Geotourism:The Tourism of Geology and Landscape* area at the publisher's website, http://www.goodfellow.com.

3 Australia's geological heritage: a national inventory for future geoparks and geotourism

Bernard Joyce, University of Melbourne, Australia

Introduction

Australia has a coastline of around 32,000 km, with varying rock types and structure, coastal types and climate. Outstanding and representative coastal sites form a significant part of the Australian inventory. Major terrains include inland deserts (for example the Simpson Desert dune field), northern tropical savannah (the Kakadu World Heritage Region), glacial and periglacial uplands in the far south (southwest Tasmania), broad inland riverine plains (Murray-Darling river system), and the young volcanic provinces of southeastern Australia and northeastern Australia. There are also many karst and cave sites (for example the Nullarbor Plain), and many palaeoweathering landforms in central Australia (for example Uluru) as well as representative stratigraphic sites, rock and mineral sites, and structural and tectonic sites. Viewpoints are also included in this list, and also sites related to the history of geology, for example Charles Darwin and the Blue Mountains near Sydney (Figure 3.1). Important fossil sites range from the Proterozoic stromatolites of the Pilbara of northwestern Australia to the World Heritage Tertiary mammal fossils of Riversleigh and Naracoorte, and the Devonian fossil fishbeds of Canowindra in New South Wales (Figure 3.2).

Australia is often referred to as 'the oldest continent'. Zircons dated between 4300 and 4200 million years have been found in the Archaean rocks of the Mt Narryer area of Western Australia, and the microfossils and stromatolites of the Pilbara, also in Western Australia, are amongst the earliest known life on earth. The old shield which forms a major part of the Australian continent is mainly a flat and low-lying plateau, tectonically quiet and with one of the lowest erosion rates known. Deep weathering profiles dating to the Mesozoic and even earlier have survived over long periods of geological time, as have relics of corresponding ancient landscapes (Joyce 1999). This contrasts with the northern hemisphere continents, where late Tertiary and Quaternary uplift and extensive glacial erosion have given very different landscapes. Only in Tasmania and the higher parts of the southeastern Australia mainland can landscapes similar to those of much of Europe be found.

The study of geological heritage in the former Gondwana continents such as Africa, South America, India and Australia may well need a different approach to that used elsewhere (Joyce 1999). Following the Permian Gondwana glaciation, the Australian

Figure 3.1: World Heritage Area of the Blue Mountains, near Sydney, New South Wales; a site of historic geological interest, visited by Charles Darwin in January 1836. On seeing the steep-sided valleys, Darwin first suggested the striking erosional landforms had been formed by the sea, but later began to argue that fluvial erosion over long periods of time could have been sufficient to produce the striking landscape, although finally and reluctantly he accepted 'the marine denudation explanation' following the ideas of his mentor Charles Lyell in the book *Principles of Geology* (Nicholas and Nicholas, 2002, pp. 36-43) Major lookouts provide viewpoints to spectacular valleys, scarps and plateaus developed in Triassic fluvial sandstone. (Photo E.B. Joyce).

Figure 3.2: Devonian fossil fish beds outside the small town of Canowindra in New South Wales, with its excellent Age of Fishes Museum (Photo E.B. Joyce).

continent had a long period of weathering and limited erosion, and was little affected by Quaternary glaciation, so that deep weathering mantles and leached soils are widespread. Thus the thematic frameworks commonly used to select global geosites may also need to be different to those used in Europe and elsewhere.

For Australia it is important to have an agreed listing of major geological sites (Joyce 2005, 2006b), sometimes referred to as geosites, as in the UNESCO Global Geosites program (Joyce 2007). The Geological Society of Australia, as the major organisation in this field for over 40 years, is a body well placed to set up and maintain such a database.

Australian geological heritage studies

Geological heritage studies in Australia go back more than 40 years to the first work by local Geological Society of Australia (GSA) groups in Queensland and South Australia in the 1960s. Even earlier, efforts had been made in promoting local reserves, and setting up notice boards and signs on individual sites.

In the mid-1960s, divisions of the Society (corresponding to the Australian states and territories) organized subcommittees of interested geologists and began a programme of seeking out and promoting individual sites. Correspondence and visits to the UK by Maud McBriar of South Australia and other workers helped provide new ideas. In the mid-1970s, with the aid of government grants, programmes of identifying, documenting, evaluating and recommending management of sites began across Australia (see historical review in Joyce 1994c). Joyce (1980 and 1995b) provides further details of work in Australia, as do papers from two international conferences, the first held at Digne in France in 1991 and the second at Malvern in the UK in 1993 (McBriar 1991; McBriar and Hasenohr 1994; Joyce 1994a, b).

Figure 3.3: Well-studied lunette and palaeolake floor of Lake Mungo, in the Willandra Lakes Region World Heritage Area, New South Wales, showing the 40,000 BP burial sites of the oldest human remains in Australia. (Photo J.M. Bowler).

Douglas (2006) has recently provided insight (Box 3.1) about geological heritage, concentrating on three landscapes in Australia – Adelaide's Hallett Cove, inland South Australia's Lake Callabonna Fossil Reserve and the World Heritage listed Willandra Lakes of western New South Wales (Figure 3.3). Once thought of as 'wasteland, desert, forsaken, degraded, unproductive and isolated' such features have now become of 'world renown' or 'classic ground'. Douglas points to an evolving methodology of geological heritage in Australia, citing the work of the GSA and the AHC. An extensive bibliography on heritage and geology in Australia is included.

Box 3.1 Geological heritage in Australia

The scarcity of navigable rivers and elevated mountain ranges in Australia encourages an aesthetic fashioned by the monumental scale represented by deep-time landscapes and objects instead of geography. This study seeks to construct a theory of geological heritage and the redemptive or recuperative power of material remains of the deep past, concentrating on three landscapes.

The South Australian Division of the Geological Society of Australia has played a central role in the preservation of geological heritage in that state since 1966 when the glacial pavements of Adelaide's Hallett Cove became the movement's flagship. The 44,800-hectare Lake Callabonna Fossil Reserve, a dry lake in the state's arid far east, has been celebrated by vertebrate palaeontologists as a significant landscape since the 1890s. The dry Willandra Lakes of western New South Wales were inscribed on the World Heritage List in 1981 for their cultural, archaeological and geological significance. These three celebrated areas have been variously described as wasteland, desert, forsaken, degraded, unproductive and isolated. Geological perspectives provide a new lexicon for the appreciation of Australian landscapes as the deep past is mobilised to turn them into regions of 'world renown' or 'classic ground'.

Extract derived from Douglas (2006)

Douglas (2006: 275) writes 'Despite its philosophical links to eco-tourism and World Heritage, the language of Geoparks, at least in Australia, is still notably utilitarian, again focused on finance, education, training and sustainability rather than aesthetics.' In her conclusion, Douglas (2006) notes that geological heritage in Australia can be hard to divorce from tourism, politics and nationalism, and that landscapes may need more than their geological significance to be celebrated, and gives as an example the World Heritage nomination of the Willandra Lakes, which had to harness archaeology, patrimony, landscape aesthetics and cultural heritage to ensure the preservation of important geological features.

The growth of geological heritage work in Australia

By the 1970s, each division had an active subcommittee, with work being carried out in each of the six states and also the Australian Capital Territory and Northern Territory. The establishment of the National Estate Grants Program in 1973 and the Australian Heritage Commission (AHC) in 1975 provided the first of a long series of Australian Government grants for the study of features of Australia's National Estate, and nomination of these to the then newly established Register of the National Estate. Grants totalling more than $320,000 over the next 25 years resulted in more than 30 substantial volumes of documentation.

A standing committee of the GSA was established in 1974 under Dr Colin Branch (Joyce 1994c) to help with the exchange of ideas between the seven subcommittees operating at that time – Queensland, New South Wales, Australian Capital Territory (with Northern Territory), Victoria, Tasmania, South Australia and Western Australia. Later the formation of a separate GSA Division in the Northern Territory, and so a new subcommittee, brought the number of subcommittees to eight. The history of the standing committee has been reviewed by Joyce (1994c) and a related timeline published (Joyce 2006a).

The state-based subcommittees each developed their own approaches to heritage studies. Some produced overall inventories in one volume while other systematically worked across their state producing a series of volumes. Some volumes were printed in hundreds of copies and distributed and sold widely, while others were only in a few reference copies, for example in South Australia only 16 copies of each report were printed, but with photocopies of appropriate sections sent to selected state government and local government bodies. A list of reports by the subcommittees and the standing committee is given in Appendix 5 in Joyce (1995b). A full list of 'Geological monuments in South Australia' (Parts 1 to 9, with details of 432 sites) has recently been issued on DVD (Hiern and Cowley 2008). Some subcommittees have made many nominations to the Register of the National Estate in Canberra, while others have made few. Where state registers are available, they have sometimes been used to register geological sites.

Books and leaflets on local geology, including geological heritage information, have been produced in Queensland and other states (Joyce 2007). Recent guidebooks sponsored by the Geological Society of Australia on scenery in National Parks in southern Queensland are part of a series prepared and published by the Queensland Division of the Geological Society of Australia. For the recently-declared World Heritage area of the Blue Mountains in NSW, a 34-page A4 colour booklet has been prepared by the NSW Department of Mineral Resources, in conjunction with the Geological Society of Australia, NSW National Parks and Wildlife Service, and the University of Sydney (Pickett and Alder 1997).

The major icons of central Australia, Uluru and Kata Tjuta, listed as World Heritage in 1987, have a detailed geological account as the first in a number of publications by the Australian Geological Survey Organisation (now Geoscience Australia). This series includes the relatively newly-recognized Bungle Bungle Range, in the East Kimberley of Western Australia, only proclaimed as the Purnululu National Park in 1987. With the Geological Society of Australia as a sponsor, a guide for the World Heritage area of Kakadu and Nitmiluk National Parks, in the Northern Territory of Australia, was published in 2000, and covers rocks, landforms, plants, and animals, the Aboriginal culture of the region, and the effects of human impact.

Methodology used in geological heritage studies in Australia

Initially GSA subcommittees in each state of Australia independently developed methods of identifying, documenting and determining the significance of a geological heritage site or feature. Methods of assessing significance, from local or regional to national or international level, were also developed by the Australian Heritage Commission for the Register of the National Estate, building in part on the expertise of the GSA subcommittees. The AHC approach to the classification and assessment of natural sites, using a detailed set of criteria, in turn exerted its influence on Society work. Techniques developed by the UK's Nature Conservancy Commission were also an important influence on GSA work in Australia. For a review of early Australian geoheritage work and its background up to 1980 see Joyce (1980).

Each Australian state and territory GSA subcommittee also looked to some extent at the work of subcommittees in other parts of Australia, and in two workshops sponsored by the Australian Heritage Commission (AHC) and held in Canberra in 1982 and 1984, discussions were held between the subcommittees in an attempt to achieve some degree of uniformity. However state and territory subcommittees continued largely to follow their own methods. The two workshops however did lead to the preparation of a report on sites of international and national significance in Australia. This report summarized the approaches used up to that time by each GSA subcommittee, and provided a consolidated list of Australian sites of international and national significance, drawn from published and unpublished subcommittee documentation (Cochrane and Joyce 1986).

GILGES

In 1991, a list of 28 geological sites of possible World Heritage significance was prepared by Joyce (1991) for the meeting of a UNESCO group in Paris in February 1991 to discuss the Global Indicative List of Geological Sites (GILGES) (see Table 3.1). GILGES was an initiative of UNESCO and ICSU to prepare a list of geological sites which might be considered for adding to the then current list of 30 geological sites on the World Heritage List (Cowie and Wimbledon 1994). The GILGES programme was replaced in 1995 by the UNESCO Global Geosites programme (Joyce 2007). Following discussion at the Paris meeting, a revised list of 26 sites for Australia appeared in the report by Cowie (1991). A related but more detailed list of 16 sites also appeared in McBriar and Hasenohr (1994).

The following list of sites is based on detailed work carried out in Australia by regional subcommittees of the Geological Society of Australia over more than 15 years. The list was prepared on 12 December 1990 in Canberra in discussions between Bernie Joyce, Federal Convener of the Geological Monuments Committee of the Geological Society of Australia, and Wanda Filsell, Jo Mummery and Phil Creaser, of the Department of the Arts, Sport, the Environment, Tourism and Territories. Since then Lake Callabonna has been added at the request of Maud McBriar, Convener of the S.A. Subcommittee.

Table 3.1: Global Indicative List of Geological Sites (GILGES) for Australia: extract from Joyce (1991: 2-4).

All the sites in this first list are documented elsewhere for the Working Group use.

1. Devonian reef complexes and Gogo fossil fish sites, W.A.
2. Ediacara Fossil Reserve, S.A.
3. Koonwarra Cretaceous fossil locality, Vic.
4. Lake Acraman meteorite crater and related depositional sites in Bunyeroo-Brachina Gorge, Flinders Ranges, S.A. Two separate localities.
5. Lake Callabonna, S.A.
6. Lord Howe Rise, N.S.W. On World Heritage List.
7. Macquarie Island, Tas. Being nominated to World Heritage List.
8. Mt Narryer and Jack Hills, W.A.
9. Naracoorte, S.A. Major fossil vertebrate site in Victoria Fossil Cave.
10. Archaean Microfossils and Stromatolites of the Pilbara, W.A. Includes North Pole site.
11. The Raak and Boinkas of the Sunset Country, Victoria.

12. Riversleigh, Qld. Cenozoic fossil sites.
13. Shark Bay, W.A. Being nominated to the World Heritage List.
14. Uluru (Ayers Rock), N.T. On World Heritage List.
15. Undara Crater and lava tubes, Qld.
16. Willandra Lakes, N.S.W. On World Heritage List.

Further possible sites - not proposed above - have been suggested by others.

17. Heard Island. Forms part of the Territory of Heard Island and McDonald Islands, and thus of the area recognized as Australian Territory; an oceanic island on the Antarctic plate. The largely Holocene cone of Big Ben is a currently active volcano, with a small lava lake at Mawson Peak, small cones along the coast, fringing moraine deposits, coastal plains, and outcrops of underlying Cainozoic limestone and volcanic deposits.
18. Blue Mountains, N.S.W. Large-scale landforms, with major weathering and erosion processes.
19. Lake Eyre region, S.A. Includes the Cainozoic Fossil Reserve of Lake Palankarinna and Dalhousie Mound Springs.
20. Flinders Ranges, S.A. Significant major Precambrian/Cambrian boundary site.
21. Hallet Cove Conservation Park, S.A.

Other sites included in the final list of sites

22. Yea Limestone, Victoria.
23. Wolf Creek Meteorite Crater, W.A.
24. Fraser Island and the Great Sandy Region, Queensland. On World Heritage List.
25. Nullarbor Plain, S.A. and W.A. This is probably the world's largest single area of karst and the largest and most significant arid karst area. Heritage Significance of the Nullarbor Plain Region in South Australia and Western Australia. Being prepared for nomination to World Heritage List.
26. Bungle Bungles, W.A.
27. Darwin meteorite crater, Tasmania.
28. Bitter Springs.

A review of the work of the GSA and the AHC in assessing the significance of geological heritage sites in Australia, from the local level to World Heritage, was published in 1994 (Joyce 1994b). In 1994, the GSA was commissioned by the AHC to prepare a methodology volume which would detail techniques for locating, describing, classifying and assessing sites and features of geological and geomorphological significance. As well as rock, mineral and fossil sites, this methodology was also to cover landforms, dynamic processes, and viewpoints, including evaluating their vulnerability to natural and human activity. A grant from the AHC enabled the GSA's standing committee members and other interested heritage workers to meet at a workshop in Canberra in 1994 and led to the preparation of a two-volume methodology report, which was to assist with future geological heritage work in Australia. The assessment volume (Joyce 1995a) was prepared in limited numbers, but its contents are available on disk and CD, and on the Web (see Joyce 1995a). The report includes a review of geological heritage methodologies used in Australia and overseas (Joyce 1995b), and a full list of heritage publications by the GSA to that time.

Geomorphological sites as well as geological sites can be classified using the methodology developed for the Australian Heritage Commission by Joyce (1995a), and a geomorphological and landscape approach has been discussed further by Joyce (2003). Themes are also being considered for use in Australian heritage work (see below) and lend themselves to a landscape approach to heritage. Cochrane and Joyce (1986) listed 'geomorphic' as the second of twelve geological types to be used in the assessment of geological significance, and in their list of important Australian sites, 70 of 229 are landforms or landscapes.

Based on the methodology approach discussed in Joyce (1994a and 1994b) and elaborated in Joyce (1995a, 1995b) the procedure can be referred to by the acronym IDEM, and summarized as Identification (of a site or feature of possible significance), Documentation (of its details), Evaluation (assessment of its geological significance), and Management (recommendations for protection and conservation). The case study in Box 3.2 illustrates the process of assessing geological significance.

Box 3.2: An example of the evaluation (assessment of geological significance) of an area: the Newer Volcanic province of southeastern Australia (based on Joyce 1994a, 1995b)

The young volcanic province of southeastern Australia provides an instructive example of how significance can be assessed (Figure 3.4). There are nearly 400 volcanoes, including about 40 maar craters (Maars are landforms caused by volcanic explosion and consist of a crater which extends below ground level and is considerably wider than deep, with a surrounding rim (tuff ring) constructed of material ejected from the crater). Extensive basaltic lava flows, some containing lava caves, cover a large part of western and central Victoria, and an adjacent part of South Australia. These have been identified and documented over many years (see for example Joyce 1975). The significance of about 25 volcanoes was assessed in an initial inventory (Joyce and King 1980). Included were volcanoes with young, morphologically well-preserved lava flows, including some with lava caves.

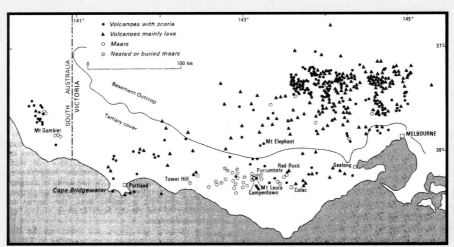

Figure 3.4: The Newer Volcanic Province of southeastern Australia

The initial assessment was of individual features such as cones, craters, flow features and lava caves. The possibility and indeed the necessity for further management planning to assess the whole of a particular eruption became evident, so that the cone and crater, flows, and any related features such as lava-dammed drainage were then looked at together.

An example is the Mt Napier volcanic complex (Joyce and King 1980: 116-120) consisting of a main volcanic centre with several eruption points, a broad area of lava flows forming a shield, several constricted valley flows with one flow having a major set of lava caves, and an unusual group of lava tumuli. Each set of features (cone, flows, caves, tumuli) initially was given its own significance level. The complex as a whole was later given a national significance.

In assessing the significance of features of the province beyond the local or state level, it was necessary to compare them with areas of similar volcanicity found in northern Queensland. In assessing their significance at international or world level, it was necessary for the assessor to have a good understanding of young basaltic lava fields around the world, such as the Auvergne in France, the Eifel in Germany, and areas in the United States of America, Mexico, New Zealand, and also the area of current activity in Hawaii. It was also possible to distinguish groups of possible higher significance within the province, such as the 40 or so maar volcanoes, which in variety, size and exposure rival those of the type area in the Eifel.

Another group that can be distinguished is that of the lava caves, which are found in several localities in the province, and in a variety of geomorphic settings including valley flows, flank flows, within a cone, and as part of an open vent. These caves are widely known in the geological literature, and one of the main theories for lava cave formation has been based on the study of the caves of this province.

A panel trying to assess the whole province, or its parts, would require local detailed knowledge (a field geologist, geological survey staff member, a geology teacher active in the area), and a knowledge of comparable areas elsewhere (perhaps a geomorphologist, especially if also a physical volcanologist). It would also help to commission a special study, and this has now been done in Victoria under the sponsorship of the Geological Society of Australia and the Victorian Branch of the National Trust of Australia, with funding from the government, and a discussion of the methodology used is given in Rosengren (1994a). At the final stage, a panel was used to check the assessment of significance carried out by the consultant, justifying significance levels in the broader context of the whole of Victoria, Australia or the world.

In this example it is possible to see how the process of identifying, documenting, and assessing individual features or sites, such as a scoria cone or lava cave, has been followed by the grouping of features, such as the Mt Napier complex, and then by the need to perhaps assess the whole volcanic province, or at least substantial sub-sets such as all lava caves, or all maar craters, at the international level.

Recommendations for future management should then follow.

Sites or features are classified as a geological or geomorphological type, for example stratigraphy, rocks and minerals, fossils and palaeontology, karst, glacial and so on. (Joyce 1995a), They can be representative of a group of similar sites, or they may be classed as outstanding. Assessment is carried out by a committee whose members have a wide range of geological experience and expertise. Sites or features are assessed at a level of significance, ranging from local, through regional, state, national, to international (see discussion in Joyce 1995a). The most recent discussion of the current procedure and protocol for the documentation and assessment of geological heritage sites in Australia is by White and Mitchell (2006). The most recent discussion of geological heritage work in Australia can be found in Brocx (2008). Chapter 5 in this book (pp.81-116) gives a historical review of initiatives and principles that underpin the conservation of geoheritage significance in Australia.

A review by Gray (2004: 249-254) described the GSA's work on geological heritage in Australia, especially in South Australia and Victoria. Gray discussed the criteria used by the AHC to assess geological features and sites for the Register of the National Estate, and the methodology developed for the AHC by Joyce (1995a), and he compared the work of the GSA with the work done by Tasmanian Government departments, discussing a code of practice developed in Tasmania. Finally, he discussed organisations such as the National Trust which are also interested in geological sites and features across Australia. The report by Rosengren (1994a) on the volcanoes of Victoria is an example of the landscape-related work carried out by the GSA with the Victorian section of the National Trust. Further examples are given in Bird and Joyce (2006). The result of the Geological Society of Australia's work is that Australia has for many years been recognized both within Australia and internationally as a leader in the field of geological conservation (see Geological Society of Australia Inc. web site).

Heritage registers

When the Australian Heritage Commission was set up by the Australian Government in 1975, one of its tasks was to compile a Register of the National Estate. This was to include places of natural, historic and Aboriginal heritage which should be kept for present and future generations. The GSA's heritage subcommittees soon became regarded by the AHC as expert nominators to the Register of the National Estate, and a total of 691 geological sites are currently on the Register (Creaser 2008).

Several Australian states also have heritage registers. In South Australia, natural sites including geological sites can be listed on the State Heritage Register, but in Victoria the register grew out of an historic buildings register, and so far only archaeological sites and shipwrecks have been added, and geological sites normally cannot be registered.

The National Trust of Australia consists of largely independent organizations in each state, and while mainly concerned with historic buildings and related heritage such as gardens, state national trusts may also study and classify landscapes, including their geological aspects, and include these landscapes on their registers (Bird and Joyce 2006).

Some other government-sponsored geological heritage studies

A major government sponsored study by Davey and White (1986) discussed the evaluation of the significance of caves and karst in the state of Victoria. Work at state government level includes consultant projects such as those of Rosengren in Victoria, including his study of the Late Cainozoic basaltic eruption points of Victoria (Rosengren 1994a) and its use in the management of scoria and tuff quarrying (Rosengren 1994b); the study was carried out jointly for the GSA's Victorian Subcommittee and the National Trust of Australia (Victoria), under an AHC grant.

In Tasmania, the Forestry, and Parks and Wildlife agencies of the Tasmanian Government have developed a methodology which includes geomorphological and soil features (Dixon et al., 1997), and a Tasmanian Geoconservation Database is available on the web at: http://www.dpiw.tas.gov.au/inter2.nsf/WebPages/LBUN-6TY32G?open (See also: http://www.dpiw.tas.gov.au/inter.nsf/WebPages/SJON-57W4FD?open.) White

(2008), current Convener of the GSA's Geological Heritage Standing Committee, has recently described the Tasmanian work and compared it with the work of the GSA.

Australian Natural Heritage Charter

An Australian Natural Heritage Charter was funded by the AHC and published in 1996 (Australian Committee for IUCN 1996). It was based in part on the Australia International Council on Monuments and Sites (ICOMOS) Charter for the Conservation of Cultural Significance ('Burra Charter' of 1992), which provided guidelines for places with both natural and cultural values. The Natural Heritage Charter provides standards and principles for the conservation of places of natural heritage significance. A Natural Heritage Places handbook published in 1998 provided further assistance in applying the Charter to determine significance and prepare conservation and management plans.

Australian parks and reserves, including geoparks

National parks in each state and in the territories provide valuable protection and management for many geological heritage sites; indeed the initial impetus for setting up such parks has often been their geological features and landscape values. However, few parks services employ or work with geologists, and management and interpretation is strongly biased towards biological and ecological aspects. Geological research including sampling is also restricted in national parks. There have been significant problems of management in World Heritage areas such as the Willandra Lakes (see Figure 3.3), and many national parks are poorly funded and interpreted (Joyce 1999).

There is a need for new groupings which emphasise geological and geomorphological sites, and the concept of *Geoparks* can be usefully applied in Australia to such areas as the youthful Western Volcanic Plains of Southeastern Australia, a closely settled agricultural region, which in June 2008 was accepted as the Kanawinka Global Geopark and thus Australia's first Geopark (McKnight 2008, Joyce and Bröhl 2008, Lewis 2008). Such regions, generally not suitable for national parks, can provide useful groupings of geological sites for future geotourism (Joyce 2007).

The new Australian Government approach to heritage

The Australian Heritage Commission has now been replaced by the Australian Heritage Council, and from 1 January 2004 a new National Heritage List of places with outstanding heritage values to Australia is being developed by the Australian Government. The values of places on the new National Heritage List will be protected under the Environment Protection and Biodiversity Conservation Act 1999 and later amendments.

The new National Heritage List will be made up of outstanding places with values to be protected by the Australian Government. These places will highlight the major stories of Australia – the evolution of the land, the qualities of its people and the diversity of its culture. All Australians will be able to nominate places, but nominations will be sought from professional groups such as the Geological Society of Australia. The earlier Register of the National Estate included many geological heritage sites but this Register was frozen on 19 February 2007, meaning that no new places can be added or removed. It continues to be available online (http://www.environment.gov.au/cgi-bin/ahdb/search.pl).

After five years there are now 100 properties on the National Heritage List, but so far there are only 20 or so geological or geomorphological places on the List. The Dinosaur Stampede National Monument in Queensland was one of the first three places to be listed on the National Heritage List in July 2004. Located at Lark Quarry Conservation Park, 110 km south of Winton in Central Queensland, the site features unique evidence of a dinosaur stampede with almost 4000 dinosaur footprints clearly visible in an area of just 210 square metres. Two archaeological sites, in the Budj Bim National Heritage Landscape, are part of the young Mt Eccles volcano and associated lava flows in southwestern Victoria, which are of geological heritage significance. Further fossil sites (Naracoorte, Riversleigh, Yea, Ediacara) have been now added, and World Heritage places such as the Great Barrier Reef, Greater Blue Mountains, Kakadu, Purnululu, Uluru–Kata Tjuta, and the Willandra Lakes have also been included on the National Heritage List.

The use of themes

The concept of themes 'telling a story' is a recent AHC approach, and is similar to concepts used by World Heritage. This approach can help link individual sites to the landscape, to processes past and present, and cultural aspects, across large areas. Two examples of themes are *The onset of aridity in Australia* (dry lakes and lunettes of the World Heritage area of the Willandra Lakes in New South Wales, and desert dunes of the inland e.g. the Simpson Desert); and *Young volcanicity and tectonics in an active Australian landscape* – volcanoes, lava flows and ash deposits of the last million years in Victoria, and also in northern Queensland (Joyce 2003).

Figure 3.5: The famous Twelve Apostles rock stacks developed in Tertiary marine limestone, Port Campbell National Park, western Victoria, with active coastal erosion illustrated with before and after photos taken seconds apart at 9.16 am on 3 July 2005 (Photos Parks Victoria, but taken by a tourist visiting the area). The 'Twelve Apostles' rock stacks of the Port Campbell coastline (Bird 1993: 61-84) have a long history of studied and recorded coastal change over more than 70 years, with a deduced abrupt 'erosion rates of 1 or 2 metres once a century'.

In Australia it is important for future geoheritage understanding to be able to explain to the public the story of the continent's changing landscape – the marks left by the climate of the last ice age, the effects of aboriginal occupation, sea level change, and European arrival. The present landscape should be linked to aboriginal dreaming and indigenous archaeology, to past and present climate, and finally to current and active landform changes (see Figure 3.5). Links can also be made to European 18th and 19th century exploration, and finally to the understanding of the Australian landscape developed over the past 200 years through the experiences of early settlers, miners and farmers, builders and architects, gardeners and landscape planners, poets and painters, and musicians and writers. This thematic approach is ideal for the selection and setting up of geoparks, and their use in geotourism.

Recent reviews and evaluations

The Australian Heritage Commission has commissioned an independent review of geological heritage sites in Australia, providing from its resources a list of sites to be investigated. A two-volume report has been prepared, listing, describing and evaluating sites of possible international and national significance. The first volume covered 198 Australian rock and landform sites (Yeates 2001a), and a companion volume (Yeates 2001b) provided a similar assessment for 150 fossil sites (see summary of numbers in Table 3.2, suggesting that not all states have been adequately covered).

Table 3.2: Number of fossil sites in each state/territory of Australia, from Yeates (2001b).

New South Wales	52
Queensland	28
Western Australia	18
Northern Territory	14
Victoria	13
Tasmania	9
South Australia	9
Australian Capital Territory	0
TOTAL	143
No of sites considered	150

Between 2005 and 2007, the AHC commissioned palaeontologists from seven state and territory museums to conduct a comprehensive comparison of outstanding fossil sites, in addition to a report that provided a comparison of the most important plant fossil sites nationally. These eight documents were then peer reviewed and edited to produce a single document, titled *Australian Fossil Sites for Potential National Heritage Listing* (Cook 2007). This draft report will enable strategic assessment of fossil sites for the National Heritage List by providing a shortlist of places that best demonstrate the evolution of Australia's biota.

The AHC also held expert workshops in 2006 and 2007 to establish a national framework for the assessment of important karst and pseudokarst sites. Results from both workshops will allow the effective comparative assessment of karst and pseudokarst sites around Australia, and produced a shortlist of important sites that illustrate the range of karst and pseudokarst features in Australia, along with a strategy for further research (Ambrose and Douglas 2008).

Geotourism in Australia

In 1996 the conference of the Geological Society of Australia was held in the national capital Canberra, and two presentations were concerned with geotourism – perhaps the earliest mention of the term amongst the Australian geological community. Casey and Stephenson (1996) spoke from their practical experience and provided 'tips and practical experience' on putting geology in tourism. They argued for the use of simple explanations of geology, avoiding the use of jargon, and they suggested including links to indigenous (aboriginal) legends, and also making use of the public's interest in orchards and wineries. W. Mayer's 1996 paper discussed geology and tourism, and suggested Australia was well-suited to nature tours, for example in areas such as Kakadu and the Great Barrier Reef. Mayer (1996) also referred to geotours in the Hamersley and Pilbara regions of far northern Western Australia, and argued that geotourism needed 'small, compact, but well-illustrated guidebooks'; he suggested that the Geological Society of Australia might help produce these.

Geotourism, or tourism related to geological sites and features, including geomorphological sites and landscapes, can be seen as a new phenomenon, and also a subset of geology and tourism. In the Australian context, the definition of geotourism has been explored, and a working definition of *geotourism* suggested:

> *people going to a place to look at and learn about one or more aspects of geology and geomorphology*
>
> (Joyce 2006b, c)

A recent book (Dowling and Newsome 2006) discusses geotourism across the globe, but unfortunately the section on Australia fails to acknowledge the work of the GSA, thus demonstrating the need to make databases of Australian geosites better known and more freely available (see discussion in Joyce 2008).

In August 2008, the Inaugural Global Geotourism Conference, 'Discover The Earth Beneath Our Feet,' was held in Fremantle, Western Australia, and several presentations reviewed the work of the GSA and the AHC over the past 40 or more years and its importance for future geotourism in Australia (Ambrose and Douglas 2008, Creaser 2008, Joyce and Bröhl 2008, Lewis 2008). These papers show how geological heritage studies in Australia are being applied to local geotourism.

Current listings of major geological heritage sites in Australia

A number of listings of the main Australian geological heritage sites have been prepared over the last 20 years:

1. **Cochrane and Joyce (1986).** This was the first report to list sites of International and National Significance for all of Australia, with 76 International sites.

2. **Joyce (1991).** In 1991 a list of 28 geological sites of possible World Heritage significance was prepared for the GILGES meeting in Paris in February 1991 (see Table 3.1). Following discussion at that meeting, a revised list of 26 sites for Australia appeared in the report by Cowie (1991). A related but more detailed list of 16 sites also appeared in McBriar and Hasenohr (1994).

3. **Yeates (2001a, b).** An independent review of geological heritage sites in Australia for the AHC listed, described and evaluated sites of possible International and Na-

tional significance (see Table 3.2). A further development is the listing of major fossil sites by Cook (2007).

4. **The current World Heritage Area list for Australia** (UNESCO World Heritage List website) shows 17 properties of which 12 are major geological sites.

In summary, the various documents listing geological heritage sites in Australia suggest there may be a total of 100 or more sites of international significance, including rock, mineral, stratigraphic, landform and process sites, and fossil sites. The actual numbers in Yeates (2001a and b) are not clearly presented. Comments by Yeates (2001a, b) also suggest additional sites may need to be added to the current listings to approach a level of completeness. In particular, he suggests further fossil sites may be needed, especially in some parts of Australia, and for certain types and ages of fossils. Yeates (2001b) noted that documentation was not complete for many fossil sites, making assessment difficult. It is likely that further landform and process sites, including coastal, tropical savannah, and weathering (regolith) sites in northern Australia, will also need to be added. Finally, in a recent study for the Australian Government expert workers selected and discussed ten fossil sites from each of Australia's seven states, giving a total of 70 sites. Some additional fossil sites were included in the related report compiled and edited by Cook (2007).

Geosites for Australian geotourism – how can geotourism workers find and use this information?

The Geological Society of Australia and the Australian Heritage Commission have been the main bodies concerned with geological heritage in the past, and some 30 reports have been prepared, covering most parts of Australia. Several overall listings have also been prepared, and many sites have been listed on the Register of the National Estate maintained by the AHC.

A full set of the GSA's grant-supported reports is in the library of the (former) AHC in Canberra. Copies of GSA reports have also often gone to state government departments, and sometimes local government bodies. Recently these volumes have been reviewed and summarised for the AHC by Yeates (2001a, b). In Victoria, copies of some studies were printed by and offered for sale by the Geological Survey of Victoria. Details of sites were also included in a Geological Survey of Victoria database. In South Australia, details of sites were included in a Geological Survey of South Australia and South Australian Museum database. Recently a set of CDs of all the South Australian GSA heritage reports was made available. However, geological heritage publications on Australia, particularly of some GSA divisions (i.e. state branches) can be difficult to locate.

Databases of geological heritage information already online include the AHC's Register of the National Estate and the National Heritage List, Victorian Resources Online, and the Tasmanian Geoconservation Database. Other information is becoming available on CD and DVD e.g. Hiern and Cowley (2008).

An up-to-date listing of database of Australian geosites should be made available. Such a database inventory will be of significant value to future geological heritage work in Australia, and justify the work involved. To assist in this work a website has been set up through the Geological Society of Australia (Victoria Division), which will be used to provide the background to the proposed program, and begin developing and maintaining an index to current databases, and also provide a list of all publications on geological heritage sites in Australia. The URL is: http://vic.gsa.org.au/geosites.htm

These data sets will also be linked from a related *Geotourism in Australia* website (http://vic.gsa.org.au/geotourism.htm). Locating and listing all available databases, developing them further, and making them freely available is a necessary condition for the future of geotourism and geoparks in Australia.

References

Ambrose, J. and Douglas, K. (2008) 'Australia's Geological Heritage and the National Heritage List', Inaugural Global Geotourism Conference, 'Discover The Earth Beneath Our Feet,' Fremantle, Western Australia, 17-20 August 2008.

Australian Committee for IUCN (1996) 'Australian Natural Heritage Charter: Standards and Principles for the Conservation of Places of Natural Heritage Significance', Australian Heritage Commission in association with the Australian Committee for IUCN, Sydney.

Bird, E.C.F. (1993) *The Coast of Victoria*, Melbourne University Press, Carlton, Victoria.

Bird, Juliet and Joyce, Bernie (2006) 'The National Trust and landscape heritage in Victoria: recent assessments of volcanic landscapes in Western Victoria', AESC 2006 Extended Abstract.

Brocx, M. (2008) *Geoheritage: from global perspectives to local principles for conservation and planning.* Western Australian Museum, Perth, Western Australia, 175 pp.

Casey, J.N. and Stephenson, A.E. (1996) 'Putting geology into tourism – some tips and practical experience', Geological Society of Australia, 13th Australian Geological Convention, Canberra, February 1996, Abstracts 41, p.79.

Cochrane, R.M. and Joyce, E.B. (1986) 'Geological features of national and international significance in Australia', report prepared for the Australian Heritage Commission, May, 1986. Federal Committee for Geological Monuments, Geological Society of Australia.

Cook, A. (ed.) (2007) 'Australian fossil sites for potential National Heritage Listing', report for the Department of Environment and Water Resources, Australian Government, Canberra.

Cowie, J.W. (1991) Report of Task Force Meeting, Paris, France, February 1991. UNESCO World Heritage Convention, Working Group on Geological (inc. Fossil) Sites, IUGS Secretariat, Norway.

Creaser, Phil. (2008) 'Australia's geological heritage: raising awareness at a national level', Inaugural Global Geotourism Conference, 'Discover The Earth Beneath Our Feet', Fremantle, Western Australia, 17-20 August 2008, pp.135-139.

Davey, A.G. and White, S.(1986) 'Victorian caves and karst: strategies for management and cataloguing', report to the Caves Classification Committee, Department of Conservation, Forests and Lands, Victoria.

Dixon, G., Houshold, I. and Pemberton, M. (1997) 'Geoconservation in Tasmania – Wizards of Oz!', *Earth Heritage*, 8, 4-15.

Douglas, K. (2006) 'Forsaken spot' to 'classic ground': geological heritage in Australia and the recuperative power of the deep past', *Environment and History*, 12, 269–296.

Dowling, R.K. and Newsome, D. (eds) (2006) *Geotourism*, Elsevier Butterworth Heinemann, Amsterdam.

Geological Society of Australia websites:
   Heritage: http://gsa.org.au/heritage/index.html
   Policy: http://gsa.org.au/pdfdocuments/management/POL_heritage_7Mar06.pdf
   Victoria Division: http://www.vic.gsa.org.au/heritage.html

Gray, M. (2004) *Geodiversity: Valuing and Conserving Abiotic Nature*, John Wiley and Sons, Chichester.

Hiern, N. and Cowley, W. (compilers) (2008) 'Geological monuments in South Australia', Geological Society of Australia and Government of South Australia, Primary Industries and Resources SA, MEDP no. 17 (DVD).

Joyce, E.B. (1975) 'Quaternary volcanism and tectonics in southeastern Australia', *Royal Society of New Zealand Bull*, **13**, 169-176.

Joyce, E.B. (1980) 'Appendix B. Geological conservation in Australia and overseas', in E.B. Joyce and R.L. King (eds), *Geological Features of the National Estate in Victoria*, Victorian Division, Geological Society of Australia, pp. 191–202.

Joyce, E.B. (1991) 'Pacific and Antarctic areas, World Heritage List, Geological Sites', unpublished document prepared for the Meeting of the World Heritage Working Group Task Force on a Global Inventory of Geological and Fossil Sites held in Paris, 11-13 February 1991.

Joyce, E.B. (1994a) Keynote address – identifying geological features of international significance: the Pacific Way', in O'Halloran, D., Green, C., Harley, M., Stanley, M. and Knill, J. (eds), *Geological and Landscape Conservation*, Geological Society, London, pp. 507-513.

Joyce, E.B. (1994b) 'Assessing the significance of geological heritage sites: from the local level to world heritage'. Proceedings of the 1st International Symposium on the Conservation of Our Geological Heritage, Digne les Bains, 11-16 June 1991. *Mémoires de la Société géologique de France*, n.s.165, 37-43.

Joyce, E.B. (1994c) 'Geological Heritage Committee', in Cooper, B.J. and Branagan, D.F. (eds) *Rock Me Hard... Rock Me Soft... A History of the Geological Society of Australia Incorporated*, Geological Society of Australia, Sydney, pp.30-36.

Joyce, E.B. (1995a) 'Assessing the significance of geological heritage: a methodology study for the Australian Heritage Commission', report prepared for the Australian Heritage Commission by the Standing Committee for Geological Heritage of the Geological Society of Australia. (Available at: http://web.earthsci.unimelb.edu.au/Joyce/heritage/methodology1.html)

Joyce, E.B. (1995b) 'A review of geological heritage methodologies, with a bibliography of publications and reports on the methodology of geological heritage in Australia and overseas', Appendix 1 in Joyce, E.B. 'Assessing the significance of geological heritage: a methodology study for the Australian Heritage Commission', report prepared for the Australian Heritage Commission by the Standing Committee for Geological Heritage of the Geological Society of Australia, pp. A1.1-A1.23. (Available at: http://web.earthsci.unimelb.edu.au/Joyce/heritage/appendix1.html)

Joyce, E.B. (1995c) 'Geological heritage reports prepared by the Standing Committee for Geological Heritage and the subcommittees in each division of the Geological Society of Australia Inc.', Appendix 5 in Joyce, E.B. 'Assessing the significance of geological heritage: a methodology study for the Australian Heritage Commission', report prepared for the Australian Heritage Commission by the Standing Committee for Geological Heritage of the Geological Society of Australia, pp. A5.1-A5.4. (Available at: http://web.earthsci.unimelb.edu.au/Joyce/heritage/appendix1.html)

Joyce, B. (1999) 'Different thinking: The oldest continent', *Earth Heritage*, **12**, 11-13. (Available at: http://web.earthsci.unimelb.edu.au/Joyce/heritage/EHarticle.pdf)

Joyce, B. (2003) 'Geomorphological sites in Australia: heritage assessment and vulnerability', abstract for the Regional Geomorphology Conference, Section S.13 'Geomorphological sites: vulnerability and assessment', International Association of Geomorphologists, Mexico City, October–November 2003, pp.158-159.

Joyce, E.B. (2005) 'Geosites of Australia: preparing an inventory and framework for the Global Inventory of the IUGS', IV International Symposium ProGEO on the Conservation of the Geological Heritage, Abstracts, 13-16 September 2005, University of Minho, Braga – Portugal, p. 23.

Joyce, B. (2006a) 'Standing Committee for Geological Heritage, GSA Inc., History Timeline 1959 to 1993', *Earth Science History Group Newsletter*, no. 36, June, pp. 9-16.

Joyce, E.B. (2006b) 'Geological heritage of Australia: selecting the best for Geosites and World Heritage, and telling the story for geotourism and Geoparks', AESC 2006 Extended Abstract.

Joyce, E.B. (2006c) 'Geomorphological sites and the new geotourism in Australia', electronic text: http://web.earthsci.unimelb.edu.au/Joyce/heritage/GeotourismReviewebj.htm

Joyce, B. (2007) 'Geotourism, Geosites and Geoparks: working together in Australia', special report, *Australian Geologist*, Newsletter, no. 144, September, 26-29.

Joyce, E.B. (2008) *Geotourism*, Ross K. Dowling and D. Newsome (eds) 2006, book reviews', *Australian Geologist*, Newsletter, no. 146, March, 43-45.

Joyce, B. and Bröhl, Mirjam (2008) 'Geological and geomorphological features of Australia: how our geosites can be used in geoparks and geotourism to promote better understanding of our geological heritage and as a tool for public education'. Inaugural Global Geotourism Conference, 'Discover The Earth Beneath Our Feet,' Fremantle, Western Australia, 17-20 August 2008, pp. 209-214.

Joyce, E.B. and King, R.L. (1980) 'Geological features of the national estate in Victoria', inventory compiled for the Australian Heritage Commission, Victorian Division, Geological Society of Australia.

Lewis, I.D. (2008) 'Australia's Kanawinka Geopark – volcanoes and lakes, limestone and sinkholes'. Inaugural Global Geotourism Conference, 'Discover The Earth Beneath Our Feet,' Fremantle, Western Australia, 17-20 August 2008, pp. 251-256.

McBriar, M. (1991) 'Conference report: the First International Symposium on the Conservation of our Geological Heritage, Digne, Provence, France, June 1–16, 1991', *Australian Geologist. Newsletter of the Geological Society of Australia Inc.*, 80, 14–15.

McBriar, E.M. and Hasenohr, P. (1994) 'Australian initiatives in earth science conservation. Proceedings of the 1st International Symposium on the Conservation of Our Geological Heritage, Digne les Bains, 11-16 June 1991', *Mémoires de la Société géologique de France*, n.s. **165**, 75-79.

McKnight, J. (2008) 'Development of the Australian Geopark', Inaugural Global Geotourism Conference, 'Discover The Earth Beneath Our Feet,' Fremantle, Western Australia, 17-20 August 2008. pp.57-62.

Mayer, W. (1996) 'Geology and tourism. Geological Society of Australia, 13th Australian Geological Convention, Canberra, February 1996', *Abstracts 41*, p. 278.

Nicholas, F.W. and Nicholas, J.M. (2002) *Charles Darwin in Australia*, Cambridge University Press, Cambridge.

Pickett, J.W. and Alder, J.D. (1997) *Layers of Time: the Blue Mountains and their Geology*, New South Wales Department of Mineral Resources, Sydney.

Rosengren, N. (1994a) *Eruption Points of the Newer Volcanics Province of Victoria*, National Trust of Australia (Victoria) and Geological Society of Australia (Victorian Division).

Rosengren, N. (1994b) 'The Newer Volcanic Province of Victoria, Australia: the use of an inventory of scientific significance in the management of scoria and tuff quarrying', in O'Halloran, D., Green, C., Harley, M., Stanley, M. and Knill, J. (eds), *Geological and Landscape Conservation*, Geological Society, London, pp. 105-110.

White, S. (2008) 'Heritage matters', *Australian Geologist*, newsletter no. 147, September, p.11.

White, S. and Mitchell, M. (2006) 'Geological heritage sites: a procedure and protocol for documentation and assessment', *AESC 2006 Extended Abstract*.

Yeates, A.N. (2001a) 'An assessment of progress made towards the nomination of Australian geological sites having National or International significance. Volume 1: rocks and landforms', report for the Australian Heritage Commission.

Yeates, A.N.(2001b) 'An assessment of progress made towards the nomination of Australian geological sites having National or International significance. Volume 2: fossils', report for the Australian Heritage Commission.

4 Centralized data management approaches in geotourism: a view from Finland

Ari Brozinski, University of Turku, Finland

Introduction

This chapter discusses the current situation of Popularization of Geology (PoG) and geotourism with focus set on Finland. An introduction to Centralized Data Management (CDM) is given and its potential benefits for PoG and geotourism are investigated. Additionally, the pathway for producing CDM-driven geotourism is explored. Finally, practical examples that were planned and realized by the author introduce the use of CDM systems.

After explaining the distinction between geotourism and PoG some thought is given to the matter of using modern technology to develop them. Ideally, by taking advantage of today's possibilities (the Internet to say the least), we may be able to bind different instances acting within geotourism and PoG development together and thus increase the level of communication and output. This results in a positive effect on the local economy. CDM itself is no specific system designed to produce geotourism. Instead, it is an outline that describes a pathway to improve communication where the free flow of information plays a central role.

This chapter describing the use of CDM should not be considered to be a step-by-step guidebook for developing geotourism using Information and Communication Technology (ICT). However, it can and could be utilized as a tool when data management, people and businesses are bound together with geology. Finally, existing geotourism solutions can benefit from ideas presented in this chapter by taking advantage of CDM and thus strengthening current interactions between active parties involved.

The popularization of geology

It is hard to tell when geoscience popularization began. A potential candidate as a popularization pioneer was the *Penny Magazine*, published in Britain during the 1830s. One of its features was its geology-related articles which discussed scientific phenomena such as lavas use as fertilizer or the extraction of quicksilver from ore (*Penny Magazine* 1835a, 1835b). In other words, the articles explained how our Earth works by giving geoscience a context from familiar surroundings and thus connecting it to everyday life. This is pretty much what one would expect from the popularization of geology.

PoG may include a wide variety of aspects. It can be viewed as a general way to educate the public about basic geology or on the other hand to encompass very specific geological data. Although great for science popularization, PoG essentially lacks a supporting structure that allows it to be turned into a commercial touristic venue. In recent years such supporting structures have been fused into PoG thus giving birth to geotourism.

PoG and geotourism can be thought to contain the same data (Figure 4.1). However, there is a distinct difference between these two (in addition to the touristic structures). PoG only goes as far as educating people about geology whereas geotourism involves aspects familiar from other forms of tourism. Such aspects include sleeping, eating and logistic services. Also, PoG may be realized as a single entity but geotourism can bound together with neighbouring branches of tourism such as eco and active tourism. Bundling other activities together with geotourism is wise as it appears that only people with a specialist interest in geology are ready to pack their family and travel hundreds of kilometres for a specific outcrop although spectacular landscapes such as the Grand Canyon in the USA are notable exceptions.

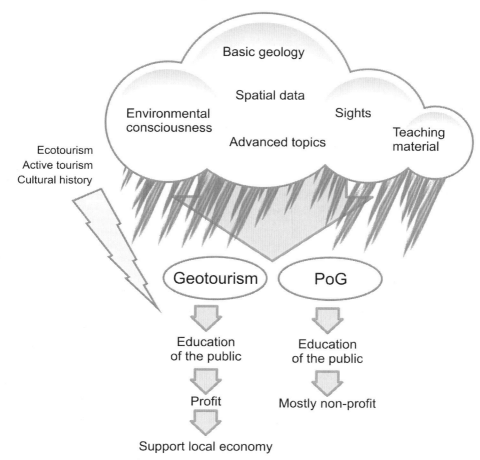

Figure 4.1: Geotourism and PoG.

Defining geotourism

Geotourism has been given many definitions over its short lifespan of little more than 10 years. Despite its relatively recent birth, it is hard to tell where the term originates from. One of the earliest references the author was able to find is a blog entry written by Jonathan B. Tourtellot in late October 2003. Tourtellot (2003) writes that he 'worked the term out on a long drive' with his wife in 1997. He also gives the term a definition by describing it as 'Tourism that sustains or enhances the geographical character of a place – its environment, heritage, aesthetics, culture and the well-being of its residents' (Tourtellot 2003). This definition is largely adopted by Stueve *et al.* (2002) in the first geotourism study where geotourism is defined to be something that is 'concerned with preserving a destination's geographic character – the entire combination of natural and human attributes that make one place distinct from another.'

National Geographic shares this viewpoint and presents it on their Center for Sustainable Destinations (CSD) home page (National Geographic 2008). Here the term 'geotourism' is broadened by coupling it with the concepts of sustainable tourism and ecotourism. Additionally, some purposes of geotourism such as economical benefit, local culture and synergy are named. It should be mentioned that National Geographic has also produced a 'Geotourism Charter'. This is an agreement between two or more parties to highlight the environment, cultural, historic, scenic and geographical assets. Although one might not agree with all of its points belonging to geotourism, the charter does include some interesting factors such as tourist satisfaction, community involvement and conservation of resources. (National Geographic 2005).

Dowling and Newsome (2006) have given geotourism a more geological character. They emphasize the appreciation of processes that created or are creating geology, geomorphology and natural resources and also mention the 'wow' factor that should belong to a geotouristic experience. Moreover, they specify geotourism as 'a subsector of natural area tourism'. This is important since many definitions seem to include a large scale of subjects ranging from culture to wildlife. Geotourism needs other branches of tourism to exist, but it should be seen as its own distinct sector of tourism.

A practical approach

Making rocks live

Essentially rocks are dead. This presents a huge dilemma when trying to turn geology into a profit making tourism activity. Prima facie the situation may indeed look difficult. There's no question that a safari in Africa with its lions and elephants instantly creates deep reaching appreciation within a visitor. But then again, the story of our Earth is very fascinating; no matter where on our planet it is observed and hence deserves to be told. After all it is something that literally involves every occupant on this planet. To overcome the obstacle of dead rock, a number of measures have to be taken to produce a comprehensive experience that doesn't just involve a random geological feature at *place X* but actually manages to tell the story about how such a feature could have formed. It should give the visitor that certain 'wow', too.

Binding people together with CDM

Geotourism isn't about a geologist reflecting his views on science popularization to the public. That would be PoG. Based on empiric research this seems to be a common misconception when the word *geotourism* is mentioned to a geologist. After all, geotourism consists of two words (at least for geologists): geology and tourism. A geologist can't do both. When thinking about the tourism industry a number of important instances that influence a touristic experience come to mind. Figure 4.2 shows a few of these. Centralized Data Management (CDM) acts as a link between instances. A dashed line is drawn to demonstrate the direct link for a geologist to produce geotourism.

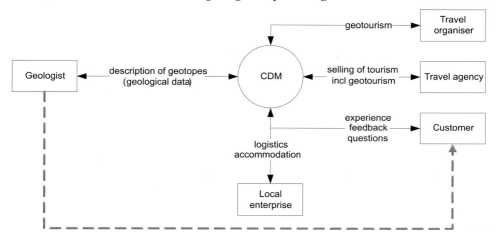

Figure 4.2: CDM and its instances.

If the context diagram was to be expanded, a sample scenario for producing geotourism could be something like this: a geologist describes geotopes of a certain area. A travel organizer produces a geotourism package by making it an 'add-on' to an already existing vacation package. The travel agency sells this add-on to the customer. A local enterprise (e.g. a bus company) receives information about sold add-on packages and arranges transportation for visitors. Based on customer feedback, all parties involved are able to shape their services towards a better end-user experience which eventually will help in turning the 'dead' rock alive.

The outcome of CDM

Geotourism, like any other branch of tourism, can have a positive influence on the local economy. This nonetheless requires its integration into the tourism infrastructure. Whereas Figure 4.2 showed instances that can be integrated using CDM, Figure 4.3 shows a possible outcome when CDM-driven geotourism is realized.

In Figure 4.3, CDM acts as a 'huge kettle' that is used in the realization phase of geotourism. First, the required elements from products, instances and development phases, are picked and then they're stirred together using CDM. Possible products may include geological booklets, walking tours, interactive multimedia kiosks and Internet services. Instances (see Figure 4.2), on the other hand are people or enterprises getting involved in project development. Development phases (see section 'Turning Finnish Bedrock into Geotourism') contain a chosen set of actions to be utilised during the project.

As the name implies CDM has three main functions: to centrally store all data produced within a project, to bind different instances acting within a project together and last, to enable free flow of information. When all data are stored centrally, the accuracy of information derived from the system is ensured. In other words all products use the latest data. Since this can be achieved in a number of ways, no specific description about the technical realization for a CDM is given. A strong possibility would be to build such a system around a Content Management System (CMS) that already is Internet-enabled. Positive experiences gathered from the Geologia.fi Internet portal that uses a CMS are discussed in the next section.

The positive feedback on the local economy mentioned above is achieved in many ways. For instance, CDM links products (e.g. geological walking tours) with companies offering them, hence improving the company's income. On the other hand, as more tourists visit an area where geotourism has been developed, other branches not directly dependent on tourism (restaurants, fuel services) also benefit.

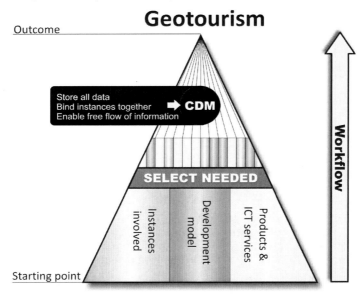

Figure 4.3: How geotourism is realised and where CDM is used.

Geologia.fi – first steps towards using CDM

Geologia.fi was started in 2006 by the Finnish National Committée in Geology. The initial goal of the project was to produce an Internet site that would hold basic geology-related content, advance the visibility of geology and improve the teaching of geology in schools (SKGK 2006). While the original feature list included a link list and very limited amount of content, the project turned out to be a lot more.

Concept and functionality

Basic functionality of Geologia.fi is illustrated in Figure 4.4. The system has four entities, the administrator, author, end user and the Finnish Museum of Natural History (FMNH). All entities have different roles: the museum supplies news, the administrator manages the system, while authors provide content (and news). Users give feedback based on the content they read. The steering committee for Geologia.fi (The Finnish National Committée in Geology) is intentionally excluded, since it has little influence on everyday routines.

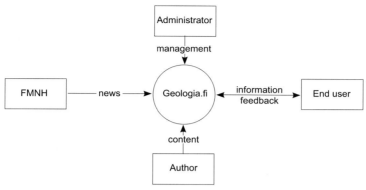

Figure 4.4: Context diagram of Geologia.fi

Figure 4.5 expands the Geologia.fi context diagram into a level 1 data flow diagram. In Figure 4.5 process 1 (Manage content) portrays the actual routine which manages all content in the system. It exchanges information between the datastore T1 and also contains interfaces for the user and administrator (front end/back end). The back end is meant solely for persons having daily management duties that require more than simply inputting information. The front end is the user interface which everyone can see. Depending on access rights, some users are able to insert data into the system through the front end. To gain a look on the mechanics operating behind this would require a deeper level data flow diagram. A separate process is used to view data and to collect feedback from the user. Authors communicate directly with process 1 when they are producing content. Also, geological news and information are automatically collected from the Finnish Museum of Natural History.

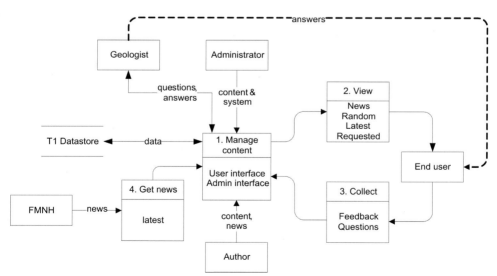

Figure 4.5: Level 1 data flow diagram of Geologia.fi

Existing features (process 2 View) include the display of news, random articles, latest addition and user requested material. In turn, the user provides feedback and asks questions (process 3 Collect). Feedback is forwarded to a geologist, who answers them, replies to the system (for a future FAQ) and also sends a reply to the user. By having a process that centrally manages content (process 1) it is easy to develop the system further by simply adding new features which receive all information from the Manage Content process. One such feature could be a photo gallery that automatically collects all geological images uploaded into the system and forms galleries based on them. When considering the concept behind this, it becomes clear that geologia.fi is a semantic system (see Figure 4.6 for details).

Even though no comment is made about the actual implementation (software) of Geologia.fi, it should be noted that geologia.fi is a semantic system. This is essential when developing CDM. When looking at the level 1 data flow diagram in Figure 4.5, it can be seen that displaying content is separated from its storage (T1). In other words, data inputs by authors are not bound to the actual web pages the users are browsing. By definition such system is semantic (e.g. Silver 2007). This is essential when thinking about CDM. The difference between a CDM system and single pages in a web environment is shown in the Figure 4.6.

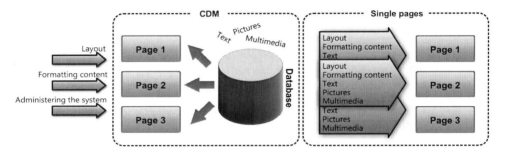

Figure 4.6: The difference between a CDM system and single pages in a web environment

In practice

In practice, Geologia.fi utilizes an open source GPL-licensed Content Management System (CMS) called Joomla. Joomla comes with necessary tools to realize a CDM system. More important, Joomla is very web-orientated (being an Internet portal) so management and updating is ideal when considering the principles of CDM. Since all communication to the datastore as well as user management and a number of other features have already been implemented under the GPL licence (White and Wallace 2008) Joomla is a natural base on which to build a CDM. A more detailed list of Joomla's benefits for Geologia.fi is published by Brozinski (2008).

When customizing Joomla to the needs of Geologia.fi, features were added and their layout was fitted to meet the graphical requirements. Thanks to the open source community, all obstacles were tackled with relatively small resources. All in all, full functionality was achieved in a very short time and the system has remained stable and robust.

An example of Geologia.fi's expandability is the geological glossary. Over 12 months after its initial launch (September 2007), the need for a Finnish geological glossary rose. Thanks to the well documented component-module-mambot-based extension scheme, a glossary component was installed and a menu link was added to the top bar. Adding the technical features quickly and easily allowed more time to be spent with the actual task: inserting geological terms and their definitions.

Basically components, modules and mambots perform different operations within a Joomla system. Components are responsible for many of the central functions like formatting content (com_content) (Hauser and Wenz 2005) whereas modules concentrate on viewing data. Often these two act together, though. Take polls, for example. Different polls are added through the Polls component at the backend of the system. Then a frontend module showing the Polls to the user is utilized. Mambots on the other hand influence content by performing automated tasks in the background. One of the mambots used in Geologia.fi resizes the pictures and creates a Lightbox popup before the content is shown to the user.

Interactive multimedia kiosk – PoG without CDM

Two interactive multimedia kiosks were built in late 2007 during the Finnish-Estonian Interreg IIIA geology popularization project. The kiosks replaced the original plan to place signs outdoors near outcrops. Potential trouble with landowners accepting bulky metal plates (and visitors) on their land and worries about maintaining the signs after the project ended led to the idea of developing a kiosk which could be easily looked after and placed inside a museum.

The prerequisite was to produce an easy-to-use interactive device that was able to display text, pictures and videos in more than one language. Maintainability and reliability were also important factors. To achieve these goals, affordably priced and standardized PC-technology was chosen. A touch screen display was implemented for user interaction. Network readiness was included for future derivations. The actual casing was build from wood by a professional carpenter to maintain an earthy and natural look.

The content of the kiosk was orientated by geological guidebooks produced within the Interreg IIIA project. To get an overview of the content a simple tree structure was created. Since the kiosk wasn't going to be a semantic system, each 'branch of the tree' holds information about its text, pictures, layout and relation to other pages. Due to this, only the administrator can manage the kiosk or add content. This, however, presents a problem when updating such a product as every page has to be edited separately.

Adding CDM features to multimedia kiosk

Assuming that the Internet portal Geologia.fi is to be expanded to show certain content (for example geological news) on the multimedia kiosk, the kiosk itself will have to be converted into a CDM system. This means that a new application must be set up in the kiosk. There are two ways to realize such application. Both have their benefits and it must be evaluated in each scenario, which of them is more useful. Figure 4.7 presents an option where a second data management process is utilized for viewing information for the end user. This is practical since one datastore is still used it can be updated by authors and administrators.

Alternatively the kiosk could be seen as an additional process connected to process 1. If this was the case, processes 2 and 3 would have to be separated (view on kiosk vs. view on webpage) but this unnecessarily complicates the system. The first scenario also has the advantage, that it doesn't require an always-on Internet connection. Process 5 can simply produce a copy of T1 and update it, for example once a week. In the other scenario an always-on Internet connection would be required since other applications, management and content production is dependent on it.

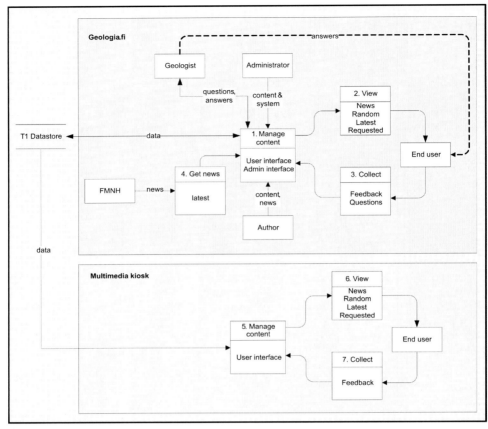

Figure 4.7: In reality the co-existence of two systems of which one is non-semantic is possible, but most likely content in the multimedia kiosk would be converted and stored in the datastore like shown in this figure.

Combining geology, tourism and CDM in the SW archipelagos of Finland

The archipelagos of Turku and Åland (Figure 4.8) are good candidates for introducing geotourism in Finland. The main language on Ålands islands is Swedish but many speak Finnish and most certainly English. In addition to beautiful landscapes, both areas contain a functional tourism infrastructure with many enterprises operating in natural and ecotourism areas (Turunmaan Seutu 2008). Geologically, the archipelagos of Turku and Åland encompass more than 1900 Ma of planetary history ranging from the Svecofennian orogeny all the way to the relatively younger (1600 Ma) Rapakivi intrusions.

The archipelago around Turku includes over 20,000 islands and it is divided into northern, western and eastern parts. Around the islands 85 bed and breakfast establishments, 12 hotels and many camping sites are available. In addition, over 60 companies or individuals offer summer cabin rentals. About 15 travel advisors and/or travel agencies operate in the area. A total of 16 natural sites (for example pathways) can be observed. (Turunmaan Seutu 2008). Large ferries that operate between the islands are free of charge.

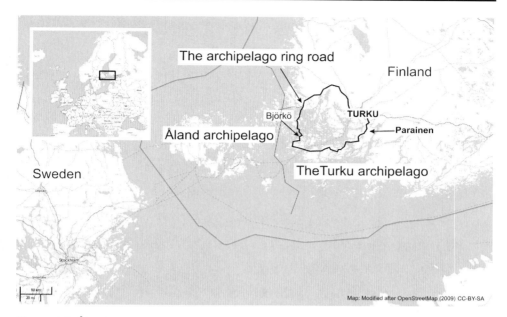

Figure 4.8: Åland and Turku archipelagoes.

Geology and other touristic activities are best enjoyed by driving along a 160 km long 'ring road' that zigzags through the maze of small and large islands. The visitor is well accommodated and catered for since there are plenty of places to rest, eat or stay overnight. Thanks to the extensive ferry network, one can also easily cross to the Åland archipelago to explore even more interesting geology. During the summer of 2008 almost 20,000 visitors toured the islands (many using the ring road).

If the Åland archipelago is included, the bed and breakfast services increases to a total of 121 and the number of hotels to 31. A total of 64 summer cabin rental offers can be found (Ålands Turistförbund 2008). A well functioning and very affordable ferry network adds value when travelling among the islands of Åland archipelago.

A short introduction to the geology of Finland

Finland occupies roughly a third of the Fennoscandian shield. Most of the Finnish bedrock was formed during the Archean and Proterozoic Eons and hence can be broadly divided into two distinct areas. The Archean craton in the north-east and younger volcanic arcs and micro-continents in the south-west welded together in a series of orogenic events referred to as the Svecofennian orogeny. The Svecofennian orogeny took place between 1800 and 1900 million years ago (Lehtinen *et al.* 1998). The main deformation phase of the Svecofennian orogeny included folding, regional metamorphism and plutonism (Simoni and Mikkola 1980). Due to the collision with the Archean craton, the Svecofennian crust thickened considerably (up to 65 km). No Archean traces have been found beneath the Svecofennian formations which hint that they weren't formed by remodelling the Archean crust. Common features of the Svecofennian orogeny include high amounts of orogenic Rapakivi granite in southern Finland as well as melted and recrystallized rocks of volcanic or sedimentary origin. These are called migmatites and they are quite common in southern Finland (Lehtinen *et al.* 1998). Following a long period of erosion, the Jotnian sediments (red arkose sandstone and siltstones) were deposited around 1300 to 1400 million years ago. They are the oldest non-metamorphic features found in south-western Finland. (Simoni and Mikkola 1980).

Around 1900 million years ago, the Svecofennides resembled the Himalayas but they have since been deeply eroded. Over time the mountains were slowly turned into sand and clay leaving a relatively flat surface behind. The current erosion level was reached some 600 million years ago and today the highest 'peaks' rise 50 metres above sea level (Hollsten and Ehlers 2000). Hence it is now possible to walk on rocks that once formed at the depth of nearly 20 kilometres.

Figure 4.9: Finnish bedrock in the Åland archipelago.

During its long geological history, Finland has been subject to many glaciations. The latest ended roughly 10,000 years ago. The remnants of glaciations can be seen on the Finnish bedrock in various forms like whalebacks and rouche moutonnees (Koivisto 2005).

One of the most interesting features of Finnish bedrock is that detailed processes can be observed *in situ*. Especially in the archipelago, outcrops are kept clean and tidy by the constant washing of the sea (and ice during winter time). Two localities near the south-western coast are presented here: the limestone quarry of Parainen and the small island of Björkö.

Limestone quarry in the Parainen area

The limestone quarry of Parainen (Figure 4.10) makes a perfect candidate for developing geotourism. Not only does the quarry have interesting geology but also free time activities take place there. Such activities occur mostly in summer and one of the highlights is the annual Rowlit festival where rock bands perform at the bottom of the quarry. Although still in operation, the semi-geological museum next to the entrance could well be transformed into an entry point for tours inside the pit. Also, the long history of mining adds to the geotouristic value of Parainen. Initially limestone was quarried for burning (Karhunen 2004) in order to produce masonry and other similar products.

The total length of the current quarry is about 2 kilometres and its width varies between 200 and 500 metres. Maximum depth is 80 metres (Glückert and Tittonen 1999). The limestone was formed roughly 1900 million years ago in a sea in front of an island arc. Finland was located close to the equator at that time (Lehtinen *et al.* 1998), giving rise to the sub-tropical temperatures required for limestone formation.

Figure 4.10: The limestone quarry of Parainen.

The Parainen area is a syncline of amphibolite with interlayers of mica schist and gneisses surrounded by microcline granite. Limestone layers of different thickness follow the strata of the amphibolite. The limestone is mostly calcite but dolomite layers occur. Quartz-feldspar-schist is also found between the limestone layers. (Karhunen 2004). The area around and in the quarry represents the southern part of the syncline where Garnet-cordierite-gneisses exist above the limestone layer. Limestone gneisses, banded diopside gneisses and amphibolites can be seen beneath the limestone layer (Glückert and Tittonen 1999). Many minerals such as scapolite, titanite, fluorite, pyroxenes, condrodite and pargasite (a fluor-rich hornblende) are found around the area. (Karhunen 2004).

Björkö

Another geotourism destination is the small island of Björkö where a number of interesting features reflecting the geological history of south-western Finland, can be seen. Strong foliation and folding represent the deformation that once took place during the Svecofennian orogeny. Even though no straight evidence such as primary structures for sedimentary origin can be seen, clear banding hints that the rocks have been originally bedded (Karhunen 2004).

The geology of Björkö can be best investigated by walking the island nature trail. In addition to geology, signs of trade that began in the 13th century and remnants of first settlements from the 16th century can be observed. Along the trail, sedimentary, plutonic and metamorphic rocks reflecting the geological history of south-western Finland are visible (Kolkka 2006).

The dominant rock along the trail is grey diorite. It represents a magma chamber that crystallised about 1880 million years ago. Its main minerals are dark mica, hornblende and light-coloured quartz and plagioclase. When walking along the trail, a Cambrian sandstone dyke is found in cracks in the red granite on the western side of the island. The red granite's minerals are clearly visible to the naked eye. They include K-feldspar, quartz, dark mica and white plagioclase. Migmatite is visible on the south-western end of Björkö. The migmatite was formed when rising temperature conditions lead to partial melting of the oldest rocks in the area (gabbro) hence producing grey plagioclase veins. Finally, younger granite intrusions intersect the migmatite sharply. (Kolkka 2006). Though not visible, post-glacial isostatic rebound still occurs in the archipelago (and on Björkö). The current pace uplift is about 3–4 mm/year (Koivisto 2005).

Turning Finnish bedrock into geotourism

Since there already is an existing well-developed tourism infrastructure along the ring road the areas described are very well suited for developing geoutourism. This chapter presents a hypothetical order in which geotourism can be developed and integrated into the existing tourism infrastructure. The working order is advisedly constructed to allow geotourism to be developed separately from other branches of tourism. The lifespan (see later) presented here is divided into seven phases called GT0–GT7 (GT being an abbreviation of geotourism). All phases can be modified to suite a wide spectrum of geoscience popularization projects. The strength of the model is that it can have a predefined timeframe. Thus overall management is easier and a clear overview of the project can be achieved.

♦   GT0 is executed before the project begins. It's a preface whose function is to find out whether there is interest towards geotourism among the local residents and tourism businesses. This phase contains an initial sketch-up of a geotourism CDM system which is used on exit polls (both locals and businesses). Figure 4.11 shows an example sub-process that can be executed furing GT0. Based on the research, adjustments are made and financial resources are evaluated. Finally a decision about system development is made. It should be noted that GT0 is also the first step of project promotion. Additionally, connections to potential key partners are made.

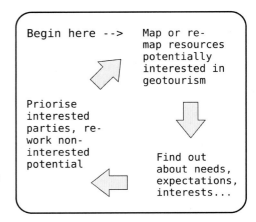

Figure 4.11: An example sub-process of phase GT0 that maps resources. Resources can be individuals or businesses interested in development.

♦   **GT1** assumes that the outcome of GT0 has been positive. At this point the actual goal of the project has to be set. Depending on information and experiences collected from phase GT0, the goal could be anything between geotourism, PoG and building a nature park. Estimates of human resources are needed too.

♦   When **GT2** has been reached, it has to be decided which products are made within the project. Even if no detailed list can be made, a tentative plan about products to be made should be drawn. When the product list is complete, financial needs can be re-evaluated. Since the products, potential key partners and goals are defined by now, the use of an existing CDM system is be investigated in phase **GT3**. If no such system exists, CDM development is continued as planned. At this point, information collected about the needs of local residents and businesses are further developed by starting co-operation projects. Also, collection and/or formatting of geological data will begin.

♦   **GT4** includes the actual building/extension of the CDM system. While the system is being built, more geological information is collected and when possible, entered into the system. Following the launch, everyone participating in the project has access to the system and interaction between local residents, communities, system developers and geologists continues to occur. This is when the production of geotourism begins. At this point promotion becomes important, too.

♦   In **GT5** the system is up and running. People are interacting and the concept is taking shape. Now is a good time to further promote the developed PoG, geotourism and/or set forth the preparation to become a geopark candidate.

♦   **GT6** is the follow-up phase. During this, it is evaluated whether the goals set in the beginning are met. Has geotourism been successfully integrated into the local tourism infrastructure, are the people functioning as a 'part of it' instead of separate instances? Are financial prospects met? If the project was realized with only PoG in mind it might be useful to ask oneself, if there is actual benefit for the people from the material published?

♦   **GT7** includes administration which begins when the actual development phase is completed. This doesn't mean that new features can't be implemented nor does it mean that interaction between entities has ceased. Instead phase GT7 should be seen more as a normal state in which the system is run on an everyday basis.

Conclusion

Even though the first steps to realise geotourism in Finland have been taken, there still is a lot to accomplish. One of the larger concerns is terminology and its use. Currently pretty much anyone can claim to develop geotourism, no matter whether it has anything to do with natural sciences. Also, some of the already realized projects have been 'filed' under geotourism even though they consist mainly of PoG.

Nonetheless, very positive feedback has been gathered from the examples mentioned in this paper. For instance, Geologia.fi had over 30,000 unique visitors during 2008 (based on the statistics so far, the number will be larger in 2009). The kiosks in turn spent over a year touring different exhibitions before being placed in museums. As a conclusion one can definitely say, that there is a strong interest among the public towards geology.

So why not take it a step further and really start developing geotourism here in Finland? It may or may not happen by the means presented here but it will happen. Finland's geology is simply too interesting to be ignored or left in the shadow of other touristic experiences. Rocks are definitely not dead!

References

Ålands Turistförbund (2008) *Åland Official Tourist Gateway*, http://www.visitaland. com/ (reviewed 4.1.2009).

Buhalis, D. (2003) *eTourism: Information Technology for Strategic Tourism Management*, Prentice Hall.

Brozinski, A. (2008) 'Geologisen tiedon esittäminen Internet-ympäristössä, esimerkkitapaus geologia.fi' master's thesis, Turku, Finland: University of Turku.

Dowling, R. and Newsome, D. (2006) *Geotourism*, Elsevier.

Glückert, G. and Tittonen, J. (1999) *Graniittikalliolta rahkasuolle*, Kaarina, Finland: Varsinais-Suomen liitto.

Hauser, T. and Wenz, C. (2005) *Mastering Mambo: A Professional Guide to Mambo's most Powerful and Useful Features*, Packt Publishing.

Hollsten, S. and Ehlers, C. (2000) *Peruskallio ja jääkausi. Geologisia retkiä Brändöm kallioille*, Mariehamn, Åland.

Karhunen, R. (2004) *Pre-Quaternary rocks of the Iniö and Turku map-sheet areas*, Espoo, Finland: Geological Survey of Finland.

Koivisto, M. (2005) *Jääkaudet*, Porvoo, Finland: WSOY.

Kolkka, M. (2006) *Björkö, luontopolkuopas*, Finland: Metsähallitus.

Lehtinen, M., Nurmi, P. and Rämö, T. (1998) *Suomen kallioperä: 3000 vuosimiljoonaa*, Helsinki, Finland: Suomen geologinen seura.

National Geographic (2005) *Geotourism Charter*, http://www.nationalgeographic.com/ travel/sustainable/pdf/geotourism_charter_template.pdf (reviewed 4.1.2009).

National Geographic (2008) *Center for Sustainable Destinations web page*, http://www. nationalgeographic.com/travel/sustainable/ (reviewed 4.1.2009).

Penny Magazine (1835) 'Mineral kingdom - section XLII, issue 215, Charles Knight.

Penny Magazine (1835) 'Fertilization of lava', issue 229, Charles Knight.

Silver, T.B. (2007) *Joomla! Template Design*, Packt Publishing.

Simoni, A. and Mikkola, A. (1980) *Geology of the European Countries: Denmark, Finland, Iceland, Norway, Sweden*, Springer-Verlag, pp. 52-126.

SKGK (2006) Minute of the Finnish National Committée in Geology (SKGK), meeting 8.1 2006. Elias Ekdahl and Sinikka Roos, Geological Survey of Finland.

Stueve, A.M., Cook, S.D. and Drewm, D. (2002) *The Geotourism Study: Phase I Executive Summary*, Travel Industry Association of America.

Tourtellot, J. (2003) *'Geotourism' Survey Shows Millions of Travelers Care*, http:// news.nationalgeographic.com/news/2003/10/1024_031024_travelsurvey.html (reviewed 4.1.2008).

Turunmaan seutu Ry (2008) *Turunmaan seutu Home Page*, http://www.saaristo.org (reviewed 4.1.2009).

White, S. and Wallace, A. (2006) *Joomla! Users Manual*, http://help.joomla.org/images/ User_manual/user_manual_v1%200%201_10%2021%2006.pdf (reviewed 1.3.2008).

5 Promoting geotourism: a case study from Northeast Iceland

John S. Hull, New Zealand Tourism Research Institute/
Icelandic Tourism Research Centre

Introduction

Iceland is becoming a popular venue for nature-based tourism enthusiasts interested in exploring Arctic environments for scenic and recreational purposes (ITB 2009; Gossling and Alkimou 2006). Visitation to Iceland is expanding exponentially, generating significant revenue and income, making tourism the third largest foreign currency earner for the Icelandic economy. In 2006, total tourism receipts were measured at 47 billion Icelandic kroner (ISK), contributing 4.1 per cent to the nation's GDP, and providing 12.7 per cent of the country's income from foreign sources (Rannsoknir and Radgjof Ferdapjonustunnar 2008). In 2007, over 530,000 international tourists visited Iceland with over 80 per cent first-time visitors mainly from Europe and North America (Rannsoknir and Radgjof Ferdapjonustunnar 2008).

The Icelandic Tourism Board (ITB 2007) identifies that the vast natural resources – glaciers, volcanoes, geysers, and untamed wilderness – are some of the most important reasons contributing to the present 7 percent annual growth rate in visitation (Gossling and Hultman 2006). The most popular leisure activity of visitors is nature observation (ITB 2007). Outdoor activities such as camping, hiking, boat tours, jeep and glacier tours, snowmobile excursions, and horseback riding are also popular throughout the island. Overall, visitor motivation to Iceland is based on romanticized notions of the unique wilderness and the grandness of the landscape and tourist experiences that recreate a 'natural' image of the island (Gossling and Alkimou 2006; Gossling and Hultman 2006).

This 'myth of Iceland' is also recognized as providing the country with the opportunity to foster visitor interest in geotourism (Dowling and Newsome 2006). Geotourism is defined as tourism with an emphasis on appreciating the geological processes that pertain to geomorphology, and the natural resources of landscape, landforms, fossil beds, and rocks and minerals (Newsome and Dowling 2006). Gudmundsson (2007) points out (p. 6), 'the country is young and active, lies on top of a mantle plume and astride a divergent plate margin, has extensive glaciers, and in addition, most geological processes are rapid and dynamic'. Running from the southwest to the northeast of the island is a supramarine section of the Mid-Atlantic Ridge (Dowling and Newsome 2006). The ridge provides opportunities for studying geological processes, developing geotourism, and understanding Iceland's 'story of formation' (Gudmundsson 2007; Dowling and Newsome 2006).

This chapter will outline the present planning and management efforts of tourism policymakers in Northeast Iceland to promote the development of a sustainable tourism industry that is integrating geotourism into its overall strategy for destination development. First a brief summary of the geology of Iceland will provide a general context for understanding destination attractions and activities linked to present visitation in Northeast Iceland. Second, the key elements of the five-year strategic plan for tourism completed in 2008 will summarize present planning efforts aimed at promoting geotourism in a context of a larger sustainable tourism framework. Finally, a number of recommendations will be identified to address future planning and development of geotourism in Northeast Iceland.

Brief summary of Iceland's geology

In geological terms, Iceland is regarded as one of the world's youngest countries emerging from the ocean around 20–24 million years ago. With an area of 103,000 square kilometres, similar in size to Ireland, Iceland boasts spreading ridge segments, intraplate lateral eruptive zones, transverse fracture zones and a hot spot (Gudmundsson 2007). Volcanic, tectonic, and glacial activities have shaped and continue to alter the present landscape.

Volcanic

More than 200 volcanoes are located within the active volcanic zone running through Iceland from the southwest to the northeast, with eruptions occurring on average every four to five years (Gudmundsson 2007). In this volcanic zone there are high-temperature areas containing steam fields with underground temperatures reaching 250°C (Figure 5.1). These areas are directly linked to the active volcanic systems as indicated by the triangles in Figure 5.1. About 250 separate low-temperature areas with temperatures not exceeding 150°C in the uppermost one kilometre of crust are mostly in the areas flanking the active zone. To date, over 600 hot springs (temperature over 20°C) have been located (Hull *et al.*, 2008a).

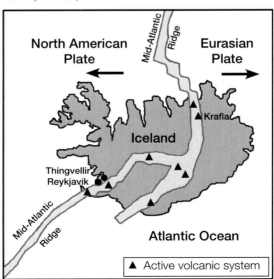

Figure 5.1: Tectonic map and active vocanic regions. Source: Wikimedia Commons.

Tectonic

The tectonic activity of Iceland refers to the forces of the North American and Eurasian tectonic plates which form part of the Mid-Atlantic ridge (Figure 5.1). Iceland is the largest island situated on the Mid-Atlantic ridge (others include Jan Mayen, the Azores, Bermuda, Ascension, Tristan da Cunha and Bouvet island). Iceland is also situated above a hot mantle plume which has created a much greater volume of volcanic emissions than anywhere else in the world (Ministry of Environment 2009; Nordal and Kristinsson 1996).

Iceland is one of the few places on earth where one can see an active spreading ridge above sea level. The boundary between the North American and Eurasian tectonic plates is moving apart at more than one centimetre per year. Iceland is one of the most tectonically active places on earth. From 1994–2000, Iceland recorded well over 25,000 earthquakes (Ministry of Environment 2009; Nordal and Kristinsson 1996).

Glacial

The Pleistocene period is dated from just less than two million years ago to around 12,000 years ago and covers most of the latest period of glaciation. As the climate cooled from the Pliocene and into the Pleistocene, repetitive glacial periods occurred which had effects on vegetation and rock formation. Studies indicate there were around 14 Upper Pliocene and Pleistocene glacial periods and Iceland was largely covered with thick ice during the main glaciations (Iceland Ministry of Foreign Affairs 2009; Gudmundsson 2007).

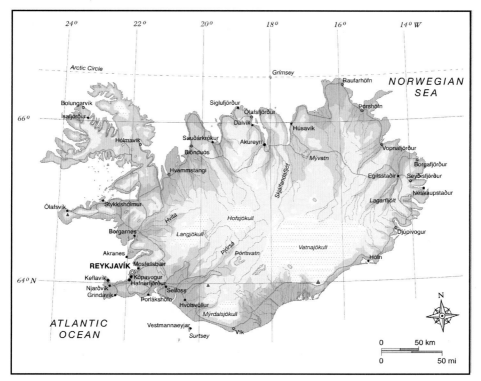

Figure 5.2: Glacial regions of Iceland. Source: Wikimedia Commons

Iceland's arctic elements include ice caps, glaciers, permafrost regions, and periglacial phenomena (Gudmundsson 2007). The total glaciated area of Iceland is 11,058 square kilometres (2005) with the number of ice caps totalling approximately 270 (National Energy Authority 2006). The Vatnajokull glacier, at 8000 square kilometres in size and over 400 metres thick, is Europe's largest glacier located in southern Iceland with ice dated at over 1000 years old (Figure 5.2) (Gudmundsson 2007).

Northeast Iceland tourism resources

Overview

Northeast Iceland is Iceland's largest Administrative District, with a land area of approximately 18,439 square kilometres comprising 18.32 per cent of the terrestrial island of Iceland (Figure 5.3). Visitors can participate in short day trips at one of the protected areas and engage in photography and interpretive walks that highlight the geological formations, waterfalls, and abundant bird life. For tourists interested in marine recreation, whale watching tours or a visit to one of the many seal or seabird colonies is possible. More demanding activities involve multi-day hikes in the mountains and volcanoes, kayaking glacial rivers and fjords, or taking a jeep tour across the unique lunar-like landscapes of the interior Highlands to Iceland's largest glacier.

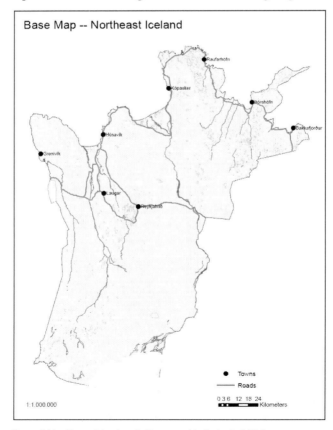

Figure 5.3: Location of Northeast Iceland. Source: Hull et al. 2008a.

Visitor demand

The region is recognized as the second most visited tourism destination of Iceland after the Capital Region of Reykjavik (Rannsoknir and Radgjof Ferdapjonustunnar 2008). It was estimated 95,000 Icelanders (approximately 35 per cent of all local tourists) visited Northeast Iceland in 2005. The demographic profile of the Icelandic visitors indicates slightly more male than female visitors. In terms of age, there is a fairly even distribution across most age groups. The majority of domestic tourists originate from Northeast Iceland and East Iceland and in general, there are more day-trippers than overnight visitors (Rannsoknir and Radgjof Ferdapjonustunnar 2008).

Of the international visitors in Iceland in July and August of 2007, over half visited Northeast Iceland with nearly 40 per cent coming during the month of June and over 25 per cent in September. The ratio drops to 14 per cent in May, 6 per cent in April and October and only 1–3 per cent in the winter months from November through March (Rannsoknir and Radgjof Ferdapjonustunnar 2008).

International visitors to Northeast Iceland totalled 116,000 with approximately half staying overnight for approximately 1.5 days while on their trip. A significant number of overnight visitors come to the region from Southern Europe, Benelux, and Central Europe. International visitors prefer guesthouses and hotels. The majority of international visitors were evenly divided between men and women, were over 55, travelling on package tours from Europe. The most popular destinations were Húsavík, Lake Mývatn, and Dettifoss. In terms of rating popular activities in the region, sightseeing, whale watching, touring Lake Mývatn, and hiking around volcanoes received the highest ratings (Rannsoknir and Radgjof Ferdapjonustunnar 2008).

In an effort to respond to the increasing visitor numbers to the region, the Regional Development Agency (Atthing), has identified tourism as a priority sector for future planning and development. The Agency is mandated to support development, employment and business life to promote and encourage innovation, co-operation and networking by working with local communities, companies, organizations and individuals to preserve the marine and terrestrial environments of the region and promote sustainable development (Atthing 2009).

Marine environment

Northeast Iceland's cultural heritage has been largely dependent on its marine heritage, supporting the livelihoods of the majority of residents in the region. Seventy five percent of all Iceland's merchandise exports are derived from marine products (UNESCO 2009). Today, recent developments as a result of the rapid growth in the service and production sectors have led to a diversification of the economy and a decline in the importance of primary resource sectors. The result has been the emergence of a well-developed marine tourism sector that is scattered along the rugged coastline (Iceland Ministry of Foreign Affairs 2009).

Húsavík on the shores of Skjálfandi Bay has become one of the leading destinations for whale watching not only within Iceland but also in Europe (Atthing 2009). Twelve species of whale visit these shores including the more popular minke whales, humpbacks, and orcas, while occasionally the blue whale, fin whale, and sei whales are spotted. Cetaceans such as the white beaked dolphins and harbour porpoises are common in addition to grey and harbour seals (Randburg.com 2009). Most of the whale watching sites and seal colonies are found along the coastal regions in the Öxarfjörðor area which attract hundreds of thousands of visitors a year for marine-based excursions.

In addition, the divergence of the Irminger Current of the Gulf Stream, and the East Greenland Current in the region create excellent conditions for all kinds of fish species and consequently very good fishing grounds. Around 320 species of fish have been recorded off the coast of Iceland, 30 of which have a part to play in the commercial and recreational fishing industries. Throughout the 20th century, the two key commercial species were the Atlantic cod and herring. More recently there has been a shift to capelin and tuna (Iceland Worldwide 2009). Arctic char, Atlantic salmon, and trout support a recreational fishery in Northeast Iceland that has gained international recognition with experienced freshwater anglers with the Laxá River being one of the most famous rivers in the region.

Terrestrial environment

Sitting upon two divergent plates, signs of the geotectonic landscape are evident over the entire region. The region's substrate is almost entirely volcanic rock, predominantly basalts (Ministry of Environment 2009; Nordal and Kristinsson 1996). The coastline has numerous inlets and fjords. Coastal lowlands, such as those around the bays of Skjálfandi and Öxarfjörður provide pasture and arable lands where grasses and low-lying shrubs predominate, providing excellent land for farming and agriculture and supporting the recent development of a small-scale agritourism industry that is highlighted by farmstays, horse riding, sheep round ups, and local cuisine including *hverab rauð* (sweet rye bread), lamb, cheese, and smoked trout (Hull *et al.* 2008a).

The northern peninsula of Melrakkaslétta (nicknamed 'Slétta') is a largely uninhabited area of basalts where a new earthquake centre has been proposed for development in the community of Kópasker. Kópasker is located on the boundary of the Eurasian and North American plates resulting in seismic activity in the area. In 1976 an earthquake of magnitude 6.25 occurred. Local residents are interested in documenting the history of earthquakes in the area and educating visitors generally about this phenomenon (Atthing 2009). The western part is dotted with lakes and streams with good fishing in amongst tundra and swamps while the eastern part is much drier. Further east is the Langanes peninsula, a historic fishing area, largely uninhabited at present, with an undulating landscape between 200–400 metres high and dominated by the 700-metre Gunnólfsvíkurfjall mountain with hiking and horse riding trails, and numerous seabird colonies, including one of the most accessible northern gannet colonies in the country (Atthing 2009).

In the east, the valleys lie in a more southwest to northeast orientation due to glaciation. In the west, the region is more mountainous, making it popular with hikers and snow enthusiasts. The region of Grenivík has become a popular ice climbing area, attracting adventurers from all over the world (Atthing 2009). Tjörnes, the mountainous peninsula east of Húsavík contains strata of Pacific fossilized marine life dating from three million years ago when there was an inflow of cold water from the North Atlantic as a result of the opening of the Bering Strait (Gudmundsson 2007).

Unique natural phenomena include Lake Mývatn, formed approximately 2300 years ago by a large basaltic lava eruption. The lake is Iceland's fourth largest and most fertile lake, known for its rich fishing and abundant concentration of water birds. The phosphate rich groundwater provides optimal conditions for the growth of aquatic plants and for nesting waterfowl (Mývatn Research Station 2009). Lake Mývatn is recognized as having one of the highest diversity of nesting ducks in the world (Environment Agency of Iceland 2009). The surrounding area is also an extremely volcanic area with numerous craters, pseudo craters, hot springs, mud pots, and the nearby Dimmuborgir and Höfdi lava fields. The Mývatn Nature Baths, which opened in 2004, attract over 60,000 visitors annually offering a unique outdoor spa and wellness experience (Mývatn Nature Baths 2007).

Further inland, the central Icelandic highlands, situated above 400–500 metres, provide the setting for an Arctic desert dotted with volcanoes, mountains, glaciers, and spectacular waterfalls. Glacial valleys run south to north and contain many pristine rivers. The Jökulsá River, with the Dettifoss waterfall, and the Ásbyrgi canyon are some of the most visited natural attractions in the region. The Highland region is also home to two large volcanoes, Askja, further to the north east is Herðubreið. In addition there is Europe's largest glacier, Vatnajokull. Several attractions are the focus of hiking and jeep tours, and are of particular note for tourism (Table 5.1).

Table 5.1: Popular attractions in Northeast Iceland

Mountain	Attraction highlights
Askja	(1500m) A massive caldera in the Central Highlands. The area was used during the Apollo program to prepare astronauts for potential lunar conditions.
Herðubreið	(1600m) A tuya volcano, flat topped and steep sided, nearby to Askja.
Krafla	(818m) A caldera volcano 10 km in diameter with a 90 km long fissure zone, is located in the Mývatn region that last erupted in 1984. Krafla includes one of the two best known Viti craters of Iceland. A popular hiking area exists around the Leirhnjúkur lava field within the Krafla caldera.
Námafjall	A geothermal area 4km south of Krafla with boiling mud pools and fumaroles.
Kverkfjöll	(1800m) A glaciated volcano on the northern edge of Vatnajökull. Mud holes, steam blowholes, luke warm lake, and an ice cavern system of several kilometers.
Gunnólfsvikurfjall	(700m) Situated on the Langanes peninsula in the north east and can be seen from Bakkafjörður.

River systems

The significant hydrographic features are listed in west to east orientation in Table 5.2. Iceland's geologically young age and volcanic substrate, in combination with the frequent precipitation and summer glacial melts, have carved a landscape punctuated by numerous rivers and lakes. These rivers are categorized into three general types: debris-laden glacial rivers draining into outwash plains in front of glaciers; direct run-off rivers draining old basalt areas; and spring-fed rivers draining post glacial lava fields and young Pleistocene rocks (Icelandic Ministry of Foreign Affairs 2009). Where rivers meet the island's numerous fault lines and fissures, spectacular waterfalls have formed; the largest by volume is Dettifoss (44 metres) in Jökulsá á Fjöllum near Ásbyrgi.

There are 18 rivers in Northeast Iceland. All are either glacial or freshwater and flow northwards into the Norwegian Sea. The Jökulsá River is the most well-known as the second longest river in Iceland, containing the Dettifoss waterfall, one of the largest waterfalls in Europe, and canyons akin to those of the Grand Canyon in the United States. The river is now the site of the annual 32.7 kilometre Dettifoss Trail Run in July that attracts hundreds of participants (Hlaup.is 2009).

Along the rivers, there are 14 major waterfalls located within the Northeast region. Iceland's geologically young age and its volcanic substrate mean that waterfalls are formed as a result of fault lines and fissures, with water flow being maintained due to frequent precipitation and summer glacial melts.

Table 5.2: Significant hydrographic features in Northeast Iceland

Hydrographic feature	Attraction highlights
Eyjafjörður	The longest fjord in Central Northern Iceland measuring 60 km and is relatively narrow. On either side of Eyjafjörður rise high, ancient mountain ranges into valleys, and in the north, marine erosion has created cliffs. The region of Eyjafjörður is Iceland's second most populous after Reykjavík.
Fnjóská	A large salmon fishing river flowing out into Eyjafjörður.
Skjálfandafljót	A glacial river that flows from the north western border of the glacier Vatnajökull in the Icelandic Highlands and into Skjálfandi Bay.
Laxá	Iceland's second largest freshwater river, renowned as one of Iceland's best and most beautiful salmon fishing rivers, also flows into Skjálfandi Bay (Nordic Adventure Travel 2009; Randburg.com 2009)
Lake Mývatn	A national conservation area - its name means 'Midge Lake' - with 15 species of breeding duck
Jökulsá á Fjöllum	The second longest river of Iceland (206 km) flowing from the glacier Vatnajökull.
Dettifoss waterfall	Fed by Jökulsá á Fjöllum which then continues into the Ásbyrgi canyon. Dettifoss waterfall is 44m (144 ft) high, 100m wide and is believed to have the greatest water volume in Europe.
Ásbyrgi Canyon	The enormous horseshoe-shaped depression is part of the Vatnajökull National Park and measures approximately 3.5 km in length by 1.1 km wide. There is also a small lake called Botnstjörn where visitors can see a variety of waterfowl species (wikipedia 2009)

Protected areas

As a result of the many unique natural attractions in Northeast Iceland, the government has designated nine protected areas in the region (Table 5.3). For these sites, management objectives are aimed at protecting natural resources, providing visitor access, and preserving sense of place in developing sustainable management options (see McCool and Moisey 2001). In Iceland, areas or sites are designated for protection under the Nature Conservation Act and upon suggestion from the Nature Conservation Agency, Icelandic Institute of Natural History, or the Minister of the Environment. This is generally due to a site's importance for its unique natural phenomenon, geological formations, scientific interest, or beauty. Areas can also be protected due to their biological value, presence of special or endangered species, unique habitat or ecosystem, and recreational use (ITB 2009). The following categories of protected areas are found in Northeast Iceland.

♦   **National parks:** Areas of state owned land considered outstanding in landscape, flora or fauna, or having special historic significance. Mandated by the Nature Conservation Agency who facilitate public access and provide relevant park information.

◆   **Nature reserves:** Areas considered important in their landscape, flora or fauna. All reserves have protected wildlife and landscape and a variable restriction on development and public access.

◆   **Natural monuments:** Natural phenomena that is unique, of outstanding beauty, or scientific interest.

Table 5.3: Protected areas in Northeast Iceland

Area type	Name	Description and highlights
National park	Vatnajökull	13,000km2, established June 7, 2008, publicly owned, under authority of Environment and Food Agency covering 13% of Iceland's land mass.
Nature reserve	Svarfaðardalur	8 km2 of wetland on both banks of the Svarfadardalur river. Over 30 bird species of migratory and breeding birds can found within the Reserve's diverse landscape from dry river-banks to bogs.
	Vestmannsvatn	A 2.5km2 lake south of Skjalfandi bay and 28km south of Husavik.
	Herðubreið	Area of around 175 km2, est 1974. Mt. Herdubreid. Diverse vegetation at high altitude on the banks of the river Lindaa and the Grafarlönd area.
Natural monuments	Dettifoss, Selfoss, Hafragilsfoss	A series of waterfalls situated on the Jökulsá á Fjöllum river running through the Ásbyrgi canyon.
	Askja	A stratovolcano within the central highlands of Northeast Iceland. The region has a series of caldera's and a geothermal lake 'Viti'.
	Dyngjufjöll	The mountain massif of 50km2 which surrounds Askja.
	Skútustaðagígar	Pseudocraters in the Mývatn region
	Lake Mývatn	'Midge Lake' 37km2 in area. Large population of birdlife and rare flora.
Other protected areas	Lake Mývatn and Laxá	Protected by Law Number 97 as from 2004. The river is the output from the lake. Surrounding area is rich in bubbling mud flats, volcanic craters and lava fields.

Tourism researchers point out that the rapid growth of tourism often results in diminished ecological integrity and degraded natural processes from habitat fragmentation and loss due to infrastructure development, travel-related air pollution, facility-related water and land pollution, and activity-related soil and vegetation damage and wildlife harassment at popular destinations (Mathieson and Wall 1982; Mieczkowski 1995; Wall 1997; Leung 2001; Newsome *et al.* 2002). The sustainability of tourism in Northeast Iceland is dependent upon how well protected area management regimes succeed in minimizing undesirable environmental effects of tourism development particularly at Dettifoss, Lake Mývatn, Ásbyrgi, the Askja volcano and Vatnajökull glacier.

Strategic plan 2009-2014

In an effort to better manage tourism's growth, the Regional Development Agency commissioned a tourism strategy in 2007 to outline a direction for future planning and development from 2009 to 2014 (Hull *et al.* 2008b). The strategy adopts the United

Nations Development Program's (UNDP) framework for sustainable tourism as its main premise. The framework is based on the belief that the tourism industry is based on the natural and socio-economic environment of a destination. These resources assist in the development of clusters of attractions and activities and secondary support services that define the supply side of the tourism industry. These services create market demand which attracts tourists from international and domestic markets as well as local residents to foster sustainable development (Inskeep 1991) (Figure 5.4).

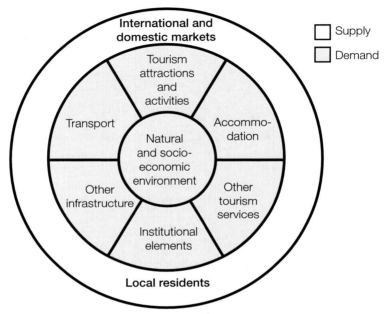

Figure 5.4: Sustainable tourism: balancing supply and demand. Adapted from Inskeep, 1991

The recommendations in the Northeast Iceland strategic plan are based on extensive research that integrates mapping tourism resources using geographic information systems (GIS) to identify gaps and weaknesses in the present tourism offer. Mapping assists planners and policymakers not only in the production of tourism spaces but also serves to assist visitors in guiding their way through a destination and learning about its histories, cultures, and environments. In addition, mapping assists in documentation of sites to inform critical thinking and decision-making (Hanna and Del Casino 2003).

Hasse and Milne (2005) have demonstrated the use of GIS as a new method to facilitate participatory community-based tourism planning through PAGIS, an abbreviation combining Participatory Approaches (PA) and Geographical Information Systems (GIS).

> *The principal idea of PAGIS is to integrate local knowledge, such as values, emotions and perceptions of a place that have been gathered in participatory mapping exercises, into GIS. This local knowledge includes the narratives of local people and reflects the diverse range of opinions of particular places in the community.*
> (Hasse and Milne 2005: 277)

In sum 'PAGIS offers a structural framework for visualizing, situating and integrating numerous perspectives on issues in tourism development' (Hasse and Milne 2005) that have been applied to tourism planning efforts in Northeast Iceland. The production of over 50 maps to document the natural and cultural heritage of the region as well as tourism supply and demand establish a baseline for sustainable tourism development that has resulted in a participatory approach to strategic planning using the PAGIS framework.

Public consultation to solicit feedback regarding the strengths, weaknesses, opportunities, and challenges of tourism were organized using the maps to identify strategic priorities for development. In addition, in-depth interviews with 20 key stakeholders were completed to verify the results of the public consultations and to further identify opportunities and needs for the tourism industry. Secondary research included a review of government reports, academic literature, and web-based information. These data generated a list of priorities and strategic recommendations for tourism development in the region from 2009 to 2014 (Hull *et al.* 2008b).

As part of the vision for tourism, it was argued by participants that marketing, product development, support services, education and training, access and infrastructure development must occur simultaneously in order to build a quality product throughout the region that supports and reinforces principles of sustainable tourism (Figure 5.5).

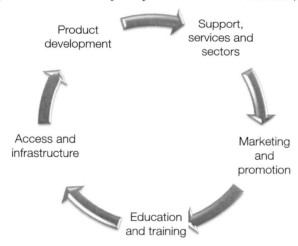

Figure 5.5: Integrating product, market, support services, access and infrastructure, education and training. Source: HUll et al. 2008b.

Based on the GIS mapping inventory, public consultations, in-depth interviews, and a secondary literature review, the overall goals for the strategic plan are to:

♦   Generate increased visitation and expenditures

♦   Increase length of stay

♦   Create jobs for local residents

♦   Generate economic activity through product development clusters

♦   Stimulate investment

♦   Provide quality products and services linked to the region's unique selling points

♦   Optimize marketing opportunities aimed at target niche markets

♦   Preserve the natural and cultural heritage of the region.

At the public consultation workshops held in the autumn of 2007, local residents were also clear and demonstrative in identifying the key issues facing Northeast Iceland that need to be addressed in becoming a tourism destination that is competitive in the marketplace. Opportunities for planning and development most often mentioned were focused largely on expanding the tourism through the development of new product opportunities along with upgrading the quality of secondary support services (Table 5.4).

Table 5.4: Opportunities for tourism

Key opportunities	Mentions
There are more opportunities to attract people/unused opportunities (untouched nature, history, culture, bird- and whale-watching, hiking, ocean/freshwater fishing, riding)	10
Better service (toilets, signs to attractions, information, education, guides, self-guiding brochures)	8
Improve road system	7
Improve marketing (brochures/website/advertisement) /create an image in people's minds	7
Be prepared for more visitors (recreation/accommodation/signs)	4
Extend season and job opportunities	4
More financial resources	3
Cooperation	3
Work on weaknesses	1
No mass tourism, but quality personalised tourism	1
Easier access for foreign tourists	1

A needs assessment of 20 tourism stakeholders in the summer of 2008 reinforced many of the points raised during the public consultations. Stakeholders mentioned most often that the needs for sustainable tourism should be focused on developing unique products, encouraging greater collaboration between the public and private sector, and building clusters of quality services to keep people in the region for longer periods of time. Stakeholders mentioned that this could be accomplished through themed touring routes and attractions that incorporate information to direct and control visitor behaviour. It was mentioned that for the independent traveller there is a distinct lack of interpretive trails and way-finding signage to guide travellers (Atthing 2008). In addition, there was also mention of the need for marketing strategies that incorporate a well-defined brand for the region (Table 5.5).

The WTO (1990: 47) argues that sustainable tourism can only be successful if carrying capacities for key tourism sites are conducted and implemented through a system of effective planning and controls. For destinations like Northeast Iceland, local tourism management strategies require the cooperation of the private sector, and participation of local communities and tourists themselves (e.g. Wearing and Neil 2001).

The challenge is to maintain the direction to sustainable tourism while providing opportunities for public deliberation and input about the meaning and actions to support continued development (e.g. McCool and Moisey 2001). Northeast Iceland has initiated a participatory approach to tourism planning that is creating resident interest and local participation. The research points out that the only forms of local participation that break existing patterns of power and development are those that originate from local communities themselves (Mitchell 2001; Mowforth and Munt 1998).

Table 5.5: Needs assessment

Key needs	Mentions
Packaging and product development that focus on the unique selling points	34
Greater participation/collaboration/cooperation in planning/management between public and private sector	26
Themed routes, walks and attractions for tourists in region	18
Marketing strategy aimed at niche markets with a well-defined brand	15
Information to direct and control visitor behavior/use of guides	14
Extending services into shoulder/winter season	14
Improve access: air/road	11
Build respect for the industry as a viable year round sector	10
Protect local natural and cultural resources that are the basis of the industry	8
Evaluate needs for secondary support services across region (hotels, restaurants, craft-shops, public washrooms, information centers)	7
Training programs needed targeted at specific needs of tourism industry/increase professionalism and customer service	4
Tourism plan that is implemented/investment in actions	4
Statistics for proper planning and management/decision-making	3

The planning and implementation of tourism development in Northeast Iceland will require that there are public–private partnerships that help to maintain the tourism industry businesses over a long time frame. For rural areas like Northeast Iceland, tourism that is small in scale and sensitive to cultural and environmental impacts which respects the involvement of local people in policy decisions is critical. Achieving sustainability will require a variety of individuals, agencies and programmes each using different forms of knowledge to work together in decision-making and policy implementation. (McCool and Moisey 2001).

Conclusions

Tourism in Northeast Iceland exists and is dependent upon the environment in which it is located. McCool and Moisey (2001) argue that the future development of tourism cannot be studied in isolation from the system in which it operates but must be integrated into broader social and economic development processes. Planning must assist in identifying sustainable tourism indicators through decision-making processes that identify desirable outcomes. Through a participatory approach to tourism using GIS, tourism policymakers in the region are actively seeking the support of local residents to advance destination development of tourism in the region using a comprehensive planning framework.

The five-year tourism development plan for Northeast Iceland is being viewed as a tool of social and economic development and as a method of protecting the region's cultural and natural heritage. Continued consensus building is necessary to implement sufficient actions proposed in the plan over the next five years. General development strategies identify the need for careful site management to inform and educate visitors to sustain geological resources in the region; to protect the region's geodiversity and biodiversity; to minimize inappropriate infrastructure development; and to ensure that the local community benefits from the economic return through product development strategies that reinforce local distinctiveness and heritage protection (Hull *et al.* 2008b; McKeever, Larwood, and McKirdy 2006).

The Icelandic Tourist Board (ITB 2007) reports that the most important factor affecting visitor's decision to visit Iceland are the natural scenery as a demand generator (Hull *et al.* 2008a). Northeast Iceland's numerous strengths as a destination are linked to the region's natural assets and unique selling points associated with the unique geology of the area. Geotourism offers a potential basis for community and regional development that is taking into account environmental conservation, community well-being, and economic benefits (Dowling and Newsome 2006) to promote more sustainable forms of tourism.

References

Atthing (2008) *2008 Northeast Iceland Guidebook*, Husavik, Iceland: Atthing.

Atthing. 2009. *Visit Northeast Iceland*. Retrieved 22 February 2009 from http://www. visitnortheasticeland.is/.

Borgþórsson, D. (2008) *Base Map, Waterfall Map*, Cultural Museum: Husavik, Iceland.

Dowling, R. and D. Newsome (2006) 'Geotourism's issues and challenges.', in R.K. Dowling and D. Newsome (eds), *Geotourism*, London: Elsevier, pp. 242-255.

Gossling, S. and A. Alkimou (2006) 'Iceland: nature-, adventure- or eco-island?', in S. Gossling and J. Hultman (eds), *Ecotourism in Scandinavia: Lessons in Theory and Practice*, Wallingford: CAB International, pp. 53-62.

Gossling, S. and Hultman, J. (2006) 'An introduction to ecotourism in Scandinavia.' in S. Gossling and J. Hultman (eds), *Ecotourism in Scandinavia: Lessons in Theory and Practice*, Wallingford: CAB International, pp. 1-9.

Gudmundsson. A.T. (2007) *Living earth: outline of the geology of Iceland*, Edda Publishing: Reykjavik, Iceland.

Hanna, S. and Del Casino, V.J. (2003) 'Introduction: tourism spaces, mapped representations, and the practices of identity', in S. Hanna and V.J. Del Casino (eds), *Mapping Tourism*, Minneapolis: University of Minnesota Press, pp. 1-27.

Hasse, J. and S.S. Milne (2005) 'Participatory approaches and geographical information systems (PAGIS) in tourism planning', *Tourism Geographies*, **7** (3), 272-289.

Hlaup.is (2009) *Running in Iceland*. Retrieved 15 February 2009, from http://www. hlaup.is/.

Hull, J.S., Patterson, C., Huijbens, E. and S.S. Milne (2008a) *The State of Affairs of Tourism in Northeast Iceland. Report #1*, Husavik, Iceland: Atthing.

Hull, J.S., Patterson, C., Huijbens, E. and S.S. Milne (2008b) *The Tourism Strategic Plan for Northeast Iceland. 2009-2014. Report #2*, Husavik, Iceland: Atthing.

Iceland Ministry of Foreign Affairs (2009) *The Official Gateway to Iceland*. Retrieved 5 August 2009 from http://www.iceland.is/.

Iceland Worldwide (2009) *Regions of Iceland*. Retrieved 25 February 2009 from http:// www.iww.is/.

Inskeep, E. (1991) *Tourism Planning: an Integrated and Sustainable Development Approach*, New York: Van Nostrand Reinhold.

ITB (Icelandic Tourist Board) (2007) *Tourism in Iceland in Figures, 2005*, Reykjavik: Icelandic Tourism Board.

ITB (Icelandic Tourist Board). 2009. 'Visit Iceland.' Retrieved 20 February 2009 from http://www.visiticeland.com/.

Leung, Y.-F. (2001) 'Environmental impacts of tourism at China's World Heritage sites', *Tourism Recreation Research*, **26** (1), 117-122.

Mathieson, A. and Wall, G. (1982) *Tourism: Economic, Physical and Social Impacts*, London: Longman.

McCool, S.F. and R.N. Moisey (2001) ' Introduction: pathways and pitfalls in the search for sustainable tourism', in S.F. McCool and R.N. Moisey (eds), *Tourism Recreation and Sustainability: Linking Culture and the Environment*, CAB International: Wallingford, pp. 1-16.

McKeever, P., Larwood, J. and A. McKirdy (2006) 'Geotourism in Ireland and Britain', in R. Dowling and D. Newsome (eds), *Geotourism*, Elsevier: London, pp. 180-198.

Mieczkowski, Z. (1995) *Environmental Issues of Tourism and Recreation*, New York: University Press of America.

Ministry of the Environment (2009) *Welfare for the future: Iceland's national strategy for sustainable development 2002-2020*. Retrieved 20 February 2009 from http://eng.umhverfisraduneyti.is/

Mitchell, R. (2001) 'Community perspectives in sustainable tourism: lessons from Peru', in S.F. McCool and R.N. Moisey (eds), *Tourism Recreation and Sustainability: Linking Culture and the Environment*, CABI Publishing: Wallingford, pp. 137-162.

Moisey, R.N. and S.F. McCool (2001) 'Sustainble tourism in the 21st century: lessons from the past; challenges to address', in S.F. McCool and R.N. Moisey (eds), *Tourism Recreation and Sustainability: Linking Culture and the Environment*, CABI Publishing: Wallingford, pp. 343-352.

Mowforth, M. and I. Munt (1998) *Tourism and Sustainability: New Tourism in the Third World*, Oxford: Routledge.

Myvatn Nature Baths (2009) *Myvatn Nature Baths: Iceland's Newest Spa*. Retrieved 20 February 2009 from http://www.jardbodin.is/English/About_us/

Myvatn Research Station (2009) *The Birds of Lake Myvatn*, Retrieved 15 February 2009 from http://www3.hi.is/~arnie/engframe.htm

National Energy Authority (2006) *Geothermal Energy and Development in Iceland*, Reykjavik: National Energy Authority and Ministries of Industry and Commerce.

Newsome, D. and R. Dowling (2006) 'The scope and nature of geotourism', in R. Dowling and D. Newsome (eds), *Geotourism*, Elsevier: London, pp. 3-25.

Newsome, D., S.A. Moore and R.K. Dowling (2002) *Natural Area Tourism: Ecology, Impacts and Management*, Channel View Publications: Clevedon, Somerset.

Nordal, J. and V. Kristinsson (eds) (1996) *Iceland the Republic*, Reykjavik: Central Bank of Iceland.

Randburg.com (2009) *Icelandic Commerce and Service Companies*, Retrieved 26 February 2009 from http://www.randburg.com/is/index/commerce.html.

Rannsoknir and Radgjof Ferdapjonustunnar (2008) *Ferðamenn í Þingeyjarsýslum 2001-2007*, Reykjavik: Rannsoknir and Radgjof Ferdapjonustunnar.

The Environment Agency of Iceland (2009) *Protected Areas*, Retrieved 19 February 2009 from http://english.ust.is/.

Tronnes, R.G. (2009) *Geology and Geodynamics of Iceland*, Reykjavik: Nordic Volcanological Institute, University of Iceland.

UNESCO (2009) *1998 International Year of the Ocean: National Contributions*, Retrieved 25 February 2009 http://ioc.unesco.org/iyo/activities/countries/iceland.htm

Wall, G. (1997) 'Sustainable tourism – unsustainable development', in S. Wahab and J.J.J. Pigram (eds), *Tourism Development and Growth: the Challenge of Sustainability*, Oxford: Routledge, pp. 33-49.

Wearing, S. and J. Neil (2001) 'Expanding sustainable tourism's conceptualization: ecotourism, volunteerism, and serious leisure', in S.F. McCool and R.N. Moisey (eds), *Tourism Recreation and Sustainability: Linking Culture and the Environment*, Wallingford: CABI, pp. 233-254.

Wikipedia (2009) *National Parks of Iceland*, Retrieved 20 February 2009 from http://en.wikipedia.org/wiki/Category:National_parks_of_Iceland.

WTO (1990) *Tourism to the Year 2000*, World Tourism Organization: Madrid.

6 The Australian Alps: opportunities and challenges for geotourism

Pascal Scherrer, Edith Cowan University, Australia and
Catherine Marina Pickering, Griffith University, Australia

Introduction

Geotourism, as the concept of tourism based on geological features, has gained growing traction in recent years as evidenced not only from contributions in this book, but also from the geopark movement and the number of recent conferences on the subject. Geotourism and particularly the geopark concept build on the notion that fundamentally, geology is the underlying, defining and connecting factor for many natural and even social features of a region, including aspects such as biodiversity, landscape, patterns of human occupancy and use and even architecture. However, today these links are seldom explored or made explicit in the general tourism product even though they have the potential to provide an avenue for a holistic view of a region and its activities, landscapes and people.

This chapter focuses on mountain areas as geotourism destinations, with specific focus on the Australian Alps. The first part of the chapter highlights the importance of mountain areas and in particular the Australian Alps for their ecological, economic and cultural values. The latter part of the chapter explores the case of Mount Kosciuszko, Australia's highest peak, as a geotourism destination. The region has a diversity of tourism attractions based on geological features which lend themselves to providing a holistic approach to the interpretation of the region's features. The chapter concludes with a discussion of some of the opportunities and challenges for geotourism and tourism in general to the region.

Importance of mountains

Geological formations such as entire mountain ranges, individual peaks and associated land formations underpin tourist attractions in many parts of the world. Mountain areas cover about 27 per cent[1] of the earth's land surface (UNEP WCMC 2002). The greatest component (12.2 per cent; 17.9 million square kilometres) is in Eurasia, while only one per cent (1.4 million square kilometres) covers the Australasian and Southeast Asia region. Mountain areas have important economic, cultural and ecological values. About 10 per cent of the world's population live in mountain regions and more than 40 per cent depend in some way on mountain resources such as water from mountain catchments for drinking and irrigation (Hamilton 2002; Messerli and Ives 1984). Some mountain areas, such as the European Alps, have been utilized sustainably for agri-

---

1 Using the UNEP WCMC definition based on elevation and slope (cf. UNEP WCMC 2002).

cultural purposes for millennia, while other areas, such as the Australian Alps, have experienced little anthropogenic alteration until relatively recently (since the arrival of Europeans) (Bock *et al.* 1995; Patzelt 1996).

Mountains are prominent geotourism destinations worldwide. The highest mountains in a range, in a country, on a continent and in the world, tend to attract far more interest than smaller peaks. At a continental scale this is seen in the focus on climbing the 'Seven Summits': the highest mountain on the seven continents. Continental Australia's highest mountain, Mt Kosciuszko at 2228 metres in the Australian Alps, is by far the lowest of the traditional 'Seven Summits'. It is much lower than the highest peaks that are at similar latitudes in New Zealand and in South America and is only a quarter of the height of Mt Everest (8848 metres) (Körner 2003).

The Australian Alps

Mt Kosciuszko is part of the Australian Alps which form the southern end of the Great Dividing Range that runs parallel to Australia's east coast for over 2000 kilometres, about 50 to 150 kilometres inland. The Australian Alps extend from the high country of the Australian Capital Territory (ACT), through the Snowy Mountains in New South Wales (NSW) to the highlands of Victoria, with some alpine areas in Tasmania (Figure 6.1).

The Australian Alps are distinctive in many ways in relation to mountain areas worldwide (Kirkpatrick 2003). Important characteristics include aspects of geology, flora, fauna, climate, and particularly their comparatively low-set topography. Many of the values of the Australian Alps are found in the differences from, rather than conformity to, the stereotypic images of steep slopes, high rocky outcrops and towering mountain peaks, which are often associated with alpine areas elsewhere (Kirkpatrick 2003). Australia's mountains are much older and, unlike the mountains of New Zealand or New Guinea which are still being uplifted, have experienced considerable weathering since their major periods of uplift (Ollier and Wyborn 1989). With milder Pleistocene conditions than in many other mountain regions, the Australian Alps experienced only weak glaciation (Good 1992). These factors all contributed to the area's rounded, soil-mantled character that stands in contrast to the icy, rugged and sawtooth-like features of alpine areas in Europe, Asia, America or New Zealand (Kirkpatrick 2003). In late 2008, the Australian Alps National Parks and Reserves were placed on the Australian Government's National Heritage List on the basis of the significance of the landscapes including its glacial features, its distinctive snow adapted flora and fauna and its human history including indigenous, pastoral, recreation and scientific use (DEWHA 2008).

The highest and largest alpine area in Australia, centred around Mt Kosciuszko, consists of an undulating plateau that gradually rises from the east to a series of north–south aligned peaks along the Main Range, and rapidly drops off towards steep valleys along the western side. The tree line is around 1850 metres which, like in many other mountain environments, coincides with a mean temperature during the warmest month of about 10°C (Costin *et al.* 2000; Körner 1999). Some of the outstanding natural features include 21 endemic flowering plant species (i.e. 10 per cent of the native flowering plants); periglacial and glacial features (which show the only clear evidence of mainland glaciation during the last glacial period and are an example of glaciation under marginal conditions); and great scenic values (Good 1992; Kirkpatrick 2003).

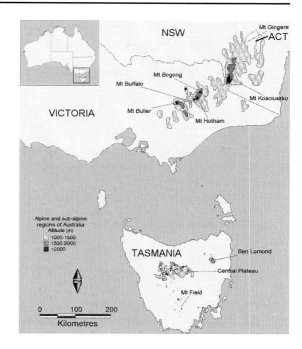

Figure 6.1: Distribution of the Australian alpine and subalpine zones across the Australian Capital Territory, New South Wales, Victoria and Tasmania (adapted from Green 1998).

The extraordinary landscape of great ecological, economic and scientific importance of the alpine area around Mt Kosciuszko is internationally recognized under the UNESCO Man and the Biosphere Program as a World Biosphere Reserve (Costin *et al.* 2000; Good 1992; Kirkpatrick 2003). In 2008, the Australian Alps were also included in Tourism Australia's National Landscapes programme and as such will feature strongly in Australia's international tourism marketing.

Human history

The Australian Alps, like most of Australia, have a long history of human use, with evidence of habitation in the general region from around 21,000 years ago during a period of glaciation (Good 1992; Sullivan and Lennon 2004). More extensive use of the higher altitude areas dates from 4000 to 3000 years ago (Good 1992; Sullivan and Lennon 2004). At least 13 linguistic and social groups visited the region with the most prominent social festivals associated with harvesting the Bogong Moths (*Agrostis infusa*) which seasonally congregate in caves and rock crevasses (Sullivan and Lennon 2004). There are also important current cultural links with the region for local Aboriginal communities. Nevertheless, unlike the region's grazing history, past and present Aboriginal association with the area is not given much prominence in tourism in the region.

Use of the region for pastoralism dates back to as early as 1823, when some of the first grazing stations were established in the region (Good 1992; Sullivan and Lennon 2004). Use of the alpine region during summer for grazing cattle and sheep was originally unregulated until the introduction of grazing leases in the 1880s, although even then illegal grazing still occurred (Good 1992). Damage to vegetation, soils and aquatic systems was extensive, with a range of impacts documented as early as the 1890s with damage still evident today (Good 1992). Some were due directly to grazing, but annual burning to promote a 'green pick' compounded impacts. It was not until the 1940s that control of grazing was instigated, with the establishment of the Kosciusko State Park in 1944 (Good 1992). Nevertheless, the legend and regional image of mountain pastoralism and brumby[2] running, instilled into the Australian psyche and folklore through the words of the poem 'The Man from Snowy River', continues to this day (Sullivan and Lennon 2004).

The main factor that resulted in limitations, and then the end of grazing, in the alpine area around Mt Kosciuszko, was the development of the Snowy Hydro-electric Scheme. Soil erosion and its impacts on water quality and potential siltation of dams lead to both the cessation of extensive grazing and the start of programs by the Soil Conservation Service of New South Wales to actively revegetate existing damage. The Snowy Hydro-electric Scheme was one of the largest-ever engineering projects in the southern hemisphere, involving the building of numerous dams and an extensive tunnel system connecting them (Collis 1990). During the construction phase from 1949 till 1972, thousands of European workers migrated to the region, contributing to the region's community fabric. The scheme and numerous sites throughout the region also lend themselves to geological interpretation from macro (e.g. landscape formation) to micro level (e.g. mineral composition of tunnel spoils).

Tourism to Mt Kosciuszko

Today, the key tourism attractions of the Australian Alps include Mt Kosciuszko and its surrounds (for its height, scenic values and hiking), snow skiing, features of the snowy hydro scheme and its development, and significant karst systems and caves. Tourism to the Kosciuszko alpine area (Figure 6.2) really commenced with the completion of the 53 km Summit Road from the town of Jindabyne to the top of Mt Kosciuszko in 1909. In 1930 (rebuilt in 1939) a Chalet was built at Charlottes Pass on the edge of the alpine area, principally to provide accommodation for ski tourism. It was also used in summer for a range of activities including bushwalking, horse riding and car touring (Walkom 1991). A small 'emergency' hut was built in the alpine area in 1929, followed by the Lake Albina and Kunama ski lodges completed in 1951 and 1952 (Hueneke 1987). Ski tourism took off in the 1950–60s partly as a result of the interest of post war migrants who worked on the Snowy Hydro-electric Scheme. Several ski resorts in the subalpine areas were established and developed during this time including Thredbo Village (1958), and Perisher Valley (1959) (Hueneke 1987). The Kunama lodge was destroyed by an avalanche in 1956. Lake Albina Lodge was acquired by the parks service in 1969, and removed in 1984 (Worboys and Pickering 2002).

The Summit Road was the main access route in summer to Mt Kosciuszko with private cars initially able to access the very summit. An informal walking track was also used from Thredbo, with the completion of a Chairlift from Thredbo Village to the edge of the alpine area in around 1962 (Worboys and Pickering 2002). In 1972, a car park was constructed below the summit of Mt Kosciuszko at Rawson's Pass, with people walking to the summit using a direct walking track through sensitive snowbank vegetation. In 1976, the Summit Road was closed between Charlotte Pass and Rawson Pass to private vehicles, with buses providing tourist access during peak periods (Worboys and Pickering 2002).

2 A brumby is a wild horse which descended from domestic horses introduced to Australia by European settlers. The management of brumbies in Kosciuszko National Park today is a highly controversial issue. The hard-hoofed feral animals cause considerable damage to the native alpine environment although they have a highly romanticized place in Australian history and are seen by some as a cultural asset.

Figure 6.2: Summit area, Mt Kosciuszko, Australian Alps

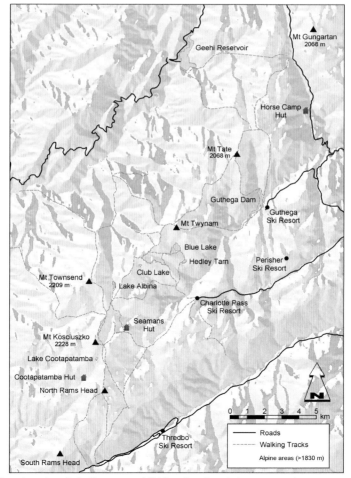

Figure 6.3: Road and walk trail access, Mt Kosciuszko alpine area

In 1978, the direct walking route from Rawson Pass to the summit was closed, with access via the old closed road. The Summit Road was closed to all vehicles (excluding management access) in 1982, and construction of a new steel mesh walkway from the top of the chairlift at Thredbo to Rawson's Pass started, with associated rehabilitation of the old track (Worboys and Pickering 2002). As a result, the main route for people walking to Mt Kosciuszko changed from Charlotte Pass to Thredbo Village, and from a car–bus–short walk, to a chairlift ride and six-kilometre walk (see Figure 6.3). At Charlottes Pass, a short interpretative raised wooden boardwalk was installed along with other upgraded facilities. Other upgrades of walking tracks also occurred between the early 1980s and the present, with the use of a range of materials including cement pavers, gravel, gravel and geoweb, and stonework paths and steps (Hill and Pickering 2006).

Winter use of the alpine area was mainly for ski touring. Reflecting changes in tourism trends in the ski resorts, snowboarding in the alpine area is increasingly popular, with some ski touring, and a limited amount of ice climbing around Blue Lake. Little detailed information is publically available about winter use of the alpine area, compared to two detailed surveys that have been conducted during the snow-free period. The first of these surveyed general visitors to the alpine region during the snow free period of 1999/2000 (Johnston and Growcock 2005), while the second focused on collecting information about visitors on top of Mt Kosciuszko itself during peak time of summer visitation (2005–2006, Dickson 2007).

Summer is the main period of visitation to the alpine area with an estimated 100,000 people visiting during the snow free period (Johnston and Growcock 2005). Walking is the most popular activity (43 per cent long walks, 36 per cent short walks), with other activities including sightseeing (12 per cent), mountain biking (3 per cent) and camping (2 per cent) (Johnston and Growcock 2005). The most popular route to access the alpine area is from the top of a commercial chairlift from Thredbo Village (67 per cent), with about a third of people accessing the region from Charlotte Pass (32 per cent) and the summit of Mt Kosciuszko being by far the most popular destination (Johnston and Growcock 2005). For general visitors to the alpine area, climbing Mt Kosciuszko was the third most common motivation for visiting the area (27 per cent, Johnston and Growcock 2005). For people surveyed on Mt Kosciuszko, 78 per cent had decided to climb the mountain before leaving home (Dickson 2007). For summiteers, important motivations for their visit were *scenic beauty/naturalness*, *to enjoy the outdoors*, and *to climb Mt Kosciuszko* (Dickson 2007). The more often people reached the summit, the less important climbing the mountain became. Of particular interest is that 63 per cent of summiteers expected wilderness on the mountain, and 62 per cent experienced wilderness, even though the area is not a designated wilderness area and often they were on top of the mountain at the same time as hundreds of others. Visitors were highly satisfied with their visit and many had a strong attachment to the region, particularly if they were return visitors (Dickson 2007). This is an important consideration for successful geotourism interpretation as it could further build on linking the area's geoheritage with people's personal values and experiences. Indeed, while Mt Kosciuszko and the surrounding national park already offer many visitor attractions/destinations that focus on geological features, including Australia's highest peak and surrounding glaciated landscapes, caves, and the Snowy Hydro-electric Scheme, current visitation is not focused on geotourism *per se*.

Environmental impacts of tourism

Impacts of tourism use of Mt Kosciuszko include direct impacts such as damage to vegetation, soil hardening and the introduction of weeds, while there are also indirect impacts such as those associated with the construction and maintenance of the infrastructure provided for tourists (Pickering *et al.* 2003; Scherrer and Pickering 2001). As walking is one of the most popular activities in the region, a major direct impact of visitors is from trampling on native vegetation. This results in reduced cover of native vegetation, reduced native species diversity compaction of soils, changes in hydrology and soil erosion (Growcock 2005). Although the main vegetation type, tall alpine herbfield, is relatively resistant to trampling compared to other vegetation types in the region and vegetation in many other areas (Hill and Pickering 2009), it is also very slow to recover once damaged (Growcock 2005; Scherrer and Pickering 2006). For example vegetation and soils on the old walking track from the Thredbo Chairlift to Rawson's Pass remained highly degraded after more than 15 years since closure and rehabilitation efforts, with significant differences to adjacent natural vegetation in terms of soil nutrients, species composition and cover (Scherrer and Pickering 2006).

The main management response to trampling damage has been to harden walking tracks using a variety of materials. However, the construction and use of these tracks have their own impacts, with some requiring the removal of all vegetation along the track and with some introduced track materials resulting in distinct weedy verges. As a result, the area of impact varies from negligible for the steel mesh walkway to 4290 square metres per km for wide gravel tracks and 2940 square metres per km for narrow gravel tracks (Hill and Pickering 2006). For non-hardened tracks there was an average of 270 square metres of disturbance per km of track (Hill and Pickering 2006).

The cover and diversity of weeds in the alpine area is strongly associated with visitor use and infrastructure (Hill and Pickering 2006; Johnston and Pickering 2001, Pickering *et al.* 2007). Eleven exotic plant species have been recorded in the alpine area (Bear *et al.* 2006), predominantly along road and track verges (Pickering *et al.* 2007). Eight of these that are common in the Kosciuszko alpine area are also recorded in other alpine areas of the world, indicating they are part of a general alpine weed flora (Pickering and Hill 2007). Although weeds introduced during grazing period and then for restoration of eroded areas, tourists themselves, as well as the equipment, materials used for the provision of infrastructure are also sources of weed seed (Johnston and Pickering 2001; Whinam *et al.* 2005). For example over 1700 seeds were collected from the socks of ten people going out for a half day walk in the Kosciuszko alpine area (Mount and Pickering, 2009).

Future of this geotourism destination

The future of geotourism to Mt Kosciuszko will be very dependent on the direct and indirect impacts of climate change. The latest climate change scenarios for the Kosciuszko area are based on the CSIRO temperature and prediction models for 2001. As current climatic conditions are at the high end of predictions, it is likely that future climatic change will parallel high impact scenarios. Based on these values, changes in temperature of $+1$°C by 2020 and $+2.9$°C by 2050 under a high impact scenario are predicted (Hennessy *et al.* 2002). Consequent reductions in snow cover resulting from changes in temperature and precipitation will be dramatic with a 60 per cent (2020) to 96 per cent (2050) reduction in the area that experiences more than two months snow cover a year.

For Mt Kosciuszko, the predicted changes in climate include a change in the duration of snow cover from around 183 days to 169 days by 2050. But even more dramatic is the change in the peak snow depth from over 2 m to under 50 cm by 2050 (Hennessy *et al.* 2002). Another way of viewing the change is to consider that +2.9°C is approximately the equivalent of a 377 m change in altitude (using a 0.77°C lapse rate; Brown and Millner 1989). Therefore under the worst case scenario in 43 years, conditions equivalent to the current tree line at around 1830 m altitude would be found a metre above Mt Kosciuszko.

The predicted changes in winter and summer temperatures and the duration of snow cover are likely to have dramatic effects on the flora and fauna of the alpine region (Pickering *et al.* 2004). Changes in specialized vegetation such as that found under late lying snowbanks appear to be occurring (Green and Pickering, 2009). Increased diversity of birds and mammals (both native and exotic mammals) are likely (Green and Pickering 2002). Other changes will include an increase in the diversity of weeds (Scherrer and Pickering 2001; Pickering *et al.* 2004). But how will changes in snow cover, temperature and the flora and fauna effect tourism in the region?

One of the biggest changes to tourism is likely to come from the response of ski resorts in the adjacent area to decreases in natural snow cover. Like their counterparts in Europe and North America, they are planning for increasing summer tourism, and hence changing from snow-based resorts to more year-round destinations. Thredbo Village already heavily promotes a wide range of activities during the snow-free period including climbing Mt Kosciusko. Therefore it is likely that there may be increases in visitation to the region beyond that already occurring. However, paralleling the changes in winter that are motivating resorts to promote summer tourism, temperatures in summer will be higher and there will be less rainfall (Hennessy *et al.* 2005; Hennessy *et al.* 2002). This will result in a dramatic increase in the number of days of high fire risk weather in the region (Hennessy *et al.* 2005).

The extensive bushfires in 2006 illustrate the potential impacts of such fires on tourism in the region. The fires, started by a series of lightning strikes, burnt 1.75 million hectares of the Australian Alps in January to February 2003 (Jacobs and Walker 2004; Worboys 2003b). Only 46 per cent of the area above 1850 m burnt, reflecting the relatively low flammability of alpine vegetation (Ken Green, personal communication, 2007). However, all visitors to the Kosciuszko Park had to be evacuated the day before the fires arrived. This occurred on the start of the January long weekend, one of the busiest periods for tourism in the snow-free period. It involved the cancellation of a range of tourism events including a Jazz festival at Thredbo Village. It was estimated that the fires might have cost AU$121 million in lost income to the local tourism industry just in the state of New South Wales (Worboys 2003a). During the period of the fire, and for several weeks after, the Park was closed, with many areas within the Park remaining closed for years as the vegetation regrew. The risk of bushfires has again resulted in Thredbo Village being evacuated in 2007, even though the area did not burn in the end.

The risk of bushfires is likely to increase during the peak period of summer visitation, while there is likely to be greater promotion of the region as a summer destination. How these two factors interact, including how the park service, tourism operators, and visitors respond to these changes is not clear.

Conclusion

As visitation to the geotourism destination of Mt Kosciuszko and the Australian Alps has grown and developed, and landuse of the area has shifted from grazing to tourism, conservation and water catchment, management approaches to the area have continually had to develop, respond and adapt. The geology of the area can provide a common thread for interpretation of the region's history and its natural and human-made features to visitors. Geological features could be used to individually develop as well as link social and ecological themes such as Aboriginal festivals centred on harvesting Bogong moths (which seasonally gather in caves and rock formations); vegetation diversity and patterns (based on the underlying geology) and the effects of livestock grazing, tourism and climate change (which are linked to soil and hydrological characteristics); and the Snowy Hydro-electric Scheme and stories of the migrant workers involved in the construction of this vast network of tunnels and dams. To further develop the geotourism theme of the Australian Alps, interpretation can draw on these events and links to engage with people's individual values and instill relevance with visitors.

Climate change, nevertheless, may pose the biggest challenge to tourism management yet. Increasing visitation through an extended tourism season is likely to result in a rising demand for tourism infrastructure, increasing management responsibilities and costs and creating additional pressures on an already stressed ecosystem. At the same time, increasing risks such as from extreme weather events are predicted to further add to the expanding list of management costs and responsibilities. Given the important and in many ways unique environmental and social values at both a national and international scale of Australia's highest geotourism destination, proactive planning and management backed by a commitment for longer term resourcing of research and tourism impact prevention and mitigation measures is required.

References

Bear, R., Hill, W. and Pickering, C.M. (2006) 'Distribution and diversity of exotic plant species in montane to alpine areas of Kosciuszko National Park', *Cunninghamia*, vol. 9: 559-570.

Bock, J.H., Jolls, C.L. and Lewis, A.C. (1995), 'The effects of grazing on alpine vegetation: a comparison of the central Caucasus, Republic of Georgia, with the Colorado Rocky Mountains, U.S.A.', *Arctic and Alpine Research*, **27** (2), 130-136.

Brown, J.A.H. and Millner, F.C. (1989), 'Aspects of the meteorology and hydrology of the Australian Alps', in R. Good (ed.), *The Scientific Significance of the Australian Alps - The Proceedings of the First Fenner Conference 1988*, Australian Alps National Parks Liaison Committee, Canberra, pp. 297-329.

Collis, B. (1990) *Snowy: The Making of Modern Australia*, Canberra: Tabletop Press.

Costin, A.B., Gray, M., Totterdell, C.J. and Wimbush, D.H. (2000) *Kosciuszko Alpine Flora*, Collingwood, Victoria: Commonwealth Scientific and Industrial Research Organisation

DEWHA (2008) National Heritage Places. Accessed in February 2009 at www.environment.gov.au/heritage/places/national/australian-alps/information.html

Dickson, T. (2007) 'Mt Kosciuszko: wilderness expectations and experiences in a non-wilderness area', *Australasian Parks and Leisure*, **10** (3), 25-29.

Good, R.B. (1992) *Kosciusko Heritage*, Sydney: National Parks and Wildlife Service of New South Wales.

Green, K. (1998) *Snow - A Natural History; An Uncertain Future*, Canberra: Australian Alps Liaison Committee.

Green, K. and Pickering, C.M. (2002) 'A scenario for mammal and bird diversity in the Snowy Mountains of Australia in relation to climate change', in C. Körner and E.M. Spehn (eds), *Mountain Biodiversity: A Global Assessment*, London: Parthenon Publishing, pp. 239-247.

Green, K. and Pickering, C.M. (2009) 'The decline of snowpatches in the Snowy Mountains: importance of climate warming, variable snow and wind', *Arctic, Antarctic and Alpine Research* **41** (2), 212-218

Growcock, A.J.W. (2005) 'Impacts of camping and trampling on Australian alpine and subalpine vegetation and soils', in *School of Environmental and Applied Sciences*, p. 285. Griffith University, Gold Coast

Hamilton, L.S. (2002) 'Why mountains matter', *World Conservation*, **33** (1), 4-5.

Hennessy, K.J., Whetton, P.H., Smith, I.N., Batholds, J.M., Hutchinson, M.F. and Sharples, JJ. (2002) *Climate Change Impacts on Snow Conditions in Australia*, Canberra:, CSIRO First Interim Report.

Hennessy, K.J., Lucas, C., Nicholls, D., Batholds, J.M., Suppiah, R. and Ricketts, J. (2005) *Climate Change Impacts on Fire-weather in South-east Australia*, Canberra: CSIRO.

Hill, W. and Pickering, C.M. (2006) 'Vegetation associated with different walking track types in the Kosciuszko alpine area, Australia', *Journal of Environmental Management*, **78** (1), 24-34.

Hill, R. and Pickering, C.M. (2009) 'Differences in the resistance of three subtropical vegetation types to experimental trampling', *Journal of Environmental Management*, **90**, 1305-1312.

Hueneke, K. (1987) *Kiandra to Kosciusko*, Canberra: Tabletop Press.

Jacobs, P. and Walker, I. (2004) 'Alpine fires 2003: Rehabilitation and recovery of public land', in *Bushfires 2003 Conference Proceedings*, Canberra.

Johnston, F. and Pickering, C.M. (2001) 'Alien plants in the Australian Alps', *Mountain Research and Development*, **21** (3), 284-291.

Johnston, S.W. and Growcock, A.J. (2005) *Visiting the Kosciuszko alpine area: visitor numbers, characteristics and activities*, Sustainable Tourism Cooperative Research Centre.

Kirkpatrick, J.B. (2003) 'The natural significance of the Australian Alps', in Australian Alps Liaison Committee (eds), *Celebrating Mountains: An International Year of Mountains Conference, 25-28 November 2002*, Canberra: Australian Alps Liaison Committee, pp. 9-14.

Körner, C. (2003) *Alpine Plant Life: Functional Plant Ecology of High Mountain Ecosystems*, Berlin: Springer Verlag.

Messerli, B. and Ives, J.D. (1984) 'Mountain ecosystems: stability and instability', *Mountain Research and Development*, **3**, 2.

Mount, A. and Pickering, C.M. (2009). 'Testing the capacity of clothing to act as vector for non-native seed in protected areas.' *Journal of Environmental Management*, **91**, 168-179.

Ollier, C.D. and Wyborn, D. (1989) 'Geology of alpine Australia', in R. Good (ed.), *The Scientific Significance of the Australian Alps - The Proceedings of the First Fenner Conference 1988*, Canberra: Australian Alps National Parks Liaison Committee, pp. 25-54.

Patzelt, G. (1996) 'Modellstudie Ötztal: Landschaftsgeschichte im Hochgebirgsraum', *Mitt. Österr. Geogr. Ges.*, **138**, 53-70.

Pickering, C.M., Good, R.B. and Green, K. (2004) *The Ecological Impacts of Global Warming: Potential Effects of Global Warming on the Biota of the Australian Alps*, Canberra: Australian Greenhouse Office, p. 48.

Pickering, C.M. and Hill, W. (2007) 'Roadside weeds of the Snowy Mountains, Australia', *Mountain Research and Development*, **27**, 359-67.

Pickering, C.M., Hill, W. and Bear, R. (2007) 'Indirect impacts of nature based tourism and recreation: association between infrastructure and exotic plants in Kosciuszko National Park', *Journal of Ecotourism*, **6**, 146-57.

Pickering, C.M., Johnston, S.W., Green, K. and Enders, G. (2003) 'People on the roof: Impacts of tourism on the alpine area of Mt Kosciuszko', in R. Buckley, C.M. Pickering and D.B. Weaver (eds), *Nature Based Tourism, Environment and Land Management* New York: CABI International,, pp. 123-135.

Scherrer, P. and Pickering, C.M. (2001) 'Effects of grazing, tourism and climate change on the alpine vegetation of Kosciuszko National Park', *Victorian Naturalist*, **118** (3),93-99.

Scherrer, P. and Pickering, C.M. (2006) 'Recovery of alpine herbfield vegetation on a closed walking track in the Snowy Mountains, Australia', *Arctic, Antarctic, and Alpine Research*, **38** (2), 239-248.

Sullivan, S. and Lennon, J. (2004) 'Cultural values', in Independent Scientific Committee (eds), *An Assessment of the Values of Kosciuszko National Park*, Canberra: New South Wales National Parks and Wildlife Service, pp. 163-179.

UNEP WCMC (2002) *Mountain Watch: Environmental Change and Sustainable Development in Mountains*, Cambridge: UNEP World Conservation Monitoring Centre.

Walkom, R. (1991) *Skiing off the roof: The Kosciusko Chalet at Charlotte Pass and its place in the history of the Australian snowfields*, Arlberg Press.

Whinam, J., Chilcott, N. and Bergstrom, D. (2005) 'Subantarctic hitchhikers: Expeditioners as vectors for the introduction of alien organisms', *Biological Conservation*, **121**, 207-219.

Worboys, G. (2003a) 'A report on the 2003 Australian Alps bushfires', in *The Australian Institute of Alpine Studies* found at http://www.aias.org.au/news.html.

Worboys, G.L. (2003b) 'A brief report on the 2003 Australian Alps bushfires', *Mountain Research and Development*, **23** (3), 294-295.

Worboys G.L. and Pickering C.M. (2002), *Managing the Kosciuszko Alpine Area: Conservation Milestones and Future Challenges*, Sustainable Tourism Cooperative Research Centre.

7 Reconsidering the boundaries and applications of Geotourism – lessons learnt from tourism at Mount Vesuvius

Jonathan Karkut, London Metropolitan University, UK

Introduction

Active volcanic regions and a vibrant tourism industry may at first consideration seem to be an unlikely combination. However, even just a cursory search on the Internet brings up a whole range of tours, experiences and accommodation from Hawaii to Iceland, Ethiopia to Japan. The attraction extends beyond the dramatic landscapes of perfect cone shaped peaks, as rich volcanic soils often produce wide arrays of flora and fauna. Equally, the promise of plentiful harvests has long drawn dense human habitation around the world's volcanoes. Thus further layers of cultural, religious and agricultural patrimony can be seen to draw tourists in to visiting these potentially dangerous sites.

As documented across eruptions over the centuries, a very thin line exists between natural drama and disaster. Hence a burgeoning body of research has evolved, from the geological understanding of when and how eruptions occur, to risk management and prevention for the populations living around active volcanoes. More recently multidisciplinary teams have emerged to create bridges between the volcanologists, emergency managers, social scientists and community representatives to ensure effective transferral of information alongside the construction and implementation of robust crisis plans. However, little has been written with respect to how destinations near to active volcanic sites may mitigate often much needed economic growth through sustainable tourism development with the demands required for effective risk management.

This chapter addresses these issues using the example of Vesuvius, its national park and the surrounding municipalities, since tourism to active volcanic regions represents one of the most significant facets of geotourism (Figure 7.1). Furthermore, the juxtaposition of geological, archaeological, agricultural and other elements around Vesuvius itself, presents an opportunity to explore how a more mature geotourism destination might be defined and developed. An introduction to the general principles that currently guide volcano hazard management is first of all outlined, followed by a focusing in to explain the specific strategy constructed for the region around Vesuvius. Based upon results from two phases of qualitative field research, a description of the present structure of tourism around the volcano is then given alongside perspectives on how future forms of tourism development might be shaped in the region, as presented by some of the princi-

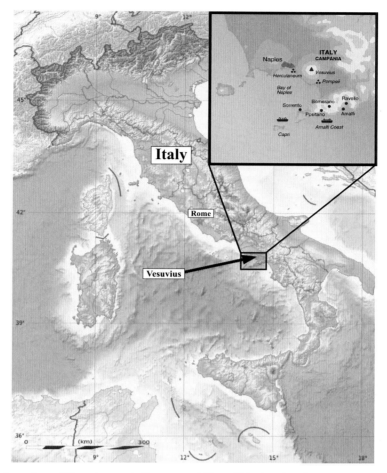

Figure 7.1: Location of Vesuvius and sites around Bay of Naples. Inset map source: http://www.exodus.co.uk/holidays/avg/itinerary

pal stakeholders involved. Subsequently we examine how a diverse geotourism product if woven into multi-stakeholder strategies may allow the crucial balancing act between development and risk management needs, to happen. Whilst making closer observations of the interconnected interests around the volcano, a more substantive understanding as to what actually encompasses geo (geological) tourism starts to emerge. In so doing, what transpires is a sector that may demonstrate considerably greater potential and possibilities than the narrow specialist tourism niche that geotourism is currently defined as representing.

Volcano hazard management

Over the latter decades of the 20th century, there has been a growing interest and understanding regarding the risks that volcanoes pose for the populations around them. As the world population has grown, urban growth particularly in developing countries, has led to a greater exposure to volcanic hazards (Chester *et al.*, 2001). The recognition of this increasing danger has been re-focused by the occurrence of numerous emergencies linked to volcanic activity and the subsequent attempts by civil authorities to lessen the impact of such eruptions. These efforts have had mixed success, from the disasters and major loss of life experienced around the 1982 eruption of El Chichon, Mexico or the 1985 eruption of Nevado del Ruiz, Colombia – to the relatively positive outcome of responses to eruptions such as 1980 Mount St. Helens, USA or 1995-98 Soufrière Hills, Montserrat (Chester *et al.*, 2002).

In response to this situation, the General Assembly of the United Nations reacted by declaring the 1990s the International Decade for Natural Disaster Reduction (IDNDR). Driven by this initiative, a whole range of studies were inspired to review how the risk to populations living in the vicinity of volcanic hazards could be significantly reduced (Chester *et al.*, 2002). Up until this point, volcanology had addressed these issues primarily from an earth sciences perspective by looking to establish the strength, nature and periodicity of major eruptive events. Through the concentrated focus of the IDNDR, a significant shift began to occur moving away from the pure science 'dominant' response, to a more applied approach involving multidisciplinary teams of volcanologists, social scientists, emergency planners, local communities and others (Aguirre and Ahearn, 2007).

In practical terms it is critical for strong lines of communication to be established between the geo-scientists, the emergency managers and contacts within the local communities themselves. As volcanic events are manifested in complex multiple cycles of raised and lessened activity followed by quiescence, one of the huge demands is for communications around known active volcanoes to remain on-going and to motivate the populations at risk even when the public perception might be that there is no danger present (Perry and Godchaux, 2005). Through observation of case studies around the world, Perry and Godchaux (2005), identify some key guidelines to appreciate when constructing a public education strategy to communicate volcanic hazard management:

1. Stress should be placed not just on 'awareness', but the transmission of actions that will ensure a greater adoption of protective measures by the affected public.

2. Communication efforts must not just be concentrated in a single campaign or event, but be longitudinal and repeat the threats and safeguards required to mitigate those circumstances.

3. It is important to ensure education flows within an inter-organizational and intergovernmental framework. The local, regional and national levels should be aware of the messages each is presenting. A further factor is for the credibility of local agencies to be ensured by establishing links with other organizations that are perceived as having specialist knowledge for specific hazards.

4. Messages need to address attitudes towards the adjustments in behaviour or actions that need to be taken, rather than solely creating hazard awareness.

5. Recognition of the roles that the media can take. Again the stress is on the long term as opposed to campaign-led processes of dissemination. Such an active programme should approach the breadth of media channels that are now available; from newspapers, magazines, radio and TV, to the Internet and e-mail. Specific audiences and sections of the community should also be identified so that specialist programmes reaching particular age, gender, ethnicity or socio-economic status may be targeted

When considering the issues and principles described above, the region around Vesuvius begins to look very vulnerable. The area represents one of the highest concentrations of predominantly urban population in Europe. Growth and rural-to-urban migration followed government funded schemes which were further fuelled by cheap but speculative, unplanned and often illegal building, which led to encroachments closer and closer to the volcano itself (Dobran, 2000). Set against this backdrop, it was recognized in the early 1990s, that a comprehensive emergency plan for the Vesuvius area was long overdue.

National Emergency Plan for Vesuvian Area (NEPVA)

The National Emergency Plan for Vesuvian Area (NEPVA), was finally agreed and published in 1995 as the first comprehensive hazard evaluation and evacuation plan for the region (Dipartimento della Protezione Civile, 1995). It is structured around a model informed by the last major sub-Plinian eruption of 1631 and assisted by computer generated maps outlining the area of hazard vulnerable to pyroclastic flow and ash fallout (Barberi et al.,1990). The plan is based on an assumption that following the pattern of warning earthquakes felt for over a fortnight before the 1631 eruption, the 700,000 residents living in the danger zone would have the opportunity to be evacuated over a seven-day period. To support this premise, it is stated that the extensive spread of different monitoring devices across the region will allow a lag of around 20 days between the first signs of movement in the magma chamber and the commencement of the eruption.

The model created three zones of hazard:

1. An inner 'red zone' that is most immediately at danger from pyroclastic flows and lahars spreading out from the cone. In the red zone there are an estimated 550,000 residents, who would have to be evacuated from the area

2. An outer far wider area called the 'yellow zone' is vulnerable to pyroclastic fallout. It is delineated based upon the spread of ash deposits laid down during former sub-Plinian eruptions of VEI (Volcanic Explosivity Index) level 4.

3. A further area of around 98 square kilometres called the 'blue zone', where it is anticipated major floods and lahars may occur.

As a result of the significant debate that arose from the presentation of the 1995 plan, there has been a further wave of information gathering and surveys to assess the volcanic risk perception of the local population. Amongst these studies, Barberi et al. (2008), have found that local communities have expressed a wish to be consulted much more, particularly through public discussions relating to emergency planning and methods to ensure better individual preparedness. The results of the survey also indicate that there is still need for a major push on education and presentation of information. Particularly working through the Vesuvius Observatory, situated high up on the flank of the volcano, extensive educational programmes have consequently targeted local schools through classes, distribution of publications and guided tours around exhibitions about the volcanic risks.

A wave of recent studies and surveys accessing the Vesuvius emergency plan, has ensured that many of the local stakeholder groups have now been consulted. However, throughout that research, little or no mention is made of one major category of temporary population, that is tourists. This is rather an alarming situation, as interviews with local municipalities, the national park and other authorities around Vesuvius have indicated that all are interested in creating a wider range of products for tourists in order to extend their stay and spend in the region. Various local, national and EU programmes are being identified through which to attract support for further tourism development. The principle motivation behind these actions is the pressing need to improve the high levels of unemployment and poor levels of return received by the local communities from the tourism industry as it is currently structured.

Placing tourism in the equation

One of the more significant questions raised by this situation, is that when apprehension is rising regarding the state of awareness and preparedness for future eruptions, can a further expansion in tourism arrivals and wider spread around the territory be mitigated against a growing geological risk? In order to explore this issue in greater detail, the present author conducted two phases of qualitative research around some of the relevant institutions linked to development in the areas adjacent to Vesuvius. The research was conducted through face-to-face interviews, participant observation, literature review and personal communications with a Naples-based company working on sustainable planning and development.

What is immediately obvious is that tourism to Vesuvius and its hinterland is not a recent phenomenon. In AD 79 Pliny the Younger became the first individual to extensively chronicle a major volcanic eruption. In so doing, the disasters that overcame the towns of Pompeii and Herculaneum were permanently lodged in our collective memory and Vesuvius became the most (in)famous volcano on the planet. Thus today the spectacular archaeological sites that have been studied and excavated for over 300 years, now attract up to 2.5 million visitors annually, whilst over a million trek up the final hundred or so metres to the main crater or 'Gran cono' of Vesuvius (see Figure 7.2).

Figure 7.2: Tourists and guide at rim of Vesuvius crater. Source: Giles Revell, 2009

Furthermore, since 1995, an area of some 8482 hectares surrounding the volcano has been designated as a national park, with the following aims outlined in its statute:

♦ Conservation of its fauna, flora and geomorphologic structures

♦ Application of administration and environmental protection programmes

♦ Promotion of educational, recreational and sustainable research activities

♦ Reconstitution and defence of hydraulic and hydrogeological balances in the area

♦ promotion of traditional cultural, agricultural and craftwork activities.

(Vesuvius National Park, 2008a).

Hence, as well as geotourism per se, the developmental priorities of the national park suggest there is the potential for a wide spread of other tourism interests to be catered for in the region around the volcano. However, the strong opinion of those interviewed by the author, was that tourism in the region continues to be poorly implemented. It was expressed that a very small percentage of what should be major benefits, ended up filtering through to the local economies and alleviating unemployment. Several interviewees indicated that central to this issue was the existence of weak and corrupt governments particularly at the local level. This meant that speculative building, illegal clearing of land and illegal dumping of waste had continued unabated, with the principle driving force and only significant beneficiary being the Campanian organized crime clans, collectively known as the *Camorra* (personal communications with Vesuvius National Park, 2008b and Legambiente Campania branch, 2008). The creation of the national park in 1995 was in part a response to this situation. The intention being that the protected area would act as a buffer zone to halt and reverse developments in increasingly hazardous locations.

Particularly in the early years after its creation, the national park authorities discovered that the touristic activities in and around Vesuvius were taken out of their control and managed directly by an external private company. For an annual contract of that was said to be approximately 15,000 euros, this company was allowed to collect all takings (personal communications with Vesuvius National Park, 2008b). Entrance fees just to the 'Gran cono' are currently 6.5 euros for adults and 4.5 euros for under 18s and students (personal observation). With over a million visitors annually passing through this entry point, this points to a sizeable profit for the management company and as indicated above, few tangible benefits for the park or the wider communities located in the territory.

When consulted about the future organization of the park and takings from tourism, the national park authorities indicated that their single greatest struggle is in levering away the influence of the Camorra and losses to the 'black' economy. This had been tackled on the political front through lobbying to the federal parliament and in the past three or four years has achieved some success. For example the management of the site is now jointly organised by the private company mentioned earlier and the national park authorities themselves. This means that the national park now receives roughly 1 euro from each of the entrance tickets sold (personal communication with Vesuvius National Park, 2008b). With this income, amongst other plans there is the intention to stop more polluting coaches coming all the way to the terrace at 1000 m. Instead vehicles would stop outside of the national park limits where passengers would then be transferred to a refurbished terrace through the use of electric shuttle buses (see Figure 7.3).

Figure 7.3: Vesuvius with entrance car park in foreground and path leading up to crater rim. Source: http://www.protezionecivile.it.

As indicated during interviews with the national park authorities, future proposals also hope to target the strengthening of links between the national park and the local municipalities, so that tourism development might incorporate local agricultural produce and traditions, along with other cultural practices and expressions. The prospects of transporting tourists to additional urban and rural locations are aided by the existence of a substantial infrastructure around the volcano. In particular, mobility is provided by a network of 96 stations and six lines that form the 'Circumvesuviana' narrow-gauge railway. This network joins up all the municipalities and main towns around Vesuvius with a service going into the centre of Naples (Circumvesuviana, 2008). It was further indicated, that a wide range of cultural traditions and experiences are embedded in the communities that inhabit the towns and countryside around the volcano, but information about these aspects of the local heritage are currently not transmitted to the tourists that arrive in the region. As a consequence, this channel for possible economic growth is barely touched (personal communication with Legambiente Campania branch, 2008).

The national park authorities, local municipalities, NGOs and other regional agencies are therefore actively looking for ways to support such tourism developments and have been considering local and national funding, plus European Union programmes that might assist such interventions. After years of disconnection from the industry, this would appear to be an useful opportunity to link and embed new tourism development proposals, which could be pursued for a broader range of beneficiaries within the Vesuvian communities. Such developments could additionally provide alternative methods of communicating more clearly and more systematically, what the hazards of the volcano are, how they are manifested and what actions all population (including tourists) would need to take in the case of a major eruptive sequence. Approaches to these issues will need to incorporate more contemporary, dynamic and interactive ways of engaging with new audiences, as many attempts to generate an interest and greater understanding of geotourism around Vesuvius, have thus far been judged by tourists visiting the site as being static and unimaginative (personal communications with tourists informally interviewed at Vesuvius in 2008 and 2009). In order to improve this situation, there has been no shortage of ideas and proposals from stakeholders active in the sector, these include:

♦ Updating and expanding existing museum spaces in the region

♦ Wider and more mobile range of exhibitions and events, taking advantage of advances in 3D computer simulations and computer generated images (CGI)

♦ Improve guiding services, including geological/volcanological guides but also linking to guides with local cultural and environmental knowledge

♦ Significant increase in the range and quality of interpretation and signage around Vesuvius

♦ Involving a wider spread of local stakeholders especially from those who can draw upon aspects of the intangible heritage of the region and present those features to touristic audiences

♦ Ensuring that local accommodation (B&Bs and hotels) are supported with further hospitality training and have access to other information on Vesuvius and to the emergency plan

(personal communication with Vesuvius National Park, 2008b and Legambiente Campania branch, 2008, 2009)

One further initiative under consideration, that is aimed at broadening the tourism offer and at the same time assisting in the transmission of information regarding volcanic risk and the attempts to alleviate this, is the development of a new 'geopark' which would link the three active volcanic sites around the Bay of Naples: Vesuvius, Campi Flegrei and Ischia (personal communication with Legambiente Campania branch, 2009). A 'Volcanoes of Campania' Geopark, would not simply highlight the only active volcanoes on mainland Europe, but offer the potential to permit elements of both tangible and intangible heritage plus a rich natural environment to be inter-woven into the overall tourism product. In so doing, information about the volcanic landscape, the flora and fauna surrounding it and insights explaining how the people occupying that landscape relate to the volcanoes, could be shared with domestic and international visitors. That process of generating further understanding and engagement with the local communities, could then lead to self-efficacy and deeper engagement with the emergency plan. Both factors that are identified as encouraging at-risk populations, not just being aware of volcanic hazards, but being prepared and knowing how to act during a crisis (Barberi *et al.* 2008).

The successful application of such ideas and initiatives around Vesuvisus, however, is far from being a straightforward task. Apart from the immediate and obvious problems of circumventing vested interests, which already benefit significantly and are content to see the existing structures of tourism development continue unaltered (personal communication with Vesuvius NP, 2008b), discussions with many of the key local stakeholders have demonstrated that there is a dearth of understanding about 'geotourism', what it constitutes and how Vesuvius could be seen as the central hub of a broad Campanian getourism product. Even institutions working directly in the field of geology, such as the Vesuvius Observatory, were unaware of the potential in utilizing geotourism around the volcano as a means to both disseminating information about hazardous geological phenomena and generating additional revenue through attracting further tourists. In part, this maybe due to limited research and communication of debates concerning geotourism beyond the attention of purely earth scientists, a situation that has only recently started to be redressed with events such as the inaugural Global Geotourism conference in Australia during 2008 and its follow-up which is to be hosted in Malaysia in 2010. With the expansion of such serious academic examination of the subject, one of the essential issues that is in need of being discussed more widely, is where do the boundaries of geotourism actually lie.

Efforts at presenting a definition have thus far placed it distinctly as a narrow subset or niche form of tourism. Dowling and Newsome (2006) restricted its borders to being a 'distinct subsector of natural area tourism and not a form of tourism that also includes wider cultural and heritage components or tourism that focuses of wildlife'. Whilst Hose (2000), indicates that geotourism represents 'The provision of interpretative facilities and services to promote the value and societal benefit of geological and geomorphological sites and their materials' and so implies that human dimensions do need to be incorporated into any consideration of the subject. Fernandez Young (2008), contests however, that the reach of geotourism should not be limited by excluding elements such as the extractive industries or the human context around which geological investigation occurs. Instead it is argued that components of geotourism should take in amongst others studies, archaeology, mineralogy and extraction, the broader 'landscape' including facets of social history and 'socioscapes' (Fernandez Young, 2008).

The influence and impact of Vesuvius on its surrounding natural and social environment and the range of groups interested in using it as a resource, does suggest that rather than treating it simply as a geological feature and linking it to tourism through the provision of hard scientific detail and interpretation, a more effective and beneficial application would be to place it at the centre of a more complex form of geotourism that incorporates cross-disciplinary elements such as archaeology, history and anthropology. In so doing, when authorities are looking to manage further tourism development in the region, by understanding this wider definition of geotourism they would address more than those who are motivated by a direct and existing interest in geology, and instead include what Fernandez Young (2008) describes as 'incidental geotourists', who travel to the location for many other reasons. By such a process the connections through the geological, environmental and social layers of a geosite such as Vesuvius could be shown, potentially providing additional benefits such as allowing economic development to reach wider strands of the community and to offer opportunities for broader awareness and understanding of geohazards.

Conclusions

At a time when global population growth is exposing more and more communities to volcanic hazards, an expanding body of work is being dedicated to lessen the impacts of major eruptions. A trend has been identified which shows a shift away from just pure earth science attempting to understand how and when eruptions occur, towards a more integrated and applied approach of risk management involving volcanologists, social scientists, emergency planners, local communities and others (Aguirre and Ahearn, 2007). The catalyst for this shift being a series of significant eruptions in the final decades of the 20th century and a focusing of minds through the UN declaration in the 1990s of an International Decade for Natural Disaster Reduction (Chester et al., 2002).

Within this framework, it would at first consideration seem to be the greatest folly for destinations near to active volcanoes to then propose expanding tourism development and thereby push further significant numbers of people into an already difficult equation. As a result, it is probably not surprising that little consideration has been given as to where tourism fits in to the burgeoning set of volcanic risk management plans and strategies. However, the natural fascination with the dramatic landscapes and experiences around active volcanoes has ensured that tourism to these sites is already a major business. It therefore follows that input from a tourism perspective has to be woven into any emergency policy and planning, otherwise a significant sector of those at risk will be overlooked.

Whilst conducting the research, the present author found that even in the case of the extensively analysed Vesuvius emergency plan, it does not currently appear to fully acknowledge that economic and cultural factors have the potential to override the best laid strategies even if there is great awareness of the volcanic risk. Furthermore, the lack of benefits to the local communities from the existing tourism products and continued high unemployment, is leading many local authorities and agencies around Vesuvius to consider new ways of developing tourism in their localities. Thus a collision course seems to be being steered between the emergency plan on one hand and social and economic necessities on the other. However, the sustainable tourism proposals mooted by agencies such as the Vesuvius National Park and environmental NGOs like Legambiente, by working to improve the chances of benefits filtering down to the local communities rather than increasing the risk to populations in an emergency situation, might actually offer additional pathways to ensure that both awareness and preparedness for the next eruption of Vesuvius are engrained in both residents' and tourists' minds

For a reworked tourism offer to succeed in playing a supporting role in the transfer of volcanic risk information and link more closely with local communities however, new approaches will have to be devised to revitalize the situation. Amongst those examined in this chapter, possibly the most effective model might come in the form of a future 'Volcanoes of Campania' Geopark. Geoparks are a framework whereby:

> geological heritage and geological knowledge is shared with the broad public and linked with broader aspects of the natural and cultural environment, which are often closely related or determined to geology and landscape.
>
> (UNESCO, 2008)

When observing the gaps between the Vesuvius emergency plan and the development of sustainable tourism development around the volcano, such a model looks to provide a helpful connection. However, the research conducted here has also identified that at present there is a limited understanding of geoparks and geotourism and their application, by many of the important tourism stakeholders in the region around Vesuvius. In part this is due to the contested nature of the term 'geotourism' and the limited transmission of debates on the subject beyond the earth sciences community. Nonetheless, one common feature of the tourism proposals that have been suggested for the region is that in one form or another the gaze is clearly towards the volcano Vesuvius. In practical and management terms, this suggests that it may be more appropriate to consider a more holistic definition for geotourism, that incorporates social and environmental layers as well as the core geological considerations. Through a more inclusive classification and application, we provide an opportunity to involve a wider range of tourists and not just those already familiar with geology. Furthermore, by presenting disciplinary linkages and connections around a geosite, we allow the local communities and other stakeholders a chance to understand geology more deeply and recognize that geotourism is relevant to them and much more than a marginal niche for those wielding a geology hammer.

References

Aguirre, J.A. and Ahearn, M. (2007) 'Tourism, volcanic eruptions, and information: lessons for crisis management in National Parks, Costa Rica, 2006'. *PASOS, Revista de Turismo y Patrimonio Cultural*, 5 (2), 175-191.

Barberi, F., Macedonio, C., Pareschi, M.T. and Santacroce, R. (1990) 'Mapping the tephra fallout risk: an example from Vesuvius (Italy)', *Nature* 344, 142-144

Barberi, F., Davis, M.S., Isaia, R., Nave, R. and Ricci, T. (2008) 'Volcanic risk perception in the Vesuvius population', *J. Volcanol. Geotherm. Res.* 172, 244-258.

Chester, D.K., Degg, M., Duncan, A.M. and Guest, J.E. (2001) 'The increasing exposure of cities to the effects of volcanic eruptions: a global survey', *Environmental Hazards*, 2, 89-103.

Chester, D.K., Dibben, C.J.L. and Duncan, A.M. (2002) 'Vocanic hazard assessment in Western Europe', *J. Volcanol. Geotherm. Res.* 115, 411-435.

Circumvesuviana (2008) Rete e Orari. http://www.vesuviana.it (accessed 12 June 2008)

Degg, M. (1998) 'Natural hazards in the urban environment: the need for a more sustainable approach to mitigation', in Maund, D.R. and Eddleston, M. (eds), *Geohazards in Engineering Geology*. Geological Society, London, Eng. Geol. Spec. Publ. 15, 329-337.

Dipartimento della Protezione Civile (1995) Rischio vulcanico - Vesuvio http://www.protezionecivile.it/minisite/index.php?dir_pk=250andcms_pk=1440 (accessed 8 July 2008)

Dobran, F. (2000) 'Mitigation of volcanic disasters in densely populated areas', http://www.westnet.com/~dobran/publ.html (accessed 30 June 2008)

Dowling, R K and Newsome, D. (2006) *Geotourism: Sustainability, Impacts and Management*, Oxford: Elsevier.

Hamilton, F.E.I. (1991) 'Global economic change', in Bennett, R.J., Estall, R.C. (eds), *Global Change and Challenge*, London: Routledge, pp. 80-102.

Fernandez Young, A. (2008) 'Geotourism: geology, industry and authenticity', paper presented at the International Geotourism Conference, Krakow, Poland.

Hose, T.A. (2000) 'Geological interpretation and geoconservation promotion for tourists', in D.Barretino, W. A.P. Wimbledon, and E. Gallego (eds), *Geological Heritage: Its Conservation and Management*, Madrid: Sociedad Geologica de Espana/Instituto Technologico GeoMinero de Espana/ProGEO, pp. 127-146.

Hose, T.A. (2007) 'Geotourism in Almeria Province, southeast Spain', *Tourism*, 55 (3), 259-276.

Legambiente Campania branch (2008) Discussions with unnamed staff on tourism developments NGO involved in and interested in Campania Geopark [Meeting] (personal communication, 9, 10 and 11 April 2008).

Legambiente Campania branch (2009) Discussions with unnamed staff on latest tourism initiatives and funding opportunities around Vesuvius [Meeting] (personal communication, 27 April 2009).

Perry, R.W. and Godchaux, J.D. (2005) 'Volcano hazard management strategies: fitting policy to patterned human responses', *Volcano Hazard Management*, 14 (2), 183-195.

UNESCO, 2008. Global Network of National Geoparks .http://www.unesco.org/science/earth/geoparks.shtml (accessed 14 July 2008)

Vesuvius National Park, 2008a. The Park. http://www.parconazionaledelvesuvio.it/grancono/index.asp#parco (accessed 10 July 2008)

Vesuvius National Park (2008b) Discussions with unnamed staff on tourism development around Vesuvius: opportunities and obstacles [Meeting] (personal communication, 10 and 11 April 2008).

8 Management of geotourism stakeholders – experiences from the Network History of the Earth

Christof Pforr, Curtin University of Technology, Australia and
Andreas Megerle, Karlsruhe Institute of Technology, Germany

Introduction

A sharp increase in interest in geotourism worldwide in recent years has transformed many suitable regions into unique geotourism destinations opening up great opportunities for geoconservation and regional sustainable development. To fully capitalize on this potential, however, it is essential to bring together the fragmented stakeholders from the public and private sectors and establish appropriate structures and processes to facilitate their effective communication and collaboration. Only through such a partnership can an adequate knowledge base, built on diverse experiences and expertise, be established to provide certainty and guidance in the sustainable development of local geotourism products. Thus, effective communication networks and an open exchange of information are cornerstones of a successful implementation of geotourism in a region. The Network History of the Earth is a case in point for such a successful geotourism partnership. It was founded in 1997 as a framework for cooperation between a range of diverse stakeholders working together to develop a high quality sustainable tourism product based on the unique georesources of South-West Germany (Pforr and Megerle, 2006).

South-West Germany mainly comprises the State of Baden-Württemberg and covers an area of 35,752 square kilometres with a population of around 10.7 million people (see Figure 8.3). A typical feature of the state is its wide variety of natural landscapes which can be subdivided into three main landforms, the Upper Rhine Graben (Oberrheingraben) in the west surrounded by the Black Forest (Schwarzwald) in the east and the Vosges Mountains (Vogesen) on the western French side, the southwestern cuesta landscape (Schichtstufenland) gently sloping towards the south-east as well as the Alpine piedmont (Alpenvorland). These diverse and distinct landscapes form the resource base of tourism, and, in some cases, like the jurassic geopark Swabian Alb and the mining areas of the Black Forest, also for geotourism (Geyer and Megerle, 2003). The service sector industries contribute almost 34 per cent to the state's economic activities with tourism being an important industry for the state in general, but especially economically significant for regional areas.

The Network History of the Earth, comprising a diverse range of stakeholders from south-west Germany, has helped to foster a creative atmosphere, to identify the hidden potential of the various network partners and to ensure the sustainability of its products and processes. To achieve this ambitious task, personal ties and frequent communication have been core elements, which often emerged from an active involvement in local projects (Megerle and Pauls, 2004a).

In the past, as part of assessing the network's actions, instruments and tools were developed to examine the transfer of know-how and the creation of competencies within the Network History of the Earth (Pauls and Megerle, 2002; Sydow *et al.*, 2003). Methodologies employed included observations from inside, interviews with network partners, and data analysis. With the help of these evaluations some difficulties have been identified over the network's ten-year lifespan as the creativity and success of the Network History of the Earth relies on the stability and quality of its relational constellations. Stakeholder interviews, for instance, unveiled that a high degree of staff fluctuation within the various partner organizations can have a negative impact on the network's performance. Furthermore, at times insufficient communication and information exchange in certain areas, for example with staff of visitor information centres, resulted in only limited transfer of know-how among tourism partners. Another significant outcome of this evaluation process was the importance of personal ties between network participants. It was found that know-how is mainly transferred informally, outside official meetings during coffee or lunch breaks, and on occasions when the various players participate in a common experience-building event (Megerle, 2005; Elsholz *et al.*, 2006). In the following, we will have a closer look at the evaluation system of the Network History of the Earth which is dynamic and integrated into the network process (Pollermann, 2007).

Designing a network evaluation system

In general, evaluation can be described as the systematic and target oriented collection, analysis and assessment of data for quality management and quality control. Its function is to help assess processes concerning planning, developing, designing and implementing offerings and/or actions (e.g. methods, programmes) taking into account quality, functionality, impacts, efficiency and benefits (evaluationsnetz.com, n.d.).

The complexity of this definition and the notion 'target-oriented' already illustrate that network evaluations have to be adapted to a certain context, to the specific demands of the respective network and its stakeholders. This is important, not only for the construction of a specific contextual evaluation design but also for its de-construction, which is a crucial step in the interpretation of evaluation results or evaluation systems and also in relation to network assessments. The framework of the network, but also the interests and motivations of its stakeholders create specific perspectives, constraints and foci of the individual evaluation system.

The specific demands on the evaluation system for the Network History of the Earth can be described by the following aspects:

♦   It had to focus on the development of competencies on all levels, i.e. core stakeholders, affiliated partners and the network as a whole.

♦   As quick and flexible reactions are imperative for an innovative network, the evaluation had to be of a formative nature.

♦   As researchers driving the evaluation process were also key stakeholders in the network, the evaluation constituted more or less an internal self-evaluation.

◆   The findings of the evaluation programme were mainly used as a general quality
control tool, as a diagnostic 'early warning' mechanism for the network's management (see for instance, Straßheim and Oppen, 2006; Megerle, 2008) and as
an instrument for the improvement of the network's products, projects and initiatives (PPIs) (Borkenhagen *et al.*, 2004).

Taking these specific requirements into consideration, an evaluation system for the Network History of the Earth was developed involving all of its stakeholders (Figure 8.1).
An important characteristic of this evaluation tool was its modular structure, which is
briefly outlined in the following section. As a basis for the different evaluation modules,
several monitoring data collection methods were employed, the most important being
network stakeholder interviews.

Evaluation system modules – some insights

One important module is the evaluation of the success and/or the benefits of different
products developed by the network. Initially, a 'product' was seen solely as a tourism
product or a combination of different products in the form of a package. This narrow
understanding was monitored by indicators like the number of bookings or the number
of overnight visitors for the respective product. With the increasing development of
competencies within the network and a greater awareness for the need of strategic al-
liances and cooperation, the perception changed towards a broader understanding of
what constitutes a product for evaluation purposes: not only packages and other tourism products but also interpretation material, such as popular geo-brochures (Hauff *et
al.*, 1999), courses for geo-guides (Megerle, 2001; Megerle and Pauls, 2004b) and quality standards, for instance for interpretation trails, were increasingly also seen as real
network products. This then necessitated the development of a new target system, new
evaluation themes and new indicators like marketing and learning effects. There were,
nonetheless, differences in the intensity of evaluation for the various network products:
some products appeared to be more difficult to assess than others (for instance some
interpretative trails), others were comprehensively evaluated, such as a training program
for geo-guides as part of a research project (Megerle, 2003). Depending on the various
products, the evaluation processes resulted in a diverse range of findings: The number of
bookings for package tours involving an overnight stay, for instance was limited whereas the success of products involving day trips (events, trails, guided tours) was in general
assessed to be satisfactory for the network partners (Megerle and Vollmer, 2005).

Another important evaluation module was the assessment of the know-how transfer
amongst the network's stakeholders. The German Federal Research Programme 'Development of Competencies within Networks' supported this aspect of the Network History of the Earth's evaluation over a four-year period. Figure 8.2 illustrates an increase
in know-how transfer activities between the network stakeholders over a period of less
than five years, which can be linked to the significant growth in PPI development activities. (A larger scale version of this figure is available online at the Goodfellow website.)
Further findings in this evaluation module include:

◆   Evidence for the importance of the network's coordination in particular for the
initiation of PPI developments.

◆   Significant increase in some stakeholders' activity driven, for instance, by the es-
tablishment of sub-networks evolving around local projects such as the 'Swabian
Alb Subnetwork', which was subsequently developed further into the 'Geopark
Swabian Alb'.

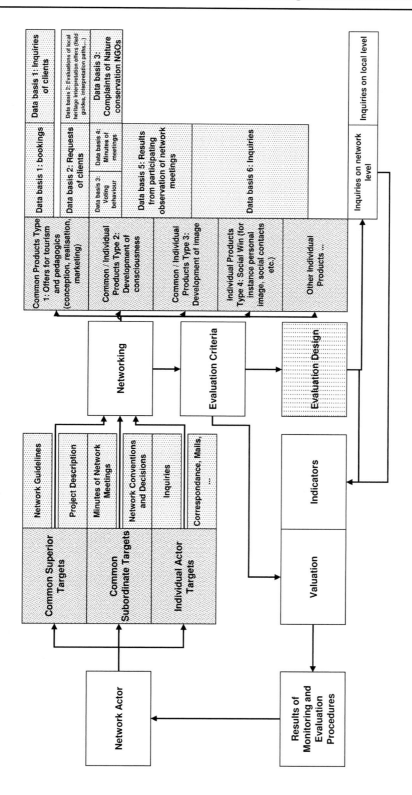

Figure 8.1: Network History of the Earth: Evaluation Concept. A larger, colour version of this diagram is available for download from the publisher's website at http://www.goodfellowpublishers.com

October 2001

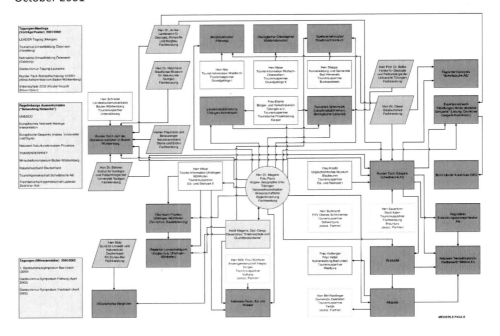

March 2005

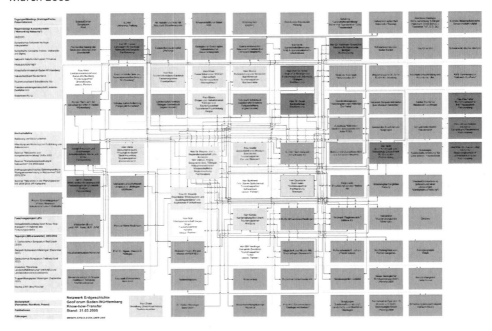

Figure 8.2: Increase in knowledge transfer in and around the Network History of the Earth over time (2001–05). Larger, colour versions of these diagrams are available for download from the publisher's website at http://www.goodfellowpublishers.com

- ♦ Identification of 'activity holes' concerning stakeholders or associated partners with limited activity within the network and 'activity centres or clusters', referring to stakeholders and partners showing strong levels of activity.

- ♦ Visualization of 'Networking networks' – strategies as an important aspect of the network's management to increase the exchange of know-how leading to innovative PPIs.

Interestingly, one of the problems identified on this particular level of evaluation was the insufficient know-how transfer between stakeholders and their colleagues within the respective institutions they are affiliated with (Megerle et al., 2004).

A third evaluation module focused on the self-evaluation of the organizational competency of the network. 'Organizational competency' means the disposition of a network as a whole to organize itself in accordance with its commonly agreed targets, available resources and within its general framework or its disposition to change this framework. This tool, also developed under the umbrella of the German Federal Research Programme 'Development of Competencies within Networks', utilized several different indicators to illustrate the competency performance of the network (see, for instance, Table 8.1). On this level of analysis, the Network History of the Earth demonstrated overall a considerable network competence, however, shortcomings were identified in its long-term financial sustainability. Consequently, the network had to opt for a low cost model as a perpetuating strategy (Elsholz et al., 2006).

Table 8.1: Network History of the Earth: evaluation of network competency (example indicator 'Dealing with targets')

Rating of network competency	Low	Middle	High
Sub-indicators	Common targets	Identification with targets	Processes for target changes
General performances of sub-indicators	Common network targets discussed, formulated and documented in an obligatory way	Targets represented outside and operationalized inside network	Success and benefits of network measured in relation to targets. If necessary, targets are modified
Performances of sub-indicators within Network History of the Earth	Common development of network targets since start of network. Known by stakeholders and documented (guidelines sustainability, medium term target system)	Intensive transfer of targets outside network by most stakeholders	Permanent adaptation of network targets to changing general conditions, e.g. extension of target system with 'geopedagogics'

Network analysis – an evaluation from outside

Although meaningful and relevant, all the above briefly described evaluation approaches were generated from within the network, taking more or less the format of a self-evaluation process from within, which was considered a limitation. An assessment of its operations from outside was therefore deemed useful to further explore the effectiveness of its communication and collaboration structures as an additional means to address some of the difficulties and shortcomings identified in the past in its operations. In the following the evaluation of the network's operations taking such an external perspective will be discussed in greater detail. This section of the chapter will present the findings of a network analysis which was designed to explore in particular how the various stakeholders within the Network History of the Earth work together and exchange information by describing and explaining the complex nature of their interactions. These findings need to be read in the context of one of the key performance indicators for its operations, namely to serve 'as a tool to develop a common language and shared aims and objectives, to create trust, and to explore its strength, available resources, competencies as well as the anticipated win–win scenario for each network partner' (Pforr and Megerle, 2006: 126). In doing so, past evaluation efforts are complemented and additional lessons might be learnt.

For assessing the network's performance from outside, a social network methodology was employed (see Wassermann and Faust, 1994; Scott, 2000) as an analytical tool to describe and explain the complex nature of the interaction between the various stakeholders within the structure of the Network History of the Earth. The focus was initially set on 'reputation', 'communication' and 'collaboration' networks (i.e. how stakeholders take each other into account in their actions), which underlie its operations. In essence, the main focus was on identifying the most influential stakeholders and how the network partners interact with each other. The aim was, thus, to map patterns of network relationships or 'relational configurations'. While various methods are available for social network analyses, this study followed initially a *structural approach*, analysing the relations between actors rather than their individual attributes. For this purpose a standardized online questionnaire was designed to investigate the nature of the interactions between the network's identified system of 45 stakeholders and its core players. The survey, which comprised four short questions, took approximately ten minutes to complete. These questions were developed to elicit how knowledge and understanding is shared between partners, in both formal and informal capacities. Hence, the survey was constructed in a way that data relating to factors such as influence reputation (defined as the perceived relative capacity of each actor to influence the operation and actions of the network), collaboration activity (defined as working together in a formal way, e.g. exchange of knowledge via meetings, seminars, workshops, sharing of resources) and participation in information exchange as part of a communication network (defined as exchange of information in terms of both information received as well as information sent among a pair of stakeholders in the network, for example, via telephone conversations, letters, emails, flyers, advertising) could be gathered. In essence, question 1 of the survey was set up to identify the stakeholders which were perceived to be the most influential within the network's partnership. Question 2 aimed to gain a clear understanding of the level of collaboration among network stakeholders, in other words, the sharing of knowledge and understanding. Questions 3 and 4 explored communication and the exchange of general information between its stakeholders. The focus here was on the activity of sending and receiving general information within the network that would normally be sent to partners, or received from them, in a more informal capacity. For the subsequent analysis, responses to questions 3 and 4 were merged and subjected to a multiplex operation, which allowed the information to be displayed in network maps with varying depth of information (e.g. general / two-way communications).

A total of 62 per cent of the network's stakeholders participated in the online survey. The network analysis was based on quantitative data using UCINET 6.0 as suitable software package (Borgatti *et al.*, 1999). In the following section, findings of this study are communicated in different ways, for instance as tables and network maps. These maps, in particular, have the potential not only to give first indications of complex realities but also aid in the exploration of questions such as 'which stakeholder relates with most other actors?' and, more importantly, 'can every stakeholder reach all other actors?' Visualization is therefore a powerful tool for displaying complexity in a very compact way.

As mentioned earlier, an initial set of 45 network stakeholders were identified and invited to participate in an online survey. They included, for instance, individuals from regional tourism businesses, environmental groups, local government, museums as well as universities (Figure 8.3). The findings of the online survey, which are presented in the following, can be used to build the base line data for any future follow-up surveys and therefore any possible longitudinal monitoring of the Network History of the Earth's communication and collaboration activities including trends or shifts in the underlying network structures over time.

An analysis of the responses to Question 1, which aimed to unveil the distribution of stakeholders identified as being most influential, defined in this context as being 'powerful, important and able to give directions', shows that within this perceived leadership group, 50 per cent of the nominated individuals are associated with the Management Team and 37.5 per cent are from academia. Most of the influential stakeholders appear to be located in four cities, Stuttgart (the State's capital city), Karlsruhe, Tübingen and Freiburg (all four being university towns, see Table 8.2).

Identifying the members of the network's management team as the stakeholders perceived to be the most influential, is no surprise and also in line with findings of earlier evaluations of the Network History of the Earth. To be able to perform successfully over the past decade or so, numerous network and project management tasks have had to be taken care of by the management team, such as coordination, moderation, mediation, documentation and information dissemination and, during some network phases, also the provision of technical input and motivation. These activities have fostered the development of a common language amongst network partners, of shared aims and objectives and of trust, they have helped to identify the network's strength but also its weaknesses, and have directed available resources to specific projects based on the competencies and capacities of the various network partners (Pforr and Megerle, 2006). Considering these tasks, it is obvious that the members of the management team need to be constantly in contact with various stakeholders and network groups and, thus, will be identified as most influential within the network. The fact that there are not only members of the formal management team but also the technical network coordinator (Actor #6) and one functional actor (Actor #17) within the group of stakeholders perceived to be most influential indicates decentralized work aspects of the network on the technical cooperation level.

Table 8.2: The most influential stakeholders ranked by their influence reputation score (sir)

sir*	Actor	Function	Organization	Region
1.00	# 22	Management	University	Karlsruhe
0.67	# 17	Management	Government	Freiburg
0.63	# 43	Management	University	Tübingen
0.38	# 6	Management	Tourism	Tübingen
0.29	# 13 # 44	Advisor Geopark	Museum Government	Stuttgart Stuttgart
0.25	# 42	Advisor	University	Karlsruhe
0.21	# 27	Advisor	Industry	Stuttgart

Note: * Rescaled to a maximum value of 1.00

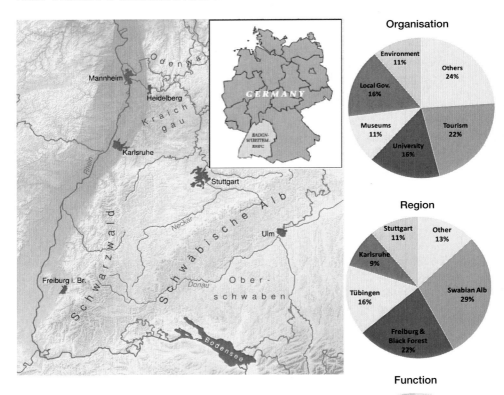

Figure 8.3: Network History of the Earth: stakeholders and their spatial centres of activity.

(Map source: http://commons.wikimedia.org/wiki/File:Karte_Baden-Wuerttemberg_physisch.png)

Based on the responses received to Question 2, which aimed to gain a clear understanding of the level of collaboration amongst network stakeholders, in other words the sharing of knowledge and understanding within the network, a network map was generated to illustrate the overall linkages and interactions amongst the stakeholders (Figure 8.4, N.B. Actors represented by numbered nodes, interactions by arrows). Despite its rather complex and active appearance, the network's density was calculated to be 0.44 (from a possible range from zero to one), hence, at present collaboration contacts amongst stakeholders do not appear to be outstandingly intensive but rather modest. One reason is that for many technical stakeholders the collaboration within the main network is less important than the collaboration in 'their' regional subnets (Megerle and Vollmer, 2005), structures which could be identified but were not further analysed as part of this study. Table 8.3 summarizes the most important stakeholders in this particular network, referred to as the collaboration elite.

Table 8.3: Collaboration elite ranked by their collaboration score (sc)

sc*	Actor	Function	Organization	Region
1.00	# 22	Management	University	Karlsruhe
0.81	# 43	Management	University	Tübingen
0.71	# 17	Management	Government	Freiburg
0.52	# 6	Management	Tourism	Tübingen
	# 13	Advisor	Museum	Stuttgart
	# 27	Advisor	Industry	Stuttgart
0.48	# 15	Advisor	Government	Freiburg
	# 44	Geopark	Government	Freiburg
0.43	# 10	Advisor	Self-employed	Freiburg
0.38	# 38	Tourism partner	Tourism	Black Forest
0.33	# 11	Tourism partner	Government	Freiburg
	# 18	Advisor	Government	Freiburg
	# 35	Tourism partner	Museum	Swabian Alb

Note: ˙ Rescaled to a maximum value of 1.00

As was the case with respect to influence reputation, the management team is again the most dominant group in collaborative activities, thus playing a crucial role in building bridges between stakeholder groups and sub-networks. It is not so much that the management team is actively involved in particular projects, but its members play a crucial role as the network's engine and a driver in drafting proposals for common strategies and projects. They also often encourage and support working arrangements within project groups and identify and promote real and potential future win–win scenarios (Pforr and Megerle, 2006). Hence, their prominent role in this collaboration network is obvious.

The organizational representation within the collaboration elite on the other hand, appears to be more balanced compared to the influence reputation elite (Table 8.2) as stakeholders with a wide range of organizational affiliations can be found (Table 8.3), most of them located in one of the state's administration and business centres.

Outside this collaboration elite, two additional sub-networks were identified which are characterized by a high level of collaborative activities. They were a regional sub-network within the Central Black Forest and a functional sub-network revolving around the 'Geopark Swabian Alb'. With respect to the latter, it comes as no surprise to find

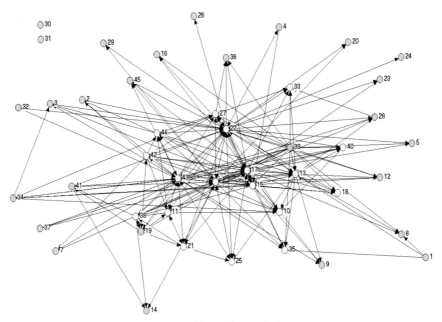

Figure 8.4: Collaboration (elite represented by white nodes)

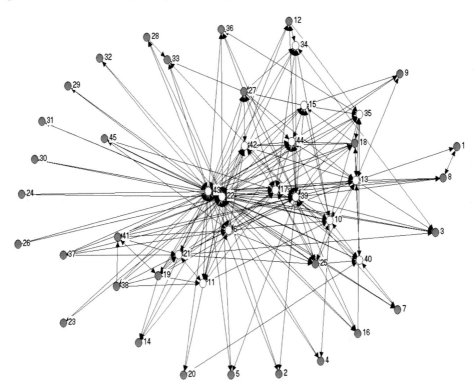

Figure 8.5: Communication network (elite represented by white nodes)

stakeholders involved in this local initiative as being particularly active. Considering the density of its geological and archaeological attractions, the Swabian Alb is rather unique on a global scale and therefore a classic geotourism destination. In fact, the Swabian Alb belongs to the most significant geotourism destinations in Germany and Europe alike and was therefore a pioneer in the German geopark movement.

Questions 3 and 4 of the survey aimed to gain information on communication and the exchange of general information between stakeholders of the Network History of the Earth. Focusing on the activity of sending and receiving general information about network activities that would normally be sent to or received from partners in a more informal capacity, responses to both questions were merged and subjected to a multiplex operation, which allowed the information to be displayed in network maps 'information exchange in general' as well as 'two-way communications only' (the latter allowing an additional level of analysis). Figure 8.5 (Actors represented by numbered nodes, interactions by arrows) illustrates the level of information exchange across stakeholders, which was found to be rather high with a density of 0.62. Overall the network composition is organisationally balanced. As was the case in the collaboration network, the management team again appears to be most active in information exchange (Table 8.4), in fact, the information exchange activities amongst the management team members were recorded with a maximum density value of 1.0. To achieve the network's objectives, the management team plays a crucial role as has been already highlighted earlier. To be able to operate successfully, its members, of course, rely heavily on close personal ties, frequent communication with various network stakeholders and effective dissemination of information. Thus, the prominent role of the management team in the communication network was somewhat anticipated considering its assigned responsibilities.

The above-mentioned sub-networks with high levels of information exchange activities and involving the stakeholders of the functional network 'Geopark Swabian Alb' seem to play an important role as they form both a communication-intensive network of tourism stakeholders and another involving university partners.

Table 8.4: Communication Elite Ranked by Their Information Exchange Score s_{ie}

sie*	Actor	Function	Organisation	Region
1.00	# 22	Management	University	Karlsruhe
0.60	# 43	Management	University	Tübingen
0.50	# 17	Management	Government	Freiburg
0.45	# 39	Geopark	Geopark	Swabian Alb
0.40	# 13	Advisor	Museum	Stuttgart
0.30	# 42	Advisor	University	Karlsruhe
0.28	# 35	Tourism partner	Museum	Swabian Alb
	# 44	Geopark	Government	Freiburg
0.25	# 6	Management	Tourism	Tübingen
	# 10	Advisor	Self-employed	Freiburg
	# 21	Tourism partner	Tourism	Freiburg
	# 40	Advisor	Environment	Swabian Alb
0.23	# 5	Advisor	Government	Freiburg
0.20	# 11	Tourism partner	Government	Freiburg
	# 34	Geopark	Volunteer	Swabian Alb

Note: * Rescaled to a maximum value of 1.00

Conclusion

In conclusion, this first online survey was successful in establishing baseline data concerning the effectiveness of collaboration and communication activities amongst stakeholders of the Network History of the Earth. It was possible to identify those stakeholders who are perceived to be the most influential. The dominant role of the management team in this influence reputation elite became apparent. These perceptions of importance were mirrored in the existing collaboration and communication networks. The survey was clearly able to highlight the crucial role of the management team in the successful operation of the network. In its leadership role it not only acts as the engine of the network by coordinating activities and disseminating information, it also plays a significant part in initiating local projects. The obtained data were also analysed with a functional, an organizational and a regional focus which allowed the identification of respective sub-networks and clusters. From these it can be concluded that an active involvement of stakeholders in regional and/or local projects such as the 'Geopark Swabian Alb' fosters collaboration and intense communication also outside the network's elites. It is also interesting to note, after having found stakeholders from academia dominating the reputational network, that the organizational representation in the various collaboration structures and communication networks appears to be much more balanced. It will be interesting to continue to monitor collaboration and communication activities of the Network History of the Earth to be able to compare and contrast findings in a longitudinal study with the aim of identifying areas requiring further improvement. The success of this undertaking, however, will strongly depend on the continuing support of all stakeholders and their willingness to participate in ongoing survey activities.

In general, the results of the combination of the different methodological modules (internal evaluation modules and external online survey) complement one another. As this methodological approach helped to identify and to analyse the structures and working procedures of the network, the combination of the two methods seems to be a practicable methodological approach for a process-orientated evaluation of collaboration networks.

References

Borgatti, S.P., Everett, M.G. and Freeman, L.C. (1999) *Ucinet 5.0 for Windows*, Natick: Analytic Technologies.

Borkenhagen, P., Jäkel, L., Kummer, A., Megerle, A. and Vollmer, L.-M. (2004) *Netzwerkmanagement* (Handlungsanleitung für die Praxis, 8), Berlin: ABWF.

Elsholz, U., Jäkel, L., Megerle, A. and Vollmer, L.-M. (2006) *Verstetigung von Netzwerken* (Handlungsanleitung für die Praxis, 12), Berlin: ABWF.

Evaluationsnetz.com (n.d.): Glossar, www.evaluationsnetz.de/index.php?cat=5&id=5& (accessed 15.07.09)

Geyer, M. and Megerle, A. (2003) 'Géotourisme et développement durable en Allemagne du Sud', in E. Reynard, C. Holzmann, D. Guex and N. Summermatter (eds), *Géomorphologie et tourisme* (Actes de la Réunion annuelle de la Société Suisse de Géomorphologie, SSGm), Lausanne: Institut de Géographie, Travaux et Recherches, pp. 177-184.

Hauff, R., Megerle, A., Megerle, H., Dieter, A., Behmel, H., Kraus, U. and Klumpp, B. (1999) *Abenteuer Geologie*, Bad Urach: Touristik-Gemeinschaft Schwäbische Alb.

Megerle, A. (2001) *Ausbildungskurs für Landschaftsführer 2001 in Tübingen und Ammerbuch* (Materialien zu Geologie/Geomorphologie), Tübingen: Universität Tübingen.

Megerle, A. (2003) *Umweltbildung als Instrument zur Akzeptanzerhöhung für den Naturschutz in der Tübinger Stufenrandbucht, Abschlußbericht*, Tübingen: Universität Tübingen.

Megerle, A. (2004) *Kompetenzentwicklung in Netzwerken – Das Netzwerk Erdgeschichte / GeoForum Baden-Wüttemberg* (Anthropogeographisches Geländepraktikum und Seminar – Ergebnisbericht), Tübingen: Universität Tübingen.

Megerle, A. (2005) 'Netzwerke als Instrumente zur Kompetenzentwicklung im Bereich Personal- und Organisationsentwicklung – Erfolgsfaktoren für ihre professionelle Nutzung durch Fach- und Führungskräfte', *QUEM-Bulletin*, 4, 11-16.

Megerle, A. (2008) 'Wissensmanagement und Netzwerke', in Deutsche Gesellschaft für Qualität (ed.), *Erfolgreiches Wissensmanagement, Methoden und Verfahren anhand von Praxisbeispielen*, Frankfurt: DGQ, pp. 208-217.

Megerle, A. and Pauls, K. (2004a) ''Geotourismusnetzwerke am Beispiel Netzwerk Erdgeschichte', in J.H. Kruhl, J. Birkenhauer, U. Lagally and G. Lehrberger (eds), *Geowissenschaften und Öffentlichkeit* (6. Internationale Tagung der Fachsektion GeoTop der Deutschen Geologischen Gesellschaft, 10. – 13.4.2002 in Viechtach. – Schriftenreihe Deutsche Geologische Gesellschaft), Hannover: Deutsche Geologische Gesellschaft, pp. 59-65.

Megerle, A. and Pauls, K. (2004b) ''GeoGuides oder Landschaftsguides? – Erfahrungen aus Landschaftsführerausbildungen in Baden-Württemberg', in J.H. Kruhl, J. Birkenhauer, U. Lagally and G. Lehrberger (eds), *Geowissenschaften und Öffentlichkeit* (6. Internationale Tagung der Fachsektion GeoTop der Deutschen Geologischen Gesellschaft, 10. – 13.4.2002 in Viechtach. – Schriftenreihe Deutsche Geologische Gesellschaft), Hannover: Deutsche Geologische Gesellschaft, pp. 12-21.

Megerle, A. and Vollmer, L. (2005) *Lernkultur Kompetenzentwicklung, Lernen im Prozess der Arbeit, Kompetenzentwicklung in Netzwerken – Netzwerk Erdgeschichte* (Abschlußbericht des vom BMBF und der EU geförderten Forschungsprojektes), Tübingen: Universität Tübingen.

Pauls, K. and Megerle, A. (2002) 'Kompetenzentwicklung in Netzwerken – Einblick in das Forschungsprojekt Netzwerk Erdgeschichte', *QUEM-Bulletin*, 3, 17-20.

Pforr, C. and Megerle, A. (2006) 'Geotourism: A perspective from Southwest Germany', in R. Dowling and D. Newsome (eds), *Geotourism*, Amsterdam: Butterworth-Heinemann, pp. 117-139.

Pollermann, K. (2007) *Prozessintegrierte Evaluationen zur nachhaltigen Regionalentwicklung*, DISP, 169, 68-79.

Scott, J. (2000) *Social Network Analysis. A Handbook*, 2nd edn, London: Sage.

Straßheim, H. and Oppen, M. (2006) *Lernen in Städtenetzwerken. Kooperation – Konflikte – Kompetenzentwicklung* (Modernisierung des öffentlichen Sektors, Sonderband 27), Berlin: Edition Sigma.

Sydow, J., Duschek, S., Möllering, G. and Rometsch, M. (2003) *Kompetenzentwicklung in Netzwerken – eine typologische Studie*, Wiesbaden: Westdeutscher Verlag.

Wassermann, S. and Faust, K. (1994) *Social Network Analysis. Methods and Applications*, Cambridge: Cambridge University Press.

9 Geotourism in the Hawaiian Islands

Lisa M. King, James Cook University, Cairns, Australia

Introduction

Situated almost in the middle of the Pacific Ocean, the Hawaiian Islands are not only one of the most isolated places in the world (Juvic and Juvic, 1998), but also one of the best known. Hawaii's acclaimed natural attractions stem from its volcanic origins – tall mountains deeply eroded by tropical rains and waterfalls into rugged gorges and valleys, a spectacular backdrop for world-class beaches, dramatic volcanic landscapes and forests. The state consists of six main islands: Kauai, Oahu, Molokai, Maui, Lanai and Hawaii Island, also known as the Big Island. Two lesser known islands, Niihau and Kahoolawe, are not open to conventional tourism. Tens of smaller, much older islands, northwest of the main island chain, are protected by-and-large within the Papahanaumokuakea Marine National Monument.

Many special interest tourists consider the Hawaiian Islands as an tropical paradise. Geotourists are especially drawn to the islands to witness their past volcanic history and experience the current eruption activity of Kilauea on Hawaii Island first hand.

This chapter is an introduction to how the Hawaiian Islands were formed and the importance of geotourism to the State's economy. The surprising diversity of geotourism-related activities available on the Hawaiian Islands is discussed along with investigating who is Hawaii's geotourist. Three case studies at the end of the chapter highlight different issues pertaining to geotourism on Hawaii Island. The first case study discusses how Hawaii Volcanoes National Park minimizes the risk to visitors in an active volcanic landscape while the second reports on how the Park rehabilitated the Sulphur Banks site from an unorganized congested visitor area to a managed natural volcanic area where visitors learn about the active volcanic processes being experienced. The last case study focuses on a small entrepreneurial business working within Kazumura lava tube, finding a balance that works for both the visitor and the resource. The chapter concludes that the Hawaiian Islands will continue to attract large numbers of geotourists in the foreseeable future.

The Hawaiian Islands – a hotspot

According to Hawaiian legend, the demi-god, Maui, raised the islands out of the ocean with his favorite fishing hook (Westervelt, 1977). Today, the theory of plate tectonics (Wegener, 1912, cited in Kious and Tilling, 1996) offers a different scenario. The theory suggests the Earth's crust is composed of huge tectonic plates slowly moving and rearranging themselves over geologic time. Volcanic activity usually occurs around the edges of these massive plates. Wilson (1963) developed the 'hotspot' theory to explain the formation of volcanic islands thousands of kilometers from the edges of tectonic plates. The hotspot theory proposes the Hawaiian Islands, and similar volcanic islands, form as a slowly moving tectonic plate intercepts a narrow stream of hot magma rising upward from the Earth's interior (Wilson, 1963). The magma from this 'hotspot' erupts from the ocean floor, building a volcano that over geologic time emerges above the surface of the ocean as an island. As the tectonic plate continues to move, the hotspot occurs beneath a new portion of the plate and repeats the island building process. For example, Kure Atoll, approximately 2100 km northwest from Oahu (Juvic and Juvic, 1998), is the oldest Hawaiian island above sea level, while Lo'ihi seamount, the newest Hawaiian volcano, is still below the surface of the Pacific Ocean and presumed by scientists to be directly over the hotspot (Anderson and Schram, 2005). Recent research is calling into question aspects of the popular hotspot paradigm (see Foulger *et al.*, 2005) and facets of the hotspot theory may undergo revision in the future.

Hawaii's economic lifeline: tourism

Hawaii's economy is based largely on tourism. Approximately 7.6 million visitors traveled to the Hawaiian Islands in 2007 with an average length of stay of slightly over nine days (Dept. of Business, Economic Development and Tourism [DBEDT] 2008a). Visitor expenditures totaled 12.8 billion US dollars in 2007 (DBEDT, 2008a).

Tourism and recreation are intimately linked to the islands' iconic volcanic features. Diamond Head, Haleakala, Molokini crater, Hanauma Bay, Mauna Kea, the Na Pali Coast and the volcanoes within Hawaii Volcanoes National Park – Mauna Loa and Kilauea, are all highly popular visitor attractions. These famous sites and landscapes help sell millions of dollars worth of tourist merchandise and memorabilia such as post cards, books and DVDs; sports equipment such as mountain bikes and hiking gear, clothing, art and real estate. Thus, geotourism is a tremendous contributor both directly and indirectly to the Hawaiian economy.

Who is Hawaii's geotourist?

Who is the geotourist in Hawaii? The simple answer is nearly everyone as almost every island visitor participates in at least one geotourism-related activity during their Hawaiian holiday. Some geotourism-related visitor statistics are collected by Hawaiian tourism agencies; others must be compiled or inferred from additional sources. See Table 9.1 for the number of people who visit some of Hawaii's most iconic geologic features.

Geotourism visitor characteristics can be identified, in part, by reviewing the State of Hawaii Department of Business, Economics and Tourism statistics through a geotourism lens. Table 9.2 shows the percentage of total visitors in various lifestyle/lifestages participating in particular Hawaiian geotourism-related activities and visitation status. For example, newlyweds and honeymooners provide a solid market for helicopter and plane tours (DBEDT, 2008b); these tours selling, in large part, Hawaii's iconic landscapes. Tour bus excursions, limousine and van tours stop, view and interpret Hawaii's famous landforms. Self-guided geotourists literally stop everywhere with their travel guidebook or with Hazlett and Hyndman's (1996) *Roadside Geology of Hawai'i* in hand. Hikers, campers and backpackers may conduct such activities to gain a more intimate connection with the land and its values, to take in less accessible views or spend a longer period of time immersed in the landscape and its contents. Public and commercial parks and gardens are often developed nestled against rugged mountains or with sea views as an additional enticement to pull visitors to the attraction.

Table 9.1: Visitation to some of Hawaii's iconic geologic features (2007).

Island	Total no. of visitors	Geosite	Description of geologic feature	Approx. no. of visitors to geosite
Oahu	4,694,750[a]	Hanauma Bay Nature Preserve	Flooded volcanic crater with one side open to the sea forming a curved beach with a protected coral reef and stunning views from the crater rim.	1,088,660[a]
		Diamond Head State Monument	Iconic volcanic crater adjacent to Waikiki.	584,909[a]
		Nuuanu Pali State Wayside Park	Deeply eroded cliffs with panoramic coastal views immediately off a major tourist route.	905,300[b]
Maui	2,463,594[a]	Haleakala National Park	Dormant volcano with colourful cinder cones and dramatic volcanic landscapes.	1,322,817[a]
		Iao Valley State Monument	Eroded caldera of the West Maui volcano covered with lush vegetation.	431,400[a]
Big Island of Hawaii	1,622,359[a]	Hawaii Volcanoes National Park	Mauna Loa and Kilauea volcanoes along with cinder cones, pit craters, active lava flows and other volcanic features.	1,467,779[a]
		Mauna Kea State Park	Mauna Kea, Hawai'i's tallest volcano at 4025m, partially protected within this park.	64,600[b]
		Akaka Falls State Park	Two large waterfalls, Akaka and Kahuna, along with several smaller waterfalls are easily viewed by visitors.	189,400[b]
		Lava Tree State Monument	Impressive lava tree molds standing where a forest once was before taken by lava.	44,400[b]
Kauai	1,200,045[a]	Na Pali Coast State Park	Deeply eroded sea cliffs resulting from of a catastrophic landslide from the north flank of the Wai'ale'ale volcano.	423,100[b]
		Waimea Canyon State Park	A gigantic volcanic erosional feature composed of thousands of lava flow layers oxidized from black to bright reds.	430,700[b]

[a] DBEDT (2008b); [b] OmniTrak Group Inc, 2007.

Table 9.2: Breakdown of the total number of Hawaii's visitors participating in some geotourism-related activities (%) (compiled from DBEDT, 2008c).

Activity	Lifestyle/lifestage segments					Visitor status	
	Wedding/ Honeymoon	Family	Young	Middle age	Seniors	First-timers	Repeat visitors
Helicopter or plane tour	19.5	10.7	10.6	13.8	13.1	14.0	11.4
Tour bus excursion	35.1	22.3	21.9	25.2	37.5	38.9	20.6
Private limousine/van tour	11.2	11.1	9.3	11.0	12.8	11.1	9.5
Self-drives	72.3	79.0	78.5	74.5	68.1	69.0	75.8
hiking/camping/backpacking	25.9	17.2	35.0	20.7	10.6	23.3	17.2
Parks/gardens	57.9	58.0	60.0	59.0	56.9	59.7	58.1

Diversity of volcanic-based geotourism activities in the Hawaiian Islands

The Hawaiian Islands offer a full range of volcanic-based formations and landscapes for the geotourist. Active volcanoes, steam vents, lava tubes, waterfalls, thermal tide pools, ocean blowholes and overlooks with panoramic cliff, sea, mountain or valley views are just a few of the features around the State for geotourists. Actually, spectacular scenery and scenic overlooks are not to be underrated. The 2007 Hawai'i State Parks Visitor Survey found scenery (61 percent) as the most important factor for the self-drive visitor in their level of park satisfaction, with scenic views (37 percent) rated second (Omni-Trak Group Inc., 2007). For example, the scenic views of Waimea Canyon are a 'must see' for geotourists on the island of Kauai (Figure 9.1).

Figure 9.1: The spectacular Waimea Canyon, often referred to as 'the Grand Canyon of the Pacific', is one of the most famous scenic views and geosites on Kauai. Photo credit: Leland Kim.

Helicopter and fixed-wing plane tours share the expansive landscapes with those who have more holiday dollars to spend. Bus and van tours provide geotourists the chance to view scenic landscapes and take pictures from overlook spots. Many geotourists choose to combine their special interests, during a holiday. For example, those geotourists hiking amongst the cinder cones within Haleakala National Park are combining their interest in geology with their affinity for multi-day backpacking trips (Figure 9.2).

Cavers can undertake tours through a limited number of lava tubes open to the public (King, forthcoming), to add them to their mental tally sheet of collected places (King and Prideaux, forthcoming). Others geotourists may opt for less strenuous options such as simply boarding a ship and cruising around the Islands, taking in the vast volcanic landscapes during the day and viewing the fiery ocean entry of Kilauea's lavas flows at night.

Figure 9.2: Geotourists hiking in the backcountry of Haleakala National Park on Maui. Photo credit: Sharon Ringsven.

Case studies

With the wide range of geologic features and ongoing geomorphological processes in the Hawaiian Islands there are also a number of geotourism management issues Statewide. The three case studies presented below focus on geotourism issues on Hawaii Island. The first two case studies highlight geotourist management issues inside Hawaii Volcanoes National Park. The first case study reports on the measures the Park has implemented to minimize risks to visitors in an active volcanic landscape. The second case study illustrates how the Park redesigned the Sulphur Banks site to reduce impacts on the fragile resource by visitors. The Kazumura lava tube cave case study highlights how a small tour operator carefully balances visitor numbers with a strong conservation ethic in order to conserve one of the most important lava tubes in the world.

Case study 1: Hawaii Volcanoes National Park

Hawai'i Volcanoes National Park is the most unique park in the U.S. National Park system (Bendure and Friary, 1997). The Park stretches from sea level to an elevation of 4169 m and encompasses the summits and rift zones of two of the world's most active volcanoes, Mauna Loa and Kilauea (U.S. National Park Service [NPS], 2008). The Park protects endemic and endangered flora and fauna including happy face spiders *(Theridion grallator)*, the Hawaiian goose *(Branta sandvicensis)* also known as the Nene, and the Mauna Loa silversword plant *(Argyroxiphium kauense)*. The Park's outstanding natural and biological resources led to its designation as an International Biosphere Reserve in 1980 and a UNESCO natural World Heritage Site in 1987 (U.S. NPS, 2008). However, the primary tourism attraction for the nearly 1.5 million annual visitors to Hawaii Volcanoes National Park (DBEDT, 2008b) is Kilauea's ongoing volcanic activity and the park's variety of dramatic volcanic landscapes.

Mauna Loa is the most massive volcano on the planet, with an estimated volume of 80,000 cubic km (U.S. NPS, n.d.). When measured from the sea floor, Mauna Loa rises 9000 m, just taller than Mt. Everest (U.S. NPS, n.d.). The two showpieces of Hawaii Volcanoes National Park are Kilauea caldera, within which is Halemaumau crater, home to the goddess of fire, Pele (Westervelt, 1977), and the dormant volcano, Mauna Loa. Kilauea has been almost continuously erupting downslope from its summit since 1983 and as of March 2008 also began emitting a substantial volcanic gas plume with occasional lava and ash being ejected from the Halemaumau crater at the summit (U.S. Geological Survey, 2008). Additional volcanic features such as pit craters, cinder cones, fumaroles, fissures and cracks, lava tubes, lava flows, black sand beaches and thermal areas are also in the park (U.S. NPS, 2008). The park's collaborative history with the U.S. Geological Survey, make Mauna Loa and Kilauea two of the most understood volcanoes in the world (U.S. NPS, 2008).

Most visitors to Hawaii Volcanoes National Park explore both the Kilauea Visitor Center and the Jaggar Museum. The Kilauea Visitor Center provides current eruption updates and cautions to visitors entering the park. It also concentrates on interpreting the natural history of Park flora and fauna including its endemic species as well as efforts to curtail human impacts such the control of feral pigs, invasive plants and other introduced species. The Center contains a movie theatre regularly playing Kilauea and Mauna Loa eruption video documentaries. Jaggar Museum highlights the Hawaiian mythology surrounding Kilauea caldera and the volcanic and scientific history of the park. It features samples of common volcanic material including lava bombs, Pele's hair and tears, 'a 'a and pahoehoe lava. Active seismometers record earthquake activity within the park as visitors watch. The museum also has a large outdoor overlook into the Kilauea caldera (see Figure 9.3) and Halemaumau providing a first hand view of the steam vents and fume plume within the caldera.

Figure 9.3: Geotourists at the Jaggar Museum overlook viewing Kilauea caldera while steam, ash and gases rise from Halemaumau crater. Halemaumau is the home of Pele, the Hawaiian goddess of fire. Photo credit: Ted Brattstrom.

Geotourists can also pursue a wide range of recreational activities depending on their interest. See Table 9.3 for the main geotourism activities within Hawaii Volcanoes National Park.

The Park's ever-changing volcanic landscape presents many visitor safety challenges for park staff. The nature of the park makes it prone to extreme natural events such as volcanic eruptions, earthquakes, high levels of dangerous fumes, bench collapses and/or fires (U.S. NPS, 2008a). The dynamic geological activity in the park requires constant risk assessment, management and evaluation by park staff in order to keep visitors safe. For example, after a swarm of small earthquakes caused cracks to open up across Chain of Craters Road in June 2007, park rangers ordered visitors to leave the area and much of the park was closed down (*Pacific Business News*, 18 June 2007).

Table 9.3: Main geotourism activities within Hawaii Volcanoes National Park (adapted from Erfurt-Cooper, 2008).

Day and night eruption viewing	Photography
Hiking up close to view eruption activities	Road cycling and mountain biking on trails
Helicopter tours and plane fly-overs to view eruption	Guided adventure caving in a 'wild' lava tube
Hiking across or around craters, steam vents, and/or old lava flows	Back country hiking up to Mauna Loa and environs
Walks to view evidence of seismic activity	Climbing and mountaineering
General walking and trekking	Scenic tours and excursions
Walking through a show cave	Ranger-led walks and hikes
Camping/picnicking	Viewing volcanic plume
Scenic overlooks	Jaggar Museum and Kilauea Visitor Center
Hiking up/down volcanic cliffs	

Volcanic fumes can also potentially affect both visitors and park employees causing respiratory illnesses, eye irritations and headaches. Thus, the direction of the volcanic plume is regularly monitored and evaluated. If a wind change brings the plume towards visitor areas, such as Jaggar Museum, and on-site instruments indicate high SO_2 levels, visitors are asked to immediately evacuate the Museum area in their vehicles with their windows rolled up (U.S. NPS, 2008). Upon occasion, the entire park is closed due to dangerous levels of sulfur dioxide in the air (*Pacific Business News*, 8 April 2008).

About 1200 visitors visit the active eruption site daily (U.S. NPS, 2008). Many visitors are unaccustomed to the local conditions near the lava flow, and are ill-prepared to walk distances over the hot, uneven terrain or are not fully informed about appropriate clothing or supplies to take out on the lava viewing trail. Hawaii Volcanoes National Park uses a variety of methods to educate park visitors and prepare hikers to view the lava flows safely (U.S. NPS, 2008). Safety information is provided upon park entry to each vehicle and every person on a tour bus. The Kilauea Visitor Center provides safety information through films, displays and signage, bulletin boards and a ranger-staffed desk. The Park also maintains a 24-hour phone hotline about park conditions, broadcasts an information loop on their own public radio channel, and closes certain areas if needed to ensure visitor safety (U.S. NPS, 2008). At the bottom of the Chain of Craters Road a ranger station is located with rangers available to provide information and answer visitor questions. When the lava flow is within park boundaries, a ranger must walk out to the flow field daily to assess safety factors and whether trail markers need to be moved to reflect the daily changes in the direction of the lava flow (U.S. NPS, 2008).

As the U.S. National Park Service's Hawaii Volcanoes National Park Business Plan (2008) notes, there is a high cost to the park for assuring visitor safety as the presence of varying volcanic activity results in ever-changing visitation patterns. Periods of high eruption activity result in personnel costs increasing making the park's overall budget difficult to calculate (U.S. NPS, 2008). Nevertheless, visitor safety is the Park's top priority.

Case study 2: Sulphur Banks

An easy walk from Kilauea Visitor Center inside Hawaii Volcanoes National Park is the Sulphur Banks, an area where sulfurous steam rises through vents and cracks in the ground. Early Hawaiians used the site for cleansing rituals while during the 19th century the area was used by visitors as a sauna and health spa (Hazlett, 2002). Known also as Haakulumanu, Sulphur Banks is a solfatara field (an area of heat and sulfur deposition) along the base of one of ring faults on the northern side of Kilauea caldera (Hazlett, 2002). The volcanic gases and groundwater steam escaping from the ground are rich in carbon dioxide, sulfur dioxide and hydrogen sulfide gas. Formed from rainwater and sulfur dioxide, sulfuric acid breaks down the basalt to clay staining it red and brown with iron oxide (U.S. NPS, 2009). Delicate bright yellow crystals of pure sulfur often encrust the surfaces around cracks and vents in Sulphur Banks (Hazlett, 2002).

Unfortunately the Sulphur Banks area had seriously deteriorated due to its popularity with visitors. The decades old Sulphur Banks road with no designated parking area, allowed cars and buses to access the fragile area. Traffic congestion was common. Vehicles regularly pulled off the narrow road and onto smaller Sulphur Bank features to go around other vehicles or to park (Hawaii Volcanoes National Park [HVNP], 2003). Tour buses left their motors running while their groups explored the site. Visitors often left the designated trail, attracted to off-trail features and scrambled onto large vent features damaging the fragile mineral deposits surrounding them. Additionally, the asphalt road laid directly on top of several geothermal features and immediately adjacent to others (HVNP, 2003). There were a lack of wayside exhibits to educate visitors about the volcanic processes they were witnessing (HVNP, 2003).The Sulphur Banks road actually contained pits which emitted steam. The Park wanted to improve the situation.

Figure 9.4: Visitors exploring the rehabilitated Sulphur Banks area with the new boardwalk clearly defining where visitors should walk. Photo credit: Ted Brattstrom.

When funding became available, Park management immediately asked staff to conduct an environmental assessment of the Sulphur Banks site. The resulting report recommended scrapping the road and rehabilitating the area with native vegetation, better defining the trail and including wayside exhibits to educate visitors about the geologic processes being observed (HVNP, 2003). A plan was drawn up to implement the recommendations made by environmental assessment. The road was scrapped and the area replanted with native trees and grasses. The trail was redesigned and included a meandering boardwalk (HVNP, 2003) to define where visitors could walk, protecting the geological points of interest from damage by curious visitors while enhancing the aesthetics of the site. A trail linking the Kilauea Visitor Center to the Sulphur Banks trail was developed to provide easy site access to visitors. Today, the natural values of the Sulphur Banks area are better protected and visitors learn about the site while safely strolling on the award winning boardwalk (Figure 9.4).

Case study 3: Kazumura Lava Tube

The Big Island of Hawaii offers a variety of cave experiences for visitors. However, most visitors and island residents only visit Nahuku, also known as Thurston lava tube, located inside Hawaii Volcanoes National Park. This 'show cave' is included in a range of tourism media, the Park's official website and numerous other websites and links. The first 110 m of Nahuku is the most heavily visited and includes a metal entrance bridge, interior electric lighting, improved walking surface and exit stairs. Visitors walk through the lava tube (see Box 9.1) unguided and with minimal interpretation (King *et al.*, 2008).

Box 9.1: Formation of lava tubes

There are two types of basaltic lavas: 'a'a and pahoehoe. 'A'a lavas have a rough, sharp clinkery surface while pahoehoe lava is smooth or ropey-looking. Lava tubes occur much more often in pahoehoe flows than 'a'a flows (Macdonald and Abbot, 1970).

In Hawaii, two processes most commonly form lava tubes. In the first, flowing lava quickly crusts over from contact with the surrounding cooler air, creating an insulating tube the lava continues to flow through. Once the flow subsides, the lava tube empties until the last remnants of the flow hardens to form its floor (Macdonald and Abbott, 1970). In the second process, a crust rapidly forms over slowing lava as it creeps farther away from its source. When the crust reaches 2-5 cm in thickness, it is strong enough to retain incoming lava, creating a hydrostatic head at the flow front (Hon *et al.*, 1994). The entire sheet lifts up as a result of the pressure and hardens. Breakouts of fresh lava may occur and the process repeats itself. The process can form lava tubes in only a few weeks (Hon *et al.*, 1994).

Few visitors are aware of the various guided tours through sections of lava tube caves on the Big Island of Hawaii. Minimal promotion of these adventure cave tours is one way to control demand yet still provide limited access to these sensitive underground environments.

Kazumura lava tube is currently the longest (65.6 km) and the deepest lava tube (vertical descent of 1100 m) in the world (Allred and Allred, 1997). Currently, Kazumura is the world's most scientifically significant lava tube (Halliday, 2004). The lava tube's

350-700 year old geologic formations include lava stalagmites, stalactites, lavacicles, soda straws, lava blades, bathtub rings, lava falls, lava plunge pools, stacked lava tubes (Allred and Allred, 1997) and many more features (Shick, 2008). The unique fauna which have evolved in such a specialized environment include underground crickets, flightless flies and beetles and cave spiders (Stone and Howarth, 1994; Howarth, 2004) along with a number of yet to be described slime molds, bacteria and other microbes (Shick, 2007). Unusual plant communities grow around cave entrances. In addition, native Hawaiians used the cave for a number of cultural purposes and sme sections contain significant artifacts (Hawaii Speleological Society, 1997).

Kazumura has natural surface openings of various sizes and accessibility about every two kilometers, making it especially vulnerable to entry by recreational cavers with little caving skill. Sections of the tube have been degraded from vandalism, sewerage deposits, solid waste dumping, road fill (Allred and Allred, 1997), graffiti (Shick, 2008), and no doubt souvenir collecting and clumsy cavers as well. Still, only a few hundred people explore most sections of the Kazumura annually (Shick, 2008).

The owner of one of the exceptional parts of the Kazumura lave tube, after working extensively with cave experts and himself becoming an expert, Harry Shick started Kazumura Cave Tours (www.fortunecity.com/oasis/angkor/176/), a small business conducting adventure tours via a natural entrance on his property since the mid-1990s. A deliberate business decision was made to keep tour group size small, infrastructure minimal, not to pay for direct advertising and to maximize interpretation while on tour. Minimal infrastructure, such as PVC ladders carefully bolted into the walls, were strategically installed in the tour section of Kazumura – sufficient to ensure visitor safety. Maximum tour size is limited to five with one guide, seven with two guides. Visitors must wear long pants and closed-toed shoes. Proper caving etiquette is reviewed before going underground and the modest fee is collected. Visitors are provided with hard hats, gloves and lights, and the all important opportunity to use a toilet before entering the tube. While walking the short distance to the Kazumura cave opening and throughout the tour, visitors learn how lava tubes form and different cave formations are pointed out and discussed. The tour guide keeps visitors an appropriate distance from fragile features and only briefly illuminates cave fauna when chanced upon. Tour participants learn not only about Kazumura's physical features and environment but also about threats to Hawaiian lava tubes and what is being done to protect them. At the end of the two-hour tour, participants return the loaned equipment. They leave with a much greater appreciation of lava tube environments and increased interest in protecting the fragile environments (King, *et al.* 2008).

Conclusion

Few locations on Earth allow for closer or more impressive views of the planet's dynamic geological forces than the active volcanoes of Hawaii (Hazlett, 2002). However, Hawaii's geological tourism extends far beyond mere volcano-watching and includes a diverse range of outdoor activities. Almost every visitor is involved in at least one geotourism activity during their stay.

Risk management plays a pivotal role within Hawaii's geosites. The centerpiece of Hawaii's geotourism, Hawaii Volcanoes National Park, is a case in point. Managing visitor risk in such a dynamic landscape requires constant assessment by park staff. Another consideration is protecting the georesource from overuse and abuse. For decades, Sulphur Banks suffered from inappropriate infrastructure and poor visitor behaviors. However, redesigning the visitor infrastructure turned Sulphur Banks into a model for rehabilitating overused sites and educating visitors on geologic processes. Finding a balance between the risks to on-site visitors and protecting the resource is essential for the long term sustainable use of geosites. Kazumura Cave Tours is a stellar example of balancing resource protection with low impact geotourism in a highly specialized environment.

References

Allred, K. and Allred, C. (1997) 'Development and morphology of Kazumura Cave, Hawaii', *Journal of Cave and Karst Studies*, 59 (2), 67-80.

Anderson, D. and Schramm, K. (2005) 'Global hotspot maps', in G. Foulger, J. Natland, D. Presnall and D. Anderson (eds.), *Plates, Plumes and Paradigms*, Boulder, CO: Geological Society of America, pp. 19-29.

Bendure, G. and Friary, N. (1997) *Hawaii*, Oakland, CA: Lonely Planet.

DBEDT (Department of Business, Economic Development and Tourism) (2008a) 'Annual Visitor Research Report – 2007'. [Electronic Resource]. Retrieved 10 November 2008 from website http://Hawaii.gov/dbedt/info/visitor-stats/visitor-research/

DBEDT (2008b), '2007 State of Hawaii Data Book, Section 7: Recreation and Travel', Retrieved 10 November 2008 from website http://hawaii.gov/dbedt/info/economic/data-book/db2007/section07.pdf

DBEDT (2008c) 'Visitor Satisfaction & Activity Report – 2007' Retrieved 7 November 2008 from http://hawaii.gov/dbedt/info/visitor-stats/vsat/2007-vsat-final-web.pdf.

Erfurth-Cooper, P. (2008) 'Geotourism in volcanic environments: destinations with a risk factor?', handout provided at the Inaugural Global Geotourism Conference, Fremantle, Western Australia.

Foulger, G., Natland, J., Presnall, D. and Anderson D. (eds.) (2005), *Plates, Plumes and Paradigms,* Boulder, CO: Geological Society of America.

Halliday, W. (2004) 'Hawaii lava tube caves, United States', in J. Gunn (ed.), *Encyclopedia of Caves and Karst Science*, London: Fitzroy Dearborn, pp. 415-416.

Hawai'i Speleological Society. (1997) *The Kazumura Cave Atlas*, Hilo, HI: Hawaii Speleological Society.

Hawai'i Volcanoes National Park (2003) 'Environmental Assessment: Rehabilitate Sulphur Bank Road and Trail', February 2003, Hawai'i Volcanoes National Park.

Hazlett, R. (2002) *Geological Field Guide: Kilauea Volcano*, Hawaii Natural History Association.

Hazlett, R. and Hyndman, D. (1996), *Roadside Geology of Hawaii*, Missoula, MO: Mountain Press Publishing Company.

Hon, K., Kauahikaua, J., Denlinger, R. and Mackay, K. (1994) 'Emplacement and inflation of pahoehoe sheet flows: Observations and measurements of active lava flows on Kilauea Volcano, Hawaii', *Geological Society of America Bulletin* 106 (3), 352-370.

Howarth, F. (2004) 'Hawaiian Islands: Biospeleology', in John Gunn (ed.), *Encyclopedia of Caves and Karst Science*, London: Fitzroy Dearborn, pp. 417-418.

Juvic, S. and Juvic, J. (1998), *Atlas of Hawaii*. 3rd edn, Honolulu: University of Hawaii Press.

King, L. (2010), 'The lure of lava tubes: Exploring lava tube tourism on the Big Island of Hawai'i', in P. Erfurt-Cooper and M. Cooper (eds.) *Volcano and Geothermal Tourism: Sustainable Geo-Resources for Leisure and Recreation*, London: Earthscan.

King, L. and Prideaux, B. (forthcoming), 'The special interest tourist collecting places and destinations: A Queensland World Heritage case study', *Journal of Vacation Marketing*.

King, L., Shick, H., and Brattstrom, T. (2008) 'Lava tube cave tourism on the Big Island of Hawaii: A low impact tour model', in R. Dowling and D. Newsome (eds.), *Inaugural Global Geotourism Conference Proceedings*. Fremantle, W.A.: Promaco Conventions, pp. 225-230.

Kious, J. and Tilling, R. (1996), *This Dynamic Earth: The Story of Plate Tectonics*. Washington DC: U.S. Government Printing Office.

Macdonald, G. and Abbott, A. (1970) *Volcanoes in the Sea*, Honolulu: University Press of Hawaii.

OminTrak Group Inc. (2007), '2007 Hawaii State Parks Survey', prepared for the Hawai'i Tourism Authority, December 2007. Retrieved 28 November 2008 from http://www.hawaiitourismauthority.org/documents_upload_path/reports/HTAPRO-Report-12-01-2007.pdf

Pacific Business News (Honolulu) (2007) 'Much of volcanoes park closed to visitors', 18 June 2007. Retrieved 2 November 2008 from http://pacific.bizjournals.com/pacific/stories/2007/06/18/daily7.html

Pacific Business News (Honolulu). (2008) 'Sulfur dioxide fumes close Big Island park' 8 April 2008. http://pacific.bizjournals.com/pacific/stories/2008/04/07/daily19.html

Shick, H. (2007) Kazumura Cave Tour, Hawaii

Shick, H. (2008) *Understanding Lava Tubes and Lava Caves*, Bloomington, IN: Trafford Publishing.

Stone, F. and Howarth, F. (2005) 'Hawaiian cave biology: Status of conservation and management', paper presented at the *National Cave and Karst Management Symposium*, 31 October- 4 November, Albany, NY.

U.S. Geological Survey (2008) '2008 marked by significant changes on Kilauea'. Retrieved 9 November 2008, from the U.S. Geological Survey website: http://hvo.wr.usgs.gov/

U.S. National Park Service (2008) 'Hawai'i Volcanoes National Park Business Plan'. Retrieved 12 October 2008 from http://home.nps.gov/havo/parkmgmt/upload/havo_manage_2008_businessplan.pdf

U.S. National Park Service (n.d.). *Hawai'i volcanoes*. Visitor park entry brochure, obtained 2008.

U.S. National Park Service (2009), 'Hawaii Volcanoes National Park: Steam Vents, Steaming Bluff and Sulphur Banks'. Retrieved 8 August 2009 from http://www.nps.gov/havo/planyourvisit/craterrimtour_steam.htm

Westervelt, W. (1977) *Hawaiian Historical Legends*, Rutland, VT: Charles E. Tuttle Press.

Wilson, J. (1963) 'A possible origin of the Hawaiian Islands', *Canadian Journal of Physics*, **41** (6), 863-870.

10 The Cretaceous fossil sites of South Korea: identifying geosites, science and geotourism

In Sung Paik, Pukyong National University, Korea,
Min Huh, Chonnam National University, Korea,
Hyun Joo Kim, Pukyong National University, Korea,
Sook Ju Kim, Pukyong National University, Korea, and
David Newsome, Murdoch University, Australia

Introduction

There are a range of natural resources for geotourism in Korea, including scenic mountains with variable geological histories, hot springs, and coastline environments. Many of the national and provincial parks and natural monuments in Korea have been designated because of their geological values. Three sites on Jeju Island have been inscribed on the World Heritage list largely for geological values such as volcanic features and landscape and associated scenic values. Furthermore, there are many geological heritage sites designated as natural monuments in Cretaceous sedimentary basins in Korea. They include dinosaur fossil sites and geologically scenic sites. The former are of great scientific importance and many have the potential to be developed into geotourism destinations of global significance. Five sites, on the Korean Cretaceous Dinosaur Coast which have been very important for regional tourism, are currently being nominated as World Heritage for their highly significant fossil trackways and dinosaur eggs.

The full gambit of geotourism potential for Korean geological heritage has rarely been studied (Jeong, 2000; Heo *et al*., 2006a; Heo *et al*., 2006b; Heo, 2007). In this chapter the Cretaceous geosites in Korea are summarized in respect to their importance as globally significant geotourism resources.

Cretaceous geological setting in South Korea

Since the late Paleozoic the eastern margin of the Asian continent, including the Korean Peninsula, was an Andean-type continental margin (Choi, 1986; Watson *et al*., 1987). During the Early Cretaceous, northward subduction of the Paleo-Pacific (Izanagi) Plate located in the oceanside of Asia resulted in sinistral strike-slip movement on the continental margin (Watson *et al*., 1987; Okada and Sakai, 1993), and generated a number of Cretaceous non-marine pull-apart basins in South Korea (Lee, 1999; Chough *et al*., 2000). These basins consist of alluvial fans, fluvial plains, lacustrine deposits, and volcanic rocks. The Gyeongsang Basin located in the southeastern part of Korean

Peninsula is the largest, comprising about one fourth of South Korea and a 9000-metre-thick sequence of deposits assigned to the Gyeongsang Supergroup. It is divided into the Sindong, Hayang, and Yucheon groups, in ascending stratigraphical order (Chang, 1975).

To the north and west of the Gyeongsang Basin, more than 10 isolated, small and exclusively non-marine Cretaceous sedimentary basins occur along two to three north-east-southwest-trending megafaults, They are filled with tuffs, lava flows, and epiclastic deposits. The frequent intercalation of volcanic rocks in these basins indicate that they are time-correlated with the upper part of the Hayang Group to Yucheon Group in the Gyeongsang Basin.

The geological age of these Cretaceous deposits in South Korea ranges from Aptian to Maastrichtian (Paik *et al.*, 2001a; Jwa *et al.*, 2004; Kim *et al.*, 2005; Paik *et al.*, 2006; Lee *et al.*, 2008). During the Cretaceous, the Korean Peninsula was situated in mid-latitudes as it is today (Lee *et al.*, 1987; Kim *et al.*, 1993), and the general palaeoclimatic regime has been interpreted to have been warm and dry (Paik and Kim, 1997; Paik and Lee, 1998; Paik and Kim, 2006; Paik *et al.*, 2007). In these Cretaceous continental deposits, diverse paleontological and sedimentological records are preserved and are a rich source of Korean geoheritage for our understanding of the Cretaceous terrestrial environments of South Korea. Sites include fossils of dinosaurs, crocodiles, turtles, fishes, molluscs, insects, and wood and a variety of paleosols and sedimentary features.

Cretaceous geosites

The Cretaceous sites stand out amongst the geological heritage sites in South Korea. These include dinosaur, invertebrate, and plant fossil sites, inorganic sedimentary structure sites, unique geological feature sites, and scenic view sites (Figure 10.1).

Dinosaur sites include bone sites, egg sites, and footprint sites, with the dinosaur footprint sites being the most common. Eleven of the nation's Natural Monuments are designated as such for the unique and world-class scale of preservation of dinosaur footprints. Some of the dinosaur footprint sites are associated with bird-footprints. Gajinri is the largest of these sites (Figure 10.1). Most of the Cretaceous bird foot print taxa have been identified in Korea. At the Uhangri site, the largest pterosaur footprints and webbed bird-foot prints are associated in the same horizons (Hwang *et al.*, 2002). The representative dinosaur egg site is Bibongri site at Boseong County, in which dinosaur egg clutches are repeatedly preserved in several horizons and in association with turtle and dinosaur bones. Very extensive dinosaur trackways and egg sites exist mainly along the southern coast of the peninsula in Jeollanam-do and Gyeongsangnam-do provinces over a distance of about 180 kilometres. Some of the sites are protected as National Monuments and have been developed for public education.

Among these Cretaceous geosites, eight sites are particularly suitable for geoheritage status and geotourism development. The geological characteristics of each will now be considered in turn.

Haenam dinosaur site

The Haenam site is located along the Uhangri coast (Fossil site No. 9, Figure 10.1), and is renowned for the preservation of the first pterosaur tracks (*Haenamichnus uhangriensis*) ever discovered in Asia (Hwang *et al.*, 2002), the largest pterosaur tracks (about 30 cm long) ever found in Cretaceous rocks, the first discovery of web-footed bird tracks

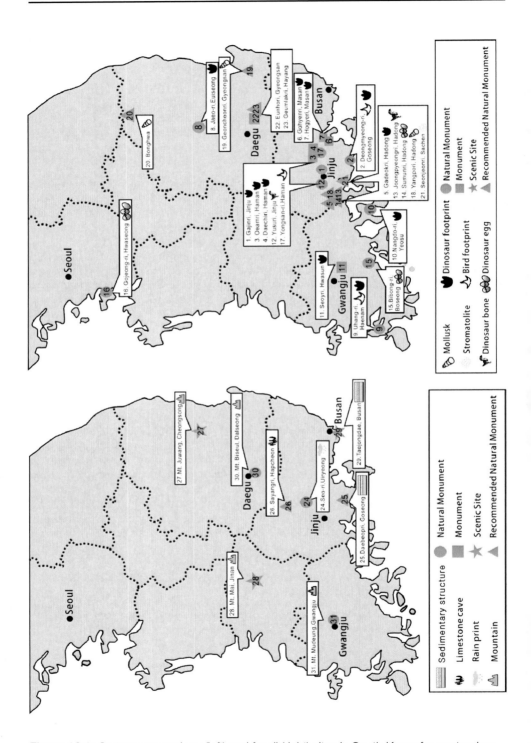

Figure 10.1: Cretaceous geology (left) and fossil (right) sites in South Korea for geotourism.

(*Uhangrichnus chuni* and *Hwangsanipes choughi*) (Yang *et al.*, 1995, 1997), and the first locality from which pterosaur and web-footed bird tracks have been reported together (see Figure 10.2 A–C). In addition, arthropod traces (*Diplichnites*) occur extensively on the bedding planes of mudstone along the prolonged outcrop exposures which are more than several hundred metres in length.

The Haenam site is composed of various types of tuffaceous epiclastic rocks that accumulated in a fluvio-lacustrine environment (Chun, 1990), and these deposits are named as the Uhangri Formation of the Late Cretaceous. Chun (1990) described the geological origin of Uhangri Formation as the result of the activity of rivers and lake systems in active volcanic terrain.

Diverse kinds of sedimentary features and fossil records are observed in the outcrops of the Uhangri Formation exposed along the coast. The sedimentary features include diverse modes of stratification and ripple marks and synsedinentary deformation structures and sedimentary dykes of paleoseismic origin. These sedimentary records are very helpful keys not only for geologists to interpret paleoenvironmental conditions of the fluvio-lacustrine Uhangri Formation but also for the visitors to understand the geologic history of this area.

The Uhangri track site is one of the world's most interesting, and scientifically most important, fossil footprint sites that provides an understanding of how the paleoecosystem around a lake was influenced by volcanic activities during the Late Cretaceous (Lockley *et al.*, 2006).

Hwasun dinosaur site

The Hwasun site (Fossil site No. 11, Figure 10.1) is characterized by approximately 1500 well-preserved dinosaur footprints, including more than 60 trackways in a small area (around 5000 square metres). Unlike other dinosaur fossil sites in South Korea, most of the tracks found in the area belong to theropods (Figure 10.2 D, F and G), especially small-sized theropods, of which tracks are classified as to *Magnoavipes* and *Ornithomimipus* or *Xiangxipus* (Huh *et al.*, 2006). An unusual trotting locomotion of a small theropod is preserved at this track site (Huh *et al.*, 2006), and unique elongate sauropod tracks can also be observed (Figure 10.2E). An additional unique feature of this track site is the concurrence of ornithopod, sauropod, and theropod tracks in a single bedding plane in an area less than 1000 square metres in size (Figure 10.2 D). On this bedding plane a few hundred tracks of several kinds of herbivorous and carnivorous dinosaurs are preserved in various orientations.

The Hwasun track-bearing deposits are composed of lake margin to shallow lake deposits, and dinosaur tracks mostly occur in lake margin deposits. Polygonal desiccation cracks are common in the track-bearing deposits. Subaerial lenticular cracks originating from the dissolution of evaporite minerals (Paik and Kim, 1998) are present in places, and the traces of evaporite minerals are also associated with underlying and overlying deposits (Paik *et al.*, 2006). Ripple marks are associated with desiccation cracks. Invertebrate body fossils are lacking in the track-bearing deposits, and bioturbation features are also very rare. The frequent intercalation of tuffaceous deposits indicates that volcanic activity took place intermittently in the vicinity of the lake during deposition of lake sediments. The Hwasun site also provides a good opportunity to understand theropod locomotion and to observe the behavioural records of diverse dinosaurs crowded in a lake margin in order to obtain water.

Yeosu dinosaur site

The Yeosu site (Fossil site No. 15, Figure 10.1) consists of five islands in the coastal zone of Yeosu City (Figure 10.2, H). There are more than 3500 tracks and 82 track ways that have been created by theropod (Figure 10.2, I), ornithopod (Figure 10.2, J), and sauropod dinosaurs (Huh *et al.*, 2003). One ornithopod track way at 85 metres length (Figure 10.2, J) is the longest trackway of this species anywhere in the world. The K-Ar age of the Yeosu tracksite is determined as 81 Ma to 65 Ma. It indicates that the Yeosu track site contains the youngest records of dinosaurs living in Asia during the Cretaceous (Paik *et al.*, 2007). The prevalence of ornithopod tracks and the limited occurrence of sauropod tracks at the Yeosu site evidently reflects decreased sauropod diversity in the Upper Cretaceous. All ornithopod trackways represent bipeds, and most of the ornithopod tracks are similar to *Caririchnium* as seen from other sites of the Korean peninsula.

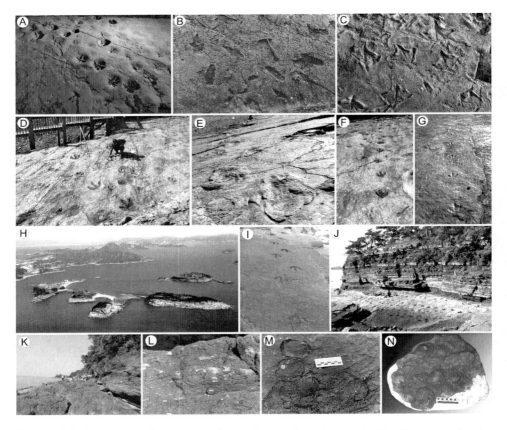

Figure 10.2: Cretaceous dinosaur geosites on the southwestern part of the Korean peninsula. A-C. Haenam site. Unique orinthopod tracks (A), pterosaur tracks named *Haenamichnus uhangriensis* (B), and web footed bird tracks. D-G. Hwasun site. Co-occurrence of theropod and ornithopod tracks (D), elongate sauropod tracks (E), and long trackways of theropods (F and G). H-J. Yeosu site. Scenic overall view of the site located in the islands (H), theropod tracks (I), and long trackway of ornithopod (J). K-N. Boseong site. Scenic overall view of the site located in the rocky coast (K), clutches of dinosaur eggs in outcrops (L and M), and an excavated clutch (N).

Most dinosaur tracks occur in lake margin deposits which display polygonal desiccation cracks and traces of evaporite casts. The rhythmic deposits of this site resulting from short-term climate change and fluctuating volcanic activity also characterize this site. (Paik *et al.*, 2009). Consequently the Yeosu site is one of the best places in the world to understand the palaeoenviroments of the last period of the dinosaur age (Cretaceous).

Boseong dinosaur site

The Boseong dinosaur sites (Fossil site No. 10, Figure 10.1) are distinguished by the preservation of intact clutches, which have been identified as belonging to ornithopod and sauropod dinosaurs (Huh and Zelenitsky, 2002). In addition, the egg-bearing deposits are well exposed along the coast at the Boseong sites (Figure 10.2, K). Dinosaur bones, turtle bones, and turtle eggs were also found at Boseong. More than 200 dinosaur eggs in clutches of three to 16 have been discovered at Boseong (Huh and Zelenitsky, 2002).

All eggs have been preserved in the hatched state (Figure 10.2, L, M, N) and site fidelity is demonstrated by the stratigraphic superimpositon of nests, that is, repeated occurrence of clutches within a few decimetre thickness of deposit (Paik *et al.*, 2004). The nesting sites occur in diverse stratigraphic and sedimentological settings thus providing an opportunity to understand palaeogeographic and palaeonenvironmental conditions in Late Cretaceous times. There are also turtle eggs and bones evident at this site as well as a well-articulated portion of a hypsilophodontid dinosaur.

The sedimentary sequences at the Boseong sites consist of epiclastic, pyroclastic, and intermediate to acidic volcanic rocks. The egg-bearing deposits are sandy mudstone, and the eggs occur at five sites located along a three-kilometre stretch of the coast of Bibon-gri of Boseong-Gun. Eggs found *in situ* occur in at least six separate horizons.

The nesting area is interpreted to have been situated on temporarily stable fan surfaces that were buried by sheet flood deposits. The preservation of the dinosaur egg clutches in calcic and vertic palaeosols indicates that the palaeoclimate of the nesting area was semi-arid and seasonal with regard to water availability (Mack and James, 1994). The Boseong site is considered to have been preferred by dinosaurs as a nesting area and to have been a suitable place for the preservation of eggs. This geosite provides an ideal opportunity to understand the palaeoenvironment of nesting Cretaceous dinosaurs.

Goseong dinosaur site

The Goseong site (Fossil site No. 2, Figure 10.1) on the scenic coastline (Figure 10.3, A) is a renowned world-class dinosaur track site including 410 track ways on up to 320 stratigraphic levels in association with numerous bird tracks (Lim *et al.*, 1994; Lockley *et al.*, 2006). This is the largest dinosaur track preservation site in a single geological formation (Jindong Formation; Late Cretaceous) (Paik *et al.*, 2001a). Many of the sauropod and ornithopod trackways (Figure 10.3, B,C) have parallel orientation indicating gregarious behavior, and dinoturbation can be observed (Figure 10.3, D). In the vicinity of the Goseong site numerous dinosaur and turtle eggs and dinosaur teeth can be found. The general depositional environment of the dinosaur track deposits was lake-margin to shallow lacustrine (Paik *et al.*, 2001). All of the dinosaur track ways in these deposits are preserved in lake margin deposits (Paik *et al.*, 2001). The trampling traces of dinosaurs are also commonly observed both on bedding surfaces and in sections of the Jindong Formation. It is thought that the extensive and frequent preservation of dinosaur

Figure 10.3: Cretaceous geosites on the southeastern part of the Korean peninsula. A-D. Goseong site. Scenic overall view of the site located in the rocky coast (A), multiple sauropod trackways (B), ornithopod trackway (C), and dinoturbation site (D). E-H. Gajinri site. Bedding surfaces of the dinosaur and bird footprint bearing deposits preserving diverse types of ripples and dessication cracks (E), colonial occurrence of bird footprints named *Koreanornis* (F and G), and feeding traces of birds associated with the web footed bird tracks (H). I-L. Yusuri site. Scenic overall view of the site located in the rocky valley (I), profile of meandering channel (lower) and floodplain (upper) deposits (J), profile of calcic (lower) and vertic (upper) paleosols (K), and paleoweathering surface in the floodplain lake depsoits (L).

tracks in these deposits is the result of repeated deposition by sheet floods on a mudflat around a shallow lake, which was utilized by dinosaurs as a reliable water source during drought. There has been subsequent development of calcareous pedogenesis in an arid climate which was prevalent at the time (Paik *et al.*, 2001b). Consequently the Goseong site provides the best opportunity to experience a diversity of dinosaur tracks along with interpretation and understanding of the palaeoenvironments of their habitat during the Cretaceous.

Sihwa dinosaur site

The Sihwa site is located in the middle western coast of the Peninsula (near to Seoul, the capital of South Korea). In this site more than 140 dinosaur eggs occur in either channel-fill conglomerate or in the massive gravelly siltstone of a braided stream environment (Kim *et al.*, 2009). The outcrops of this site are exposed on a tidal flat, which provides the opportunity to experience not only ancient environments of dinosaur age but also a modern coastal ecosystem.

In addition to those sites described above, some of the sauropod track ways exposed on road-cuts in the vicinity of Masan City (Hwang *et al.*, 2002; Hwang *et al.*, 2004) provide good examples as to how dinosaurs walked at the time (Figure 10.4).

Figure 10.4: Well-preserved dinosaur trackway sites at Docheonri preserving multiple sauropod trackways (A) and Hogyeri preserving crossing sauropod trackways (B) in the vicinity of Masan city.

Bird footprints site at Gajinri, Jinju

Diverse ichnospecies of bird footprints were discovered at many sites in the Cretaceous deposits in South Korea, including *Koreanaornis hamanensis*, *Jindongornipes kimi*, *Uhangrichus chuni*, *Hwangsanipes choughi*, *Goseongornipes markjonesi*, *Ignotornis yangi*, along with some unnamed bird tracks (Kim, 1969; Chun, 1995; Yang *et al.*, 1995; Baek and Yang, 1998; Kim *et al.*, 2006; Kim *et al.*, 2008). The named ichnospecies from South Korea occupy the greater part of avian ichnospecies reported in Cretaceous deposits throughout the world. Cretaceous bird footprint-bearing deposits in South Korea consist of alluvial plain deposits and lake margin deposits, which were formed under seasonal climates with alternating wet and dry periods.

In this site (Fossil site No. 1, Figure 10.1) several thousands of bird footprints occur in a relatively small geographic area. They are preserved in alluvial plain deposits (Figure 10.3, E), and consist of four kinds (Baek and Yang, 1998; Lim *et al.*, 2000) including *Koreanaornis hamanensis* (Figure 10.3F) and web-footed (Figure 10.3, G) tracks. The feeding traces of birds with the shape of arcuate parallel lines (Figure 10.3, H) are, in a number of places, locally associated with the bird footprints. Small theropod tracks and invertebrate trails occur together with these bird footprints, and small-scale ripples, polygonal desiccation cracks, and rain prints can also be observed in these deposits. The occurrence of innumerable bird tracks in this site with the association of diverse paleontological and sedimentological records provide an immense opportunity to study and understand the paleoecological and paleoenvironmental conditions of bird habitats in the Cretaceous.

Fluvial ecosystem site at Yusuri, Jinju

In this area (Fossil site No. 12, Figure 10.1), the upper part of the Hasandong Formation (Sindong Group) of the Gyeongsang Supergroup is well-exposed along a 100 m wide and 1 km long stream valley (Figure 10.3, I). This site consists of massive channel sandstones with point bar deposits (Figure 10.3, J), floodplain sandy mudstones, crevasse channel/splay fine-grained sandstones, and floodplain-lake deposits. In the floodplain deposits, calcic palaeosols with various types of calcretes are common, and some show vertic features (Figure 10.3, K). Rhizocretions, circumnodular cracks, septarian cracks, and coarsening-upward calcrete profiles are really visible in the calcic paleosols (Paik and Kim, 1994). Pseudoanticlines (Figure 10.3, K), pedogenic slickensides, and deep desiccation cracks, which are typical features of the vertisols, are easily recognized in the vertic paleosols (Paik and Lee, 1998). In the 4.6 m-thick floodplain-lake deposits, short-term climatic changes have been preserved (Paik and Lee, 1994). The lake deposits contain *in situ* carbonized tree stumps and wood fragments, stromatolites, oncoids, *Diplicraterion* burrows, and paleoweathered surfaces (Figure 10.3, L), all of which are important evidence of dynamic paleoclimatic conditions. Non-marine bivalve fossils of *Trigonioides* and *Nagdongia* and fragments of dinosaur bones and teeth and turtle carapace occur in a dark grey shale (Paik and Lee, 1994; Park *et al.*, 2000). Dinosaur skeletons and bone fragments are found in some calcic palaeosols and floodplain-lake deposits. It is characteristic that most of the bone fragments are encrusted by micrite with thicknesses of a few mm to over one cm. Small bone fragments thus appear as calcareous nodules (Paik *et al.*, 2001a).

The sedimentological and paleontological records preserved in this site demonstrate features that aid in the understanding of ancient fluvial environments inhabited by dinosaurs, turtles, bivalves, and gymnosperm trees under a semi-arid climate characterized by dry and wet periods. In addition to the sites mentioned above, diverse geotourism resources including stromatolites, mollusc fossils, petrified wood, paleosols, variegated scenic outcrops, and unique geomorphology are present in the Cretaceous geological heritage of South Korea. Among them the oldest records of microbial-caddisfly bioherms (Paik, 2005).

Developing geotourism in Korea

Geotourism is to travel with the intention of viewing, experiencing, and learning about geology and geomorphology. For geotourism to be successful there also needs to be adequate access, site management and educational facilities as well as other tourism resources such as transport and accommodation. Geotourism therefore draws on the expertise of two professional 'communities', the geological community and the tourism industry, who need to work together in order to provide the necessary geosite inventories, site facilities and educational resources along with tourism infrastructure such as the accommodation sector (Hose, 2007).

Scientific values

One of the essential features of a geosite, which is to be presented for geotourism is its scientific value. The significance of a geosite can be ranked according to various degrees or levels, e.g. international, national, state-wide, regional, and local (Sharples, 2002; Brocx, 2003). The Cretaceous geosites in South Korea mentioned here have diverse levels of significance, and their scientific importance has been recognized by the publication of scientific accounts of these sites in international and domestic journals.

The dinosaur geosites including Haenam, Hwasun, Boseong, Yeosu, and Goseong have been nominated as World Heritage because of their international significance in regard to outstanding and unique dinosaur fossil records. The Gajinri bird footprint site is of global significance in regard to innumerable footprints of four kinds of Mesozoic birds in association with various ichnological and sedimentological records. The Sihwa site is of international and national significance in that it provides a record and some understanding of the various nesting environments of dinosaurs. The Yusuri site has national and international significance in that it provides a record and understanding of Cetaceous fluvial environments and semi-arid ecosystems during the Cretaceous.

Tourism infrastructure

Transportation and accommodation are important aspects of tourism planning. In South Korea there are sealed roads for all vehicle access, and access to most sites is only a few hours from major metropolitan areas. In addition accommodation facilities are located in the vicinity of the geosites, and other tourism facilities and enterprises such as climbing, cruise tours, temple-stays, hot-spa bathing and bird-watching are also available around some geosites (e.g. Haenam, Boseong, Yeosu, and Hwasun).

Academic infrastructures

The development and management of interpretive programmes is one of the basic elements of geotourism. Scientific data are required for geosite interpretation. Many research projects have been undertaken on diverse aspects such as paleoenvironments, paleoecology, ichnology, vertebrate paleontology, geochemistry, and absolute age measurement. On the basis of scientific research and publications interpretive explanation, displays, trails, and guided tours can be developed for various geosites. At the Haenam, Goseong, and Gajinri geosites exhibition facilities have been established providing for the understanding of earth history (Figure 10.5).

Geotourism visitor profiles

According to Hose (2007) there appear to be two kinds of geotourist. One is the dedicated geotourist who visits geosites for the purpose of personal educational or intellectual improvement and enjoyment, and the other is the casual geotourist who visits geosites primarily for the purpose of pleasure and some limited intellectual stimulation. The tourists visiting the Cretaceous geosites in South Korea are mostly casual geotourists, while students and teachers fall into the dedicated geotourist category as they have

Figure 10.5: Exhibition and walk-trail facilities in the Cretaceous geosites of South Korea. A and B. Haenam site. C. Hwasun site. D and E. Boseong site with photo spot (E). F and G. Goseong site. H. Gajinri site.

more interest in the scientific meaning of the geosites they are visiting. Most casual geotourists visiting Korean geosites have little knowledge and experience of geology and geomorphology, but still appreciate scenic views and unique features of geology and geomorphology. In order to improve scientific understanding and appreciation of Korean geosites for all visitors, an active programme of geotrail development and interpretive guiding is required. Achieving this will require the training of well-educated guides and a combination of generalized and carefully designed interpretive trails that cater for diverse levels of geotourist background.

Geoconservation and management

All of the Cretaceous geosites described in this chapter are designated as Natural Monuments by the Cultural Heritage Administration of Korea, and Cultural Property Protection Laws and Codes have been legislated in order to conserve them. Financial and personnel support is requisite for the effective protection and management of Korean geosites. The management of Cretaceous geosites is the responsibility of local governments (city or county) in which the geosites are located. Money for geosite management is assigned in annual budgets and staff are assigned to manage the geosites. However, at present budgets are limited and there are a limited number of often poorly trained officers for the management of geosites. Notwithstanding this, most local governments involved in geosite management are intending to improve management strategies and are aiming to promote geotourism.

Economic merit

All of the geosites listed in this chapter are located in rural and agricultural areas in which the mean annual income of residents is less than the national average. The promotion of geotourism which is supported by local government authorities can thus facilitate the creation of jobs and subsequently increase the income of residents. For example, the exhibition events and festivals based on dinosaur geosites in Goseong have brought in over one million visitors. Furthermore the Yeosu dinosaur geosite is to be one of the main attractions of the World Expo, which is to be held in Yeosu in 2012. Over the past several decades, the tourism industry in South Korea has increasingly become a significant segment of the national economy. However, a gradual increase of outbound travel by Korean tourists has resulted in seven consecutive years of deficit in the national balance of payments in travel accounts from 2000 to 2006 (Seo *et al.*, 2009). In particular, the Korean leisure tourism demand for east and southeast Asian countries has markedly increased since 1992, confronting domestic Korean tourism with the challenge of promoting Korean destinations to domestic tourists (Seo *et al.*, 2009). Conversely the promotion of geotourism at the Cretaceous geosites of Korea has the potential to generate new inbound tourism from neighbouring Asian countries. However, compared with geotourism resources in China, South Korean geotourism has some weak points in terms of scale, diversity, and touring expense. Notwithstanding this, the strong points for geotourism in South Korea are very easy access to geological sites compared with China and lower geotourism expenses as compared with Japan. In addition, the Cretaceous dinosaur track sites along the southern rocky coasts in South Korea are world-class unique geotourism resources that neighbouring countries do not possess. Consequently the promotion of geotourism around Korean geosites has the potential to become a significant part of an emerging international nature-based tourism industry.

Conclusions

In terms of past and current international visitation it might be considered that the South Korean Cretaceous geosites do not have the scale and diversity to attract large numbers of foreign visitors as compared with established world-class geotourism sites like the Grand Canyon and Yellowstone in USA, Rocky Mountain in Canada, Jungfrau in Switzerland, Halong Bay in Vietnam and Uluru in Australia. However, the Korean Cretaceous geosites have many attributes in terms of accessibility, unique and significant attractions and low tour expenses compared with many other world-class geotourism destinations.

With regard to accessibility, the Korean Cretaceous geosites are located within a few hours by road from major metropolitan areas as compared with many of the world-class geotourism sites such as the Grand Canyon (USA) and Uluru (Australia) that are located in remote areas. Moreover, the Korean sites provide world-scale footprint records of dinosaurs and Cretaceous birds that cannot be observed at geotourism destinations anywhere else in the world. Although there are many geosites in China and Mongolia with abundant dinosaur bones and eggs, they are also in remote locations and footprints of dinosaurs and Mesozoic birds are very rare. In summary, the visitors to the Korean Cretaceous geosites can observe unique, diverse and world-class paleobiological and geological records. In terms of fostering sustainable geotourism and geotourism development, local authorities have constructed and maintained geological museums and exhibition halls at some geosites. This coupled with promotion by local government and the media is attracting an increasing number of domestic tourists. In conclusion, geotourism centered around the South Korean Cretaceous geosites is readily available and marketable for both international and domestic tourists seeking the unique experience of the 'age of dinosaurs'.

Acknowledgements

This work was supported by the Pukyong National University Research Abroad Fund in 2008 (PS-2008-041).

References

Baek, K.S. and Yang, S.Y. (1998) 'Preliminary report on the Cretaceous bird tracks of the Lower Haman Formation, Korea', *Journal of the Geological Society of Korea*, 34, 94-104.

Brocx, M. (2003) 'Geoheritage: from global reviews and the Australian experience to guiding principles for coastal Western Australia', unpublished honours thesis, Murdoch University, Perth, Australia.

Chang, K.H. (1975) 'Cretaceous stratigraphy of Southeast Korea', *Journal of the Geological Society of Korea*, 11 (1), 1-23.

Choi, H.I. (1986) 'Sedimentation and evolution of the Cretaceous Gyeongsang Basin, Southestern Korea', *Journal of Geological Society (London)*, 143, 29-40.

Chough, S.K., Kwon, S.T., Ree, J.T. and Choi, D.K. (2000) 'Tectonic and sedimentary evolution of the Korea peninsula: A review and new view', *Earth Science Reviews*, 52, 175-235.

Chun, S.S. (1990) 'Sedimentary processes depositional environments and tectonic setting of the Cretaceous Uhangri Formation', unpublished PhD thesis, Seoul National University.

Dixon, G. (1996) Geoconservation: an international review and strategy for Tasmania. Miscellaneous Report, Parks & Wildlife Service, Tasmania, 101.

Heo, C.H. (2007) 'A study on the possibility as a site for geopark in Korea: Byeonsan-bando National Park', *Journal of Korean Earth Science Society*, **28** (1), 136-141.

Heo, C.H. and Kim, S.Y. (2005) 'The study on the development of geological and geomorphological landscape resources to promote tourism geology – A case study in the Naejangsan national park', *Economic and Environmental Geology*, **38** (3), 355-367.

Heo, C. H., and Choi, S. H. (2007) A Study on the Development of Geological Geomorphological landscape resources to promote Tourism Geology: A Case Study in Taean Seashore National Park. *Journal of Korean Earth Science Society*, **28** (1), 75-86.

Hose, T.A. (2007) 'Geotourism in Almeria Province, southeast Spain', *Tourism* **55**, 259-276.

Huh, M., Hwang, K.G., Paik, I.S. and Chung, C.H. (2003) 'Dinosaur tracks from the Cretaceous of South Korea: distribution, occurrence and paleobiological significance, *Island Arc*, **12**, 132-144.

Huh, M., Paik, I.S., Lockley, M.G., Hwang, K.G., Kim, B.S. and Kwak, S.K. (2006) 'Well-preserved theropod tracks from the Upper Cretaceous of Hwasun County, Southwest South Korea, and their paleobiological implications', *Cretaceous Research*, **27**, 123-138.

Huh, M. and Zelenitsky, D.K. (2002) 'A rich nesting site from the Cretaceous of Bosung county, Chullanam-do Procince, South Korea', *Journal of Vertebrate Paleontology*, **22**, 716-718.

Hwang, K.G., Huh, M., Lockley, M., Unwin, D. and Wright, J.L. (2002) 'New pterosaur tracks (Pteraichnidae) from the Late Cretaceous Uhangri Formation, SW Korea', *Geological Magazine*, **139**, 421-435.

Hwang, K.G., Huh, M. and Paik, I.S. (2002) 'Sauropod tracks from the Cretaceous Jindong Formation, Hogyeri, Masan-city, Korea', *Journal of the Geological Society of Korea*, **38**, 361-375.

Hwang, K.G., Huh, M. and Paik, I.S. (2004) 'Sauropod trackways from the Cretaceous Jindong Formation at Docheon-ri, Changnyeong-geun, Gyeongsangnam-do, Korea', *Journal of the Geological Society of Korea*, **40**, 145-159.

Jeong, G.H. (2000) 'The study on the "Tourism market analysis" and "dvelopment of tourism programs and events" to promote the sites of geoutourism', *Tourism Sciences Society of Korea*, **31**, 281-296.

Jwa, Y.J., Lee, Y.I. and Orihashi, Y. (2004) 'Discussion on the U-Pb ages of zircon minerals from the Gusandong Tuff and the Jindong Granite and the age of the Jindong Formation', *59th Symposium of the Geological Society of Korea (Abstract)*, p. 73.

Kim, B.K. (1969) 'A study of several sole marks in the Haman Formation', *Journal of the Geological Society of Korea*, **5** (4), 243-258.

Kim, C.S., Park, K.H. and Paik, I.S. (2005) '$^{40}Ar/^{39}Ar$ age of the volcanic pebbles within the Silla Conglomerate and the deposition timing of the Hayang Group', *Journal of Petrological Society of Korea*, **14**, 38-44.

Kim, H.J., Paik, I.S., Lee, J.E. and Huh, M. (2008) 'Bird footprint fossils from the Upper Cretaceous Jindong Formation at Hogyeri, Masan city, Gyeongsangnamdo, Korea: occurrences and paleoenvironmental implications', *Journal of the Geological Society of Korea*, **44**, 729-745.

Kim, I.S., Kang, H.C., Lee, H.K. (1993) 'Paleomagnetism of Early Cretaceous sedimentary rocks in Chingyo-Sachon area, southwestern Gyeongsang Basin', *Journal of Korean Institution of Mining Geology*, 519-539.

Kim, J.Y., Kim, S.H., Kim, K.S., and Lockley, M.G. (2006) 'The oldest record of webbed bird and pterosaur tracks from South Korea (Cretaceous Haman Formation, Changseon and Sinsu Islands): more evidence of high avian diversity in east Asia', *Cretaceous Research*, **26**, 56-59.

Kim, S.B., Kim, Y.G., Jo, H.R., Jeong, K.S. and Chough, S.K. (2009) 'Depositional facies, architecture and environments of the Sihwa Formation (Lower Cretaceous), mid-west Korea with special reference to dinosaur eggs', *Cretaceous Research*, 30, 100-126.

Lee, D.W. (1999), 'Strike-slip fault tectonics and basin formation during the Cretaceous in the Korea Peninsula', *Island Arc*, 8, 218-231.

Lee, G., Besse, J. and Courtillot, V. (1987) 'Eastern Asia in the Cretaceous: new paleomagnetic data from South Korea and a new look at Chinese and Japanese data', *Journal of Geophysical Research*, 92, 3580-3596.

Lee, Y. I., Choi, T. J., Lim, H. S. and Orihashi, Y. (2008) Detrital zircon geochronology of the Cretaceous Sindong Group, SE Korea: Implications for a new view on the depositional age and provenance. 63rd Symposium of the Geological Society of Korea (Abstracts), p. 25.

Lim, S.K., Lockley, M.G., Yang, S.Y., Fleming, R.F., Houck, K. (1994) 'A preliminary report on sauropod tracksites from the Cretaceous of Korea', *GAIA*, 10, 109-117.

Lockley, M.G., Houck, K., Yang, S.Y., Matsukawa, M. and Lim, S.K. (2006) 'Dinosaur-dominated footprint assemblages from the Cretaceous Jindong Formation, Hallyo Haesang National Park area, Goseong County, South Korea: Evidence and implications', *Cretaceous Research*, 27, 70-101.

Mack, G.H. and James, W.C. (1994) 'Paleoclimates and the global distribution of paleosols', *Journal of Geology*, 102, 360-366.

Okada, H. and Sakai, T. (1993) 'Nature and development of Late Mesozoic and Early Cenozoic sedimentary basin in southwest Japan', *Palaeogeography, Palaeoclimatology, Palaeoecology*, 105, 3-16.

Paik, I.S. (2005) 'The oldest record of microbial-caddisfly bioherms from the Early Cretaceous Jinju Formation, Korea: occurrence and palaeoenvironmental implications', *Palaeogeography, Palaeoclimatology, Palaeoecology*, 218, 301-315.

Paik, I.S. and Kim, H.J. (1997) 'Paleoclimatic records of the Gyeonsang Supergroup', in Woo, Y.K. (ed.), *Collected Monographs for Memory of Retirement of Professor Hee In Park*, pp. 111-118.

Paik, I.S. and Kim, H.J. (1998) 'Subaerial lenticular cracks in Cretaceous lacustrine deposits, Korea', *Journal of Sedimentary Research*, 68, 80-87.

Paik, I.S. and Kim, H.J. (2006) 'Playa lake and sheetflood deposits of the Upper Cretaceous Jindong Formation, Korea: Occurrences and palaeoenvironments', *Sedimentary Geology*, 187, 83-103.

Paik, I S. and Lee, Y.I. (1994) 'Paleoclimatic records in floodplain lake deposits of the Cretacesou Hasandong Formation in Jinju area, Korea', *Journal of the Geological Society of Korea*, 30 (4), 410-424.

Paik, I.S. and Lee, Y.I. (1998) 'Desiccation cracks in vertic paleosols of the Cretaceous

Hasandong Formation, Korea: genesis and palaeoenvironmental implications', *Sedimentary Geology*, **119**, 161-179.

Paik, I.S., Kim, H.J. and Lee, Y.I. (2001) 'Dinosaur track-bearing deposits in the Cretaceous Jindong Formation, Korea: occurrence, palaeoenvironments and preservation', *Cretaceous Research*, **22**, 79-92.

Paik, I.S., Huh, M. and Kim, H.J. (2004) 'Dinosaur egg-bearing deposits (Upper Cretaceous) of Boseong, Korea: occurrence, palaeoenvironments, taphonomy, and preservation', *Palaeogeography, Palaeoclimatology, Palaeoecology*, **205**, 155-168.

Paik, I.S., Huh, M., Park, K.H., Hwang, K.G., Kim K.S. and Kim, H.J. (2006) 'Yeosu dinosaur track sites of Korea: the youngest dinosaur track records in Asia', *Journal of Asian Earth Sciences*, **28**, 457-468.

Paik, I.S., Huh, M., So, Y.H., Lee, J.E. and Kim, H.J. (2007) 'Traces of evaporites in Upper Cretaceous lacustrine deposits of Korea: origin and paleoenvironmental implications', *Journal of Asian Earth Sciences*, **30**, 93-107.

Paik, I.S., So, Y.H., Kim., H.J., Lee, H.I., Yoon, H.I., Lim, H.S. and Huh, M. (2009) 'Rhythmic deposits in the Upper Cretaceous lacustrine deposits at Yeosu area, Korea: occurrences and origin', *Journal of the Geological Society of Korea*, **45** (2), 85-105.

Park, E.J., Yang, S.Y. and Currie, P.J. (2000) 'Early Cretaceous dinosaur teeth of Korea', *Paleontological Society of Korea, Special Publication no. 4*, 85-98.

Seo, J.H., Park, S.Y., Yu, L. (2009) 'The analysis of the relationship of Korean outbound tourism demand: Jeju Island and three international destinations', *Tourism Management*, **30**, 530-543.

Sharples, C. (2002) *Concepts and Principles of Geoconservation*. Hobart: Tasmanian Parks and Wildlife Service.

Waston, M.P., Hayward, A.B., Parkinson, D.N., Zhang, Z.H.M. (1987) 'Plate tectonic history, basin development and petroleum source rock deposition onshore China', *Marine and Petroleum Geology*, **4**, 205-225.

Yang, S.Y., Lockley, M.G., Greben, R., Erikson, B.R., Lim, S.K. (1995) 'Flamingo and Duck-like bird tracks from the Late Cretaceous and Early Tertiary: evidence and implications', *Ichnos*, **44**, 21-34.

Yang, S.Y., Lockley, M., Lim S.K., Chun, S.S. (1997) 'Cretaceous bird tracks of Korea', *Journal of the Paleontological Society of Korea, Special Publication*, **2**, 33-42.

11 Geotourism and geotourist education in Poland

Tadeusz Slomka and Wojciech Mayer, AGH - University of Science and Technology, Poland

Introduction

Since its appearance in 1990s, geotourism has gained many, sometimes misleading definitions. An excellent overview of the genesis of geotourism has been recently given by Newsome and Dowling (2006) and Hose (2008). Hose (2008) provided the first sensible explanation of geotourism as:

> *The provision of interpretive and service facilities to enable tourists to acquire knowledge and the understanding of the geology and geomorphology of a site (including its contribution to the development of the Earth sciences) beyond the level of mere aesthetic appreciation*

For further explanation see Hose (1995).

In Poland geotourism has been defined by Slomka and Kicinska-Swiderska (2004) as:

> *Geotourism is an offshoot of cognitive tourism and/or adventure tourism based upon visits to geological objects (geosites) and recognition of geological processes integrated with aesthetic experiences gained by the contact with a geosite.*

Slomka and Kicinska-Swiderska (2004) also introduced some new terms:

♦ **geotouristic object (geosite)** is a geological site, which may become a tourist product after proper development and promotion,

♦ **geotouristic event** is a recent geological process which may become a tourist product,

♦ **geotouristic attraction** is a sum of geotouristic objects and events.

Geotourism emerged in early 1990s as a response to several factors among which the most important were:

♦ the growing and changing demand of the tourist industry, particularly specialized tourism,

♦ the growing understanding of the importance of the Earth heritage,

♦ the evolution of Earth sciences into more interdisciplinary issues including geology, geomorphology and environmental sciences.

The rapidly expanding tourist industry has been looking for new offers attractive for the growing number of tourists who were interested in something more exciting than a 'classic' formula of leisure holidays. Hence, attention has been paid to specialized tourism, including visits to objects of abiotic nature where elements of geology and geomorphology could be seen 'on site' and basic knowledge could be gained at the level available for non-professionals. Such world-famous tourist sites as the Grand Canyon or Yellowstone National Parks in the USA have received a new role as educational centres where knowledge can be effectively communicated about the Earth, its history, evolution, relationships between geology and environment, and its future. Moreover, such a formula has provided an opportunity to develop thousands of abiotic nature objects all over the world as tourist attractions, even if these are not extraordinary as the two national parks mentioned above.

In 1991, a new initiative appeared during the Digny Conference: the 'International declaration of the rights of the memory of the Earth'. This provided suitable frames leading to international projects focused on the protection of geological heritage. As a result, in 2000 the European Geopark Network was established, followed by the Global Geopark Network (2004) (for details see, for example, Zouros, 2004, 2008). Both the protection and promotion of geosites has gained a new formula, much wider and comprehensive than just a simple sightseeing of geological/geomorphological sites, as it includes elements of history and cultural heritage as well as important economic and social issues in terms of revitalization of local economy and communities (Zouros, 2008). Finally, in the 1990s geological sciences gained a new impetus towards more interdisciplinary issues when environmental geology emerged as a response to new challenges including sustainable development, natural hazards and general shift from reactive to proactive involvement of the applied nature of Earth sciences (see, for example, Bennett and Doyle, 1997).

The appearance of geotourism has resulted in a growing demand for a new specialist – a BSc and/or MSc graduate who has knowledge of the principles and practice of the tourist industry combined with reasonable level of understanding and experience in Earth sciences, including geology, geomorphology and environmental protection. Such a specialist should be qualified not only to run a tourist business in all aspects but also to prepare a specialized geotouristic offer (product) and to guide geotouristic trips, explaining the details of geology and geomorphology of a particular site to a wide spectrum of visitors – from non-professionals to Earth sciences students and specialists. Such a demand led the authors to propose and develop in 1999, the MSc and engineer course in applied geology with specialization in geotourism.

Geodiversity in Poland

In Poland three principal structural units meet: the Precambrian East European Platform, the Paleozoic orogens of Central and Western Europe and the Alpine orogenic belts of Southern Europe (Pozaryski, 1990; Guterch and Grad, 1996; Znosko, 1998; Stupnicka, 2007, Slomka, 2008), (Figure 11.1).

The northeastern part of Poland belongs to the East European Platform, which includes Precambrian magmatics and metamorphics covered by Paleozoic and Mesozoic sediments. From the southwest, the Platform is cut by the Trans-European Suture Zone (TESZ), which is a system of deep fractures and faults. The huge central and southwestern portion of Poland is occupied by Paleozoic orogenic belts of both Caledonian (about 490–390 Ma) and Variscan (about 380-280 Ma) ages. These rocks are covered by thick sedimentary pile of Permian, Mesozoic and Cenozoic sediments. Only parts of these orogens are exposed in southwestern (the Sudety Mts), central (the Holy-Cross Mts) and the southern (the Upper Silesian Coal Basin and the uplifted part of the Silesian–Kraków Upland) parts of Poland.

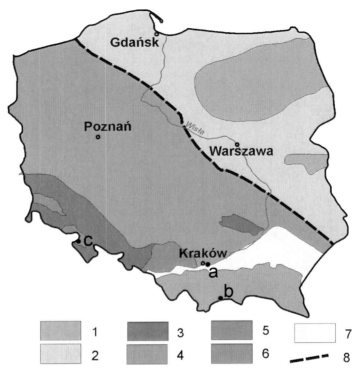

Figure 11.1: Structural map of Poland (after Znosko 1998, simplified):
Precambrian platform; 1. depressed fragments of crystalline basement; 2. uplifted fragments of crystalline basement.
Paleozoic fold belts; 3. uplifted Paleozoic units; 4. Paleozoic platform; 5. Variscan depressions; Alpine fold belt; 6. The Carpathians; 7. The Carpathian Foredeep; 8. The Trans European Suture Zone (TESZ).

a – The Wieliczka Salt Mine, b – The Dunajec River Gorge, c – The Table Mountains.

Southern Poland is covered by a large part of the Carpathians – the Alpine fold belt (about 70-1.5 Ma) with a vast foreland depression named the Carpathian Foredeep. The Carpathians extend over some 1300 kilometres, from Vienna in Austria to southern Romania. Three principal zones are present: the Outer (Flysch) Carpathians composed of alternating sandstone-shale successions ranging in age from Cretaceous to Tertiary and organized in several, stacked, strongly deformed nappes; the Pieniny Klippen Belt, which is a narrow tectonic zone of complicated internal structure in which Mesozoic and Cainozoic carbonates and clastics are strongly deformed; the Inner Carpathians being composed of Paleozoic crystalline basement with a Mesozoic sedimentary cover.

The morphology of Poland appears as a vast lowland (Paleozoic/Mesozoic platform overlying the buried Paleozoic orogens) bordered from the south by the Carpathians – an Alpine thrust-and-fold orogenic belt, and from the southwest by the Sudety Mts – a multistage, Variscan orogen of complicated internal structure and geological history. The final relief is a result of both the endo- and exogenic processes which have been active during the last several Ma and controlled by abrupt climatic changes (Mojski, 2005). The principal geomorphological factor was the Pleistocene glaciation during which almost whole area of Poland was covered with a thick ice sheet prograding from

Scandinavia. The ice sheet and its meltwaters deposited a thick pile of various glacial and post-glacial sediments together with their typical landforms, e.g. glacial rafts and lakes, ridge crests and proglacial valleys. The combined, land-shaping effects of glaciation coupled with basement structures, fault tectonics and resultant vertical, neo-tectonic movements of amplitudes over 100 metres are still insufficiently understood (Liszkowski, 1982; Mojski, 2005).

Both the shallow geological structures and the morphology recently observed in Poland are the effects of various geological and climatic processes, and are responsible for the geodiversity of Poland. Geosites, which can be readily developed as touristic products (Slomka and Kicinska-Swiderska, 2004) have resulted from both ancient and recent geological processes: weathering, erosion, mass wasting and human activity, e.g. agriculture and the mining industry. Below three examples of geosites are briefly characterized as samples of geodiversity of Poland.

The historical rock-salt mine and underground saltwork museum in Wieliczka

The Carpathian Foredeep is a broad foreland depression formed during the folding and thrusting of the Carpathian flysch nappes. Sea level rise, which flooded the depression in the Miocene left behind a succession of clays, sands, carbonates and evaporites totaling a thickness of up to 1500 metres. The evaporite member (Badenian, Miocene) includes chloride facies (rock salt), which has been mined since the Neolithic period in the vicinity of Wieliczka and Bochnia towns (some 15 kilometres east from Kraków), first as brine collected from seeps and dug wells, then, since the 11th century, as rock salt extracted from underground. For centuries both the Wieliczka and the Bochnia mines have been royal properties and the salt trade provided for a significant part of the income of the Polish Kingdom. In fact, the Wieliczka Mine is the oldest, continuously operating underground mine in Europe (it finally closed in 1996). After centuries of mining activity the Wieliczka Mine appears as a labyrinth of galleries and chambers (nearly 3000 open spaces) of total length about 300 kilometres, with a vertical extent from about 60 to more than 300 metres below the surface. Due to the specific properties of rock salt, and its propensity for deformation, the mine workings must be continuously monitored and maintained or backfilled (Alexandrowicz, 1994; Garlicki, 2008).

The Wieliczka Mine and the Saltwork Museum are world-class geotourism attractions visited each year by over 1 million tourists. In 1978, the mine was included into the UNESCO First World List of Cultural and Natural Heritage. In 1994 it was officially recognized as a Monument of National History (as was the adjacent Bochnia Salt Mine in 2000). The underground trail is about 3.5 kilometres long and includes shafts, chambers and galleries, and even an underground pond. The museum offers a unique exhibition: from historical documents and maps through rock-salt sculptures, minerals and rocks to original mining equipment. At the lower levels, which are closed to the ordinary tourists but may be visited by specialized groups, outcrops of Miocene evaporites and examples of salt tectonics can be examined.

The leading attraction of the underground tourist trail is the St Kinga Chapel (Fig. 11.2). Located at a depth of 101 metres, the chapel was continuously carved in a worked-out rock salt block between the years 1896 and 1963, although the last sculptures were placed in 2003. The chapel, over 50 metres long, about 20 metres wide and up to 12 metres high, still plays a religious role but is also a unique exhibition of rock-salt sculptures and a concert hall.

Figure 11.2: The Saint Kinga Chapel in Wieliczka Salt Mine – a chamber cut in a single block of rock-salt and decorated with sculptures and bas-reliefs (photo Krzysztof Slomka).

The other outstanding features of the Wieliczka Mine and Saltwork Museum are the 'Crystal Caves' – two large cavities encrusted with perfect, cubic halite megacrystals and showing the examples of salt karst. In 2000, the caves were granted the status of nature reserve. Both are permanently closed to the public in order to protect the sensitive microclimate which the highly soluble halite crystals require for stability (Alexandrowicz, 2000). Details of the geology of the Carpathian Foredeep and the Wieliczka Mine and Saltwork Museum can be found in, for example, Garlicki (2008 and references therein). The official website of the Saltwork Museum: (www.kopalnia-wieliczka.com.pl) provides additional information.

The Dunajec River Gorge

The Pieniny Klippen Belt is a low (about 1,000m above sea level) mountain range (the Pieniny Mts) sandwiched between the Outer (Flysch) and the Inner Carpathians. It extends along some 600 kilometres, from Vienna in the west to Romania in the southeast, and is from 1 to 20 kilometres wide,. The belt is built of Early Jurassic-Late Cretaceous, deep and shallow-marine carbonates, clastics and siliceous sediments forming a number of structural sub-units and intruded by rare volcanics. The sediments were laid down in an extended marine basin, then were deformed into a kind of diapir, then some successions were overthrusted as nappes. The boundaries of the belt are Tertiary vertical faults (strike-slip from the south) and shear zones. The internal structure of the belt is extremely complicated and is still a matter of discussion (Birkenmajer, 1986; Krobicki and Golonka, 2008).

Although low in relief, the Pieniny Mts are valued by tourists because of panoramic views of peaks towering over the Dunajec River Gorge and other, smaller gorges, along with steep rock walls and pinnacles built of white limestone. Additional sites of interest are medieval castles, mountain villages which still preserve traditional architecture, small town spas with characteristic architecture and mineral waters of high therapeutic value.

The Pieniny Klippen Belt (Krobicki and Golonka (2008) is partly protected as the Pieniny Mts National Park in Poland and its Slovakian partner – the Pieninsky Narodny Park. The prime geotourism attraction of the Pieniny Mts is the Dunajec River Gorge (Golonka and Krobicki, 2007). Here, the river cuts through limestone formations forming a meandering, antecedent gorge which is almost vertical, with rock walls over 100 metres high (Figure 11.3). There is 15-kilometres-long rafting route down the meandering gorge.

Figure 11.3: The Dunajec River Gorge (photo are Robert Karpowicz).

The Table Mountains

The Sudety Mts are a multistage orogen composed of magmatic, metamorphic and sedimentary rocks ranging in age from the Upper Proterozoic to the Cenozoic. They were formed mainly during the Variscan orogeny and were subsequently affected by intensive Alpine (Neogene) block tectonics, and young basaltic volcanism. The final effect of these processes is a mosaic of structural units (terranes) of various ages, comprising a variety of rocks. The recent morphology of the Sudety Mts resulted from the combined effects of climate change, long-lasting weathering, erosion and denudation. However, the complicated structure of the orogen and its diversified lithology gave rise to the formation of numerous, outstanding morphological forms which are excellent geotouristic objects, for example, monadnocks, ravines, caves and waterfalls. Also of interest are the occurrences of rare minerals and rocks accessible in natural exposures as well as in quarries and in underground workings. Some of the old mines were developed as underground tourist trails (as for example, the historical gold mine in Złoty Stok). The Sudety Mountains also have many health resorts providing high-class therapeutic waters.

The Table Mountains are one of the leading geotourism attractions of the region. Located in the central part of the Sudety Mts, this is a NW-SE-trending plateau, over 40 km long, shared by Poland and Czech Republic. The highest peaks reach elevations up to about 900 metres a.s.l. The Table Mts are built of Upper Cretaceous, flat-lying, shallow-marine, thick-bedded sandstones and marls. Three complexes of sandstones can be distinguished: lower (glauconitic, clayey and calcareous sandstones, Cenomanian), middle (arcosic sandstones, Lower/Middle Turonian) and upper (quartz sandstones, Upper Turonian), the latter two each up to 100 metres thick. Thickness of marl intercalation exceeds 30 metres. Sandstone complexes are cut by three systems of regular joints

(Cwojdzinski, 2007). The outstanding features of the Table Mts are isolated, flat-topped mountains resembling mesas, rising up to 200 metres above the surrounding plateau. The most popular is the Great Szczeliniec (919 meters a.s.l.) with its spectacular cliffs, panoramas and systems of regular joints enlarged by weathering (Figure 11.4).

Figure 11.4: Vertical, nearly 150-meters-high walls of Cretaceous sandstones at the top of the Great Szczeliniec – the tallest peak of the Table Mts (photo by Karolina Slomka-Polonis).

The relief of the Table Mts originated from intensive, physical and chemical weathering processes, that commenced in Oligocene and had been particularly active during periods of cold climate. Regular joint systems have allowed the penetration of rain water, which has facilitated mechanical and chemical weathering. The Table Mts are perfect examples of weathering processes followed by erosion and mass movements. In Poland, a significant part of the Table Mts is protected as a national park. Details of geology can be found in, for example, Gawlikowska (2008).

Geotourism in national parks in Poland

According to Polish state regulations, a national park is the area of the highest and most strict protection of nature along with its scientific, social, cultural, educational and scenic values. Protection of biotic natural resources and biodiversity in the national parks is generally well understood by the public. However, the preservation of abiotic nature is commonly underestimated or even neglected. In all 23 national parks in Poland a wide variety of abiotic natural sites occur. These sites exhibit the high geodiversity of the country and are important targets of geotourism. Examples include the following:

♦   Baltic Sea coast with a spectrum of coastal and aeolian processes, and landforms (cliffs, coastal dunes, playas),

♦ alpine-type mountains with a number of glacial landforms (cirques, glacial valleys and lakes, moraines), and perfect examples of lithologically and tectonically controlled morphology,

♦ lowlands with a variety of glacial sediments and ice-sheet-originated landforms (moraine hills, kames, eskers, kettle holes),

♦ river valleys and glacial lakeland,

♦ karst terrains with typical landforms and amazing caves.

Tourist flow in the selected national parks in Poland is shown in Figure 11.5. Statistical analysis was based upon the attendance data provided by park authorities in the years 1999– 2003 (see Slomka *et al.*, 2006).

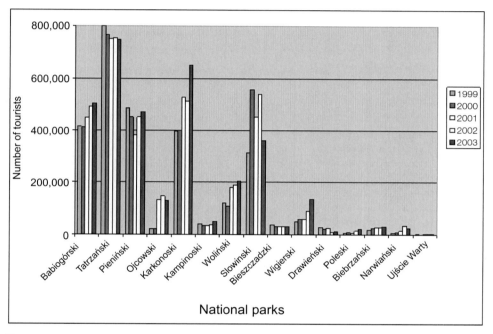

Figure 11.5: Tourist flow in the selected national parks in Poland in the years 1999-2003 (after Słomka et al. 2006)

Statistical analysis of tourist flow has revealed a strong correlation between the number of geotourism attractions and the number of visitors. Four out of the five parks occupying the leading positions include the largest number of high-class geotourism attractions (Slomka *et al.*, 2008). For instance, in the Tatra Mts National Park has the most used tourist trail (about 10,000 visitors per day in summer) leads along the glacial valley towards the famous 'Eye of the Sea' cirque lake. In the Pieniny National Park the major tourist attraction is the Dunajec River gorge, which can be visited by rafting or by a hike/bike trail built along the southern shore of the river. The Karkonosze National Park is well recognized for a hiking trail which leads along the crest of the main granite ridge where erosional and glacial features can be easily identified. Finally, in the Slowinski National Park the geotourism attractions are coastal lakes, migrating sand dunes and peat bogs.

Recent developments in geotourism in Poland

The International Association for Geotourism

The International Association for Geotourism (IAGT) was established in 2007, in Kraków – a historical capital of Poland. Kraków seems to be a good site for such an organization as it is one of the most popular tourist centres in Europe with a number of historical monuments, museums and cultural events, with important scientific and educational institutions active also in the Earth and environmental sciences, and with a number of geotourism attractions.

The IAGT aims to integrate the Earth and environmental sciences, mining heritage and tourism by:

♦   promotion of universal beauty of inanimate nature and mining heritage;

♦   promotion of interdisciplinary studies on preservation of inanimate nature and mining heritage;

♦   promotion of business activity in the field of geotourism;

♦   granting of scholarships for students of geotourism and junior scientific staff active in nature and mining heritage protection research.

The IAGT organizes conferences, symposia, workshops and professional training as well as preparing databases related to abiotic nature and mining heritage sites. Membership is open to any person ready to cooperate and contribute to the IAGT activities within the framework of its statute. The first President of IAGT was Professor Tadeusz Slomka from AGH – University of Science and Technology in Krakow, Poland. Currently, the President of the IAGT is Professor Pavol Rybar from the Technical University in Kosice, Slovakia.

The Catalogue of Geotourism Objects in Poland

In 2006 the Catalogue of Geotouristic Objects in Poland was issued as a result of the joint efforts of a working group in geotourism from the AGH-University of Mining and Metallurgy in Krakow (Faculty of Geology, Geophysics and Environment Protection) and the Ministry of Environment (Slomka *et al.* 2006). The Catalogue was the first such initiative in Poland. The project aimed to select and describe in detail a representative sample of geotouristic sites in all districts, best-illustrating the geodiversity of Poland. From about 600 initial proposals a group of 100 geosites were carefully selected and described using a standardized data sheet. These sites represent a wide spectrum of geological structures, lithostratigraphic units, fossils, minerals and rock occurrences, mineral deposits, landforms as well as geological and geomorphological processes, both recent and active in the past. Simultaneously, the selected geosites present the beauty of abiotic nature seen in natural and anthropogenic exposures (Slomka *et al.*, 2008). The Catalogue is public-oriented, that is, it may be a valuable source of information for both amateurs and professionals, including tourist agencies. It also plays an educational role as it spreads knowledge of Earth heritage. Moreover, it provides a suitable exemplar for future developments, as many interesting geosites still await recognition from local authorities, tourist agencies and local communities.

The Geoturystyka-Geotourism Quarterly

In 2004 the working group in geotourism from the Faculty of Geology, Geophysics and Envrionment Protection, AGH-University of Science and Technology in Krakow, commenced publishing a new periodical *Geoturystyka-Geotourism*. The journal is published quarterly and is devoted to popularization of abiotic nature objects in Poland and worldwide as tourist attractions. Up to the time of writing 15 volumes have appeared with over 70 papers. Initially, papers were published in Polish with extended English summaries. Recently, papers in English have prevailed, each with an extended Polish summary. It is expected that in the future the journal will become the statutory periodical of the IAGT and will also be available on-line.

The websites geoturystyka.pl and GeoTourismOnline.com

In 2005, a new website was initiated: www.geoturystyka.pl. Its aim was to integrate all those who are interested in tourism, in general, but are also interested in the Earth and environmental sciences and, who travelled around Poland, Europe and/or over the world and now wish to share their experiences and knowledge of specific sites. It is also suitable for those who are planning their future travels, and seeking relevant information and knowledge of specific geosites (Slomka *et al.*, 2005).

The website has been created with modern, standard tools: HTML, PHP, Javascript, Flash and Mysql. The main part of the website is the library of reports and essays concerning journeys to various parts of the world. It includes descriptions of geosites and links to photo galleries. Photographs can be browsed as parts of relevant reports or can be viewed independently.

The Sudetic Geostrada

The idea of a tourist trail along the Sudety Mts (southwestern Poland) was raised many years ago by Dr Leszek Sawicki from the Lower Silesian Branch of the Polish Geological Institute. In 2008 the working group on geotourism from the Faculty of Geology, Geophysics and Environment Protection, AGH-University of Science and Technology in Kraków started a new project scheduled over three years, named 'The Sudetic Geostrad' (Sudetic Geo-highway). The project is roughly linked to the previous idea and is run in cooperation with the Lower Silesian Branch of the Polish Geological Institute. Funds are provided by the Ministry of Environment.

The Sudetic Geostrada starts near the Polish-German border in the west and terminates close to Glucholazy village in the east. It very roughly follows the main ridge of the Sudety Mts (in a geographical sense) both in Poland and the Czech Republic. The general idea of the Sudetic Geostrada project is to select secondary roads within a corridor running roughly west–east, about 400 kilometres long and 10 kilometres wide, close to which most interesting geosites are located. Selected points will be described in detail from a geological, geographic and tourist industry point of view, in a form suitable for the future planning of tourism development. Additionally, the project will include historical monuments, cultural centres, regional events and infrastructure in order to provide full information suitable for motorized tourists, bikers and even hikers. The corridor will avoid the main highways, large towns, popular tourist centres and health resorts in the area, and will focus on less-popular roads and small villages where interesting geological and geomorphological sites occur. Redirection of tourist flow from the popular centres to lesser-known (or even unknown) sites would solve visitor satisfaction issues and avoid potentially damaging effects of overcrowding at popular tourist centres and trails It would also provide stimulation of social and economic development of local communities. This idea has strong links to the European geoparks concept and to the concept of Scenic Byways developed in the USA.

Education in Geotourism

A changing environment

In 1999, education in geotourism had commenced at the Faculty of Geology, Geophysics and Environment Protection, AGH-University of Science and Technology in Krakow, as a specialization in the frame of the Applied Geology course. The reasoning being that the links between geology, geomorphology and tourism are obvious. A large part of the most popular tourist sites visited each year by millions of people are, in fact, geological objects or geologically-controlled landforms of various scales, from regional, as for example, mountain ranges, islands, sea coasts to local, e.g. volcanoes, lakes and caves. Also sites of mining heritage, which become more and more popular tourist targets, are closely linked to interesting geology in various parts of the world. Thus, geotourism defined colloquially as visits to geosites for knowledge and pleasure (see Slomka and Kicinska-Swiderska, 2004) has almost naturally emerged and has quickly expanded at the geological faculty, despite some resistance from more conservatively minded staff. Simultaneously, the new specialization (accompanied by other proposals, e.g. environmental protection and computer geoscience courses) enabled the faculty to provide new, attractive educational options for students.

The appearance of new education proposals was closely correlated with changes at the university and at the faculty. Changing demands of the industry, changing labour markets and resulting reorientation of candidates' preferences forced the evolution of the university towards a more diversified formula. Still keeping alive the 'traditional' courses: mining engineering, applied geology, iron and base-metal metallurgy, both the educational and research activities moved decisively towards material sciences, computer science, new technologies, applied mathematics and physics, environmental protection and environmental engineering and, in recent years, to the human sciences.

The early education in geotourism

The geotourism specialization was implemented in 1999 within the MSc/engineer course in applied geology. The general idea was to create a new type of graduate – a fully qualified geologist with additional, broad knowledge of the tourist industry. The intention was to educate a specialist who was able to prepare a tourist product based on geosites, who was trained to promote such products and who was fully qualified to guide a trip and to explain to the participants what the site is, how and when was it formed, how it evolved and why it formed at this particular place in the world. Simultaneously, our graduates were prepared to modify their explanations depending on the educational level of participants – from full amateurs to professional geologists and to be fully prepared to answer even the most surprising questions.

The course included three groups of topics: (1) state standard topics, (2) faculty standard topics and (3) specialized topics. The state standard topics are obligatory for all students in the Applied Geology course at all university-level schools in Poland and include over 500 teaching hours of basic topics including mathematics, physics, chemistry, computing, general geology and some other Earth sciences, principles of economy and management, principles of mining engineering and drilling engineering, and foreign languages. Most of the state standard topics were taught during the first three semesters. The standard faculty topics included a wide range of applied Earth sciences: geophysics, geology of mineral deposits, geological mapping, hydrogeology, engineering geology and Quaternary geology. These topics were taught mostly in semesters IV–VI and amounted to about 1000 teaching hours.

The specialized topics (totalling about 1000 teaching hours) taught mostly at semesters VIII–X were dealing directly with various aspects of the tourist industry (e.g. geography of tourism, preparation of the tourist product, tourist service, management in tourism) and with geotourism itself. Moreover, several optional topics were included (to be chosen by students), related to various detailed aspects of tourism and geotourism (e.g. world museums, coasts, and even world cuisine). During specialized topic tutorials emphasis was put on the student's own projects and presentations prepared under the supervision of tutors. The course was supported with a number of field training sessions including the faculty standards (e.g. field training in general geology and in geological mapping) as well as geotouristic attractions of Poland and of Europe (two field sessions, eight days each) run usually in the mountainous regions of southern Poland and in the eastern Alps. Up to now, about 300 graduates of the geotourism specialization have been granted the MSc/engineer degree. Most of them found jobs in the tourist industry in Poland and in the European Union or in state and local administration agencies dealing with tourism, its regional and local promotion and development.

The environment protection-geotourism alliance

In 2005 the university accepted the principles and practice of the so-called 'Bologne Process,' which resulted in implementation of a new, three-level education system. Simultaneously, the new state standard topics were issued for all courses run at Polish universities. The new applied geology course standards have been extended leaving limited space for specialized tourism topics. Moreover, new trends have emerged in the tourist industry, related to ideas of geoconservation, protection of Earth heritage and geoparks. Thus a demand has been generated for specialists with broader knowledge and understanding of environmental problems. As a result, the Geotourism specialization has been shifted to the environment protection course.

The alliance between environment protection and geotourism enabled academics to improve education in geotourism. Graduates still obtain a relevant knowledge of Earth sciences, which enables them to develop tourist products linked to geosites, which lead to specialized excursions and interpretation of the geological and geomorphologic features as seen by participants. However, students also gain an extended knowledge and better understanding of environmental issues and, of course; they are well-educated in tourism industry topics.

The tourism and recreation/geotourism alliance

Although studies in geotourism at the faculty appeared to be the great success, in September 2009 a new course in tourism and recreation commenced. This course is quite popular at human-science-oriented universities but had never been implemented up to now at the Technical University in Poland. This is an entirely different proposal to the courses described above as it is directed towards those candidates who are keen to study geotourism but are unable to satisfy the requirements of an engineer degree course. This quite sizeable group of potential students has always been present in the educational market but this market has expanded significantly after an unfortunate reform of the Polish education system in 2002 when mathematics was excluded from obligatory topics of the high school state certificate examination, which resulted in a dramatic decline in knowledge and competence in mathematics. The course is, however, consistent with the 'Bologne Process' and includes six semesters of I level studies leading to the BSc degree followed by four semesters of II level studies leading to the MSc degree.

At the beginning of this new teaching experiment I level studies will commence. The structure of the course includes the package of state standard topics and specialized topics. The state standard (semesters I–III) amounts to 1000 teaching hours dealing mostly with various aspects of tourism industry in abroad sense, supported by human sciences, economy and a foreign language course, which at the faculty contains an extended number of teaching hours of obligatory English. The specialized topics (semesters III–VI) comprise the Earth sciences package (e.g. basic geology, applied geology, geological and tourism mapping, totalling about 350 teaching hours), the tourism package (the next 350 teaching hours) and the optional topics (additional Earth, environmental and human sciences issues extending the knowledge of graduates, total 120 teaching hours) to be chosen by the students. Moreover, the course contains about 300 teaching hours of field practical training (including basic geology, tourism mapping and tourist attractions of Poland and Europe).

Discussion and conclusions

Geotourism is a relatively new aspect of tourism. It is directed towards the more ambitious tourists who are interested in Earth and environmental sciences and who seek more detailed knowledge of abiotic nature. Geotourism opens new fields of activity for the tourist industry due to the great number and extreme diversity of abiotic nature objects (geosites), which can be found in any country in the world and which can be relatively easily developed and offered as tourist products. Simultaneously, geotourism helps to spread knowledge and understanding of the Earth heritage and acceptance of public opinion for the protection of geodiversity.

The future of geotourism in Poland depends on the new initiatives undertaken by various institutions and working teams. Three groups of such initiatives have recently emerged in Poland: large-scale – geoparks, medium-scale – thematic trails and small-scale – geosites. The most comprehensive form of popularization and protection of the Earth heritage – and, simultaneously, the best geotouristic targets – are geoparks. Currently, at least six geoparks are at various stages of planning and organization in Poland. However, a geopark is a complicated structure. Its organization and final acceptance as a member of the European Geopark Network require long and laborious procedures with many formal (bureaucratic) steps to be resolved. It also needs thorough planning, efficient management, significant investments as well as acceptance by and close cooperation with the local communities and local authorities (see Zouros, 2008).

The medium-scale initiatives are for thematic trails. Such trails are definitely less expensive and easier to organize than the geoparks as these are based mostly upon the existing tourist infrastructure. An example is 'The Petroleum Trail' – an initiative undertaken by the Local Tourist Institution in Krosno (southeastern Poland) in cooperation with local authorities and its Ukrainian partners (Radwanski, forthcoming). The project was financed by the European Union and completed in 2005. This trans-border trail is directed generally to motorized tourists and cyclists, and leads from Jasło town in Poland to Lviv in Ukraine. It includes several sites related to the birthplace and early stages of the world petroleum industry in southeastern Poland and western Ukraine, supplemented by leading historical and cultural monuments in the area.

The small-scale initiatives can be developed at any place in the country where geotouristic objects exist. The identification and assessment of such sites have already started with the 'Catalogue of Geotouristic Objects in Poland' and, hopefully, will be continued in the future. An example of a small-scale proposal, currently under discussion, is the educational trail 'The Cradle of World Petroleum Exploitation' (Radwanski, forthcoming). It is a short, thematic round trail based on the famous Open-Air Museum of the Petroleum Industry in Bobrka – the site where the world petroleum industry was born in 1854. The trail, addressed to motorized tourists as well as to cyclists and hikers, leads through a few towns and villages where early petroleum exploration, drillings and exploitation of oilfields took place in the 19th and 20th centuries and where the relics of equipment and machinery can be seen. Such local initiatives can be easily and quickly developed at low expense, and promoted via the Internet.

Education in geotourism responds to the new employment opportunities which have emerged at the beginning of the 21st century as a result of both the rapidly growing tourist industry and rapidly expanding developments in Earth heritage protection and conservation. The entirely new proposal of MSc/engineer geological studies merged with tourism has been the great success at the AGH-University of Science and Technology in Krakow within a difficult educational market in Poland, in which state-owned universities had to undertake tough competition with rapidly growing private schools. It was shown that the Technical University itself and engineer degree studies can be a productive environment for education of specialists for the tourism industry in the same way as for the mineral industry, metallurgy or material science. Its success has been noticed by other universities and currently geotourism specializations are run at several, state-owned and private universities in Poland.

The geotourism specialization created a new type of specialist, well-educated in Earth/environmental sciences and in tourism. Most of the graduates (about 300 in 10 years) found jobs in the tourism industry in Poland and in Europe. The changing educational and labour market forced the faculty to move geotourism from applied geology to environmental protection courses and, finally, to initiate tourism and recreation studies. However, all these alternatives were (and are) deeply rooted in Earth sciences, as expressed by a large number of geological topics, because such knowledge is crucial for successful operation within a competitive market of tourism services, particularly in the specialized area of geotourism.

References

Alexandrowicz, Z. (ed.) (1994) '*Magnum Sal* – monument of world nature heritage', *Chronmy Przyrode Ojczysta*, 50, 7–20 (in Polish).

Alexandrowicz, Z. (2000) 'Crystal caves at the Wieliczka Salt Mine', *Studia Naturae*, 46, 7–10 (in Polish).

Bennett, M.R. and Doyle, P. (1997) *Environmental Geology*, Wiley and Sons.

Birkenmajer, K. (1986) 'Stages of structural evolution of the Pieniny Klippen Belt, Carpathians', *Studia Geologica Polonica*, 88: 7-32.

Cwojdzinski S., 2007. Stolowe Mts (Klodzko-Scinawka Dolna and Srednia-Radkow-

Karlow-Radkow-Tlumaczow-Nowa Ruda), in S.Cwojdzinski and W.Kozdro, *The Sudetes Geotourist Guide*, pp.167-172.

Garlicki, 2008. 'Salt Mines at Bochnia and Wieliczka', *Przegl.Geol.* [*Polish Geological Review*], **56**, 8/1: 663-669.

Gawlikowska, E. (2008) 'Stolowe (Table) Mountains' *Przegl.Geol.* [*Polish Geological Review*], **56**, 8/1: 699-705.

Golonka, J. and Krobicki, M. (2007) 'Dunajec River rafting as one of the most important geotouristic object of the future trans-bordering PIENINY Geopark', *Geoturystyka I[Geotourism]*, **3** (10): 29-44.

Guterch, A.and Grad, M. (1996) 'Seismic structure of the Earth's crust between Precambrian and Variscan Europe in Poland', *Publ. Inst. Geoph. Pol. Acad. Sc.*, M-18: 273.

Hose, T.A. (1995) 'Selling the story of Britain's stone', *Environmental Interpretation*, **10**, 16-17

Hose, T.A. (2008) 'Towards a history of landscape appreciation', *Proceedings of the Inaugural Global Geotourism Conference*, 17-20 August 2008, Fremantle, Western Australia, pp. 9-18.

Krobicki, M. and Golonka, J. (2008) 'Geological history of the Pieniny Klippen Belt and Middle Jurassic black shales as one of the oldest deposits of this region – stratigraphical position and palaeoenvironmental significance' *Geoturystyka* [*Geotourism*], **2** (13): 3-18.

Liszkowski, J. (1982) 'Genesis of recent vertical movements of the Earth crust in Poland', *Rozpr.Uniw.Warsz. [Transactions of the Warsaw University]* **174**, 7-179.

Mojski, J.E. (2005) 'Polish lands in the Quaternary. Outline of morphology', *Wyd.PIG*, pp. 404.

Newsome, D. and Dowling, R.K. (2006) 'The scope and nature of geotourism', in R.K.Dowling and D. Newsome (eds), *Geotourism*, 3-25.

Pozaryski, W. (1990) 'Caledonides of Central Europe as a transpressional orogen composed of terranes', *Przegl. Geol* [*Polish Geological Review*], 1 (in Polish).

Radwanski, A.B. (forthcoming) 'The Ignacy Lukasiewicz Memorial Museum of Oil and Gas Industry in Bobrka and relics of petroleum industry in the vicinity of Krosno (the Polish Fore-Carpathian region)', *Geoturystyka* [*Geotourism*].

Rybar P. and Slomka, T. (2008) 'International Association for Geotourism IAGt', *Proceedings of the Inaugural Global Geotourism Conference*, 17-20 August 2008, Fremantle, Western Australia, pp. 341-346.

Slomka, E., Slomka, T. and Mayer W. (2006) 'The influence of geotouristic attractions on tourist flow in the national parks', in G.M.Timcak (ed.), *Perspectives of Rural Tourism in the New Europe*, 5th International Conference GEOTOUR 2006, 5-7 October , Kosice, Slovakia: pp. 175-180.

Slomka E. and Slomka, T. (2008) 'Selected geotouristic attractions in national parks of Malopolska (southern Poland) and their impact on tourist flow', in T.Slomka (ed.), *Geotourism and Mining Heritage*, 4th International Conference GEOTOUR 2008, 26-28 June, Krakow, Poland, 64-65.

Slomka, T. (2008) 'Geodiversity of Poland', *Przegl.Geol.* [*Polish Geological Review*], **56**, 8/1: 584-587.

Slomka, T.and Kicinska-Swiderska, A. (2004) 'Geoturism – the basic concepts', *Geoturystyka [Geotourism]*, **1**: 2-5. (in Polish only).

Slomka, T., Ptaszek, I., Slomka, K. and Stasiak, M. (2005) www.geoturystyka.pl, in M.Doktor and A.Waskowska-Oliwa (eds), *Geotourism – New Dimensions in XXI Century Tourism and Chance for Future Development*, 2nd International Conference GEOTOUR 2005, 22-24 September, Krakow, Poland pp.104-106.

Slomka, T., Kicinska-Swiderska, A., Doktor, M. and Joniec, A. (2006) *The Catalogue of Geotouristic Sites in Poland*, (in Polish, English summary), AGH, Krakow, Poland.

Slomka, T., Doktor, M., Joniec, A., Kicinska, A., Mayer, W. and Slomka, E. (2008) 'Development of geotourism in Poland and examples of geosites from the catalogue of geotouristic objects in Poland', *Przegl.Geol. [Polish Geological Review]*, **56**, 8/1: 588-594.

Stupnicka, E. (2007) 'Regional geology of Poland', *Warszawa*, (in Polish only).

Znosko, J. (ed.), (1998) 'Tectonic atlas of Poland', *Panstw. Inst. Geol., Warszawa*. (in Polish only) pp. 253.

Zouros, N. (2004) 'The European Geoparks Network. Geological heritage protection and local development', *Episodes*, 27 (3), 165–171.

Zouros, N. (2008) 'European Geoparks Network: transnational collaboration on Earth heritage protection, geotourism and local development', *Geoturystyka (Geotourism)*.

12 Geotourism product interpretation: Rangitoto Island, Auckland, New Zealand

Christian Wittlich, Johannes Gutenberg-Universität Mainz, Germany and Sarah Palmer, Murdoch University, Australia

Introduction

Rangitoto Island, an island of volcanic origin, is a unique geotourism attraction and landmark of Auckland, New Zealand, capturing the attention of tourists since 1890. The island's symmetrical cone and lava slopes rise gradually from the sea, making the shield volcano an iconic landmark for Auckland residents and a popular urban recreation area for domestic and international visitors. This chapter focuses on the effectiveness of different types of interpretive media (e.g. information signs and guided tours) as educative tools for geotourism which occurs in an urban context. It is based on a study which investigated which media were used most, how much visitors learned from them and whether visitors had a preference for a particular medium. While a number of publications address cultural and historical aspects of the island (Murdoch, 1991; Graham, 2005; Philips-Gibson, 2006; Kearns and Collins, 2006) and Rangitoto's natural history (Wilcox, 2007), no publications have investigated tourism on the island and there has been no visitor evaluation of the island and its interpretive media.

Study area

Auckland, New Zealand's largest city, is situated in the upper part of the North Island. With a population of about 1.3 million, the Auckland region accommodates 32.4 per cent of New Zealand's population (Statistics New Zealand, 2008). Although the region is quite densely populated, it offers numerous possibilities for tourism in natural environments. The research location – Rangitoto Island – lies in the Hauraki Gulf and is accessible by a ferry which can transport visitors from Auckland in about 10 minutes (Figure 12.1).

Rangitoto is a shield volcano – a landform characterised by broad, gently sloping sides formed by lava flows that spread in all directions from a central summit vent (Wilcox, 2007) – and is connected by a small land bridge to neighbouring Motutapu Island. It is by far the largest of the 50 cones and craters belonging to the Auckland volcanic field (Wilcox, 2007).

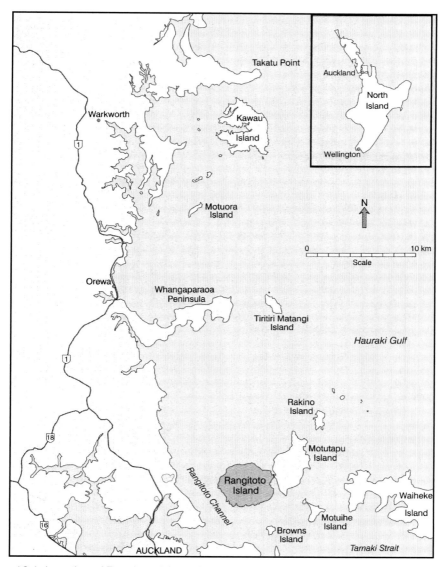

Figure 12.1: Location of Rangitoto Island (Source: Wilcox, 2007)

The Auckland volcanic field has been characterised as dormant and an eruption could therefore theoretically occur at any time. The Auckland volcanoes originate in a zone of melting about 100 km beneath the surface and have been classified as small and monogenetic volcanoes because every eruption springs from a separate batch of magma making its way to the surface (Jamieson, 2004; Wilcox, 2007). It is difficult to predict where and when an eruption in this field will take place. On the isthmus, where most of Auckland's city and suburbs lie, 48 volcanoes have erupted within the past 150,000 years. Most eruptions date from only 10,000–50,000 years ago (Ell, 2004). Although the exact year of Rangitoto's last eruption has not yet been identified, it is widely acknowledged that Rangitoto arose from the sea just 600 years ago, making Rangitoto the youngest volcano of the Auckland volcanic field (Ell, 2004; Wilcox, 2007).

Figure 12.2: Geodiversity of Rangitoto. Top left: The shield volcano with lava flows reaching the sea. Top centre: Vesicles (trapped gas bubbles) in lava near Rangitoto Wharf. Top right: Scoria slope, north of summit. Bottom left: Pahoehoe lava near the coast. Bottom centre: Slab lava flow. Bottom right: Baked mud in lava flow. Source Wilcox, 2007.

Rangitoto offers a rich natural diversity of geological, geomorphological and soil features (see Figure 12.2). Its emergence from the sea started with an explosive, phreatomagmatic eruption (involving external water) forming a low cone, and depositing ash and volcanic mud over the neighbouring and much older Motutapu Island (Wilcox, 2007). These early and largely ferocious eruptions were followed by fire fountains of scoria. At least two phases of scoria cone building can be seen in the summit topography of Rangitoto Island, the earlier phase forming the outlying hills and the later phase creating the main crater and the central cone (Jamieson, 2004). As a result, there are many different volcanic rocks to be found on the island. The basaltic slopes consist mostly of a'a flows[1] of three types:

♦ block a'a flows
♦ clinkerly a'a flows (broken into smaller pieces)
♦ slab flow lava (large pieces of lava 2–10 m across)

The latter represents the broken crust that sat above the underlying moving lava (Homer *et al.*, 2000). Another type of lava, the ropier and slicker pahoehoe, is present in places along parts of the track leading to the summit and is considered to be from the earliest

---

1 There are two major types of lava flow, referred to around the world by their Hawaiian names: pahoehoe, a more fluid flow with a smooth to ropy surface; and aa (or a'a), a more viscous flow, rough and scoriaceous, whose surface is covered by thick, jumbled piles of loose, sharp blocks. Both types have the same chemical composition; the difference seems to be in the eruptive temperature and the speed of movement of the flow (Encyclopaedia Britannica, 2009).

phase of lava outpouring (Wilcox, 2007). In addition, there are lava caves on the island, some of which are accessible via small holes in the rock.

In addition, Rangitoto illustrates how the geological evolution of a volcanic landscape has led to diverse landforms serving as habitats in which an even richer biodiversity has evolved. Botanically, Rangitoto is an outstanding example of primary succession – the colonisation of ground by vegetation for the first time. This is despite the lack of water, the limited availability of soil and the dark lava reaching surface temperatures up to 70°C (Jamieson, 2004; Wilcox, 2007).

Tourism on Rangitoto Island

Rangitoto Island has been a popular day-trip destination for Auckland residents ever since it was designated a public domain in 1890. The opening of the first track in 1897 attracted 2500 people to the island (Jamieson, 2004). In an era of poor infrastructure and few cars, when holidays afar were beyond the reach of most, the opportunity to get away from everything in the proximity of Auckland was embraced enthusiastically (Jamieson, 2004). During the 1920s and 1930s, prisoners were brought to the island where they built the main infrastructure (Wilcox, 2007). Furthermore, holiday home sites were leased to help finance the island's development. For more than 80 years, there have been small numbers of people on the island, including a few permanent residents (Department of Conservation, 2003). Nowadays, Rangitoto tourism has a more international focus with around 80,000 people visiting the island per year (Wilcox, 2007).

Resources facilitating public education

A variety of interpretive media (see Figure 12.4) can be found on the island (on-site), such as information signs and guided tours, but visitors may have also accessed media located away from the island (off-site). It covers a variety of topics including the natural history (geology, volcanism, vegetation, flora and fauna) and the cultural history (Maori and European) of the island. Sources of off-site media include:

♦ Guide books (e.g. Lonely Planet series)
♦ School books
♦ School field trips
♦ Tourism brochures
♦ Friends and family
♦ Auckland City Council
♦ Computer information at Sky Tower observation deck
♦ I-Site (New Zealand-wide tourism information centre)
♦ Department of Conservation website
♦ Informational films
♦ Auckland Museum (at the time when field work was conducted, an exhibition focused on volcanoes and Rangitoto Island)

Sources of on-site interpretive media – the focus of the study – are guided tours (a temporary and regular operator), trail-side information signs and information shelter posters.

Guided tours

♦   **Regular tour:** The tractor tour operated by the ferry company is a fully commentated guided tour of four to five hours' duration, including the ferry transfer to and from Auckland or Devonport, a tour of the island in a 'carriage' pulled by the tractor, and a hike to the summit of the volcano via the 900 m boardwalk. Each tour caters for up to 50 people and operates daily on weekdays and twice a day on weekends. It costs NZ$55 per adult and $27.50 per child. The tour guide drives the tractor and uses a microphone to talk to tourists about the natural features (geology, geodiversity, biodiversity) and cultural features (Maori and European history) of the island. At this stage the visitors have no opportunity to ask questions of the guide, but are able to do so during the hike to the summit.

♦   **Temporary tour:** During the study period, a free guided tour was offered in conjunction with Auckland's Heritage Festival (15–30 September 2007). This was led by Dr Mike Wilcox (author of the book *Natural History of Rangitoto Island*) and Susan Yoffe (an expert on the cultural history of Rangitoto).

Trail-side information signs

There are several tracks for hikers who want to explore the island on their own (see Figure 12.3). Information signs along the Coastal Track, along the Summit Track and at the summit explain the natural and cultural features of the island.

Information shelter posters

There is an information shelter close to Rangitoto Wharf containing material not directly addressed by the other signs. The posters in the shelter also include some general safety and environmental rules and guidelines which apply to the whole island.

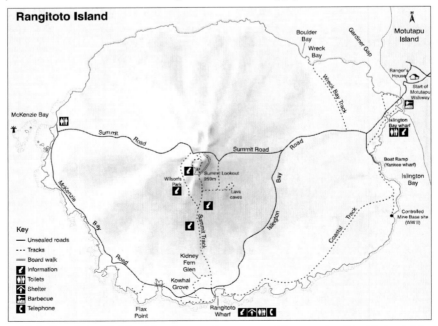

Figure 12.3: Rangitoto Walking Map (Source: Department of Conservation, New Zealand, http://csl. doc.govt.nz/parks-and-recreation/places-to-visit/auckland/auckland-area/rangitoto-island-scenic-reserve)

Figure 12.4: Rangitoto's interpretive media (Source: C. Wittlich)

A: Tourists on the guided tractor tour
B: Tourists reading information on the self-guided trail
C: Information sign on a walk trail
D: Information shelter
E: A poster in the information shelter

Testing the effectiveness of on-site interpretive media

It has been widely acknowledged that interpretive facilities play a central role within geotourism, potentially expanding a tourist's aesthetic appreciation of a site to an understanding of its geology and geomorphology (Dowling and Newsome, 2006). Within the broader ecotourism literature, there is also acceptance that interpretation can achieve learning (Lee and Balchin, 1995; Weaver, 2001; Lück, 2003; Fennell, 2003). Additionally, it is suggested that interpretation will not merely expand knowledge but that this increased knowledge may translate into an attitude change towards the environment (Phillips, 1989; Butler, 1993; Orams, 1997). Whether attitude change can result in behaviour change is contentious, and linear models suggesting that this is the case have been criticised as simplistic in social and educational psychology (Russell, 1999; Lee and Moscardo, 2005). However, whether or not this is the case, a starting point is to assess the degree to which interpretive media has been effectively conveyed to a visitor (Phillips, 1989).

The Rangitoto study focuses only on knowledge gain and attitudes to the interpretive media itself, and does not attempt to measure (environmental) attitude or behaviour change. There are two ways to assess the effectiveness of knowledge gain – one which measures conceptual learning (how visitors receive underlying interpretive messages and relate it to existing knowledge) and one which measures the acquisition of facts (Tubb, 2003). The latter was employed in this study.

Approach and methods

The voluntary and transient nature of tourists as learners presents a challenge in assessing the effectiveness of interpretive media and whether any learning has taken place. However, the pre-visit/post-visit survey is an accepted method of measuring knowledge gain in terms of acquisition of factual knowledge (Hughes and Morrison-Saunders, 2002; Tubb, 2003). Using this method, visitors complete a quiz before visiting a site and again after visiting the site, having been exposed to the interpretive media. Although testing the same group of people would seem to provide the best means of comparison, Lee and Balchin (1995) note that this method can create bias because the respondent's awareness of the displays has been heightened by the pre-visit test. Studies such as that by Tubb (2003) purposely use different (but statistically comparable) samples for the pre- and post-tests to avoid this issue. This was the approach adopted for this study. A pilot study which indicated that visitors to Rangitoto were reluctant to complete the same test twice confirmed that this was also a practical approach.

The pre-visit group was defined as those who had not visited the island but were willing to do so. This sample was drawn randomly from tourists waiting at Auckland Harbour for the ferry to Rangitoto Island. The post-visit group was defined as those who had just visited Rangitoto and were expected to have gained knowledge about the site. This sample was drawn randomly from tourists at Rangitoto summit. At this location participants had already been exposed to the various interpretive media (signs and/or guided tour). The quiz consisted of 10 statements about cultural and natural aspects of Rangitoto, to which respondents could answer 'True', 'False' or 'Don't Know'. The statements were formulated from a convergence of what visitors can learn from the guided tractor tour and from the information signs. If a visitor had carefully listened to the guide or carefully read each information sign along the path to the summit, it would be possible to answer all questions correctly. The quiz was pre-tested by a tour guide who answered all questions correctly.

Participants were also asked their reason for visiting, if they had visited the site before, if they had prior media experiences, if they had any prior knowledge about Rangitoto and how this knowledge was sourced. (Only visitors who indicated that they were first time visitors and had never heard about Rangitoto were candidates for the measurement of knowledge gain.) Additionally, post-visit participants were asked what sources of information they had used to complete the quiz, if they had read the information signs on the Summit Track and to what degree, and suggestions for possible improvements to the site (open-ended question). They were also asked to indicate the extent to which they felt four statements regarding environmental education applied (from 'Strongly applies' to 'Doesn't apply at all'). Another question asks participants to indicate issues that are important in a tourism context, with seven possible responses including 'conservation of nature', 'recreation' and 'education'.

A small number of face-to-face semi-structured interviews were conducted with tourists at Rangitoto Wharf after they had completed their tour of the island, and with participants in the Heritage Festival free guided tour. These provide interesting insights which help to contextualise the questionnaire results.

Results

Of the 310 questionnaires which were correctly filled out, 108 were from the pre-visit group and 202 were from the post-visit group. Around 45 per cent came from New Zealand, reflecting domestic tourism, while 55 per cent were international tourists (mainly from Europe). About 30 per cent indicated that they were returning visitors. The majority of visitors (75.2 per cent) indicated that their main reason for visiting Rangitoto was for leisure, followed by hiking (36.5 per cent), learning (10.6 per cent) and other (9.7 per cent) (see Figure 12.5).

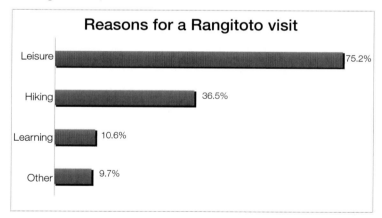

Figure 12.5: Main reasons for a Rangitoto visit – multiple responses were possible (*n* = 310)

Knowledge gain

Using cross-tabulation to compare the quiz results of the pre- and post-visit groups, the proportion of correct answers was shown to be higher (about 20 per cent) in the post-visit group for all questions, and statistically significant for two of the questions (numbers 2 and 6).[2]

---

2 The *p*-value is 0.034 for question 2 and 0.024 for question 6 (significant at the 0.05 level).

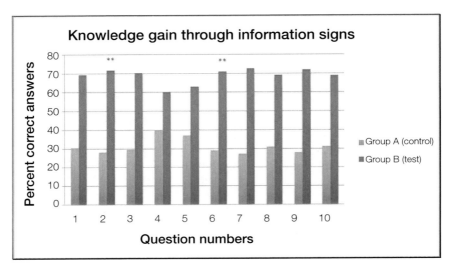

Figure 12.6: Knowledge gain through information signs – a comparison of pre-visit (A) and post-visit (B) groups to Rangitoto Island.** significantly different at 0.05 level (*n* = 167)

The most effective medium?

Although visitors often prefer putting questions to a knowledgeable guide, so that guided tours are a suitable on-site medium (Lück, 2003), the questionnaire data showed that self-guided tours using trail-side information were more popular with tourists. The results of the question 'What sources of information did you make use of today?' show that most respondents (69.3 per cent) made use of the information signs, while only 6.9 per cent (14 people out of 202) had tickets for the guided tractor tour (Figure 12.7). At least 19.3 per cent of respondents made use of the information shelter at Rangitoto Wharf, while some respondents had other sources of information and some did not make use of any source of information.

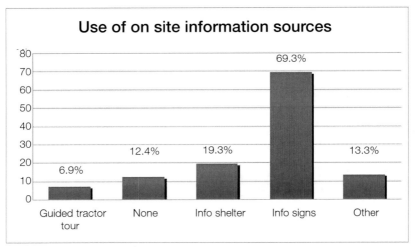

Figure 12.7: Sources of on-site information Rangitoto visitors made use of before completing the survey – multiple responses were possible (n = 202)

While it was the intention to compare the effectiveness of the different media using the knowledge gain quiz results, there were insufficient tractor tour participants for a meaningful statistical comparison with the group which used only information signs. However, comments from the interviews help provide insight into visitors' preferences for one medium over another, or indeed for a combination of interpretive media.

Information signs

The Summit Track was walked by 88.1 per cent of the (post-visit) surveyed population. Almost two-thirds of participants (64.4 per cent) said they read the signs along the track while only about a quarter read every sign from beginning to end. More than half (55.4 per cent) said they enjoyed reading the signs.

Comments from the interviews suggest that younger hikers were more focused on walking than on reading, perhaps motivated by the physical challenge, while older hikers – with perhaps a lower level of fitness – welcomed the chance to pause to read the signs. A possible link between age/fitness and attention to information signs is worth probing.

Information shelter with posters

Only 19.3 per cent of visitors made use of this facility, while more than 80 per cent did not pay attention to it. Comments from the interviews show that there is a need to direct visitors' attention to the information shelter to provide more people with important details:

> *The posters are very good. I think only from what we have seen they could be a little bit more informative about the state of the path … I think this [information shelter] could be set out a little bit more clearly and a little bit more to draw you in before you set off on the walk. To be honest, we walked straight past it this morning because we did not realise it was what it was.* (Patt, 57)

To attract visitors to this shelter may be challenging but worth undertaking. In addition, this part of the infrastructure has considerable potential to increase interpretation on the island, by such means as more informal hands-on education to engage youngsters. A teacher from the UK suggested:

> *interactive things where they can have their hands on … You would probably almost need a little mini cinema, an I-Max, to attract youngsters. An educational facility like that would be nice and could be placed where the information shelter is.*

Guided tours

It seems surprising that only 14 out of 202 visitors took part in the guided tractor tour. Without further investigation, it is only possible to speculate as to the reasons for this. Some interviewees cited price as a deterrent, particularly for locals. An Auckland resident commented:

> *I like guided tours … but I would not pay NZ$30 or $40 just to go on a guided tour. I think the tractor tour is too expensive, especially for a family.*

Another comments:

> *Because we live in Auckland, I would rarely pay for a guided tour, but if I was not from around the area I would probably be happy to come over and go for the tour.*

It may be the case that international tourists would be more willing to pay for a tour because they do not have the opportunity to easily return on another occasion. Some comments were related to safety and guidance. A young English couple stated:

> *We enjoyed the tractor tour and the good comments but there is a lack of instructions. For instance, when the guide gives us some time to explore the lava caves we would have appreciated to know if we are allowed to crawl into the dark caves or not.*

In general, however, interviewees who participated in the tractor tour or the free tour (as part of the Heritage Festival) enjoyed their tours, appreciating the interaction with a knowledgeable guide.

An ecotourism student commented:

> *a guided tour offers a much deeper learning experience – one that is hard to forget. Through a guided tour a visitor can become a mindful visitor. This is more important than just learning from the media.*

The reference to being a 'mindful visitor' echoes a concept spoken about by Moscardo (1996) and Tubb (2003). The latter suggests that interpretation aims to produce 'mindful' rather than 'mindless' visitors – that is, visitors who will be prompted to reassess their views by engaging with information that is intellectually and emotionally stimulating. 'Mindfulness' is most likely to be related to the tourist's level of control or influence over the situation, the relevance and variety of the information, and novelty value (Moscardo, 1996).

Combination of media

A recent investigation by Smith and Weiler (2009) found a clear relationship between the number of interpretive experiences visitors had and the kind of knowledge they took away from their visit. That is, the more interpretive experiences visitors were exposed to, the better the outcome. Some interviewees expressed a preference for a combination of media, recognising the strengths of each:

> *They all [interpretive media] have their advantages and disadvantages. The guided tour is good because you hear and learn things that are not in the signs. Then again the guided tour is restricted in where they are going and you can not go off. The signs and the posters are good because it means that you can go at your own pace and choose to read it or not and move on to the next one.*
>
> (Norman, 60)

> *I actually quite like both [guided tour and information signs] and it is good to have more opportunities. If you choose to go on your own you can pick up the information from the signs or you can go for the guided tour if you want.*
>
> (Bridget, 52)

Suggested improvements

Visitors' responses to the open-ended question 'What are your suggestions for improvement of the site?' are presented in Table 12.1. Many respondents suggested multi-lingual information signs and the provision of more information – about birds, plants, geology and history for example. A common suggestion also was the installation of a sign at the summit pointing out the surrounding areas and places of interest. There are spectacular

360° views from the summit, stretching over the surrounding islands and the mainland. Such a sign could highlight the other volcanic cones in sight, placing Rangitoto Island within the context of the Auckland volcanic field.

Table 12.1: Visitors' comments regarding possible improvements to Rangitoto on-site media. (Comments which appeared more than once have been marked with an asterisk – *).

On-site media
Brochures
- Have information brochure available at Rangitoto wharf in waterproof case
- Small information book on the island

Guides
- Guided walking tours discussing geology and plant life
- Robot guides

Information signs
- More information along route
- The information signs could be less extensive and more comprehensive instead
- Update the information signs along the track. More fun facts, not so boring
- Need more information sign boards along the tramping track
- All of the sign content was very basic
- Give brief summaries
- Upgraded signs
- The information signs are a bit old and tired
- Multi-lingual information signs*

Direction signs
- More direction signs
- Get walking times correct.
- Add maps to show the route

Content
- At the summit there should be a sign pointing out the geography and names of all the surrounding islands and which way is north*
- Photographic satellite map at top to show geographic locations towards view of city
- More information about birds/history
- More detailed information about geology on notices*
- I'd like to see some labelled plants*
- Sign at bottom describing the exact terrain of the upward paths

The following suggestions could be considered to improve the quality of geo-interpretation on the island:

♦ Interpretive media, signs in particular, should offer a broad and a narrow focus on geological issues, emphasising Rangitoto's uniqueness but also the island's place as one of about 50 volcanic cones in the Auckland field (and in relation to the Pacific 'Ring of Fire')

♦ Since maps are an important way of introducing a geologically significant area, at Rangitoto summit a sign with a map pointing out the neighbouring islands and other specific geological features within sight would be useful

♦ Often interpretive signs are installed at locations that are easy to access. However, it would be better to place them directly at the points of interest (e.g. explaining the different kinds of rock or how lava caves have been formed).

Conclusion

In this comparison of interpretive media on the volcanic island of Rangitoto near Auckland, New Zealand, three types of interpretive media were investigated: information signs, posters at an information shelter and guided tours. The main aims were to determine which medium was used most by tourists, how much visitors learned from each type and if there was a clear preference for one particular medium.

The information signs were the medium used most by visitors (almost 70 per cent). Many people appreciated the information signs because they were able to see as much or as little as they desired at their own pace. A knowledge gain quiz revealed an increase in knowledge of nearly 20 per cent between the pre-visit group and the post-visit group, indicating that interpretation can achieve learning (as per Lee and Balchin, 1995). It was not possible to statistically determine which medium achieved the greatest degree of knowledge gain, due to the low number of participants on the guided tour. Nevertheless, interview participants who participated in guided tours stated a clear preference for these, mainly because they allowed interaction between the participant and the guide.

Although there are clearly many positive interpretive experiences on Rangitoto, comments from more than 50 questionnaires and about a dozen visitor interviews provide a good starting point for ideas to improve interpretive media on the island, and indeed at other geotourism sites. Many respondents expressed a desire for more information about the geography and geology of the island. Rangitoto's location - so close to a major urban centre - affords a unique opportunity to develop volcano tourism as an exciting aspect of geotourism.

Acknowledgements

Thanks to Michael Lück, Manfred Domrös, Richard Le Heron, David Newsome, Stephan Heym and Geoffrey Miller for their constructive criticism and support, and to the German Academic Exchange Service (DAAD) for funding Christian Wittlich's academic year in New Zealand.

References

Butler, J.R. (ed.) (1993) *Tourism and Sustainable Development: Monitoring, Planning, Managing*, Department of Geography Publication Series Number 37, University of Waterloo.

Department of Conservation (2003) Hauraki Gulf Marine Park brochure.

Dowling, R. and Newsome, D. (eds) (2006) *Geotourism*, Oxford: Elsevier.

Ell, G. (2004) 'The curious life of Rangitoto', *Forest and Bird*, **311**, 26-32.

Encyclopaedia Britannica (2009) 'Science and technology – Pahoehoe', accessed from http://www.britannica.com/EBchecked/topic/438352/pahoehoe, on 19 June 2009.

Fennell, D. (2003) *Ecotourism: an Introduction*, 2nd edn, London: Routledge.

Graham, P. (2005) *Maori Legends of the Land – Maori Tales and Traditions*, 2nd edn, Takapuna: Bush Press of New Zealand.

Homer, L., Moore, P. and Kermode, L. (2000) *Lava and Strata. A Guide to the Volcanoes and Rock Formations of Auckland*, Wellington: Landscape Publications.

Hughes, M.J. and Morrison-Saunders, A. (2002) 'Impact of trail-side interpretive signs on visitor knowledge', *Journal of Ecotourism*, **1** (2/3).

Jamieson, A. (2004) 'Rangitoto: island volcano in the City of Sails', *New Zealand Geographic*, **68**, 17-37.

Kearns, R., and Collins, D. (2006) ' "On the rocks": New Zealand's coastal bach landscape and the case of Rangitoto Island', *New Zealand Geographer*, **62**, 227-235.

Lee, T. and Balchin, N. (1995) 'Learning and attitude change at British Nuclear Fuel's Sellafield visitors centre', *Journal of Environmental Psychology*, **15**, 283–298.

Lee, W. H. and Moscardo, G. (2005) 'Understanding the impact of ecotourism resort experiences on tourist's environmental attitude and behavioural intentions', *Journal of Sustainable Tourism*, **13** (6), 546-565.

Lück, M. (2003) 'Education on marine mammal tours as agent for conservation – but do tourists want to be educated?', *Ocean and Coastal Management*, **46** (9-10), 943-956.

Moscardo, G. (1996) 'Mindful visitors: heritage and tourism', *Annals of Tourism Research*, **23** (2), 376-397.

Murdoch, G. (1991) 'He Korero Tawhito Mo Rangitoto - A brief outline of the Maori Historical Associations with Rangitoto Island', unpublished document.

Orams, M.B. (1997) 'The effectiveness of environmental education: can we turn tourists into "greenies"?' *Progress in Tourism and Hospitality Research* **3** (4), 295–306.

Phillips, A. (1989) 'Interpreting the countryside and the natural environment', in D. Uzzell (ed.), *Heritage Interpretation – the Natural and Built Environment*, London: Belhaven.

Phillips-Gibson, E. (ed.) (2006) *Tamaki-Makaurau. Myths and Legends of Auckland Landmarks*, Auckland: Reed Publishing (NZ).

Russell, C.L. (1999) 'Problematizing nature experience in environmental education: the interrelationship of experience and story', *Journal of Experiential Education*, **22** (3), 123-128.

Smith, L. and Weiler, B. (2009) 'Does more interpretation lead to greater outcomes? An assessment of the impacts of multiple layers of interpretation in a zoo context', *Journal of Sustainable Tourism*, **17** (1), 91-105.

Statistics New Zealand (2008) Quick Stats about Auckland Region, accessed from http://www.stats.govt.nz/census/censusoutputs/quickstats/snapshotplace2.htm?id=1000 002andtype=regionandParentID, on 18 April 2008.

Tubb, K.N. (2003) 'An evaluation of the effectiveness of interpretation within Dartmoor National Park in reaching the goals of sustainable tourism development', *Journal of Sustainable Tourism*, **2** (6), 476-498.

Weaver, D.B. (2001) *The Encyclopaedia of Ecotourism*, Milton: John Wiley and Sons Australia.

Wilcox, M.D. (ed.) (2007) *Natural History of Rangitoto Island*, Auckland: Auckland Botanical Society.

13 Geotourism potential in North Carolina: perspectives from interpretation at state parks

Stacy Supak and Yu-Fai Leung, North Carolina State University
and Kevin Stewart, University of North Carolina at Chapel Hill

Introduction

Established in 1789 as the 12th state, North Carolina lies in the eastern seaboard of the United States of America between the Appalachian mountain range and the Atlantic Ocean. It is ranked 28th with respect to its size (139,389 square kilometers) and is the 10th most populated state with 9.1 million residents as of 2007 (US Census Bureau, 2008). The state was known for its farming/tobacco, textile and furniture industries, but substantial transformation has taken place over the past few decades and now the service industry, led by tourism, is the major part of the state's economy (Gade, 2008).

North Carolina has a unique and rich natural heritage which includes geological, landscape and biological resources that span three physiographic regions: the Appalachian Mountains, the Piedmont Plateau and the Coastal Plain (Horton *et al.*, 1991; Stewart and Roberson, 2007). This natural heritage forms an integral part of the network of attractions enticing local, out-of-state and international tourists, who spent over $17 billion in the state and generated almost 200,000 jobs in 2007 (TIA, 2008). Indeed, North Carolina's tourism promotional material (e.g., travel guides, brochures, websites) routinely highlight physical landscapes such as the Great Smoky Mountains, peaks like Pilot Mountain and geomorphic features such as waterfalls. Many of these geological features and attractions can be found in North Carolina's state park (NCSP) system, which received over 12.8 million visitors in 2007– 2008 (Leung *et al.*, 2009), with an estimated annual economic impact of $289 million to local economies (NCDPR, 2009). Landform-dependent recreation opportunities draw tourists to the state as well, with skiers enjoying the mountains and kitesurfers flocking to sandy beaches at the Outer Banks. In addition, mineral hunting has become a popular tourist activity with several independent contractors offering mine tours, cave tours and gemstone mining.

The geodiversity of North Carolina supports not only aesthetic and economic values, it also offers tremendous potential for research, education and recreation (Gray, 2004). The state capital city of Raleigh hosts the Museum of Natural Science, while the Museum of North Carolina Minerals is located along the Blue Ridge Parkway. Bulletins published by the North Carolina Geological Survey (NCGS) describe the geology at Eno River State Park, Gorges State Park, the Blue Ridge Parkway and the state park system as a whole (Carpenter, 1989; Carter *et al.*, 2001; Wooten *et al.*, 2003; Bradley, 2007).

Although the Roadside Geology Series has decidedly overlooked the southeast with the exception of Florida, other guides are being published to fill the need. Recently, the first geology guide book for North and South Carolina was published with the state-park visiting public as the target audience (Stewart and Roberson, 2007).

In pursuit of an eco-friendly path to development, North Carolina is embracing sustainable forms of tourism, in which geotourism, or tourism based on geoheritage and its conservation (Dowling and Newsome, 2006) seems to have a significant role to play. Similar to ecotourism, geotourism has the potential to support sustainable economic development while cultivating public support for geoheritage conservation (Burek and Prosser, 2008). However, these goals can be attainable only if geotourism opportunities are communicated to nature-seeking as well as causal tourists. Hence, interpretation is the key to connecting sustainable tourism with geoheritage conservation (Hose, 1996, 2006).

While there is a wealth of information about the resource base (geoheritage) and park facilities (infrastructure) that are important for geotourism development, we know far less about interpretation services that facilitate geotourism experiences. Two published studies seem to be particularly relevant to our discussion. Hose (1996) reports results from visitor studies on three geoheritage sites in the UK, which suggest a need for more interpretation and using appropriate vocabulary in interpretive materials. In China, Wei and Wang (2007) evaluated the effectiveness of interpretive materials and programs in Yuntaishan World Geopark using a visitor survey. The respondents were found to have a strong preference for interactive interpretation through interpreters or multimedia, and they were more interested in the scientific explanation on Yuntaishan's landform than in the fairy tales related to the site. These two studies point to the need for more evaluation of interpretive programs and materials in support of geotourism.

The purpose of this chapter was to take a first look at the current status and potential of geotourism in North Carolina from an interpretive perspective using state parks as an example. We were interested in the extent to which North Carolina's geoheritage is communicated to state park visitors and in what ways. We begin with a concise review of geoheritage in North Carolina. The rest of the chapter focuses on the results of a recent survey of state park managers on geoheritage resources and their interpretation. Implications to management and research are discussed in light of survey results.

Geoheritage in North Carolina

The varied landscapes in North Carolina are controlled for the most part by the underlying geology (Figure 13.1). The Blue Ridge Mountains make up the westernmost part of the state and include over 40 peaks that reach 1800 m in elevation. East of the Blue Ridge, the Piedmont is characterized by rolling hills and subdued topography, although there are several locations in the Piedmont with high elevations (over 900 m). The Coastal Plain makes up the eastern half of the state and has low elevation (about 120 m down to sea level) and low topographic relief. The Atlantic Ocean coast of North Carolina is marked by a chain of narrow barrier islands.

The rocks that make up the Blue Ridge mountains are metamorphic rocks that were created during a series of plate tectonic collisions beginning about 1 billion years ago with the assembly of the ancient supercontinent of Rodinia during an event known as the Grenville orogeny. Billion-year-old metamorphic rocks are ubiquitous in the western part of the Blue Ridge (Hatcher, 1989; Horton et al., 1991).

Rodinia began to rift apart beginning about 700 million years ago, and as the crust stretched, it broke along a series of faults. Crustal blocks slipped down along these faults creating basins that received thousands of meters of sediment. These rift-basin sedimentary rocks, now metamorphosed, are well-exposed in the Great Smoky Mountains and on Grandfather Mountain and the surrounding area. Igneous rocks, such as granite and basalt, were also created during this rifting and can be found scattered through the western Blue Ridge. The rifting eventually led to the complete breakup of Rodinia and the creation of an ancient ocean, known as Iapetus (Hatcher, 1989).

The eastern Blue Ridge also contains metamorphic rocks, but these are younger than those in the western Blue Ridge. Iapetus began to close beginning about 500 million years ago, and a continental fragment, now exposed in the western Piedmont, collided with North America about 460 million years ago (Hatcher, 1989). This event is known as the Taconic orogeny, and the eastern Blue Ridge is mostly made of metamorphosed sediments that were originally deposited on the Iapetus Ocean floor and were then scraped off as the continental fragment collided. The highest point in eastern North America, Mount Mitchell, is made of these metamorphosed ocean floor sediments. As the Taconic collision progressed, rocks of the North American continental margin were overridden and deeply buried. Some of the rocks melted and the rising bodies of magma intruded the metamorphosed sediments. These igneous rocks are now exposed in the eastern Blue Ridge at Whiteside Mountain (Miller *et al.*, 2006).

The Iapetus Ocean continued to close, and parts of the edge of the ancient continent of Gondwana, the continental land mass that consisted of South America and Africa, broke away and eventually collided with North America. These exotic fragments of crust are known as peri-Gondwana terranes and make up the bedrock geology that underlies the eastern half of the Piedmont. These rocks are mostly metamorphosed volcanic rocks and sediments that formed when these terranes were still attached to Gondwana, between about 550 and 650 million years ago. The collision between the peri-Gondwanan terranes and North America is possibly associated with the Acadian orogeny, which is a well-documented orogeny in the northern Appalachians, but its existence in the southern Appalachians is not well-established (Trupe *et al.*, 2003).

Final closure of Iapetus occurred about 330 million years ago when Gondwana collided with North America creating the supercontinent of Pangea. This major continent–continent collision is known as the Alleghanian orogeny and created a Himalayan-scale mountain range in the southern Appalachians. The effects of this collision are well-preserved in the Blue Ridge and in parts of the Piedmont. Major Alleghanian faults separate kilometer-scale sheets of metamorphic rock that were thrust over one another. A spectacular example of one of these thrust faults is exposed at Linville Falls along the Blue Ridge Parkway (Trupe *et al.*, 2004). As happened during the Taconic orogeny, thickening of the crust during the Alleghanian orogeny caused localized melting in deeply buried rocks. These rising bodies of magma crystallized and are now preserved throughout the Piedmont and Blue Ridge, including Stone Mountain State Park (Miller *et al.*, 2006).

North Carolina was tectonically quiet for about 100 million years following the Alleghanian orogeny. Pangea began to rift apart beginning about 220 million years ago during the Triassic period and a series of fault-bounded rift basins formed. Eventually, Africa separated from North America and the Atlantic Ocean was born. Since about 200 million years ago, there has been no active plate boundary in North Carolina. The high mountains have been eroding, and the sediments from this erosion have been deposited on the Coastal Plain and along the Atlantic continental shelf.

The Coastal Plain is underlain by sedimentary rocks that range in age from the Late Cretaceous period (~100 million years old) up to modern sediments that are being deposited along the Atlantic Ocean coast. The low topographic relief of the Coastal Plain is due to the presence of thick, easily erodible sediments that have been deposited on top of the metamorphic rocks of the Piedmont. The barrier islands that line the coast are Pleistocene features that have been actively moving at least since 18,000 years ago and continue to move today, primarily as a result of storms and sea-level rise.

Not only has this series of geological events created the landforms and landscapes which we see today, they have also shaped the ecosystems and play an important role in the development of urban and rural communities in the state. Some of the best examples of natural history and the interplay between nature and culture can be found in North Carolina's parks, natural areas and historic sites, of which the state park system is a major component.

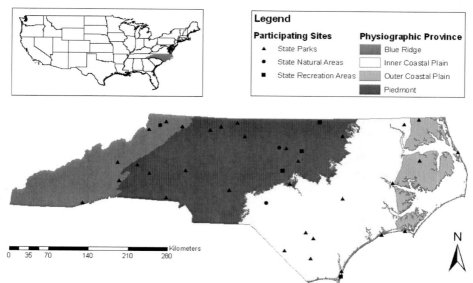

Figure 13.1: Physiographic regions and state parks in North Carolina.

Geotourism: a survey of state park managers

Purpose and methods

In order to gauge the extent to which geotourism in North Carolina is facilitated through interpretation of the state's geoheritage to park visitors, we conducted a survey to examine state park managers' perceptions of the occurrence of geological features and the interpretation of those features. The entire NCSP System consists of 66 different units, covering about 83,000 hectares of lands and waters (Leung *et al.*, 2009). This online survey included managers of 39 North Carolina state parks, state recreation areas and state natural areas (state park units hereafter) which are accessible to the public.

In February 2009, the NCSP system's Lead Interpretation and Education Specialist sent an e-mail request on our behalf to park superintendents urging them to take the 'Geotourism at North Carolina State Parks' online survey. The survey instrument consisted of 10 questions and addressed the following items:

♦   The park's major interpretive themes.

♦   Identification of geologic features and existing interpretation related to a set of 22 basic geologic features listed in the survey. These included 10 landscape elements related to rock outcrops and large boulders and 12 general features such as hills and valleys, erosional features, sand dunes and estuaries. Survey participants also were given an opportunity to identify and comment on features not listed.

♦   Missed educational opportunity in the indoor or outdoor displays.

♦   Perceptions of the level of geotourism interest among the visiting public.

The survey was available online for three months and phone calls were conducted with non-respondents. At the end of the survey period, managers from all 39 target state park units had responded.

Survey results

Of the 39 North Carolina state park units participating in the survey, 15 superintendents responded themselves, while 24 passed the request along to a park ranger who completed the survey. The respondents were asked to rate their own geology knowledge and 21 percent reported moderate geology experience, 69 percent reported limited geology experience and 10 percent reported no geology experience. No respondent self-reported to have extensive geology experience or to be a geology expert.

Despite the low level of self-identified geologic knowledge, the respondents believed that the park system as a whole provides a variety of interpretation of geologic features across the state. Of the 289 total identified features at North Carolina state park units, 46 or 16 percent of the features were declared to have no interpretation. Interpretive talks were identified by the respondents as the most common form of interpretation, connecting to 181 or 63 percent of the identified features. Other forms of interpretation selected included exhibits (25 percent), outdoor signs (12 percent), indoor signs (2 percent) and websites (2 percent). Of the total identified features, 40 or 14 percent were identified as having other forms of interpretation and some respondents described additional publications, external websites or educational programs in which state park units are used for activity-based field trips. Morrow Mountain State Park, for example, conducts one such geology based program entitled 'Old as the Hills.' Pilot Mountain State Park in the Piedmont conducts a hands-on simulation of the process of creating sedimentary and metamorphic rocks and another discussing water quality and how the surrounding terrain affects water quality.

Of the 22 features presented to the survey respondents, creeks, streams or rivers had the highest occurrence, with 82 percent of the parks responding positively with interpretation such as talks, exhibits and outdoor signs offered to visitors. The least commonly reported feature in the state park system was earthquakes, with only two parks identifying and interpreting this occurrence. Only 62 percent of the total parks have exposed rock and park managers believe that 28 percent of the total parks have igneous rocks, 36 percent have metamorphic rock and 38 percent have sedimentary rock. Of the geologic features listed in the survey, respondents said they did not know if their park contained rocks that had been dated, unconformities or fossils more than the other features. The features that are most prevalent, with the least amount of interpretation, are hills and valleys. From this study we also have learned that creeks, rivers and streams along with water-related erosional features are the most interpreted features in the NCSP system.

Each park unit within the NCSP system has its own unique physical features, biota, biology, ecology and cultural history. When a state park is established, a set of interpretive themes are developed as well. These themes provide the foundation from which programs, exhibits and educational publications are promoted. The major interpretive themes for NCSPs vary widely and encompass, geology, ecology, wildlife, water related issues, plant life and culture as reported by the respondents. Each respondent was asked to identify the major interpretive themes of their park and geology or geological features were reported as being a major interpretive theme at 46 percent of the parks.

When respondents were asked for their perceptions of missed educational opportunities in the indoor or outdoor displays, several responses were geologically based. These opportunities included increasing general knowledge of geologic history, coastline erosion processes, lake processes and employing basic learning aids for geology or offering fossil displays. Park specific suggestions included desires to add interpretation of the local mountain formations (Morrow Mountain State Park) and to have 'a knowledgeable geologist to periodically offer geology walks and talks in the park' (Gorges State Park). Missed educational opportunities in some cases were related to perceptions of the public's aptitude and the need to simplify the information presented, so that the 'majority of people can quickly read, understand and remember.' Another respondent claimed that 'visitors don't actually take the time to read the indoor or outdoor displays.'

Without directly surveying tourists at state parks, it is hard to gauge geotourism interest from the visitor's perspective. Park managers were asked for their perceptions of the level of geotourism interest among the visiting public. Only 5 percent believed the public to be very interested, 44 percent somewhat interested and 15 percent not interested. Almost one third of the respondents were uncertain about the geotourism interest of their visitors.

Some examples: the good, the bad and the possible

North Carolina state park units are dispersed across the state and although they are not a random sample of the statewide geology, many were chosen to showcase a portion of the state's natural beauty (Carpenter, 1989). Prior to this study, there was very little known about the geoheritage interpretation in the state park system. We have examined what a geotourist can expect in terms of geology and interpretation. A large disconnect that falls out of this survey is that geology or geological features were reported as being a major interpretive theme at 46 percent of park units, yet the level of geologic knowledge of park superintendents and rangers is self-reportedly low. In many cases the rangers have a strong educational background in natural resources management, with strong foundations in wildlife management and ecology. This disconnect in part is being bridged by the NCGS's willingness to assist state park staff with educational content and activities.

Although geoheritage interpretation is prevalent throughout the NCSP system, one place where geotourism can be better promoted is Stone Mountain State Park, which only offers one paragraph on the general park display interpreting the park's namesake. It reads:

> One of the park's most spectacular features is Stone Mountain, a 600-foot granite dome. This magnificent feature is part of a 25-square-mile pluton, an igneous rock formed beneath the earth's surface by molten lava. Over time, wind, water and other forces gradually eroded the softer layers of rock atop the granite block and exposed the outcrop we see today. Wet weather springs continually carve troughs in the granite as water runs down the mountain's sloping face.

Interestingly, several state parks have taken a more active approach to offering geoheritage interpretive materials and programs which correspond to their respective geologic interpretive themes (Figures 13.2 and 13.3).

Figure 13.2: Geoheritage and its visual interpretation in four North Carolina state park units (also refer to Figure 13.3 for interpretive themes, identified features and interpretations).

Mount Jefferson State Natural Area

Geologic Interpretive Themes: "Mount Jefferson appears to be an inselberg, an isolated mountain surrounded by mountain ranges. The outcrops provide an excellent opportunity for interpretive study of the formation and subsequent erosion of the southern Appalachian Mountains."

Survey results:
- Talks and/or outdoor signs cover topics such as the network of waterways, water and wind erosional features, weathered rocks, monadnocks, cliffs, signs of faulting, interesting minerals, metamorphic rocks and geologically dated rocks.
- There is additional interpretation for the rock cycle, the mountain vista, frost wedging, Lichens and air quality.

Eno River State Park

Geologic interpretive theme: "The metavolcanic rock lying under the water's surface and scattered about the valley tells the story of the Eno River's formation. Lying within the Carolina Terrane, the park contains many interesting geologic features that have enhanced the interpretive opportunities offered. Current programming focuses on the basics of geology, identification of rocks and minerals, and the park's geologic history. Occoneechee Mountain State Natural Area includes the highest point in Orange County at 867 feet and numerous rock outcrops demonstrating evidence of ancient volcanic activity. The recent publication by the North Carolina Geologic Survey, *A Geologic Adventure Along the Eno River*, interprets the many geologic features found along the park's trails and is an invaluable resource for park staff and the public."

Survey results:
- Talks and/or outdoor signs cover topics such as the topography, the network of waterways, water and wind erosional features, monadnocks, cliffs, dykes/sills, interesting minerals, signs of faulting and igneous, sedimentary and metamorphic rocks.

Carolina Beach State Park

Although the interpretive themes for this park are plant related, several geological features were identified through this survey. Additionally, the park's indoor displays highlight the important role of geology in creating distinct habitats within the park.

Survey results:
- Talks and/or exhibits cover topics such as the network of waterways, sand dunes, estuaries, weathered rocks, sedimentary rocks and sink holes.

Cliffs of Neuse State Park

Geologic interpretive themes: "The main feature of the park is the multi-layered cliffs along the banks of the Neuse River. The steep, colorful cliffs are not only an important scenic resource; they are also a valuable educational resource that provides visitors with a view back through time. Most of the exposed cliff layers belong to the Black Creek Formation, which was deposited during the late Cretaceous period more than 66 million years ago. The cliffs present a challenge to park interpreters because they are fragile and difficult to view from overlooks in the park. Therefore, exhibits and creative programming techniques must be used to make the cliffs and their geologic history come alive for park visitors. Activities help students learn how geologists and paleontologists use observations of landforms and fossils to create a picture of the

Cont...

local geography, climate and life forms of the Cretaceous period. The park museum provides models and dioramas that further illustrate this geologic age. Other park programs and museum exhibits demonstrate the geologic processes that formed the cliffs and continue to shape them today."

Survey results:
- Talks and/or exhibits cover topics such as the topography, the network of waterways, water erosional features, weathered rocks, fossils, interesting minerals, sedimentary rocks, cliffs and unconformities.

Figure 13.3: Interpretive themes and survey results for four selected North Carolina state park units.

Implications: a call for geotourism as an educational tool

This survey is reflective of managers' perceptions and may not be a comprehensive look at the geology statewide. Additionally, state parks may not be a complete sampling of statewide geology. Although some parks were established for distinctive geology, many were established for cultural significance, wildlife, ecological value or flora and fauna, as discovered in this survey. Despite these limitations, this exploratory study has identified where geotourism is well promoted and where it can better be promoted at state parks.

For instance, North Carolina should be known for its breadth of landscape from the slowly eroding Blue Ridge Mountains across the hilly river-filled piedmont to the estuaries and sand dunes of the coastal plain. With only a few books published as guides for geology tourism in NC, more must be done to recognize the value of geotourism. The geoheritage discussed in this chapter highlights geotourism assets such as evidence of the Taconic orogeny and associated metamorphic rock formations or the barrier islands that line the coast. These are the resources that can be promoted, which represent the unique types of geotourism opportunities in the state.

Given the discrepancy between the geologic points of interest at state parks and the self-identified lack of geologic knowledge of park managers, the burden of cultivating geotourism infrastructure and interest falls to those who have been geologically trained. The NCGS recognizes this discrepancy and beyond conducting research on state park land, they assist state park staff with educational activities. Furthermore, they have published additional geologic guides to various state parks and protected lands in North Carolina (Bradley, 2007; Carpenter, 1989; Carter et al., 2001; Wooten et al., 2003).

There is great potential for fostering environmental knowledge through tourism, but we must find ways to engage the public for geotourism to flourish. With the large tourism industry and a wide range of natural resources, North Carolina is an ideal backdrop for this agenda. Efforts to engage the public in the enjoyment of geotourism at state parks include a range of interpretive experiences, but new efforts to foster geotourism interest are always needed. Currently one such effort is being made by the NCGS, whose staff is developing a web-based interface for interactive geologic information (Bradley, personal communication). Eno River State Park was chosen as the pilot project for this effort because a significant amount of content already exists (Bradley, 2007). The links for Eno River Interactive can be found at http://www.ncgeology.com/pages/Index_eno.html. The long-term goal is to provide this service for each state park in which geology plays a major role in the significance of the park. The findings from this study will potentially be used in this endeavor.

Concluding remarks

This chapter is a small step toward better understanding of the link between geoheritage and geotourism opportunities in North Carolina. The findings may inform actions taken to better service the geotourism community by increasing availability of interpretation of geologic features and ensuring that the most prominent of geologic features are well represented to the public. This also could include more interactive ways to disseminate information about the geoheritage at state parks such as the Eno River example.

Improving visitor experiences through geotourism promotion will educate and inspire visitors about geoheritage and the value of its protection. When action is taken with the intent of conserving and enhancing geologic and geomorphological features, processes, sites and specimens for the future, it has been termed geoconservation (Burek and Prosser, 2008). Geotourism and geoconservation can be mutually beneficial. The initial activities leading up to geoconservation are in many ways synonymous with the steps leading to cultivating geotourism, such as initial awareness and appreciation of the existence of features, processes, sites and specimens, examination, description, scientific audit and valuing and communication of value with others. A difference occurs in the later steps of geoconservation with the awareness of a threat, conservation audit and protection through policy means (Burek and Prosser, 2008). The development of geotourism can lead to the awareness of threats and the geoconservation efforts at specific sites offering opportunities for geotourism. The use of geoheritage can contribute to the environmental, social and economic pillars of sustainable development through conserving and promoting educationally, scientifically, recreationally and culturally important features.

North Carolina, like the rest of the eastern seaboard of the United States, is on a tectonic passive margin with no 'flashy' geologic phenomena such as active volcanoes or large earthquakes. However, there are other very active geologic processes at work which can affect the lives of many who reside in the region such as river flooding, landslides and beach erosion. All of the geologic process, whether previous or ongoing, impact geoconservation and sustainable development objectives. Other issues happening in states such as New Jersey include the problem of urban sprawl obscuring the majority of interesting geological features (Gates, 2006). With increasing levels of population growth and urbanization in North Carolina, its geoheritage may also be threatened by similar pressure. Public support for geoconservation and for sustainable development of geoheritage-based tourism in NC is therefore critical for both to prosper, and, as Hose (2006) warns us, the absence of interpretation at geoconservation sites might lead to threatened geoheritage. Geotourism not only requires an appreciation or learning infrastructure, but it also requires tourists' interest and their cooperation with respect to appropriate behavior at geoheritage sites.

To understand tourist interest, further studies including visitor surveys may elucidate questions such as how interested is the visiting public in geoheritage and how could geotourism interest be cultivated. These questions would inform the development of tailored and effective interpretive programs to promote scientific understanding and a conservation ethic that would more likely result in positive learning and conservation outcomes. These studies would then help realize the potential to turn regular tourists into geotourists, thereby making mass tourism more sustainable.

Acknowledgements

We appreciate the information and support provided by Siobhan O'Neal and Sean Higgins of the NCSP Service, Phil Bradley of the NCGS and Del Bohnenstiehl of NC State University.

References

Bradley, P.J. (2007) 'A geologic adventure along the Eno River', *North Carolina Geological Survey Information Circular 35*, Raleigh, NC: NC Department of Environment and Natural Resources, Geological Survey Section.

Burek, C.V. and Prosser, C.D. (eds) (2008) *The History of Geoconservation*, London: Geological Society.

Carpenter, P.A. (ed.) (1989) 'A geologic guide to North Carolina's state parks', *North Carolina Geological Survey Bulletin* 91, Raleigh, NC: NC Department of Environment and Natural Resources, Geological Survey Section.

Carter, M.W., Merschat, C.E. and Wilson, W.F. (2001) 'A geologic adventure along the Blue Ridge Parkway in North Carolina', *North Carolina Geological Survey Bulletin* 98, Raleigh, NC: NC Department of Environment and Natural Resources, Geological Survey Section.

Dowling, R. and Newsome, D. (eds) (2006) *Geotourism*, Amsterdam: Elsevier.

Gade, O. (2008) 'The evolving urban and economic structure since 1900', in D.G. Bennett and J.C. Patton (eds), *A Geography of the Carolinas* Boone, NC: Parkway Publishers, pp. 95-140.

Gates, A.E. (2006) 'Geotourism: a perspective from the USA', in R. Dowling and D. Newsome (eds), *Geotourism*, Amsterdam: Elsevier, pp. 157-179.

Gray, M. (2004) *Geodiversity: Valuing and Conserving Abiotic Nature*, New York: John Wiley.

Hatcher, R.D., Jr. (1989) 'Tectonic synthesis of the U.S. Appalachians', in R.D. Hatcher, Jr., W.A. Thomas and G.W. Viele (eds), *The Appalachian-Ouachita Orogeny in the United States. The Geology of North America*, vol. F-2, Boulder, CO: Geological Society of America, pp. 511-535.

Horton, J.W., Jr. and Zullo V.A. (1991) 'An introduction to the geology of the Carolinas', in J.W. Horton, Jr. and V.A. Zullo (eds), *The Geology of the Carolinas*, Carolina Geological Society 50th Anniversary Volume. Knoxville: University of Tennessee Press, pp. 1-10.

Hose, T.A. (1996) 'Geotourism, or can tourists become casual rock hounds?', in M.R. Bennett, P. Doyle, J.G. Larwood, and C.D. Prosser (eds), *Geology on Your Doorstep: The Role of Urban Geology in Earth Heritage Conservation*, London: Geological Society, pp. 207-228.

Hose, T.A. (2006) 'Geotourism and interpretation', in R. Dowling and D. Newsome (eds) *Geotourism*, Amsterdam: Elsevier, pp. 221-241.

Leung, Y.-F., Siderelis, C., and Hoffbeck, D. (2009) 'Statistical report of state park operations: 2007-2008', Raleigh, NC: National Association of State Park Directors.

Miller B.V., Fetter A.H., and Stewart K.G. (2006) 'Plutonism in three orogenic pulses, eastern Blue Ridge Province, southern Appalachians', *Geological Society of America Bulletin*, **118** (1-2), 171-84.

NCDPR (NC Division of Parks and Recreation) (2009) *North Carolina Division of Parks and Recreation, 2009 Annual Report*, Raleigh, NC: NC Department of Environment and Natural Resources, Division of Parks and Recreation.

Stewart, K. and Roberson, M.-R. (2007) *Exploring the Geology of the Carolinas: A Field Guide to Favorite Places from Chimney Rock to Charleston.* Chapel Hill: University of North Carolina Press.

TIA (Travel Industry Association) (2008) *The Economic Impact of Travel on North Carolina Counties 2007*, Washington, DC: Travel Industry Association.

Trupe, C.H., Stewart, K.G., Adams, M.G., and Foudy, J.P. (2004) 'Deciphering the Grenville of the southern Appalachians through evaluation of the post-Grenville tectonic history in northwestern North Carolina', in R.P. Tollo, L. Corriveau, J.B. McLelland, and M.J. Bartholomew (eds), *Proterozoic Tectonic Evolution of the Grenville Orogen in North America, Geological Society of America Memoir*, **197**, 679-695.

Trupe, C.H., Stewart, K.G., Adams, M.G., Waters, C.L., Miller, B.V. and Hewitt, L.K. (2003) 'The Burnsville fault: evidence for the timing and kinematics of Acadian dextral transform tectonics in the southern Appalachians', *Geological Society of America Bulletin*, **115** (11), 1365-1376.

U.S. Census Bureau (2008) *Statistical Abstract of the United States: 2009*, 128th edn, Washington, DC: U.S. Census Bureau.

Wei, D. and Wang, M. (2007) 'Evaluation of the validity of interpretation system for the visitors to Yuntaishan World Geopark in China', in X. Zhao, J. Jiang, S. Dong, M. Li, and T. Zhao (eds), *Proceedings of the Second International Symposium on Development within Geoparks*, Beijing: Geological Publishing, pp. 158-162.

Wooten, R.M., Carter, M.W. and Merschat, C.E. (2003) *Geology of Gorges State Park Transylvania County North Carolina. North Carolina Geological Survey Information Circular*, 31. Raleigh, NC: NC Department of Environment and Natural Resources, Geological Survey Section.

14 Interpretation rocks! Designing signs for geotourism sites

Karen Hughes and Roy Ballantyne, School of Tourism,
University of Queensland

Introduction

Nature-based tourism experiences are attracting increasing numbers of visitors world-wide, a phenomenon that has been attributed to a range of factors including greater flexibility in terms of leisure, mobility and disposable income; a growing public awareness of environment issues; and the desire to escape from 'everyday' routines (Waitt, 2000). Researchers have termed the learning that occurs in these tourism settings 'free-choice learning' because people are free to choose what, where, when and with whom they learn (Falk, 2001).

Information and educational activities delivered during free-choice learning experiences are generally referred to as interpretation. A term originally coined by Tilden (1957), interpretation is a form of communication that presents ideas and concepts in a format that is designed to interest, entertain and inspire visitors (Ballantyne *et al.*, 2000). Unlike education in formal settings, interpretation does *not* consist of lists of facts, figures, and dates but rather, uses illustrative media, first-hand experiences and original objects to impart meaning and demonstrate relationships (Tilden, 1977).

The aim of this chapter is to outline the process of developing interpretive plans and signage for geotourism attractions. Discussion focuses on the importance of understanding and appealing to target markets and the principles and procedures underlying the development of interpretive materials. Wherever possible, examples are provided to illustrate concepts and techniques.

First things first: Developing an interpretive plan

Regardless of the site and/or content, interpretive signs and exhibits should always be guided and supported by an interpretive plan. There are many models and systems for developing interpretive plans (see Trapp *et al.*, 1994; Knudson *et al.*, 1995; Brochu, 2003; Ham *et al.*, 2005), but all have three steps or phases in common:

♦ Defining the objectives of the interpretation
♦ Turning objectives into themes
♦ Selecting the best interpretive medium

1. Defining the objectives

In order to scope out interpretive objectives, interpreters should ask themselves the following questions.

Who are the target audience?

The increasing popularity of nature-based tourism suggests that visitors are no longer likely to be people with specialist knowledge of, or interest in, the natural environment. Indeed, it is widely documented and accepted that visitors to ecotourism attractions (including geological sites) are heterogeneous comprising tour groups, independent travellers, older people travelling independently (grey nomads), backpackers, historians, archaeologists, families with young children, community groups, and school groups all having a wide range of interests, experiences, needs and expectations. Thus, any discussion of what should and should not be offered to visitors must first consider *who* actually visits these sites and *why*. In particular, interpreters need a clear understanding of their main visitor groups – their knowledge, motives, experiences and interests – prior to designing interpretive materials and experiences. If this initial step is ignored, considerable time and effort could be wasted designing materials that visitors are either already familiar with or have little interest in (Chhabra *et al.*, 2003).

Information about key target audiences can be obtained from commercial tourism statistics as well as in-house surveys. If these indicate that potential visitors have limited knowledge of the topics, features and/or processes being interpreted, introductory signs that provide sufficient background knowledge to understand the topics being discussed will be required. This particularly applies if the concepts and processes being interpreted are complex. While geologists can 'read' a landscape and explain the geological processes or events that created certain rock formations and features, most visitors will lack the knowledge and experience to appreciate the significance of the site's features and formations. Thus, as geologists and interpreters we need to 'paint pictures' and create stories to help visitors 'see' and appreciate the significance of what created the landscapes around them. Techniques for achieving these outcomes will be addressed later in the chapter.

What is special about this place?

Answering this question requires ascertaining which features or properties make the geotourism site important, attractive or unique in some way. These could include elements such as geological formations or features, escarpments and views; landscape evolution; cultural traditions and celebrations; artefacts; historic events and/or stories (Ham *et al.*, 2005). This process will assist in identifying possible foci for interpretation.

What are the constraints of the setting or place for the interpretation?

While it might be tempting to interpret many features or rock formations at a site, this is often not practical or desirable. Issues that need considering in the selection of the most appropriate features or areas to interpret include:

1.   Are there extreme weather conditions (e.g. harsh sunlight, severe winds) that make interpretation difficult? Could placing signs in a particular spot cause discomfort for visitors (e.g. reflective glare, sunburn, exposure to wind/rain/cold)?

2.   If tour groups visit the site, is there enough space for large groups to see signs and/or the feature being interpreted?

3.   Does the site have alternative uses which might interfere with the interpretive experience?

Are there visitor management issues?

Many geotourism sites are fragile – effective interpretive planning can ensure these resources are protected by encouraging visitors to behave in ways that minimize negative impacts. Thus, interpretation can include messages relating to touching surfaces, walking on artefacts, and souveniring rocks and other geological artefacts. It is important, however, that infrastructure at the site supports these messages – asking visitors to stay on trails is unlikely to work if trails are poorly defined, difficult to traverse or in need of maintenance.

2. Turning objectives into themes

Once objectives have been defined, interpretive themes can be developed. Themes are the 'big picture' concepts that form the foundation of a site's interpretation – essentially, the ideas that interpreters try to get across to visitors. Themes should encourage visitors to want to learn more about the site, feature, object or event being interpreted. Strong themes present a single idea; they connect audiences to the site by telling them what's important; and they act as a single thread that ties together different pieces of information presented (Regnier *et al*.,1992; Knudson *et al*., 1995; Serrell, 1996, Ham, 1992). Themes also provide a framework that informs the content of interpretive signs and activities (Ham *et al*., 2005).

Several themes can be developed from a single topic, as demonstrated in Table 14.1. The theme chosen should be based on what aspects interpreters want to highlight, how they want visitors to view the site, and what messages they want to convey to visitors.

Table 14.1: Developing Interpretive Themes

Topics/subjects	Themes
Rivers	Rivers: Nature's architects Erosion and deposition – landscape 'engineering' River transport: the brown beneath the blue
Sedimentary rocks	Sedimentary landscapes: layer upon layer Sedimentary rocks: natural recycling
Limestone	Limestone comprises shells and skeletons of snail-like animals Stalagmites and stalactites grow drip by drip

3. Selecting the best interpretive medium

Interpretation can take many forms – talks, discussions, activities, audio-visual presentations, displays, signs and self-guided walks, to name a few. The remainder of this chapter focuses on the design and production of interpretive signs – for an in-depth discussion and practical examples relating to the development of oral presentations see Ballantyne *et al*., (2000).

The key advantages and disadvantages of interpretive signs are listed in Table 14.2. Arguably, the greatest advantage of installing signs at geotourism sites is that they provide a cost-effective method of reaching large audiences in settings which may be remote, difficult to access or simply not suitable for other forms of interpretation such as presentations and audio-visual displays. The main drawback of using signs is that once installed, they are difficult to update or adjust. Issues of on-going maintenance also need to be considered as poorly maintained signs are difficult to read (Merriman and Brochu, 2005).

Table 14.2: Advantages and disadvantages of interpretive signs

Advantages	Disadvantages
Can be used by a large number of visitors	Difficult to alter and/or update
Can be used in almost any setting	Cannot be adapted to seasonal or other
Are available whenever the site is open	regular changes
Are usually cheaper in the long run than staff	Cannot answer questions or adapt informa-
Can provide access to visitors who speak	tion to specific visitors
other languages and, if properly designed,	Can be intrusive in some settings
can provide access for hearing and sight	Must be concise and to the point therefore
impaired visitors.	may not be suitable for complex messages
Can be read by visitors at their own pace	Require effort from the visitor
Are silent and, if well designed and posi-	May not be read in entirety
tioned, can be unobtrusive	
Provide optional interpretation – visitors	
can choose whether or not to access the	
information	

Adapted from Moscardo et al., 2007.

'Connecting' with visitors

Much current research in 'free choice' learning environments focuses on how visitors make sense of the information they encounter (Ballantyne and Packer, forthcoming). Falk and Dierking's (2000) Contextual Model of Learning is widely used to investigate and understand 'free choice' learning. This model assumes that learning is a cumulative process that draws from a wide variety of sources over long periods of time. Thus, visitors' prior experiences and motives for learning influence how they experience particular events, information and environments.

When visitors encounter interpretive signs, 'new' information enters their short-term store. It can only be held here for a few minutes – if it is actively processed it enters their long-term memory but if it is not, it is forgotten. To actively process 'new' ideas, visitors must connect the pieces of new information to each other and to things they already know. This process can be facilitated by linking the unfamiliar or new to something familiar or common. The better interpreters are at designing signs that place objects, features and events into a meaningful context, the greater the chance visitors will assimilate the new information (Falk and Dierking, 1992). If these links are not present, visitors will struggle to make sense of the information presented – the messages will not connect together in any meaningful way; nor will they connect with anything in visitors' existing schemata. As a result, it is unlikely much will be remembered or learnt from the experience.

While it is impossible to design interpretive signs that 'connect' to every visitor, there are a range of techniques and approaches that can be adopted at geotourism sites that will help make material relevant to the majority of audiences. These include using analogies, metaphors and humour; telling stories, particularly those with realistic characters; encouraging visitors to actively participate in activities; and offering suggestions about how to use new information to 'make sense of' other sites, situations and experiences. These techniques are discussed and demonstrated below.

Using analogies, metaphors and humour

Analogies and metaphors inject colour and movement into topics and signs and provide visitors with realistic visual images and reference points. Essentially, analogies and metaphors highlight the similarities between what visitors already know and the topic, event or experience being interpreted. These techniques help visitors take the step from the familiar to the unfamiliar; the known to the unknown. To do this effectively, however, it is important to select common objects and examples – sedimentary landscapes can be compared to layers in a cake; volcanoes compared to a boiling kettle; tectonic plates compared to pieces of a jigsaw puzzle and so on. The sign in Figure 14.1 draws a comparison between stone tools and modern pocket knives.

Figure 14.1: Using analogies to 'connect' with visitors. The text reads:

Ice age pocket knife?

Imagine you had never seen a pocket knife before. The sharp blade suggests it's used for cutting - but cutting what?

Look closely, you might find traces of wood shavings, orange peel or even fish scales on the knife....

....stone tools found in some Aboriginal campsites in south west Tasmania date back to the ice age. Traces of ancient blood found on some of them tell us they were probably used as knives to skin animals and as scrapers to skin animals.

Humour has wide appeal but tends to be subjective so should be used judiciously. Puns are generally safe, as are carefully worded riddles and witticisms. Jokes that ridicule individuals from particular ethnic, social or religious backgrounds are likely to offend visitors and should be avoided (Beck and Cable, 2002).

Telling stories

Stories are powerful interpretive techniques because they encourage visitors to become emotionally involved in the topics being discussed (Regnier *et al.*, 1992). The key to effective story telling is to find human experiences or characters that are related to the topic. In a geotourism context, interpretive signs could explain that much of what we use in everyday life – diamonds, concrete, oil, salt, marble, petrol – comes from geological processes. Alternatively, signs could focus on a particular mineral by asking visitors questions such as 'Did you know that limestone is an ingredient in cement, paper, plastics, paint, tiles, toothpaste and bread?' In terms of human characters, interpretation could focus on the lives of pioneers in the gold rush, scientists who discovered minerals, farmers who introduced irrigation and so on. All such stories relate to how people have used and thus shaped the landscape. Stories about the impact of people on the landscape and the landscape on the people bring a human dimension to the events being interpreted and are thus likely to engage and interest visitors.

Stories can also be used to convey information about non-human topics. For example, canyons could be explained by ascribing human qualities to rivers and describing the erosion processes from the perspective of either the river or the surrounding rocks. Alternatively, interpreters could tell the story of one particular rock, outcrop or other feature over a period of hundreds or even thousands of years. Through this process, interpretive signs can 'teach' visitors about the process of erosion.

Encouraging visitors to actively participate

Research exploring the relationship between interactive elements and learning indicates that visitors enjoy participating in interactive activities; that interactive elements generate positive visitor attitudes; and that memories of such experiences are long-lasting (Caulton, 1998; Falk *et al.*, 2004; Spock, 2004). A common axiom in interpretive circles is that visitors remember 10 per cent of what they hear; 30 per cent of what they read; 50 per cent of what they see; and 90 per cent of what they do (Hooper-Greenhill, 1994).

Successful interactive activities have variable, open-ended outcomes and should be challenging but not threatening. Signs can incorporate interactive components such as features visitors can touch or manipulate, sliding or hinged panels that move to reveal more information, quizzes and puzzles. It is important that these have an underlying educational purpose and are clearly linked to the topics or objects being interpreted. For instance, classifying rocks by looking closely at their structure and composition would be effective, as would asking them to consider which of the 'culprits' (river, wind, ice) formed particular landscapes. Alternatively, asking visitors to order rocks in terms of their weight or preferred colour is unlikely to generate much thought and/or discussion.

Another way of engaging visitors is to ask them questions. This reinforces messages given on-site and helps to consolidate learning. For instance, visitors could be asked to note changes in vegetation, rock strata, and colour of river water, and to reflect upon possible causes of these.

As an example:

> Cliffs near the start of this walk showed the effects of weathering.
> - Can you see similar signs of weathering here?
> - Where is it most evident?
> - What do you think caused this?

It should be noted, however, that this approach is only effective if the answers can be found in the site's interpretation – asking visitors questions they cannot hope to answer is not recommended!

Discuss implications

There is increasing evidence to suggest that interpretation can encourage visitors to adopt environmentally-friendly practices such as staying on paths, not souveniring rocks and flora, and not touching fragile formations (Ham and Krumpe, 1996; Weiler and Ham, 2002). This is important for geotourism as many sites are fragile and require considerable protection. Research also suggests that interpretation has the potential to influence visitors' behaviour after their visit, provided visitors are given specific examples of what they can do to help (Beaumont, 2001; Ballantyne *et al.*, 2007; Ballantyne and Packer, forthcoming). For example, visitors could be asked to consider where petrol comes from, how much they use per week, the cumulative impact this has on the natural resource, what is likely to happen if supply runs out, whether (and how) they could reduce their usage to lessen the impact.

The nitty gritty: text, illustrations and other design issues

As mentioned throughout this chapter, interpretation aims to form connections between new information and something within the visitors' experience. Besides using the techniques described above, interpreters also endeavour to use words, examples and illustrations that are widely known and likely to resonate with a range of target audiences. The following section describes these practices, presenting examples where appropriate.

Selecting effective text

Literacy research suggests that interpretive signs are most effective when they incorporate text that can be understood by 10–12 year olds. The occasional complex word or expression can be added for colour and variety, provided that sentences still make sense if these complex words are not clearly understood (Serrell, 1996). Consider the sign in Figure 14.2 – while factually correct, much of the information would be of little interest to the 'average' visitor and some of the terms are likely to cause confusion.

The following guidelines for crafting text that is easy to read are based on research by Dean (1994); Knudson *et al.* (1995); Punt, (1989) and Serrell (1996).

- Keep sentences short (maximum of 15 words);
- Limit the number of qualifying phrases;
- Use familiar words – avoid technical terms and complex geological explanations;
- Write in concise sentences as complex and/or detailed explanations are unlikely to attract or interest many visitors;
- Express statements in the positive rather than the negative; and
- Use verbs rather than nouns or adjectives derived from verbs.

Figure 14.2: Jargon and technical terms make signs difficult to understand. This text reads:

This granodiorite (a granite rock) formed from a molten magma intrusion deep into the surrounding Neranleigh-Fernvale beds about 220 million years ago (Triassic period). The molten magma, being insulated by the surrounding rocks, cooled very slowly and formed relatively large crystals. The solidified rock has since been uncovered by erosion. Dark fragments of slightly earlier diorite can be seen in places. Hard rounded boulders set in decomposed material beneath sandly soil is typical of weathering granite rocks.

Signs that 'converse' directly with visitors tend to be the most engaging and interesting. One of simplest ways to achieve this is to use active sentence structure and present information as though it were part of a conversation. Signs using active, vivid verbs and pronouns such as 'you', 'me', 'I' and 'we' are particularly effective (Heintzman, 1988; Serrell, 1988; McManus, 1989; Zehr *et al.*, 1991; Ham, 1992). One of the simplest ways to ensure that signs are clearly expressed is to read them out aloud – if the combination of words is rhythmic and easy to say, the sign will be easy to read.

Table 14.3: Rules for making text easier to read

Rule	What to avoid	What to replace it with
Keep it simple	Indicative of…	Shows
	Has been known to be …	Is
	Due to the fact that…	Because
	…must be sufficiently high so as to …	…must be high enough to….
Limit qualifying phrases	Aluminium, making up over 8 percent of the earth's crust, is more abundant than iron, but workable deposits are limited.	Aluminium makes up over 8 percent of the earth's crust. It is more abundant than iron but workable deposits are limited.
Use familiar words	Magnitude	Size
	Terminate	End
	Permeate	Penetrate
Write concisely	Volcanoes assume different shapes according to the relative amount of the various materials they eject. The ejection of abundant solid matter from volcanoes produces a steep cone of cinders.	The shape of a volcano is determined by the type of material ejected. A large amount of solid matter produces a steep cone of cinders.

Rule	What to avoid	What to replace it with
Express statements in the positive.	This area would be infertile if it were not for these ancient irrigation systems.	This area is fertile because of these ancient irrigation systems.
Use verbs rather than nouns or adjectives from verbs.	Land clearing has lead to a reduction in the number of species that grow in this region. Geologists' estimation is that…	Land clearing has reduced the number of species growing in this region. We estimate that…

The sign in Figure 14.3 shows how the topic of glaciers can be 'brought to life' using expressive verbs such as 'rushing', 'pluck', 'spread' and 'gouge' and colourful adjectives such as 'awesome power' and 'vast quantities'.

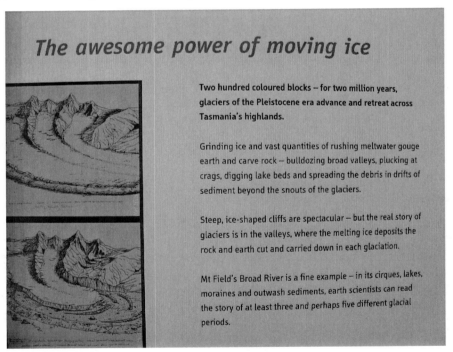

Figure 14.3: Attracting attention with titles and active verbs

Creating eye catching titles

Titles introduce and help to set the 'mood' of the sign. In most instances, visitors are attracted to signs that are headed by eye catching and interesting titles. Compare the two titles 'Faults in the earth's crust' and 'So whose fault is it anyway?' Both mean the same thing but the second is more likely to attract attention than the first. Titles should be short (no more than ten words) and should introduce visitors to the theme of the sign and/or site (Dean, 1994). As illustrated in Table 14.4, titles can include quotes, common expressions, metaphors, alliteration, provocative questions, idioms and other clever turns of phrase (Moscardo *et al*, 2007).

Table 14.4: Examples of attractive titles

Original	Improved version
Nature formed this landscape	Mother Nature flexes her muscles
Rocks evolve over many years	Rock of ages
Glaciers scour out valleys	Glaciers: Nature's bulldozers
Silt is finer grained than sand or gravel	Silt, sand or gravel: Size *does* matter!
Graphite is a key ingredient in lead pencils	2B or not 2B: What's in a pencil?
Changes in pressure create metamorphic rocks	Under pressure: The creation of metamorphic rocks

'Chunking' information

Visitors prefer and are more likely to read signs that seem to have fewer words. One way of making signs appear short is to include only two or three topics or pieces of information in each sign. Some researchers also recommend limiting the number of words per sign, particularly if they are to be read while standing or if visitors are likely to have been at the site for several hours (Bitgood and Woehr, 1986; Serrell, 1996).

Signs can also appear shorter if they are broken up with headings and subheadings. Using headings and subheadings improves visual appeal by dividing information into chunks or layers. This not only helps visitors understand and recall interpretive content (Hartley and Trueman, 1983; Serrell, 1996; Cross, 1998), it also enables them to select the level of detail they wish to read. This is important, as research shows that visitors rarely read *everything* on interpretive signs (Falk and Dierking, 1992; McManus, 1994). By presenting information in chunks or layers, interpreters can arrange text so that visitors only have to read the top layer to understand the sign's main message. Visitors who are interested in a detailed explanation will read subsequent layers; those who only want a brief overview of the site or topic will only read the top layers. To illustrate, in Figure 14.4 the main message that the cave floor is comprised of discarded objects and soil is presented in bold type.

Figure 14.4: Using layering to make text easier to read. This text says:

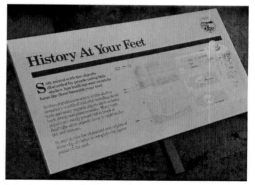

History At Your Feet

Soil, mixed with the objects discarded by people using this shelter, has built up over the years to form the floor beneath your feet.

Archaeological excavations in this shelter revealed a wealth of material including stone tools and many organic objects such as bone, bark, string and plant remains. These objects are rarely preserved in tropical Australia because organic decay is rapid in the hot, wet climate.

Research into the placement and origins of these objects helps to complete the jigsaw puzzle of the past.

Illustrations and colour

Illustrations are particularly effective for showing visitors features, processes or objects that they can't actually see (e.g. inside a volcano, the process of glacial erosion, contour lines,) or to give them an idea of what a particular structure may once have looked like (e.g. landscapes prior to erosion). Illustrations should support themes and messages by enhancing and simplifying information, as is shown in Figure 14.5.

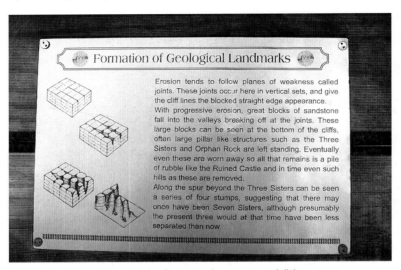

Figure 14.5: Illustrations work well for features that are not visible

Prior to including illustrations, consider the following:

♦ *Are the illustrations relevant to the text?* If there is no logical link between text and illustrations or the illustration does little to enhance or explain the text, illustrations will be redundant.

♦ *Are the illustrations clear and simple?* Illustrations should not require explanatory text and should enable non-readers or those with limited language skills to grasp the sign's main concepts.

♦ *Do illustrations demonstrate one main idea?* It is important not to bombard visitors with too much visual information. Figure 14.6 shows the common practice of displaying every photograph available – the result is often information overload.

Colour can be used to 'set the scene' of interpretive topics and themes. 'Warm' colours (reds, yellows, purple) are often used to attract visitors' attention. These colours suggest that the interpretive topic and associated materials are dynamic, interactive, controversial and/or stimulating (Dean, 1994). 'Cool' colours (blues, greens, violet) are regarded as more relaxing (Denton, 1992; Falk and Dierking, 2000) and consequently, tend to be associated with quiet, more reflective activities. Choice of colour may also depend on the sign's surroundings – signs in bright sunlight are easiest to read if they have light coloured lettering on dark backgrounds, while those in shaded areas are easier to read if they have dark lettering on light backgrounds (Trapp *et al.*, 1994).

Figure 14.6: Too many illustrations can be overwhelming

Arranging sign elements

To prevent signs looking crowded, there should be more rather than less white space around the edges. White space between the components of a sign, such as paragraphs and/or illustrations, should be just enough to make it clear that the components are separate. Visual appeal can be heightened by selecting illustrations of various sizes, though it is important to ensure that the final result appears balanced. Thus, if a large illustration is placed on one side of a sign it should be balanced with a large body of text on the other side or a smaller piece of text and another smaller illustration. Note in Figure 14.7 how the panel holding the text is the same size as the adjoining illustration – even though the body of text is smaller than the photo, the display appears balanced.

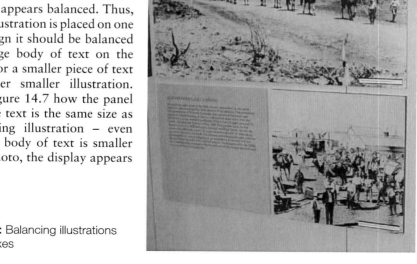

Figure 14.7: Balancing illustrations and text boxes

Designing signs for trails

Many geotourism sites feature trails or boardwalks that rely on several signs or sets of signs to convey interpretive messages. To signify that they belong to a set or series, signs should be linked by a common underlying theme and have similar design elements (e.g. borders, materials, logos). The procedure for designing signs for interpretive trails is described below.

1 Plan the route

♦　Define the purpose and theme.

♦　Select a route that will deliver a variety of features and views. Ensure the physical effort required will be within the capabilities of key target audiences. If possible, use a 'loop' configuration with the same entrance and exit to facilitate transport access.

♦　Identify possible places to position signage – natural stopping points and common decision points such as forks in the paths, lookouts, picnic and seating areas are often the best locations for signs.

♦　Make note of any signs that are likely to face bright sunlight as these will need to be constructed from materials that are non-reflective and fade-resistant.

2 Write the text

♦　Using everyday language, catchy titles, analogies, metaphors, stories, questions and illustrations, write the interpretive content.

♦　If possible, incorporate multi-sensory activities that encourage visitors to experience the landscape using senses such as touch and smell.

3 Design an introductory sign

♦　Trails should be introduced by a welcome sign that describes the route's length and degree of difficulty as well as its interpretive theme (Ham, 1992). If the route is best walked in a particular direction at a particular time of day, this needs to be included.

♦　Introductory signs can also define key topics/terms, especially if this will facilitate comprehension of subsequent signs.

4 Design and test mock signs prior to installation

♦　Mock signs should be evaluated in-situ to ascertain whether themes, ideas and concepts 'flow' from one sign to the next and whether the proposed sites for installation are appropriate.

♦　Evaluation can be formal (e.g. through interviews or surveys) or informal (through observation of whether or not visitors stop to read trailside signs).

Signs in situ: Getting pole position

The effort and expense of designing, illustrating and constructing interpretive signs is of little value if they are placed where few visitors see them. To determine the best location, it is necessary to have an understanding of how visitors move through the site or attraction. This can be gained through observation studies and/or by recording signs of wear and tear such as worn patches on the grass and erosion on paths, outcrops and other surfaces. Places where people already stop to rest, admire the view or simply catch their breath are often the best places to locate signs. Research shows that signs installed perpendicular to visitors' line of approach such as in Figure 14.8 are more likely to attract attention than those placed parallel to pathways (Korn, 1988).

Figure 14.8 Signs should be placed at an angle to attract attention

Signs interpreting particular features of the landscape should be within easy viewing distance of the interpreted feature as visitors will soon tire of walking back and forth between the sign and the feature or view. While placing a sign in the centre of visitor's line of vision will attract their attention, it is important not to position it where it is likely to interfere with their view of the feature, object or vista being interpreted. Regardless of where they are positioned, signs can be very intrusive if they do not blend in with their surroundings. This particularly applies to geotourism settings – nature should always dominate, regardless of the interpretive message (Gunn, 1994).

Concluding comments

Geotourism offers unprecedented opportunities to educate the public about the natural landscape, and when accompanied by well-designed interpretation, can foster a life-long appreciation and respect for nature. It is argued that by adopting the principles and practices described in this chapter, geotourism sites will be well-positioned to offer interpretive experiences that develop visitors' skills, knowledge and/or understanding of geological concepts and thereby help them find meaning in the landscape.

References

Ballantyne, R. and Packer, J. (forthcoming) 'Post-visit "action resourcing": promoting and supporting visitor adoption of environmentally sustainable behaviours', *Environmental Education Research*.

Ballantyne, R., Crabtree, A., Ham, S., Hughes, K. and Weiler, B. (2000) *Tour Guiding: Developing Effective Communication and Interpretation Techniques*, Brisbane, Queensland: Queensland University of Technology.

Ballantyne, R., Packer, J., Hughes, K. and Dierking, L. (2007) 'Conservation learning in wildlife tourism settings: lessons from research in zoos and aquariums', *Environmental Education Research*, **13** (3), 367-383.

Beaumont, N. (2001) 'Ecotourism and the conservation ethic: Recruiting the uninitiated or preaching to the converted?', *Journal of Sustainable Tourism*, **9** (4), 317-341.

Beck, L. and Cable, T. (2002) *Interpretation for the 21st century: Fifteen Guiding Principles for Interpreting Nature and Culture*, Champaign, IL: Sagamore Publishing.

Bitgood, S. and Woehr, D. (1986) 'Design and evaluation of exhibit labels', *Technical Report No87-40c*, Jacksonville, AL: Center for Social Design.

Brochu, L. (2003) *Interpretive Planning: The 5-M model for Successful Planning Projects*. Colorado: National Association for Interpretation.

Caulton, T. (1998) *Hands-on Exhibitions: Managing Interactive Museums and Science Centres*, London: Routledge.

Chhabra, D., Healy, R. and Sills, E. (2003) 'Staged authenticity and heritage tourism', *Annals of Tourism Research*, **30** (3), 702-719.

Dean, D. (1994) *Museum Exhibition: Theory and Practice*, London: Routledge.

Denton, C. (1992) *Graphics for Visual Communication*, Dubuque, IA: Wm. C. Brown Publishers.

Falk, J. H. (2001). *Free-choice science education: How we learn science outside of school*. New York: Teachers College Press.

Falk, J.H. and Dierking, L.D. (1992) *The Museum Experience*, Washington DC: Whalesback Books.

Falk, J.H. and Dierking, L.D. (2000) *Learning from Museums: Visitor Experiences and the Making of Meaning*, Walnut Creek, CA: AltaMira Press.

Falk, J.H., Scott, C., Dierking, L., Rennie, L. and Jones, M.C. (2004) 'Interactives and visitor learning', *Curator*, **47** (2), 171-198.

Gunn, C.A. (1994) *Tourism planning: Basics, Concepts, Cases*, Washington DC: Taylor and Francis.

Ham, S.H. (1992). *Environmental Interpretation: A Practical Guide for People with Big Ideas and Small Budgets*, Golden, Colorado: North American Press.

Ham, S.H. and Krumpe, E.E. (1996) 'Identifying audiences and messages for nonformal environmental education – a theoretical framework for interpreters', *Journal of Interpretation*, **1** (1) 11-23.

Ham, S.H., Housego, A. and Weiler, B. (2005) *Tasmanian Thematic Interpretation Planning Manual*, Tourism Tasmania.

Hartley, L. and Trueman, M. (1983) 'The effects of headings in text on recall, search and retrieval', *British Journal of Educational Psychology*, **53** (2), 205-214.

Heintzman, J. (1988) *Making the right connections: a guide for nature writers*. Stevens Point, WI: The University of Wisconsin.

Hooper-Greenhill, E. (1994). *Museums and their Visitors*, London: Routledge.

Knudson, D.M., Cable, T.T. and Beck, L. (1995) *Interpretation of Cultural and Natural Resources*, State College, PA: Venture Publishing.

Korn, R. (1988) 'Self-guiding brochures: an evaluation', *Curator*, **31**, 9-19.

McManus, P.M. (1989) 'Oh yes they do: how museum visitors read labels and interact with exhibit texts', *Curator*, **32** (3), 174-189.

McManus, P.M. (1994) 'Families in museums', in R.Miles and Zavala, L. (eds) *Towards the Museum of the Future: New European Perspectives*, London: Routledge, pp. 81-97.

Merriman, T. and Brochu, L. (2005) *Management of Interpretive Sites: Developing Sustainable Operations through Effective Leadership*, Colorado: National Association for Interpretation.

Moscardo, G., Ballantyne, R., and Hughes, K. (2007) *Designing Interpretive Signs: Principles in Practice*, Colorado: Fulcrum Publishing.

Pierssene, A. (1999) *Explaining our World: An Approach to the Art of Environmental Interpretation*, London: E and F.N. Spon.

Powell, R.B. and Ham, S.H. (2008) 'Can ecotourism interpretation really lead to pro-conservation knowledge, attitudes and behaviour? Evidence from the Galapagos Islands', *Journal of Sustainable Tourism*, **16** (4), 467-489.

Punt, B. (1989) *Doing it Right: A Workbook for Improving Exhibit Labels*, Brooklyn: Brooklyn Children's Museum.

Regnier, K., Gross, M. and Zimmerman, R. (1992) *The Interpreter's Guidebook: Techniques for Programs and Presentations*, Madison: University of Wisconsin, UW-SP Foundation Press.

Serrell, B. (Ed.) (1998) *Paying Attention: Visitors & Museum Exhibitions*, American Association of Museums.

Serrell, B. (1996) 'In search of generalizability: new tools for visitor studies', *Journal of Museum Education*, **21** (3), 11-18.

Spock, D. (2004) 'Is it interactive yet?', *Curator*, **47** (4), 369-374.

Tilden, F. (1957) *Interpreting Our Heritage*, Chapel Hill: University of North Carolina Press.

Tilden, F. (1977). *Interpreting our Heritage*, 3rd edn, Chapel Hill: University of North Carolina Press.

Trapp, S., Gross, M. and Zimmerman, R. (1994) *Signs, Trails, and Wayside Exhibits: Connecting People and Places*, Stevens Point, WI : UW-SP Foundation Press.

Waitt, G. (2000) 'Consuming heritage: perceived historical authenticity', *Annals of Tourism Research*, **27** (4), 835-862.

Weiler, B. and Ham, S.H. (2002) 'Tour guide training: a model for sustainable capacity building in developing countries', *Journal of Sustainable Tourism*, **10** (1), 52-69.

15 The Jurassic Coast World Heritage Site: understanding the nature of geotourism

Sally King, Anjana Ford, Richard Edmonds, Dorset and East Devon Coast World Heritage Site, United Kingdom

Introduction: What makes this coast so special?

The Dorset and East Devon Coast World Heritage Site (also known as the 'Jurassic Coast'), stretches for 155 km across the southern English coastline, encompassing one of the most spectacular geological sequences in the world. The internationally renowned coastal exposures of the Jurassic Coast were awarded World Heritage Site status in 2001 based on a near complete sequence of Mesozoic rocks, which record evidence and development of early reptiles through to the age of the dinosaurs. For a site to obtain World Heritage Site status, it must exhibit cultural or natural features that are of 'outstanding universal value' and must be protected for present and future generations of all humanity. Protecting the integrity (or condition) of the site is essential for maintaining the qualities that led to site inscription. Coastal erosion maintains the geological integrity of the Jurassic Coast by exposing fossils that are then washed out onto the beaches. The fossils are an important part of our geological heritage.

The Jurassic Coast is a long narrow linear site (Figure 15.1). The World Heritage Site boundary is designated from the top of the cliffs to the low water mark. For some World Heritage Sites an official 'buffer zone' strengthens conservation measures. Since the Jurassic Coast lies within the designated Dorset and East Devon Areas of Outstanding Natural Beauty, as well as 13 Sites of Special Scientific Interest, these additional layers of designation afford statutory protection for the site's setting. The World Heritage Site Management Plan (Jurassic Coast Team, 2009) guides the work of the Jurassic Coast Steering Group and partners in managing the Site now and into the future. The Steering Group consists of broad stakeholder involvement and is the main body responsible for the delivery of the World Heritage Site Management Plan. The Jurassic Coast team and associated partners deliver the work programme.

Like most beautiful and accessible natural environments, the coastline has also attracted visitors since the earliest days of tourism. Now, as then, many of these visitors are interested in fossils and geology, but the majority come to enjoy the peace, beauty and coastal land and seascapes. With visitors come benefits, but also challenges and pressures which have to be carefully managed.

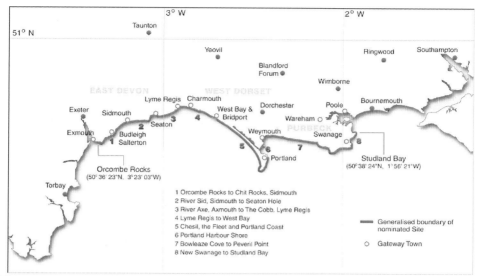

Figure 15.1: Jurassic Coast World Heritage Site

In this chapter, we will explore how the management of the Jurassic Coast has success-fully balanced the challenges of encouraging people to enjoy, learn from and appreciate the World Heritage Site, while at the same time, conserving the integrity of one of the world's most important geological sites.

A slice of Mesozoic life – telling the story

The Jurassic Coast encompasses the Triassic, Jurassic and Cretaceous periods of geologi-cal time; 185 million years of the Earth's ancient history – known as the Mesozoic era. The key to understanding this geodiversity is that overall, the rocks dip very gently to the east. As a result, the oldest rocks are found in the west with progressively younger rocks forming the coast to the east. Therefore each section of the coast contains part of a much larger story and the coast as a whole represents a 'walk through time'.

In some areas, the story stands out before your eyes – fossils at Charmouth and the Lulworth Crumple (see Figure 15.2) for example, but in many other areas, it is far more subtle and there is a need for the story to be 'brought to life'.

Along the coast, there are visitor centres, tourist information centres, museums and other outlets which provide information and attempt to help people understand, learn from and enjoy the Jurassic Coast. There are aspirations to develop interpretation cen-tres in areas along the coast where there are gaps in provision, but funding remains an issue. Examples of interpretation centres that do exist are listed below:

♦ Beer Quarry Caves – guided tours explaining the story of quarrying for Beer stone – privately owned.

♦ Charmouth Heritage Coast Centre – one of the flagship Jurassic Coast centres, providing information and advice on fossil collecting, plus guided walks – oper-ated and owned by an independent trust.

♦ Dorset County Museum – although located inland in Dorchester, the museum opened a Jurassic Coast Geology Gallery in 2006 which tells the story of the whole World Heritage Site – operated and owned by a charitable trust.

♦　Lulworth Heritage Centre – tells the story of the Jurassic rocks around Lulworth Cove and Durdle Door, offers guided walks and school field trips – privately owned

♦　Durlston Country Park – at the eastern extreme of the site. The site of a former restaurant that is currently (2009) being converted into a Jurassic Coast World Heritage Centre, which will tell the story of the entire World Heritage Site and focus on the key interests in Purbeck. Set in a 280-hectare country park landscape, this is the only Jurassic Coast centre which is owned and managed by a local authority – Dorset County Council.

Figure 15.2: Lulworth Crumple

Marketing, visitor management and access

A key task at hand for site managers is how to attract visitors to the Jurassic Coast, while at the same time ensuring the integrity of the site remains intact. This section will look at issues of marketing, visitor management and access.

Engaging the audience

The Dorset and East Devon coastline has always been a popular holiday destination. The responsibility of the Jurassic Coast team is not so much to encourage more visitors to the coast, but to promote the interests in respect to the site's geological credentials. In other words, rather than marketing the location, the team markets the geological and associated elements of the product offer. This approach poses numerous challenges mainly because geology and the earth sciences can often be an inaccessible and abstract subject area for non-specialists.

The first step is perhaps to examine ways in which the geological stories can be interpreted in an accessible way which seeks to engage the audience on a variety of levels which they can relate to. In 2003, the Jurassic Coast team commissioned the Natural History Museum to investigate how this could be done. The scoping study revealed that written interpretation should be targeted to an audience aged between 7 and 14 years of age and that there were a variety of geological stories that could be told with site-specific elements (Natural History Museum, 2003).

To this end, the interpretation provided by the Jurassic Coast team is designed to be accessible to a broad audience, often without specialist scientific knowledge. Examples include a series of leaflets that are reprinted and revised on an annual basis (budgets allowing). For example, *The Dorset and East Devon Coast, England's First Natural World Heritage Site* leaflet pulls out some of the key stories and briefly gives an overview of the whole site, within the context of the international 'family' of World Heritage Sites. *Explore the Jurassic Coast Without Your Car* leaflet is an attempt to encourage visitors to leave their cars behind and use public transport, walk or cycle. The *Fossil Collecting Along the Jurassic Coast* leaflet gives advice for safe, responsible fossil collecting and is based on the Fossil Collecting Code of Conduct which is in existence along the West Dorset section of the coastline.

In addition, a series of publications for sale include a guide to the Jurassic Coast (Brunsden, 2005) and a series of more detailed site-specific books such as Edwards, (2007) which looks at the interests along East Devon's red Triassic landscape and Edwards (2008) which focuses on the biodiversity found along the site. Income generated from these sales is managed by the Jurassic Coast World Heritage Site Trust and goes towards reprints, distribution, and supporting conservation and education projects.

As a World Heritage Site, the Jurassic Coast attracts interest on a global scale. The Jurassic Coast website (www.jurassiccoast.com, Jurassic Coast team, 2006) contains a wealth of information to inspire, inform and engage potential audiences of all ages. As new technology continues to emerge, such as the new generation of 3G mobile devices, the scope for providing visitors with current, up-to-date and personalised information is constantly evolving. It is important to recognise that not all visitors will have access to these new and emerging technologies so high quality, physical on-site interpretation will always be needed.

Along the coast, outdoor interpretation panels have been located in appropriate locations (such as car parks) but care has been taken to avoid imposing on the tranquillity of the natural environment. In many cases, natural, local materials (e.g. setting a panel in a local stone plinth) have been used that complement the surrounding environment. Recently there has been a move towards using more creative means for conveying messages about the Jurassic Coast to the general public. The Jurassic Coast Arts Programme has been specially created to deliver this objective. Recently commissioned work includes a site-specific arts project called 'Universal Value' which explored the interrelationship between people and the environment they live in. The artist recorded interviews with local residents along the Jurassic Coast and then projected his edited film with no sound and in slow motion onto a rugged cliff face (Figure 15.3). The result was a stunning visual portrayal of people's reaction to their natural heritage, played out on the very environment which stimulated their reactions in the first place.

Arguably the best way to truly engage with any audience is through first person interpretation. Experiencing a guided walk and learning how to find fossils with an expert is much more evocative and memorable than reading about it in a book or online. The visitor centres and museums showcase some of the key interests of the World Heritage Site and most of them offer visitors the chance to experience guided walks, evening talks and seminars.

Figure 15.3: The 'Universal Value' arts project

Visitor management

The Jurassic Coast team is also concerned with the flow and spread of visitors across the area and throughout the year. Efforts are made to alleviate the pressure of large numbers of visitors at 'honey pot' sites, i.e. those locations which are so popular, they are potentially close to or at their capacity. Usually, locations along the coast are under most visitor pressure in the summer months between July to the end of August. However there is now a growing trend towards taking short trips during half-term school holidays (particularly October, when the weather on the south coast can still be very favourable) and during Easter.

Capacity is notoriously difficult to measure. Perception often interferes with real issues of capacity; for example, what to one person might constitute unacceptable levels of congestion, may well seem perfectly acceptable to another. The question can arise as to whether one is monitoring capacity or managing the perception of capacity. Both are important, but neither are easily resolved.

What is clear is that some parts of the Jurassic Coast are much busier than others. Often this is due to the accessibility of a site and the provision of facilities (car park, toilets, cafes), but it can also be down to historical factors (e.g. Lulworth Cove has been a popular holiday destination for centuries), media coverage and a destination's marketing strategy. For example, if every brochure, website and newspaper article on the Jurassic Coast uses Durdle Door as the accompanying image, that location will (and has!) become a heavily visited site. Sometimes, extreme action is required – for example, Avebury World

Heritage Site, also in the south west of the UK, has a non-marketing policy, as the site managers, together with the community, took the decision that the sensitive landscape setting was nearing capacity. To further complicate matters, while some parts of the Jurassic Coast may well have the capacity to receive more visitors, we cannot forget that tranquil zones along the coast are an integral part of its appeal and indeed, integrity. But should tranquil zones remain as they are so that visitors are encouraged to descend on the traditionally busy parts of the coast?

Careful marketing clearly has a role to play and for the Jurassic Coast team, this means influencing and providing advice for other marketers who wish to use the Jurassic Coast in promotional material, be they accommodation providers, local authority tourism officers or businesses seeking involvement with the brand.

A Jurassic Coast Quality Business Scheme was set up in 2006 to encourage business involvement with the coast. It aims to support businesses to be in part responsible for the management of what is, essentially, 'their' World Heritage Site. Many of the businesses involved are accommodation providers, recognising that they are often the first point of contact with a visitor to the area. By 2009, sixty businesses had been accredited and have thereby gained a number of benefits including use of a logo closely associated with the Jurassic Coast. Of those businesses accredited, 69 per cent felt the Jurassic Coast was 'very important' to their business and 30 per cent felt it was 'quite important'. It is hoped the numbers involved will continue to increase and create Jurassic Coast ambassadors who will be advocates for the World Heritage Site and all that it stands for.

Engagement with the wider community has always been at the core of the principles of the Jurassic Coast. We endeavour to work with local communities to generate a sense of pride and ownership about their environment. Local communities are increasingly gaining confidence with their role in the management of the site and working more closely with other partners and stakeholders.

Buses and boats ... or the car? Managing access

Access to the Jurassic Coast is complex due to various factors, including erosion, the physical geomorphology and the fact the coast has multiple landowners. To preserve the integrity of the site, it is important that access is given due regard within the remit of visitor management.

Generally speaking, the British love the convenience and independence of travelling by car. Some 80 per cent of visitors to the Jurassic Coast come by car and the coastal roads have seen a significant increase in traffic. For example, in Dorset as a whole, traffic grew by 5.5 per cent between 1999–04; whereas on roads servicing the Jurassic Coast, it grew by 8.6 per cent in the same time frame. Traffic growth is undoubtedly part of a national trend, but that does not make it of any less concern. Changing attitude and behaviour towards travel is a huge challenge but one which those involved in the management of the Jurassic Coast, are attempting to tackle.

A starting point has been to try to get people to leave their cars behind once they are on holiday in the area. This can be marketed as an appealing option (avoid traffic jams, no need to pay for parking, more relaxing) and has been especially successful where the alternative to the car is seen as an 'experience' or 'attraction' in its own right.

In 2002, an existing bus service was the beneficiary of a successful three-year Rural Bus Challenge grant submitted by Dorset and Devon County Councils and First Bus company. First Bus increased the frequency to a two-hourly service between Exeter and

Poole and six new, low floor, double-decker buses were purchased and branded in an engaging and distinctive 'Jurassic' livery. The buses have been named by local people through a competition and the drivers have taken part in training courses which aim to raise their awareness and understanding of the Jurassic Coast. Passenger usage has increased fourfold.

The potential for waterborne transport along the Jurassic Coast has only recently begun to be explored. While boat trips do operate out of several harbours, they are currently seen more as an excursion rather than a means of travelling from one place to another. They have an important role to play in demonstrating the coastline to visitors – probably the best way of seeing the Jurassic Coast's unique geology is from the sea – and local operators have benefited from Jurassic Coast training. The Jurassic Coast team, together with the Dorset Area of Outstanding Natural Beauty team , is currently investigating the potential for waterborne transport, as opposed to boat trips. Issues to consider include supply versus demand, weather, tidal and wind constraints and physical opportunities and limitations. Promoting waterborne transport is particularly timely given that Weymouth and Portland on the Jurassic Coast are to be the setting for the sailing events for the London 2012 Olympic Games.

Other than from the sea, the second best way to see the World Heritage Site is to walk along it. The South West Coast Path National Trail runs along the entire length of the Site. Recreational counters to monitor path use are in place at key locations along the route and provide valuable information for monitoring and managing the trail. A challenge is the expense associated with the on-going erosion of the coast path and the necessity to create diversions to maintain the accessibility of the route. Management of coastal defences is directed by Shoreline Management Plans prepared for South Devon and Dorset Coastal Authorities Group (Halcrow Group, 2008) and for the Poole and Christchurch Bays Coastal Group (Royal Haskoning, 2008) which encourage a policy of 'no active intervention' along the majority of the Jurassic Coast. Since erosion is a key process that maintains the natural beauty and integrity of the World Heritage Site, there is a conflict with maintaining and safely promoting the coastal footpaths.

The work of the huge number of partners involved in the management of the coast and its hinterland is coordinated through a Coastal Corridor Action Plan (Butler *et al.*, 2009) which is managed and led by the Dorset Area of Outstanding Natural Beauty team.

Conservation and conflicts

Heritage is our legacy from the past, what we live with today, and what we pass on to future generations. Our cultural and natural heritage are both irreplaceable sources of life and inspiration. Certainly in this respect, World Heritage Sites need to be protected to maintain the very quality that makes them unique. It is our duty to ensure that the geology along the Jurassic Coast remains exposed and retains its natural quality and condition.

Coastal defence structures interfere with natural coastal processes and therefore could threaten the integrity of the site. Such intervention obscures the rock sequence and prevents erosion and therefore the exposure of fossils. But at the same time coastal towns are an integral part of the coast; they are the places where people stay, learn about and access the site. With ongoing erosion, which is likely to be accelerated by climate change, this is a constant challenge and conflict. The Shoreline Management Plans mentioned above will identify the risks and management prescriptions for the next 100 years.

Landslips and coastal erosion are not welcomed by everyone (particularly private landowners) and can be a cause of conflict between local people, engineers, planners and conservation managers. Controlling these processes can often conflict with what we value in our environment; the dilemma being that the natural erosive processes of our coastline are essential to maintain the unique quality and beauty of the site. We need to find a balance between the needs of the environment with the needs of its users in order to maintain a sustainable future.

Although conservation methods can be implemented to ensure protection of the site, preservation is a very different issue altogether. Preservation not only encompasses protecting the site from loss or damage, but it also raises issues about whether that site can *or should* be protected from change. In the case of the Jurassic Coast, preservation is not appropriate since we need change to maintain the integrity of the site. Erosion is the process that gives the site its value. Coastal defence structures would disrupt these natural processes, the geological value of the site could be harmed and ultimately the World Heritage Site status could be put at risk. The fossils which are revealed are a direct result of these erosional processes and provide the key to understanding past environments.

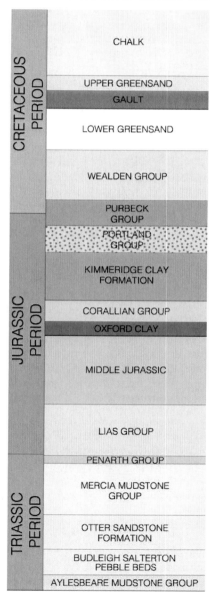

The fossil heritage of the Jurassic Coast

The geological sequences (see Figure 15.4) along the Jurassic Coast chart monumental changes encompassing hot deserts, deep oceans, shallow warm seas, dense forests, swamps, lagoons and salt lakes. The fossils revealed along the site are crucial to our understanding not only of past environments but also how life adapted and evolved over time.

Finders-keepers?

What is the best way to ensure that fossils are saved? Coastal erosion is an ongoing, natural process and once fossils are released onto the beach, they are at the mercy of the ocean which inevitably damages them and washes them out to sea. Once this happens, potentially scientifically valuable specimens could be lost forever. For this reason, responsible fossil collecting is deemed to be acceptable along certain parts of the Jurassic Coast.

Figure 15.4: Stratigraphic sequence of the Jurassic coastline

While it may seem surprising that people are allowed to 'take away' a part of our natural heritage, the history of fossil collecting along this coast has always followed the premise that collectors are only collecting that which would otherwise disappear for ever. Fossil collecting has been an important part of the culture of the Jurassic Coast for well over 200 years, a long time before the term 'Geotourism' was ever developed. Numerous specimens that are important to science have been rescued from damage or loss by collectors with open access to the site.

In fact, some of the specimens found by renowned fossil hunter Mary Anning from Lyme Regis, 200 years ago, still help to answer key scientific questions today. Precisely when scientifically significant fossils emerge along the Jurassic Coast is impossible to predict. We do not know which cliffs or geological sections will yield a specimen that will be new to science. For visitors, ammonite and belemnite fossils are easily found on the beaches, particularly in winter and early spring. Having an activity which is appealing to visitors in the off-peak seasons is a bonus in terms of sustainable tourism. The Jurassic Coast is well placed in that one of its key interests is far more readily accessible in winter than in the already extremely busy summer months and gives us an opportunity to promote the coast out of season.

But who owns these fossils? Under English law, fossils *in situ* belong to the owner of the mineral rights who is also usually the landowner. Once the fossil is washed out onto the beach, then it may be regarded as abandoned by the owner, and can be freely collected. Fossils are collected by a wide range of people such as casual collectors, keen amateurs and professionals. Collecting fossils from a World Heritage Site raises certain ethical and controversial issues. If we don't allow visitors to take away bits of the Taj Mahal World Heritage Site, why should we allow collectors to search for, collect and even sell Jurassic Coast fossils? The answer lies in the characteristics of the site. The Taj Mahal is a unique building; its beauty lies completely in its structure and form. It is perfectly obvious that removing blocks of marble would ruin its integrity. However, the Jurassic Coast is dynamic and robust, every year producing a renewed supply of fossils due to coastal erosion. The fossils that are collected on the Jurassic Coast represent a tiny fraction of what will be available thousands of years in the future. For professional collectors, significant time is required to search for and clean specimens. This serves as a source of income supporting a range of cottage industries for a number of local people. Professional collectors are often in the position to find the more scientifically valuable fossils along our coast that many academic palaeontologists (who are constrained by time and funding) cannot. In many cases, important finds are donated to museums or universities by collectors. There have been many unqualified collectors who have made major contributions to palaeontology, such as Mary Anning.

In some countries, unauthorised fossil collectors can be fined or even jailed. In the United States, many fossil-rich areas fall into national parks which are owned by the federal government. These large expanses of land are patrolled by a few rangers who can arrest and prosecute anyone who tries to illegally remove fossils. Along the West Dorset coast there is a Fossil Collecting Code of Conduct (Appendix 4 of the World Heritage Site Management Plan; Jurassic Coast Team, 2009) by which landowners agree to transfer ownership in fossils to the finder provided they are collected according to the terms of the code. Collectors who do not abide by the code may be regarded as stealing the fossils. The terms of the code state that 'scientifically important finds' should be registered. The fossil is photographed, a record is taken and then the specimen is handed back to the collector. Collectors and visitors alike should not collect fossils *in situ* (stable cliff exposures) and advice is given on safe and sustainable methods of collecting. Over the last 12 years, fossil collectors have helped to discover several new species of Ichthyo-saur that have contributed to our understanding of the Jurassic Period (Fossil Database, Charmouth Heritage Coast Centre, 2006). Another collector has saved possibly one of the largest and best preserved skulls of a Pliosaur (not yet officially recorded – October 2009) over a five-year period, as it fell out of the cliffs.

Balancing the issues

Natural World Heritage Sites are subject to change from physical or biological process-es, so it is important to ensure that conservation is tailored to that environment. There is no 'one-size-fits all' management strategy that we can apply to the care of our World's heritage. For example, protecting rare petroglyphs on a cave wall from being washed or eroded away would require a very different approach from that of managing natural cliff erosion. The former has a very high sensitivity to change while the latter does not. Sites need to be classified according to their sensitivity to collecting pressure and the nature of the exposure. A fossil site in a cave would be sensitive to change since the resource is bound to be limited (finite). In this case, access and entry into the site should be controlled and collecting should almost certainly be restricted to scientists. Disused quarries would also be sensitive to collecting since this type of fossil resource is not be-ing continuously renewed. Robust sites such as the Jurassic Coast or a working quarry are constantly under change and renewal, exposing new discoveries. Fossils are either being washed away by natural processes in the former or crushed to form aggregate in the latter. Building sites or road cuttings can also offer opportunities for timely fossil ex-plorations. These temporary exposures can yield rare finds that would otherwise remain undiscovered. In such cases, the challenge is to ensure that any specimen retrieval for the benefit of science is carried out as quickly as possible. One way of controlling fossil col-lecting is by restricting access to sites. In a quarry or enclosed environment access can be monitored. However it is impossible to do this along the 155 km of the World Heritage Site. Attempting to police the coastline will not stop collecting, but drive it underground and many specimens would not then come to the attention of scientists.

Heritage under threat?

Balancing the value of natural heritage against the needs of the local community is dif-ficult. World Heritage Site status provides an opportunity to protect the environment against damage or exploitation. However for local communities struggling to make ends meet, it may mean a challenge to their source of income. How would restricting and controlling fishing in a World Heritage Site affect local fishermen? Would they share the same ethic as an environmentalist who wanted the coral reef protected from exploita-tion? What if a large reserve of oil was discovered beneath a rich dense tropical forest? Would more local jobs and an increase to the global oil reserve outweigh environmental concerns to protect our natural heritage? The biggest danger to the beauty and integrity of the Jurassic Coast is coastal development, and this can generate conflicting views on what has more value (long term heritage protection or shorter term considerations). The World Heritage Convention strives to ensure that countries adopt suitable management plans to care for the World's heritage. It exists to give protected status to natural envi-ronments and cultural landscapes that are constantly under threat from development, exploitation or modernisation.

Conclusion: Keeping the Jurassic Coast special now and into the future

As stated in the introduction, the World Heritage Site Management Plan (Jurassic Coast Team, 2009) will continue to guide the work of the Jurassic Coast Steering Group and partners to ensure the integrity of the Jurassic Coast remains intact. It is, however, the duty of all of us to help manage and protect the integrity of World Heritage Sites.

An important aspect for the Jurassic Coast is ensuring the natural erosional processes are allowed to continue. Erosion is what gives the site its value; without it, we wouldn't have World Heritage Site status. Articulating this to local and global audiences and stakeholders, and changing the common perception that natural processes (including erosion) must be stopped, is an important part of the management of the Jurassic Coast.

Visitor management will continue to be one of the most important areas of concern within the remit of managing the Jurassic Coast. Communicating and marketing information to visitors is key to engaging respect and understanding of the environment they are visiting. Helping people travel to and around the coast without increasing congestion remains a challenge but the potential for waterborne transport is an exciting one which will hopefully be developed further in the near future.

Fossil collecting is one of the major aspects of the World Heritage Site which really bring it to life for visitors, communities, site managers and perhaps especially, young people. It is vital that this engaging and historically important activity continues. Rather than damaging the site in any way, if carefully managed, fossil collecting can only enhance the site's integrity as new specimens come to light and as more people recognise the value of heritage, in all its forms, whether cultural or natural.

Through stimulating this shared sense of pride and ownership about our environment, we can ensure that the Jurassic Coast World Heritage Site will continue to be available and valued for generations of people who come to enjoy its beauty and its amazing geology, fossils and geomorphology.

References

Brunsden, D. (2005) *Official Guide to the Jurassic Coast* 2nd edn, Wareham: Coastal Publishing.

Butler, R., Roberts, C. and Harman, D. (2009) *Dorset and East Devon Coastal Corridor Action Plan*, report prepared for Coastal Corridor Steering Group.

Charmouth Heritage Coast Centre (2006) *Fossil Database*, www.charmouth.org.

Edwards, R.A. (2007) *Red Rocks Revealed*, Wareham: Coastal Publishing.

Edwards, B. (2008) *Wildlife of the Jurassic Coast*, Wareham: Coastal Publishing.

Halcrow Group (2008) *South Devon and Dorset Shoreline Management Plan*, report prepared for South Devon and Dorset Coastal Authorities Group

Jurassic Coast Team (2006) *www.jurassiccoast.com*

Jurassic Coast Team (2009) The *World Heritage Site Management Plan* (2nd rev).

Natural History Museum (2003), *Jurassic Coast World Heritage Site: Scoping Study on Interpretation Facilities*, report prepared for World Heritage Steering Group.

Royal Haskoning (2008) *Two Bays Shoreline Management Plan*, report prepared for Poole and Christchurch Bays Coastal Group.

16 USA scenic byways – connecting people to places

Judy Walden, Walden Mills Group, Wesley Hill, the Geological Society of America and Sally Pearce, Scenic Byways Program Coordinator, State of Colorado

Scenic byways in America: a national collection

International tourists who are seeking America's most scenic roads and geotravelers who are searching for America's most significant geological sites can both find reliable guidance in America's Scenic Byways program. This program presents to travelers 151 scenic roadways and the landscapes that surround them. These national scenic roadways were first nominated by local community groups, then officially designated by commissions in each of the 50 states, and finally presented for national recognition and branded as America's Byways®. Now 18 years after the program began, these 151 acclaimed highways have produced increased tourism and economic development for the regions that they pass through. Each has written guidelines for continuing local management and each has provided interpretive materials that assist the traveling public (e.g. Figure 16.1). All are a source of considerable regional pride.

Figure 16.1: Lake Lenore caves signage.

Program history and goals

The program was established in December 1991 when the United States Congress created a new program for designating National Scenic Byways within the Intermodal Surface Transportation Efficiency Act. This program was continued within the Transportation Equity Act for the 21st Century in 1998 and in the Safe, Accountable, Flexible, and Efficient Transportation Equity Act of 2003. The goals of the National Scenic Byways Program were to provide a high quality visitor experience, to strengthen local economies, and to develop ways to manage the irreplaceable assets of the corridor.

An annual discretionary grant program established by Congress supports both state and nationally designated byways. In 2008 over $US38 million was available for grant projects. The grant program is administered by the Federal Highway Administration, and funds are passed through the State Transportation Departments to local byway organizations. Since the program's inception in 1992, $US346,999,974 has been awarded to 2672 projects in 52 states and territories. Eligibility categories include state and Native American scenic byways programs, corridor management plans, safety improvements, facilities such as pullouts and overlooks, access to recreation, resource protection, educational information and marketing programs.

Table 16.1: The six intrinsic qualities of scenic byways (Mingo, 1997)

Scenic: Beauty, both natural and human made. The qualities of the features are measured by how memorable, distinctive, uninterrupted, and unified they are.

Natural: Minimal human disturbance of geographic and other natural ecological features.

Historic: Landscapes, buildings, structures, or other visual evidence of the past. There must be something tangible and visible— not just the site of something that *used* to be there.

Cultural: Visual evidence of the unique customs, traditions, folklore, or rituals of a currently existing human group.

Archeological: Visual evidence of the unique customs, traditions, folklore, or rituals of a human group that no longer exists.

Recreational: The road corridor itself is used for recreation like jogging, biking, roadside picnics, or provides direct access to recreational sites like campgrounds, lakes, ski lodges and cabins.

Intrinsic qualities define the byways

For a route to qualify as a National Scenic Byway, a road or highway must possess one or more of the six 'intrinsic qualities' listed in Table 16.1. In this sense, an intrinsic quality refers to a feature considered representative, unique, or irreplaceable – perhaps a geological feature, a canyon, a mountain range, or a Native American trail. These features must possess major local or regional significance and have a community (or group of communities) committed to their management. A formal document called the Corridor Management Plan guides the management process.

Two tiers of national designation

The collection of All-American Roads represents the finest examples of the intrinsic resources of the nation. Designation as an All-American Road is rare; of the 151 National Scenic Byways, only 32 have achieved this highest designation. To receive an All-American Road designation, a road must possess multiple intrinsic qualities that are nationally significant and contain one-of-a-kind features that do not exist elsewhere in the United States. The road or highway must qualify as a 'destination unto itself' (Federal Highway Administration, 1994).

National Scenic Byways are considered regionally significant. Included in this collection are 119 byways. To be designated as a National Scenic Byway, a road must possess at least one of the six intrinsic qualities listed above, and the distinctive characteristics of the corridor's intrinsic qualities must be recognized throughout a multi-state region (Federal Highway Administration, 1994).

Anyone may nominate a road for national designation, but the nomination must be submitted through a state Department of Transportation. The state scenic byway coordinator then determines if the byway possesses intrinsic qualities sufficient to merit nomination as a National Scenic Byway or All-American Road. To assist the Federal Highway Administration in its review, several experts from outside the Department of Transportation provide an independent assessment using the nomination and designation criteria in Federal Highway Administration Policy. The Federal Highway Administrator and the Secretary of Transportation decide which roads are designated.

Corridor management plans guide the byways

A formal document called the Corridor Management Plan guides the management process. A corridor management plan is a community-based strategy to balance conservation of a byway corridor's intrinsic qualities with the use and enjoyment of those same resources. Corridor management planning allows communities to consider all the ways that they want to use and benefit from the scenic byway and its intrinsic qualities and still maintain the integrity and value of those qualities.

Scenic byway corridor management plans are the product of a close working and planning relationship between community groups which establish the vision and set the goals, and professionals who contribute technical expertise and formulate strategies. Creating a realistic management plan makes efficient use of community resources, both public and private, both professional and volunteer.

The Scenic Byways Advisory Committee identified 14 key elements to be included in a corridor management plan (Federal Highway Administration, 1994).

1. A map identifying the corridor boundaries and the location of intrinsic qualities and different land uses within the corridor.

2. An assessment of such intrinsic qualities and of their context.

3. A strategy for maintaining and enhancing those intrinsic qualities. The level of protection for different parts of a National Scenic Byway or All-American Road can vary, with the highest level of protection afforded those parts which most reflect their intrinsic values. All nationally recognized scenic byways should, however, be maintained with particularly high standards, not only for travelers' safety and comfort, but also for preserving the highest levels of visual integrity and attractiveness.

4. A schedule and a listing of all agency, group, and individual responsibilities in the implementation of the corridor management plan, and a description of enforcement and review mechanisms, including a schedule for the continuing review of how well those responsibilities are being met.

5. A strategy describing how existing development might be enhanced and new development might be accommodated while still preserving the intrinsic qualities of the corridor. This can be done through design review, and such land management techniques as zoning, easements, and economic incentives.

6. A plan to assure on-going public participation in the implementation of corridor management objectives.

7. A general review of the road's or highway's safety and accident record to identify any correctable faults in highway design, maintenance, or operation.

8. A plan to accommodate commerce while maintaining a safe and efficient level of highway service, including convenient user facilities.

9. A demonstration that intrusions on the visitor experience have been minimized to the extent feasible, and a plan for making improvements to enhance that experience.

10. A demonstration of compliance with all existing local, state, and federal laws on the control of outdoor advertising.

11. A signage plan that demonstrates how the state will insure and make the number and placement of signs more supportive of the visitor experience.

12. A narrative describing how the National Scenic Byway will be positioned for marketing.

13. A discussion of design standards relating to any proposed modification of the roadway. This discussion should include an evaluation of how the proposed changes may impact on the intrinsic qualities of the byway corridor.

14. A description of plans to interpret the significant resources of the scenic byway.

Corridor management plans can benefit all scenic byways programs, no matter what size or scale. The corridor management planning process establishes community-based goals and implementation strategies for the scenic byway to utilize community resources efficiently, to conserve intrinsic qualities of the scenic byway and to enhance its value to the community.

Grassroots management

The National Scenic Byway Program is a voluntary, grassroots program. The program is founded upon the strength of local leadership and passionate support for preservation of place. Through examination of a byway's corridor management plan, one can understand the community's vision for the byway and the strategies that will be used for conserving and enhancing the byway's intrinsic qualities, as well as the promotion of tourism and economic development.

Public lands and state byway systems

Although 'America's Byways' is the best known designation for distinctive roadways in America, other systems must be noted. Prior to the Federal Highway Administration beginning its designation process, the United States Forest Service and the Bureau of Land Management developed their own systems of nationally designated routes within their jurisdiction. A total of 134 National Forest Scenic Byways and 54 Bureau of Land Management (BLM) Backcountry Byways were designated before these two programs were absorbed under the brand of 'America's Byways'®. An additional 645 byways have been designated by the 50 states to date. The longest byway is Alaska's Marine Highway which traverses 3500 miles and is serviced by water ferries (Federal Highway Administration, 2009).

Colorado offers most national byways

The State of Colorado, located high in the Rocky Mountains, provides an excellent example of programs that offer many geologically rich byways. The state claims two All-American Roads and nine National Scenic Byways (more than any other state) plus 14 state-designated byways. Colorado's longest byway, The San Juan Skyway, an All-American Road, spans 236 miles and has become a national model for how byways can leverage funding for preservation. Over 18 years, this byway has raised $US41 million to purchase mining claims, preserve above-ground mining structures, and place important scenic viewsheds in conservation easements.

Colorado's Gold Belt Tour: a case study

The geological sites linked along Colorado's Gold Belt Tour National Scenic Byway include the Florissant Fossil Beds National Monument (managed by the National Park Service) where volcanics date back 34.1 million years, the Dome Rock exfoliation samples, and the Garden Park Dinosaur Fossil Quarries. This byway started as a Bureau of Land Management Back Country Byway and evolved into a partnership organization that brings together federal and state agencies, county and local governments, land trusts, historical societies and landowner associations.

The Gold Belt Tour has gained strength by tying together diverse geological features with strong sites that anchor each end of the byway. Florissant Fossil Beds National Monument is the magnet that pulls people to the area as it is one of the most diverse fossil deposits in the world, containing 1700 different species. A majority of the fossils are impressions of insects and plants with the largest being petrified Sequoia trees, some of the largest in the world.

Dinosaur Diamond Prehistoric Highway, Colorado and Utah

The Dinosaur Diamond Prehistoric Highway spans the states of Colorado and Utah and attracts many international visitors (e.g. Figure 16.2). This National Scenic Byway showcases world-class dinosaur fossils, archaeological sites displaying rock art, and provides outdoor recreational opportunities, primarily rafting, hiking, mountain biking and off-road driving. The byway links two National Parks, two National Monuments, and a Ute Indian Reservation.

Because the geologic resources along the byway are both fragile and non-renewable, protection is a key issue. Since the byway is a partnership between many federal, state, and local organizations, it is easy to communicate with relevant people when potential problems arise or suspicious activity is reported. The byway further strengthens protection of the resources by providing accessibility to important sites that can be easily patrolled, and provides multiple points of education.

The byway partnership has used the six intrinsic values as subtitles for tourist information, and offers half-day to five-day itineraries for recommended touring. The website provides fun-based activities for children, and geology lesson plans for teachers. The

Dinosaur Diamond partnership published an exploratory interactive guidebook on the 512-mile multi-state byway. The book identifies four distinct regions: Monuments and Mesas, Dinosaur Land, Utah's Castle Country, and Canyon Lands. Sites of paleontological interest, museums, and Indian rock art sites are listed for each region (Dinosaur Diamond Prehistoric Highway Partnership, 2009).

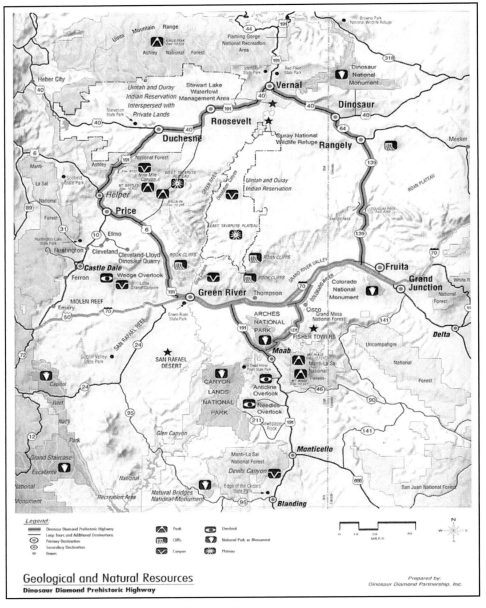

Figure 16.2: Map of the Dinosaur Diamond Byway Utah

A geology trail for the blind

The Dinosaur Diamond Byway partnership team has worked with the Bureau of Land Management and the local chapter of the Federation for the Blind to develop an educational interpretive trail at Dinosaur Hill Dig. The half mile trail includes a guided system of curbs and wire roping that leads visually impaired visitors along the trail. Interpretive signs have raised letters that describe the history and geology of the quarry, rediscovered by Elmer Riggs in 1901 (e.g. Figure 16.3). The signs also feature tactile graphics to provide a picture of the setting or the dinosaur that was discovered at the site (Figure 16.4). Two of the benches are exact replicas of the two 600-pound thigh bones of the Apatosaurus, down to the texture and color (Figure 16.5). Design of the benches were based on photographs of actual bones.

Figure 16.3: Tactile display providing information about the local geology

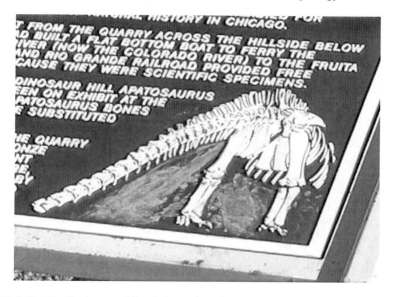

Figure 16.4: Tactile display providing information about the dinosaur site

Figure 16.5: Dinosaur bone bench design

Hard rock mining

Hard rock mining is another major geological theme in Colorado, and partnerships between the byways and working mines have become key to traveler involvement. Some byways have working mines which allow for a special kind of interactive visit, i.e. the Cripple Creek and Victor Mining Company is a major partner with the Gold Belt Tour Byway. The company has provided matching funds for grants, holds a seat on the byway board of directors, and sponsors local events. The Climax Mine Company has been an active participant with the Top of the Rockies Byway, and has provided matching funds and artifacts for an interactive interpretive site at the mine. Another example of partnership is in the National Mining Hall of Fame and Museum located in Leadville, Colorado.

Diversity and choice are key

The prime benefit that byways provide to the traveler is a diversified experience –they allow visitors to 'shop' for experiences that they are seeking. In Colorado, the landscape is a major part of that expectation – mountains, canyons, rivers, and plains. The byway ties together the geology and landscape and this combination becomes the major attraction to visitors. Linking sites also helps to spread the economic benefit to multiple regions and small communities. A visitor will have a better experience when educational interpretative tools explain the 'how and why' of the landscape, the history, and the natural environment.

Ice Age floods – Washington State

When it comes to dramatic geology along scenic byways, the Coulee Corridor National Scenic Byway has no equal. The Coulee Corridor Scenic Byway tells the story of the continental ice sheet and associated ice age floods that swept through the Pacific Northwest region some 17,000 years ago on its path to the Pacific Ocean. 'Koo'lee' is a French

Canadian word that refers to a dry canyon; however, it was the massive force of water that shaped the dry canyon landscape and formations seen today. Multiple waves of ice age floods carved through basalt flows to form a landscape of sheer cliffs, sand dunes, dry canyons and massive erratics that the locals refer to as coulees. Today, at the bottom of the canyons are depressions scoured out from the floods. Here, hundreds of species of birds and wildlife congregate, making the byway a birdwatcher's paradise.

The byway roadway stretches 150 miles (241 km) north to south, running parallel to the Columbia River. Sheer basalt cliffs, water, and grand coulees stay within sight, and the byway links these dramatic geologic sites to additional man-made and natural features. Travelers pass by the world's largest dam, the Grand Coulee Dam, and the Colville Indian Reservation whose ancestral people could have witnessed the ice age floods. Columbia National Wildlife Refuge lies under a major flyway for many species of birds, and Soap Lake offers mineral waters renowned for their healing powers. These stories linked together by the byway are often discovered by visitors who may have originally traveled to see the dramatic geological formations created by the ice age floods, but have lingered to enjoy additional experiences.

Connecting visitors with the story of the Ice Age floods

With spectacular scenery never far from the roadway or the view shed, travelers on the Coulee Corridor Byway constantly feel the dramatic presence of geologic features formed by the Ice Age Floods. The local scenic byway organization has worked to amplify this powerful geologic presence by contracting with a landscape architecture firm to produce an educational master plan and design guidelines that would help intensify a 'sense of place.' All visitor information signage, educational panels, website graphics, community signs and byway orientation maps use the same branding of colors, graphic styles, and natural materials. The colors used in the signage are the same as the colors that dominate the landscape, producing a cohesive information design (Otak, 2009).

These same design elements reassure travelers that they are still traveling on the byway; this is especially important in a landscape so grand that at times it seems overwhelming and endless. Points of interest along the byway, such as the Dry Falls Visitor Center and Pot Holes State Park, connect visitors to the landscape through profound physical experiences. Dry Falls Visitor Center hangs near the edge of an enormous cliff and a wall of windows allows visitors to look down hundreds of feet into the bottom of the canyon. Pot Holes State Park is at the bottom of the canyon and resembles a puzzle of connected lakes.

Studies have not yet been completed by the local byway organization to measure the impact of educational materials on visitor numbers or visitor behavior. The organization is tracking the visitor use of printed guides to the area including one on geologic trips in Grant County Washington (Amara, 1996) and one on a bird watching trail in Washington State (AWCCC, 2003). Communities along the byway corridor continue to strive for increased tourism and accelerated economic development along the byway.

Conclusion

Deep pride in a 'sense of place' and 'power of story' are the prime drivers that motivate communities to seek national recognition for their extraordinary roadways. Through the designation, they issue an invitation to share their special places with others. They understand that their byway is one part of a collage of roads that together represent the spectrum of America's landscapes.

The way forward

Recent studies conducted by niche marketing groups in the United States have sought demographic information that would help define the interests and travel patterns of travelers who express primary interest in experiencing nature, culture or history. These studies have been commissioned by the National Trust for Historic Preservation, *National Geographic Traveler Magazine*; Federal Highway Administration and America's Byways Resource Center; America's Byways Resource Center and Federal Highway Administration.

The results of these national studies display remarkable overlap and reveal that heritage travelers, geotourism travelers, and byway travelers share a common profile: They are older, better traveled, have higher educational levels and report higher household incomes than American travelers in general. Most important, all three niche groups expressed interest in travel experiences that ranged far beyond their primary interests. They are more likely to shop, seek culinary experiences, enjoy nightlife, and engage in active recreation than American travelers as a whole. Since Scenic Byways actively and deliberately connect visitors to the width and breadth of experiences along specific highway corridors, it is expected that visitors will turn to byways in increasing numbers in the future.

References

Amara M.S. (1996) *Geologic road trips in Grant County Washington*, Adam East Museum and Art Center.

AWCCC (Audubon Washington and Coulee Corridor Consortium) (2003) 'The great Washington state birding trail', brochure.

Bates USA Midwest (2000) 'Strategic brand analysis for national scenic byways', Federal Highway Administration.

Dinosaur Diamond Prehistoric Highway Partnership (2009) accesssed 8 October 2009, http://www.dinosaurdiamond.org.

Dinosaur Diamond Prehistoric Highway Partnership (2009) *Exploratory Interactive Guidebook*, brochure, Fruita, Colorado: Dinosaur Diamond Prehistoric Highway Partnership.

Federal Highway Administration (1994) *Scenic Byways Advisory Committee Report*, United States Department of Transportation.

Federal Highway Administration (2009) *Assessing and sustaining the quality of the America's Byways® collection*, United States Department of Transportation. Available at http://bywaysonline.org/program/reports/

Mingo, J (ed.) (1997) *Community Guide to Planning and Managing a Scenic Byway*, US Department of Transportation, Federal Highway Administration.

Otak (2009) 'Coulee Corridor National Scenic Byway interpretive plan and design guidelines', Washington:Otak. http://www.otak.com

17 The UNESCO global network of national geoparks

Patrick J. Mc Keever, Geological Survey of Northern Ireland,
Nickolas Zouros, University of the Aegean, Greece,
Margarete Patzak, UNESCO, Division of Ecological and
Earth Sciences and Jutta Weber, Geo-Naturpark Bergstraße-
Odenwald, Germany

Introduction

Today, at the start of the 21st century we can look back over a century that has seen enormous advances in our understanding of how our planet functions. While we might still not be able to predict exactly when an earthquake will happen or exactly when a volcano will erupt, we know why these phenomena occur. We know how and why mountain ranges are formed and we know how the very face of our planet changes over millions of years as the tectonic plates of the Earth's crust continue their relentless move over the surface of the planet. But it wasn't always like this. For centuries, people had no clear understanding of Earth processes. Nevertheless, people were in awe of their landscape and of the planet's natural phenomena and stories, myths and legends arose to help explain them. We, as geoscientists, now have explanations for all these phenomena. However, perhaps we should ask ourselves: How successful are we at sharing this knowledge with those with no formal geological training? Moreover, how good are we at preserving these phenomena and special landscapes for future generations. Many people today still ask the same questions our ancestors of long ago asked. Yet, all across our planet we have places where the amazing story of our planet can be told to the non-specialist without the need for the use of the esoteric language so often employed by geoscientists. Moreover these places should be conserved for the future. But it should not be our aim to conserve them in a sterile way where only the geoscientist can visit, it should be our aim to conserve in a way that the local communities can take ownership of these places and where they can feel that these places contribute positively to their everyday lives.

Local communities across Europe, China and increasingly other parts of the world, are beginning to realise that their geological heritage can provide a source of sustainable economic benefit to their area. Rather than exploit this heritage in the non-renewable fashion of the past, there is an opportunity to manage it in a way that conserves it for the future through the development of geotourism. This form of sustainable economic development has the potential to directly impact on those rural areas that have suffered from economic stagnation or demographic decline. But why should geoscientists be involved in such activities? In simple terms, we have to demonstrate to the wider public the relevance of geological science in the 21st century. We have to re-build the bridge between our knowledge of the Earth, its history and its landscape and the total dependence of modern society upon Earth's natural resources, a link that was known to generations past.

The Global Geoparks Network

In June 2000, representatives of four European territories, which had separately been pro-moting geological conservation and sustainable development, came together in Greece to discuss their common socio-economic problems (stagnant economic development, high unemployment, rural depopulation and an ageing of the remaining population) and how to address these problems through the protection of geological heritage and the promo-tion of geological tourism. The result was the signing of a convention declaring the crea-tion of the European Geoparks Network. The purpose of this new designation was to provide a network within which to share information and expertise, and to define com-mon tools in addressing the above objectives (Zouros and Martini, 2003).

In November 2000, the four members of the new network, Réserve Géologique de Haute-Provence (France), Lesvos Petrified Forest (Greece), Maestrazgo Cultural Park (Spain), and Vulkaneifel (Germany) invited interested regions and organizations from across Europe to join them in learning more about geoparks and to apply for mem-bership of the new network. From its formal beginnings in June 2000, the European Geoparks Network grew rapidly and successfully. One of the key early successes for the European Geoparks Network was the signing of an official agreement of collaboration with UNESCO (the then Division of Earth Sciences) in April 2001 which placed the new network under the auspices of UNESCO, thereby confirming its important contributions to conservation and sustainable development issues in Europe. Since then, UNESCO has played an important role in the development of the European Geoparks Network and has used the European model as the one to follow as they rolled out their Global Geoparks Network (Eder, 2004). At a meeting in UNESCO headquarters in Paris in February 2004 representatives from the scientific board of the International Geoscience Programme, the International Geographical Union and the International Union of Geo-logical Sciences along with international experts on geological heritage, conservation and promotion agreed to the establishment of a 'Global Network of National Geoparks (GGN) under the auspices of UNESCO'. This decision was endorsed by the first Interna-tional Geoparks Conference held in Beijing in June 2004. Three goals were established for the new global network, i.e. conserving a healthy environment, education about earth sciences to the wider public and fostering sustainable local economic development. Currently (May 2009) the GGN comprises 58 members in 18 nations including 34 in Europe, 20 in China and one each in Australia, Brazil, Iran and Malaysia.

But what actually is a 'geopark'? As specified in the operational guidelines, a geopark is not just a collection of geological sites, but is a territory with a particular geological her-itage of international significance and with a sustainable territorial development strategy (in Frey *et al.*, 2001). It must have clearly defined boundaries and a sufficient area to allow for true territorial economic development, primarily through tourism. Geological sites must be of international importance in terms of their scientific quality, rarity, aes-thetic appeal and educational value. Sites can not only be related to geology but also to archaeology, ecology, history and culture. All these sites in the geopark must be linked in a network and constitute thematic parks with routes, trails and rock sections that can benefit from protection and management measures.

Typical activities in a global geopark include the development of walking and cycling trails, the training of local people to act as guides, education courses, provision of in-formation signage and the development of modern museums and visitor centres (Figure 17.1). The ultimate aim of a global geopark is to bring enhanced employment opportunities for the people who live there. These opportunities are now being realized right across the expanding network but they are being created in association with the conservation of the geological heritage of the geoparks. But this conservation is not of the restrictive type. Geoparks use a holistic approach to conservation where all aspects of a geopark's natural and cultural heritage are valued, conserved and promoted under the geopark label. Three examples, from different parts of the European continent illustrate these things (see later).

Figure 17.1: A photo of a group on a geological walking route within the Réserve Géologique de Haute-Provence European Geopark visiting the in-site remains of a fossilised ichthyosaur.

Geoconservation is implicitly expressed within the operational guidelines of the Global Geoparks Network through the strong statement that no destruction or sale of the geological value of a global geopark may be be tolerated, except for scientific or educational purposes. Furthermore, a geopark has to develop and enhance methods and tools for the preservation and conservation of geological heritage, as well as to support and develop scientific research related to the various disciplines of the earth sciences. Education and training on the natural and geological environment comes as a direct consequence of conservation strategies and aims to promote knowledge and value of geological heritage, outlining the concept of geodiversity in the territory. Sustainable development is considered as an essential practice for economic development in the territory and for the strengthening of the management structure and, therefore, for the geopark itself. Geological heritage is evaluated and considered from the inhabitants' perspective, presence and needs. The contribution of the geopark is thus seen through the enhancement and promotion of a certain image related to the geological heritage and the development of tourism with related actions. This should have a direct impact on the territory influencing its inhabitants' living conditions and environment, lead to a revalidation of the values of the territory's heritage and enforce active participation to the territory's cultural revitalization as a whole. Finally, and crucially, a global geopark has to work within the network for its further expansion and cohesion, collaborate with other geoparks and local enterprises for the achievement of its objectives, create and promote new by-products linked with geological and cultural heritage in the spirit of complementarity with the other Global Geoparks Network members. In practice this is mostly done through regional networks such as the European Geoparks Network or the Asia-Pacific Geoparks and Geoheritage Network (which was founded in November 2007).

Lesvos Petrified Forest European and Global Geopark

Lesvos is a Greek island located in the northeastern Aegean Sea. It is the third largest of the Greek islands and the eighth largest in the Mediterranean Sea. It has an area of 1630 square kilometres with 320 kilometres of coastline. Its population is approximately 90,000, a third of which lives in its capital Mytilene in the southeastern part of the island. The remaining population is distributed in small towns and villages. The economy on Lesvos is largely rural based including the production of olive oil, fishing, the rearing of cattle and the production of ouzo. Tourism, while important, is on a small scale compared to other Greek islands and is largely culturally based. The economic development of the island was for decades stagnating. This was due to several reasons including the proximity of the island to the Turkish coast and the perception that the island was a dangerous place to go to due the political instability of the region. The remote western part of the island, around the small fishing village of Sigri, was especially hard hit with limited employment opportunities and rising depopulation.

Figure 17.2: An example of geoconservation from the Lesvos Petrified Forest European Geopark.

However, it was the presence of well preserved fossil trees that have helped transform the area around Sigri. Realizing the significance of this special geological heritage, the local community, spurred on by the University of the Aegean, have ensured that the so-called Petrified Forest of Lesvos is a nationally protected site. Guided tours are offered to visitors and these have expanded from the petrified forest itself to the surrounding volcanic landscape of western Lesvos (e.g. Figure 17.2). A state-of-the-art museum has been built, a key factor in keeping visitors in this part of the island. The museum not only explains the geological heritage of Lesvos, it also acts as a major retail outlet for a range of local agricultural and traditional craft products. From an area with few employment opportunities, the creation of the Lesvos Petrified Forest European Geopark, has transformed western Lesvos attracting 90,000 visitors annually and employing 35 directly with hundreds of new jobs having been created indirectly. The geopark is now the islands main visitor attraction and is an excellent example of how the holistic approach to conservation used in geoparks can be successful from the perspective of the local community and the scientific/conservation community.

Marble Arch Caves European and Global Geopark

At the opposite end of Europe, in the far north-west corner of Ireland are the Marble Arch Caves. The caves are located in County Fermanagh which covers an area of 1692 square kilometres and is home to 57,000 people, most of whom live in the county town of Enniskillen. Like Lesvos, the economy of Fermanagh is based on agriculture, mostly on beef, dairy, sheep, pigs and some poultry products.

Tourism too is important with the county often referred to as Ireland's lake district. However tourism is much less developed here than in, for example, the south-west of the country in counties Cork and Kerry and much of the tourism potential of Fermanagh is yet to be realized. The ecomony of Fermanagh, like the rest of the north of Ireland, was until recently blighted by political violence and instability. As a so-called border county, many of the small roads that led into the Republic of Ireland were blocked leading to a huge distortion of the natural economic hinterland of the region with consequential damage to the regional economy. This, coupled with on-going political violence at the time, was a huge deterrent to potential investors.

At the height of the unrest the local authority, Fermanagh District Council, made the strategic decision to develop the caves at Marble Arch into a tourist attraction (Figure 17.3). Recognizing the need for the caves to offer something special in order to attract visitors into the area, a policy of conservation and sustainable development was employed from the start. Opening in 1985, the caves have now received over 1,000,000 visitors with the annual average number of visitors running at around 60,000. The council have also taken ownership of a vast swath of Cuilcagh Mountain immediately south of the caves and have instigated an award-winning conservation scheme on the large area of blanket bog here. But again, it is not a sterile type of conservation, education groups of all ages are encouraged to visit and new walking routes have opened up the area to a new generation of visitors. Today, the Marble Arch Caves European Geopark is the main tourism hub in this part of Ireland. It employs over 50 local people during the tourism season (April–September) with a staff of 14 retained throughout the year. The indirect benefit of the geopark is also large with new accommodation providers opening for business and new restaurants opening in the nearby villages of Blacklion and Belcoo. Currently the benefits of the geopark are spreading following a two-phase expansion of the geopark's area. In 2007, the geopark expanded north across other areas of Fermanagh. In 2008, the geopark expanded south across the border into County Cavan in the Republic and across the roads that were once blocked but which now allow the movement of the benefits of geoparks across this once hostile border.

Figure 17.3: A European Geopark information corner at the visitors centre of the Marble Arch Caves European Geopark.

Bergstrasse-Odenwald Geopark

The Geopark Bergstrasse-Odenwald in the Federal Republic of Germany is located about 50 km south of the international airport Frankfurt/Main. From here, the region is just one hour away by car or train. The landscape of the geopark covers an area of 3500 square kilometres between Rhine, Bergstrasse, Odenwald, Main and Neckar. The region is characterized by over 500 million years of geological history, a multi-faceted natural landscape and a thousand-year-old culture. There are three UNESCO World Heritage sites within the boundaries of the geopark: Messel Fossil Pit in the north, Lorsch Abbey in the west and the Roman Limes in the east. The geopark rangers offer tours of the landscape and family-friendly nature, and environmental programmes under the motto 'Nature with the professional', as well as 'Geo and Enjoyment' tours (e.g. Figure 17.4). More than 30 geopark trails (e.g. Table 17.1) have been created throughout the region for those seeking to explore the landscape on their own. The rock bottle (Figure 17.5) is part of the Wine and Rocks Trail. The rocks represent a stratigraphic column of the main rock types and geological units of the Geopark territory.

Figure 17.4: Continents on the move through the ages – jigsaw puzzle for geo-educational activities with Geopark Rangers.

Table 17.1: Examples of geotrails

Amorbach: Sandstone trail through the typical landscape of the Bunter Sandstone Odenwald (Continental Triassic) with geological information, historical sandstone buildings, information about the use of sandstone in former everyday life, and beautiful scenic viewpoints.

Heppenheim: Wine and rocks adventure trail dealing with geology, soils, wine growing, climate change, grapes of the world, medieval grapes. Integrated: educational rock sculpture, arts sculptures (rock, steel, wood) which communicate the relation of man, nature and culture, and a Mediterranean garden, related to climate change and its impact on the flora and fauna. Guided tours, wine tastings, annual programme and special wine edition.

Reichelsheim: Historical mining trail with information about two major mining phases in the Odenwald area – (16th and 18th century). Geological background, mining techniques, economic impact. Additionally: regional museum in Reichelsheim with mineral and mining exhibition.

Michelstadt: Geotrail with two sections through the cultural landscape of the Michelstadt graben structure. Landscape development related to geological features, cultural highlights, mining history. Annual programme for guided tours available.

Weinheim/Schriesheim: Geotrail titled 'Rocks, Canyons and Tales' with two sections related to geological and landscape development of the Crystalline Odenwald and the Rhine Rift Valley. Canyon route (historical Baryte mining area), accessible only in dry weather conditions.

Rothenberg: Geotrail titled 'The lack of water in sandstone landscapes'. Geology of the Bunter sandstone Odenwald related to aquifers, typical strata springs, water distribution networks and landscape development. Historical techniques of water catchment and storage.

(Source: http://www.geo-naturpark.net/daten/pfade/geopfade.php)

World History Site Messel Pit, a close cooperation partner and Geopark entrance gate, still has the capacity to surprise! Besides the famous little prehistoric horse, palaetherium parvulum, just recently the world was introduced to Ida, a female primate from the Eocene epoch. The unprecedented, world-wide reaction to our oldest known predecessor comes just at the right time: the state of Hesse is currently building an information and visitor centre on the edge of Messel Pit, to be opened in summer 2010. Various topics will be grouped together under the heading 'Time and Messel Dimensions'. The visitor centre will be more than an open window into the world of 47 million years ago, as it will also reveal new dimensions for exploring the history of the Messel Pit. The centre will also house a gift shop and a bistro. Visitors, however, may enter Messel Pit only by guided tours.

Each year, the geopark recognizes a 'Geotope of the Year' (Table 17.2). Selected sites are windows in different phases of Earth history which show the strong connection with nature, culture and history of the territory. Guided tours are available by the geopark rangers, as well as comprehensive brochures and information on the geopark website.

Figure 17.5: The Rock Bottle, an educational rock sculpture at the "Wine and rocks adventure trail", filled with the typical rocks of the Geopark territory in stratigraphic order. Comprehensive explanatory panel aside. Photo: J. Weber, from: www.weinundstein.net

The European Geoparks Network: regional cooperation

As mentioned earlier, the Global Geoparks Network operates primarily through regional cooperation. Such regional cooperation is best exemplified by the European Geoparks Network which has been operating for eight years. One of its stated aims is to exchange ideas and expertise on promoting geological awareness and sustainable development. It is with this aim in mind that the members come together twice per year. One meeting is for the network on its own while the other takes place a few days in advance of the annual meeting and is open to everyone, members and non-members alike. These meetings promote the use of common tools such as the website (www.europeangeoparks. org), magazines, displays, events but also encourage members to develop exchanges or projects between smaller groups of geoparks.

Table 17.2: Bergstrasse-Odenwald Geopark: Geotopes of the Year

Geotopes of the year	Location	Age, brief description
2002	Felsenmeer, Lautertal	Crystalline rocks of Palaeozoic age (320 Ma), Crystalline Odenwald, variscian magmatic arc. Additionally: abandoned Roman quarry with more than 300 relics and Geopark information centre. Earth history and culture.
2003	Abandoned quarry Olfen, Beerfelden	Bunter Sandstone of Mesozoic age (245 Ma) Bunter Sandstone Odenwald, lithified river deposits of the German Triassic basin. Earth history and economic history.
2004	Nature conservation area "Kühkopf - landscape in a river", Stockstadt,	Sands and gravels of the river Rhine (from Pleistocene until today), creation of the Rhine rift valley (50 Ma). Additionally: nature conservation area and European bird reserve, information centre and exhibition. Earth history, landscape formation and use.
2005	Otzberg hill, Hering	Basalt columns of Tertiary age (22 Ma), volcanism related to the Rhine rift valley. Additionally: at the top of the volcano a relic medieval castle with museum and restaurant Earth history, landscape formation and culture.
2006	Eberstadter Höhlenwelten, showcave Buchen	Limestones of Mesozoic age (220 Ma). Marine deposits of the German Triassic "Muschelkalk", huge system of carst caves, one open to the public. Additionally: geological trail around the cave and abandoned quarry, and restaurant. Earth history and nature.
2007	Glockenbuckel, Viernheim	Pleistocene dune (10,000 a) of Cenozoic age. Part of the peri-glacial dune belt of the Bergstrasse area. Additionally: nature conservation area. Information: nature conservation centre Bergstrasse. Earth history and nature.
2008	Heunesäulen, Miltenberg,	Bunter sandstone columns (sedimentary rocks of Mesozoic age, 245 Ma). Historical relation: Roman or medieval age, until now not clarified. Earth history and culture.
2009	Abandoned quarry Leferenz, Dossenheim	Porphyric rocks of Palaeozoic age (290 Ma). Volcanic eruption relics and pyroclastics. Quarrying history, arts (sculpturing), outdoor museum and biotope. Earth history, economic history and culture.

Once a year all members participate in European Geoparks Week. This is a series of coordinated events (guided walks, talks, activities for children) which occur in the same week in every member of the network and which is aimed at increasing public awareness about earth science issues in general and about building awareness of the European Geoparks Network and our great shared geological heritage. Not only is the public in one geopark informed about activities occurring there but they are made aware of the fact that they are part of a much wider series of events that will be happening across Europe.

Transnational networking and sharing of knowledge will mean new concepts, outputs and results for further integration on spatial planning, transnational environmental problems and development issues. The creation of quality standards for geopark services and products is one of the key aims of the network. As part of this, an evaluation process has been established that will try to measure the level of quality in infrastructure, services and sustainable management in each member of the network. The process will be repeated every four years to ensure that the level of quality remains of the highest order. An evaluation dossier has been drawn up and the evaluation process occurs in two parts. First, the geopark subject to the evaluation completes a self-evaluation. This is followed by a visit and an evaluation by an independent referee. A geopark which fails to reach a certain quality level in the evaluation process will lose its membership of the network. To date this has happened to three former members.

The network continues to expand, drawing in new expertise and knowledge from all parts of Europe. Many new membership applications are pending and members from across the network are assisting these territories in their membership bids to ensure the overall high quality of services the network insists on is maintained. The network is still young and the coming years will continue to be one of great challenge. With the global partners in the Global Geoparks Network, the members will continue to assist UNESCO in bringing the geopark concept to all parts of the world, especially to the developing world where sustainable tourism, such as that developed within geoparks, could lead to job creation in local rural communities for the benefit of those communities.

Acknowledgements

The authors would like to acknowledge the help and advice of the members of the coordination committee of the European Geoparks Network on whose behalf this article has been written. The EU INTERREG IIIC, IIIB (North-West Europe), LEADER IIC AND LEADER+ programmes are acknowledged for their financial support of the activities of the European Geoparks Network. The Geological Survey of Northern Ireland, the Department of Geography at the University of the Aegean and the Division of Ecological and Earth Sciences of UNESCO are gratefully thanked for their continuing support for the European and Global Geoparks initiatives.

References

Eder, F.W. (2004) 'The Global UNESCO Network of Geoparks', in Zhao, X., Jiang, J., Dong, S., Li., and Zhao, T. (eds), *Proceedings of the First International Conference on Geoparks*, Beijing: Geological Publishing House, pp.1-3.

Frey, M-L., Martini, G. and Zouros, N. (2001) 'European Geopark Charter', in Frey, M-L. (ed.), *European Geoparks Magazine* issue 1, 28.

Martini, G. and Zouros, N. (2001) 'European geoparks: geological heritage and European identity – cooperation for a common future', in Frey, M-L., (ed.), *European Geoparks Magazine*, issue 1, 4.

Zouros, N. and Martini, G. (2003) 'Introduction to the European Geoparks Network', in Zouros, N., Martini, G., and Frey, M-L. (eds), *Proceedings of the 2nd European Geoparks Network Meeting*. Lesvos, Greece: Natural History Museum of the Lesvos Petrified Forest, pp. 17-21.

18 The future of geotourism: where to from here?

Ross Dowling and David Newsome

Introduction

Geotourism is on the rise the world over. Governments, tourism businesses, geological organizations, community groups, conservationists, NGOs, and individuals are seeking a future for the protection of our geological heritage and community advancement through sustainable tourism development. Countries as far apart as New Zealand and Iceland, USA and China, are getting involved and lifting our knowledge on geology and landscape, through interpretation and education. The future is exciting for geotourism as evidenced by the increased interest in geological awareness, the phenomenal rise of the Geopark Movement, and the rising interest in geotourism as a tool for conservation of our geoheritage.

But whilst in its infancy, geotourism has a number of issues to address as part of its evolving future. They include:

1. The need for a uniformly accepted definition of geotourism

2. The importance of geoheritage conservation

3. Understanding geotourism's stakeholders

4. The growth of geotourism's attractions and products

5. The importance of risk management at geotourism sites

6. Learning more about geotourists

7. The need for geotourism education

8. The importance of 'connection' in interpretation

9. The emerging role of technology in geotourism

10. Capitalizing on the power of the Global Geoparks brand

1. The need for a uniformly accepted definition of geotourism

As stated in our introduction to this book, geotourism is a distinct subsector of natural area tourism firmly entrenched in 'geological' tourism. We do not support the view of *National Geographic* that geotourism is 'geographic' tourism. From our extensive travels around the world attending geotourism and/or geopark conferences and observations in the field, it is clearly evident to us that geotourism is universally understood as 'geological' in nature and not 'geographically' oriented. It is clear that the earliest definition of geotourism was made by the English geological historian Dr Thomas Hose in a 1995 article in the journal *Environmental Interpretation*. Under the heading 'Selling the story of Britain's stone' he discussed the need for this new niche form of tourism offering both a new packaged tourism product and the potential to foster geoheritage. Under a section of his paper entitled 'Geotourism' he stated that it is:

> *The provision of interpretive and service facilities to enable tourists to acquire knowledge and understanding of the geology and geomorphology of a site (including its contribution to the development of the Earth sciences) beyond the level of mere aesthetic appreciation.*
>
> (Hose, 1995: 17)

It was a development of a working definition for research (Hose, 1994: 2) informally undertaken for English Nature on 'site-specific geological interpretation' at Sites of Special Scientific Interest (SSSIs) and subsequently developed (Hose, 1996) and refined (Hose, 2000). Thus we wish to clearly draw a line in the sand to stop the 'geologic' versus 'geographic' confusion and reemphasize that is only the *geologic* character of geotourism that is referred to:

1.   In the first recorded definition of geotourism (Hose, 1995) as later further developed by Hose (1996) and Hose (2000).

2.   In the first comprehensive book on the subject *Geotourism* (Dowling and Newsome, 2006).

3.   By UNESCO in the 'Global Geoparks Network' (UNESCO, 2006)

4.   During the 'Inaugural Global Geotourism Conference' held in Western Australia in August 2008 when over 220 delegates from 36 countries discussed geotourism as 'geologic tourism' (Dowling and Newsome, 2008).

Now taking all of the definitions into account, we have suggested that the generally accepted definition of geotourism at the start of 2010 is:

> *Geotourism is a form of natural area tourism that specifically focuses on geology and landscape. It promotes tourism to geosites and the conservation of geo-diversity and an understanding of earth sciences through appreciation and learning. This is achieved through independent visits to geological features, use of geo-trails and view points, guided tours, geo-activities and patronage of geosite visitor centres.*

Thus the character of geotourism is such that it:

1.   Is geologically based and can occur in either natural, rural or urban environments

2.   Fosters geoheritage conservation through appropriate sustainability measures

3.   Advances sound geological understanding through interpretation and education

4.   Generates tourist or visitor satisfaction.

This definition involves all of the wider aspects of tourism activity as geotourism requires transport, access, accommodation and services, trained staff, planning and management and reiterates that stakeholders in geotourism can include investors, government planners, environmental groups and universities (Dowling, 2009).

Taking the above themes further is central to the advancement of geotourism over the next five to ten years.

2. The importance of geoheritage conservation

Central to our understanding of geoheritage protection and conservation is the need to identify our geological and landscape attributes so that appropriate judgements can be made about them. Just because a site has been identified as having heritage values does not make it a candidate for development as a geosite. Malaki *et al.* (2008) state that whilst concepts such as geological heritage, geosite, geopark and geotope have been widely used over the past few years, the level of understanding of their significance and the implications of these concepts in practice is open to discussion. These authors define geosites as being derived from natural history and argue that they can help people to understand the story of the Earth and provoke an awareness of the need for their preservation.

A number of countries are preparing geoheritage inventories and assessments. In Poland a 'Catalogue of Geotouristic Objects' was established in 2006 (Slomka *et al.*, 2006). The Catalogue was the first such initiative in the country and aimed to select and describe in detail a representative sample of geotouristic sites representing the geodiversity of Poland. From about 600 initial proposals a group of 100 geosites were selected representing a range of geological and geomorphological structures, landforms and processes. The catalogue or list is viewed as being a valuable source of information for both tourists and local visitors alike and it provides an exemplar for future developments, as many interesting geosites still await recognition from local authorities, tourist agencies and local communities.

In Morocco, a survey of the Atlas Mountains has created an inventory of volcanic geosites (Malaki *et al.*, 2008). The goal of the study was to strike a balance between those sites which should be classified as having heritage conservation value as well as others with local or regional development potential. The authors suggested that the establishment of geoparks would be an appropriate tool to heighten public awareness of the values of geological and geomorphological heritage. They suggested that this would ensure the protection and promotion of the volcanic geosites whilst at the same time adding significantly to local development.

3. Understanding geotourism's stakeholders

There are a number of stakeholders in tourism development and management. Each group has a contribution to make to the nature of tourism and their own success is dependent upon the contribution of others. Tourism development involves multiple stakeholders including business and government as well as community and environmental groups. A central task in stakeholder development is to establish who the stakeholders actually are and whether or not they adequately represent the affected stakeholders. This can be done by identification, self-nomination or referral.

In the development of geotourism it is important that tourism should more equitably balance the costs and benefits of conservation, which are often borne by local communities. This balance can be achieved through the creation of mutually beneficial, self-sustaining mechanisms that support tourism, geoheritage, institutions and communities. Ensuring the long-term success of geotourism depends on creating local incentives to conserve and protect environmental amenities. The local host community and wider community groups are both included in a wider group again, that of the stakeholder. In geotourism, this group includes the tourism industry; planners and investors; protected area managers; conservation non-government organizations; the local communities; and finally, the tourists themselves.

While tourists who are on geotours are primarily interested in viewing landforms and other geological features, they are generally also interested in interacting with local communities in a sustainable manner. This can occur when visitors view geo-attractions with local guides, visit villages, sample local food and drink, or watch crafts being made, music played or dances. Local guides are often especially highly valued by geotourists as they can provide deeper understanding of the surrounding geological and biotic environment. Geotourism development represents a partnership between local people, the private sector and government and it is gaining acceptance because it makes good economic sense and can benefit all partners.

4. The growth of geotourism's attractions and products

Geotourism attractions are being developed around the world in order to foster the development of local and regional communities. Examples have been presented of selected geotourism developments in many countries, and other examples are now briefly introduced from Italy and Slovenia. (See also Dowling and Newsome, *Global Geotourism Perspectives*, forthcoming.)

Italy

Another example of developing geotourism attractions and products is from Italy. The Beigua Geopark became a Global Geopark in 2005 and since that time the region has gained increased attention from local authorities, tourist organizations and operators, entrepreneurs, farmers, universities and research institutions, schools, volunteers and environmental associations (Burlando *et al.*, 2009). In order to capitalize on their newfound status, the park administrators devised and implemented a new sustainable tourism development strategy. The strategy launched a network of touristic offers as a result of a cooperative and participative debate with all the stakeholders in the area. As a result they have connected landscape, cultural heritage, traditional foods and sports facilities with the region's unique geological and landscape features, all designed to foster regional economic growth. Cultural attractions and heritage buildings are now featuring local cuisine to add value to their products, and educational visits are targeted outside the period of peak tourist activity which should help to extend the shoulder season. As a result, geotourism activities are providing alternative opportunities to bring economic and social benefits at a local and regional level, whilst enhancing the geological, cultural and traditional heritage of the region.

Slovenia

The Idrija Municipality in Slovenia has a rich geological history based on one of the oldest mercury mines in the world (Kavčič *et al.*, 2009). The local museum offers a rich geological collection of minerals and fossils from the region and visitors have an opportunity to learn about the origin of the mercury ore deposit. In addition there are a number of walk trails based around the themes of geology, landscape and hydrology, botany and zoology. These attract a wide range of visitors including school groups, families, mountaineers, cyclists and students of natural sciences (Režun *et al.*, 2009).

5. The importance of risk management at geotourism sites

The golden rule in tourism is to put safety first, always. Tourists travelling to remote areas, active volcanoes, glaciated zones, marine areas, high mountains and hot deserts are always testing the boundaries at the interface of acceptable risk. While the adventure tourism industry has to live by this understanding, it took a while for the ecotourism industry to understand its importance. For geotourism development and a successful geotourism industry, it is absolutely essential for the full import of the centrality of risk management to be grasped at the outset.

This is well underscored by Karkut in Chapter 7 and King in Chapter 9 in relation to tourism development at active volcanic sites. Karkut states that there has been a growing interest and understanding regarding the risks that volcanoes pose for the populations around them. In response to this situation, the General Assembly of the United Nations declared the 1990s the International Decade for Natural Disaster Reduction (IDNDR) and as a result of this initiative, considerable research was undertaken by multidisciplinary teams of volcanologists, social scientists, emergency planners, and local communities. In the case of Mt Vesuvius in Italy, a National Emergency Plan for Vesuvian Area (NEPVA), was devised based on a pattern of warning earthquakes. The model created three zones of hazard – an inner 'red zone' of immediate danger, an outer 'yellow zone' of some danger, and a 'blue zone', where it is anticipated there may be some element of danger. Karkut suggests that even in the case of the extensively analysed Vesuvius emergency plan, it does not currently appear to fully acknowledge that economic and cultural factors have the potential to override the best-laid strategies even if there is great awareness of the volcanic risk.

In the USA, King discussed measures taken by the Hawaii Volcanoes National Park to minimize risks to visitors from an active volcanic landscape. She notes that risk management plays a pivotal role within Hawaii's geosites and that managing visitor risk requires constant assessment by park staff. She concludes that finding a balance between the risks to on-site visitors and protecting the resource is essential for the long-term sustainable use of geosites.

6. Understanding geotourists

According to Hose (2008) there appear to be two kinds of geotourist. One is the dedicated geotourist who visits geosites for the purpose of personal educational or intellectual improvement and enjoyment, and the other is the casual geotourist who visits geosites primarily for the purpose of pleasure and some limited intellectual stimulation. In this book Paik et al. (Chapter 10) note that the tourists visiting the Cretaceous geosites in South Korea are mostly casual geotourists, while students and teachers fall into the dedicated geotourist category as they have more interest in the scientific meaning of the geosites they are visiting. Most casual geotourists visiting Korean geosites have little knowledge and experience of geology and geomorphology, but still appreciate scenic views and unique features of geology and geomorphology. In order to improve scientific understanding and appreciation of Korean geosites for all visitors, an active programme of geotrail development and interpretive guiding is required. Achieving this will require the training of well-educated guides and a combination of generalized and carefully designed interpretive trails that cater for diverse levels of geotourist backgrounds.

Whilst there is a growing amount of research and understanding on the supply side of geotourism and geoparks (Dowling, 2008), there is relatively little known about the demand for these products (Robinson and Roots, 2008). Thus a pilot study was conducted to understand the extent of interest that Australian geoscientists have in participating in geotours either in Australia or overseas (Mao et al., 2009).

Members of the Geological Society of Australia (GSA) were surveyed in 2008 to determine their reasons for travel generally, as well as their specific interest in geotourism. Findings from the 154 respondents indicate that the most important travel purposes amongst the respondents were to increase their knowledge of geological sites and landforms, satisfy their curiosity, have memorable experiences, obtain intellectual stimulation, and visit destinations offering a unique package of features and attractions. Thus respondent's priorities were principally to increase their knowledge of geological sites and landforms.

A key finding was that respondents prefer to travel independently in Australia or overseas rather than participating in group tours. Results indicated that respondents were unlikely to join a tour to visit a geotourism site in Australia (46 per cent) or overseas (45 per cent). Conversely respondents said they were more likely to travel independently to geotourism sites either in Australia (77 per cent) or overseas (53 per cent). These results indicate that geotourism destinations have not yet been fully developed for organized tour groups and also that the members of the GSA surveyed are well-travelled and knowledgeable enough to travel independently to geotourism sites. The findings of Mao *et al.* (2009) indicate that there is a strong interest in – visiting geotourism sites, increasing knowledge in history and geology, meeting people from different cultures, enjoying outdoor activities, and staying in simple accommodation.

Thus at this point in time we are still learning about geotourists, their demographics, motivations and behaviours and it will need considerably more research to even begin to make the broadest generalizations.

7. The need for geotourism education

Whilst geology has been a primary science subject in universities for a long time, both environmental science and tourism as university disciplines are relatively new. By extension, geoconservation and geotourism education are in their infancy. In several Portuguese universities, undergraduate degrees in geology, geography and biology also include some modules on geoconservation. At the University of Minho, a master's course on geological heritage and geoconservation has been available since 2005 and in other universities, master's degree courses on geology and geography offer optional geoconservation modules (Brilha, 2009).

In Australia, at Edith Cowan University in Perth, a geotourism unit is offered in the tourism programme as part of a tourism degree in a faculty of business. As part of their course the students participated in geotourism conferences in Western Australia organized by the Forum Advocating Cultural and Eco Tourism (FACET). These included the Inaugural Global Geotourism Conference (2008) and the Regional Tourism Development Conference (2009).

Geotourism is still considered new in Brazil, but in order to foster its awareness in the region of Campos Gerais in Paraná State, the Tourism Department of the Ponta Grossa State University held a 'Tourism Studies Week (SESTUR) – Geotourism', with the support from the Araucaria Foundation (Moreira *et al.*, forthcoming). This was the first event of its kind in the country and encompassed a number of groups including those from education and government. The programme comprised lectures, seminars and fieldtrips on geotourism and geoparks. The event included over 100 participants and 27 papers and was widely covered by local media. A key goal was to inform the local community of the possibility of creating a local geopark (Campos Gerais).

Geotourism education is emerging in a number of countries at a range of levels including at both secondary and tertiary institutions. No common themes can be deduced amongst them at this time but it is clear that such education embraces an understanding of geoconservation and sustainable tourism principles. We would also argue that any geotourism course should include at least some element of field study to ensure it is related to 'real world' situations.

8. The importance of 'connection' in interpretation

A central theme throughout the book has been the importance of interpretation to the tourist's understanding of geology and the landscape. Wittlich and Palmer (Chapter 12) described information signs, posters, an information shelter and guided tours as all being part of the tourist experience on the volcanic island of Rangitoto in Auckland's Waitemata Harbour, New Zealand. A survey of tourists found that information signs were the medium used most by visitors (70 per cent) because they were able to see as much or as little as they desired at their own pace.

Hughes and Ballantyne (Chapter 14) discussed the importance of understanding in interpretation as well as the principles underlying the development of interpretive materials. They stressed the importance of a site or park having an interpretive plan, developing interpretive themes and selecting the best interpretive mediums. A key message is the need for geotourism interpretation to be used as a medium to 'connect' with visitors through stories, analogies and humour. Taken to a higher level they suggest that sound interpretation should encourage visitors to actively participate in their experience through questions or quizzes.

An example of the participation of the visitor at a geotourism attraction is illustrated through the Water Adventure Park in Eisenwurzen, Austria, which features a 9m × 11m landscape model representing a geological approach to water activities. The model is an experimental playground which has been accepted by children and adults and now attracts over 50,000 visitors per annum (Kollmann et al., 2009). For example, a thunderstorm is triggered by pushing a button, the rising of the water table in the mountains may be observed through peepholes, and springs begin to release water at hillsides. Streams merge to rivers which finally open out into the sea. Visitors are encouraged to interact with the model, and for example they may add sand to the water to experience the sedimentation in rivers and estuaries. The water flow can be regulated with locks and inundations prevented with sandbags. On a larger scale, visitors may experience the physical and biological properties of water by canoeing, operating locks in small streams, using technical devices and experiencing the importance of water in manufacturing, for which the Eisenwurzen region was famous up to the 19th century.

Our belief is that for the full connection to be made between the visitor and the landscape, the visitor must be challenged through 'Head, Heart and Hand'. This is an application long advocated in environmental education to bring greater connection in ecotourism (Dowling 1976). Put simply, the interaction created through interpretation must provide appropriate and adequate understanding (through the Head) as well as some form of connection (through the Heart). By a combination of these activities the tourist should be moved to do something for the earth (through the Hand). If this simple message is understood and applied, the geological world will better understood and cared for.

9. The emerging role of technology in geotourism

Education and interpretation may be taken to the next level through technology. Tourism is going 'hi tech' and geotourism as a niche form of tourism, is also embracing a range of technological advances. In Chapter 4, Brozinski outlined the situation in Finland through the introduction of Centralized Data Management (CDM) to drive geotourism development. CDM is a programme that outlines a pathway to improve geotourism communication using Information and Communication Technology (ICT). It may be utilized when data management, people and businesses are linked through geology.

The Adamello Brenta Geopark in Italy has a Geobrowser 3D geoguide available which has been developed by Fondazione Graphitech (Povo – TN). This new software allows three-dimensional navigation and visualization of landscapes through a film generated by the software '3D Real Time Exploration' (Ferrari and Mase 2009). A free download of the software Geobrowser 3D is possible in the website of the Park (www.pnab.it). The software, which is suitable for an MP3 audio and video player, simulates a virtual flight over the landscape and receives information about the key attractions and activities. The software allows the visitor to activate many geographical information layers including the region's geosites, hiking trails, Sites of Community Interest (SCI), Special Protection Zones (SPZ), aerial photos and maps. This information is then transferrable to a mobile phone.

Traditional interpretive tools such as field guides (books and pamphlets), interpretive panels and museums and visitor centres, all provide interesting multimedia experiences and prepare the tourists to the outdoor activities. However, according to Baucon (2009) they fail to awaken the visitor's emotions, thus highlighting a gap in the geotourist's experience. To address this situation a pocket sized hand-held device called 'TERRAGAZE mobile' has been developed. This portable multimedia system is directed specifically to geotourism and geoscience education. It is an electronic geological guide capable of displaying a range of media (texts, audio, pictures and animations). Together with GPS support, the device provides specific content to visitors depending on where they are and what they are viewing.

Specific information automatically begins to play when visitors pass a geological point of interest. The mobile allows tourists to interpret the natural and cultural heritage and creates immersive geotourism experiences. It can also locate the closest geosite relative to a visitor's position and they can also use the device to plan their route according to the features they wish to visit. With the device, visitors become engaged in the region they are experiencing by leading them to geological items of interest, listening to stories based around exhibits and attractions, and overlaying new tours on existing content to provide fresh experiences thereby, encouraging repeat visitation. The device has now been adapted for use by cyclists and also includes a location-based game turning a geotourism site into a gigantic game board.

10. Capitalizing on the power of the Global Geoparks brand

The United Nations Educational, Scientific and Cultural Organization (UNESCO), administers the World Heritage and Man and the Biosphere programmes. These programmes focus on the protection of the natural heritage of the Earth. The World Heritage List deals with the protection of cultural and natural sites only of outstanding universal value whereas the World Network of Biosphere Reserves focuses only on biological diversity conservation (fauna and flora) and not on the diversity of geology.

In 2004, UNESCO established a third conservation initiative, the Global Geoparks Network (Chapter 17). Whereas these two former programmes are funded by UNESCO, the geoparks initiative is not (Table 18.1). Geoparks are established on two levels – national and global. National geoparks are endorsed by the country they are in whereas global geoparks are endorsed by UNESCO. The International Network of Geoparks (INoG) is a UNESCO Geoparks initiative. It provides a platform of active cooperation between experts and practitioners in geological heritage. Under the umbrella of UNESCO, and through exchange between the global network partners, important national geological sites gain worldwide recognition and profit through the exchange of knowledge, expertise, experience and staff with other geoparks.

Table 18.1: Comparative UNESCO Protected Areas

Program	Sites	Countries
World Heritage	890	148
Man and the Biosphere	553	107
Geoparks	64	19

The establishment of a geopark brings development of sustainable tourism and other economic and cultural benefits for the community and the park. The inclusion of a park into UNESCO's Global Network is a sign of recognition of excellence in meeting the criteria but is not a legally or governmentally recognized brand. For a geopark to qualify in the INoG it needs to have plans for geoheritage conservation and management as well as for geotourism development.

Since the launch of the Network in 2004, 64 national geoparks have been recognized as global geoparks in 19 countries (Table 18.2). In addition there are two regional geopark networks – European and Asia-Pacific. The real power of the network lies in its global marketing strength and within the next decade we predict that there will be tourists travelling the world to experience geotourism in these parks, in the same way today that there a large number of global tourists who travel to countries solely to visit their sites of world heritage.

Geoparks are not just about rocks-they are about people. It is crucial that they get involved - we want to see as many people as possible getting out and enjoying the geology of the area. Our aim is to maximise geotourism (...) for the benefit of the local economy and to help people to understand the evolution of their local landscape.

Chris Woodley-Stewart, Geopark Manager, North Pennines AONB, UK

Table 18.2: UNESCO's Global Geoparks (Last updated: September 2009)

Countries	Geoparks	Globala Geoparks Network
Australia	Kanawinka	2008
Austria	Eisenwurzen	2004
Brazil	Araripe	2006
China	Danxiashan	2004
	Huangshan	2004
	Lushan	2004
	Shilin	2004
	Songshan	2004
	Wudalianchi	2004
	Yuntaishan	2004
	Zhangjiajie	2004
	Hexingten	2005
	Taining	2005
	Xingwen	2005
	Yandangshan	2005
	Fangshan	2006
	Funiushan	2006
	Jingpohu	2006
	Leiqiong	2006
	Taishan	2006
	Wangwushan	2006
	Longhushan	2008
	Zigong	2008
	Alxa	2009
	Qinling	2009
Croatia	Papuk Geopark	2007
Czech Republic	Bohemian Paradise	2005
France	Réserve Géologique de Haute Provence	2004
	Luberon	2005
Germany	Bergstrasse-Odenwald	2004
	TERRA.vita Naturepark	2004
	Vulkaneifel	2004
	Harz Braunschweiger Land Ostfalen	2005
	Mecklenburg Ice Age Park	2005
	Swabian Albs	2005
Greece	Lesvos Petrified Forest	2004
	Psiloritis	2004
	Chelmos - Vouraikos	2009
Iran	Qeshm Island	2006
Ireland	Copper Coast	2004
Italy	Madonie	2004
	Parco del Beigua	2005
	Geological and Mining Park of Sardinia	2007
	Adamello-Brenta	2008
	Rocca di Cerere	2008
Japan	Itoigawa	2009
	Toya Caldera and Usu Volcano	2009
	Unzen Volcanic Area	2009

Countries	Geoparks	Globala Geoparks Network
Malaysia	Langkawi	2007
Norway	Gea Norvegica	2006
Portugal	Naturtejo	2006
	Arouca	2009
Romania	Hateg Country	2005
Spain	Maestrazgo	2004
	Cabo de Gata - Nijar Natural Park	2006
	Sobrarbe	2006
	Sierras Subbeticas Natural Park	2006
United Kingdom	Marble Arch Caves & Cuilcagh Mountain	2004
	North Pennines AONB	2004
	Forest Fawr	2005
	North West Highlands	2005
	Lochaber	2007
	English Riviera	2007
	GeoMon	2009
	Shetland	2009

Conclusions

In our 2006 book on the subject we outlined a number of 'recurring themes for geotourism'. These were:

1. There is no generally accepted definition of that geotourism

2. Virtually all countries have some geological resources with the potential for geotourism development

3. The impacts of geotourism are not yet well understood

4. The key to making geotourism accepted by tourists is through proper interpretation

5. Geoparks have the potential to foster geotourism at the community, regional and national levels.

In the intervening period a number of these issues have been addressed, as evidenced by the new content we have proposed in this chapter. First, geotourism has been more clearly defined and is moving towards a more universally accepted definition. We also stated that most countries have the potential for geotourism development. This has also been borne out by the huge array of geo- attractions, products and activities which have been described in this volume, and its companion *Global Geotourism Perspectives*.

Our third point at the time was that the impacts of geotourism are not yet well understood. As we know, sustainability is desired and impacts may be environmental, social/ cultural, and economic. Such impacts can be either beneficial, neutral, or adverse. At this time they are still not addressed in any real form and we have not addressed this pressing issue in this book either. As natural scientists we see the need for a complete volume dedicated to this and so we have left this aspect of geotourism's growth and development to be explored in later research.

Whilst in our previous book we suggested that the key to making geotourism accepted by tourists is through proper interpretation, in this volume we see the huge leap forward made in geotourism interpretation. Many authors have provided sound examples of geo-interpretation while others have moved the debate forward by outlining the importance of interactive, participatory, connective experiences. Others have highlighted the role of technology in the interpretation of the landscape and geology, through the use of MP3 players and mobile phones.

Finally we suggested that geoparks had the potential to foster geotourism at the community, regional and national levels. This is clearly evident with many papers and books written on the subject due to the phenomenal growth of the Global Geoparks Movement in the intervening years. When we began writing our first book in 2003, there were no geoparks in the world. Today there are 64 in 19 countries with many others clamouring to join this global brand. Allied to this growth in geoparks has been a commensurate rise in geotourism attractions.

So where to from here? Our new list above is at least a pointer to tasks which still need to be undertaken. But since 2000 geotourism has grown as a new and emerging form of niche tourism predicated on its connection with the geological environment. Attractions have developed and tours have been set up. The seeds of this new, emerging industry have been planted and individuals, communities, regions, nations and international organizations have taken notice. We predict that geotourism will be the catalyst for the tourism industry in general to gain a greater understanding of the role of landscape and geology in their resource arsenal, just as ecotourism has proved to be the leader in the greening of tourism. Looking at the environment in a simplistic manner, we see that it is made up of Abiotic, Biotic and Cultural (ABC) attributes. Starting with the 'C' or cultural component first, we note that of three features it is this one which is generally the most known and interpreted, that is, through information about the built or cultural environment either in the past (historical accounts) or present (community customs and culture). The 'B' or biotic features of fauna (animals) and flora (plants) has seen a large focus of interpretation and understanding through ecotourism.

But it is the first attribute of the 'A' or abiotic features including rocks, landforms and processes that has received the least attention in tourism, and consequently is the least known and understood. This then is the real power of geotourism, in that it puts the tourist spotlight firmly on geology, and brings it to the forefront of our understanding through tourism. If we can follow through with the ideas in this book then the promise of geotourism and its attendant benefits to geoconservation and geoheritage will be well made. But first, those of us who work in geotourism and see ourselves as its stewards, must ensure that we provide the relevant connection from earth to humans through understanding (our Head) and connection (our Hearts), so that we may return to our places of life and work ready to do something or act (with our Hands) to help in a greater understanding and conservation of the earth's precious landforms and landscape. If we can carry this out then the promise of geotourism will have been reached.

References

Baucon, A. (2009) '*Terragaze Mobile*, A GPS-powered geological guide: information depending on where you are', in de Carvalho, C.N. and Rodrigues, J. (eds), *New Challenges with Geotourism*, (Proceedings of the VIII European Geoparks Conference), Idanha-a-Nova, Portugal, 14-16 September, pp. 56-59.

Brilha, J. (2009) 'Geological heritage and geoconservation in Portugal', in de Carvalho, C.N. and Rodrigues, J. (eds), *New Challenges with Geotourism*, (Proceedings of the VIII European Geoparks Conference), Idanha-a-Nova, Portugal, 14-16 September, pp. 31-35.

Burlando, M., Firpo, M., Queirolo, C. and Vacchi, M. (2009) 'A new strategy to promote sustainable tourism in Beigua Geopark (Italy)', in de Carvalho, C.N. and Rodrigues, J. (eds), *New Challenges with Geotourism*, (Proceedings of the VIII European Geoparks Conference), Idanha-a-Nova, Portugal, 14-16 September, p. 54.

Dowling, R.K. (1976) 'Environmental education', *New Zealand Environment* 16, 24-26.

Dowling, R.K. (2008) 'The emergence of geotourism and geoparks', *Journal of Tourism* 9 (2): 227-236.

Dowling, R.K. (2009) 'Geotourism's contribution to local and regional development', in de Carvalho, C. and Rodrigues, J. (eds), *Geotourism and Local Development*, Camar municipal de Idanha-a-Nova, Portugal, pp.15-37.

Dowling, R.K. and Newsome, D. (eds) (2006) *Geotourism*, Oxford: Elsevier/Butterworth Heinemann.

Dowling, R.K. and Newsome, D. (eds) (2008) *Geotourism* (Proceedings of the Inaugural Global Geotourism Conference, 'Discover the Earth Beneath our Feet), Fremantle, Western Australia, 17-20 August. Promaco Conventions Pty, Ltd, p. 478.

Ferrari, C. and Mase, V. (2009) 'Audio-video geoguide in the Adamello Brenta Geopark', in de Carvalho, C.N. and Rodrigues, J. (eds), *New Challenges with Geotourism*, (Proceedings of the VIII European Geoparks Conference), Idanha-a-Nova, Portugal, 14-16 September, pp.121-122.

Hose, T.A. (1994) *Hunstanton Cliffs Geological SSSI – A Summative Evaluation*, Buckinghamshire College.

Hose, T.A. (1995) 'Selling the story of Britain's stone', *Environmental Interpretation*, 10 (2), 16-17.

Hose, T.A. (1996) 'Geotourism, or can tourists become casual rock hounds?', in Bennett, M.R., Doyle, P., Larwood, J.G. and Prosser, C.D. (eds), *Geology on your Doorstep*, Geological Society, pp. 207-228.

Hose, T.A. (2000) 'European geotourism – geological interpretation and geoconservation promotion for tourists', in Barretino, D., Wimbledon, W.P. and Gallego, E. (eds), *Geological Heritage: Its Conservation and Management*, Madrid: Instituto Tecnologico Geominero de Espana. pp.127-146.

Kavčič, M., Stupar, M., Peljhan, M., Režun, B. and Eržen, U. (2009) 'Geopark Idrija – thematic trails', in de Carvalho, C.N. and Rodrigues, J. (eds), *New Challenges with Geotourism*, (Proceedings of the VIII European Geoparks Conference), Idanha-a-Nova, Portugal, 14-16 September, p. 71.

Kollmann, H.A., Mitterbäck, R. and Weiskopf, K. (2009) 'Intellect and emotion: water and geotourism in the Eisenwurzen Geopark', in de Carvalho, C.N. and Rodrigues, J. (eds), *New Challenges with Geotourism*, (Proceedings of the VIII European Geoparks Conference), Idanha-a-Nova, Portugal, 14-16 September, p. 51.

Malaki, A., El Wartiti, M., Di Gregorio, F., Zahraoui, M., Kharbouch, F., El Mahi, B. and Fadli, D. (2008) 'Volcanic geosites of the Tabular Middle Atlas of Morocco: a tool for public education, recreation and sustainable economic development', in the 33rd International Geological Congress, *IES-03 Geosites and landscape? Conservation and Management Strategies*, Oslo, Norway, 6-14 August.

Mao, I., Robinson, A.M. and Dowling, R.K. (2009) 'Potential geotourists: an Australian case study', *Journal of Tourism* IX (2)

Moreira, J.C., Jorge, M.A., Dropa, M.M., Horodisky, G.S., de Souza, L.F., Mongruel, L., Guimarães, C.J., Maio, C.A. and Stachowiak, P.R.B. (forthcoming) 'The realization of the "Tourism Studies Week – SESTUR" as a mean of disseminating Geotourism in Paraná, Brazil', paper prepared for the Second Global Geotourism Conference, Mulu, Sarawak, Malaysia, 17-20 April 2010.

Režun, B., Peljhan, M. and Kavčič, M. (2009) 'Idrija – Slovenian treasure', in de Carvalho, C.N. and Rodrigues, J. (eds), *Geotourism's Contribution to Local and Regional Development*, Camara Municipal de Idanha-a-Nova, Portugal, pp. 121-137.

Robinson, A.M. and Roots, D. (2008) 'Marketing tourism sustainably', in Dowling, R.K. and Newsome, D. (eds), *Geotourism*. (Proceedings of the Inaugural Global Geotourism Conference, 'Discover the Earth Beneath our Feet'), Fremantle, Western Australia, 17-20 August, Promaco Conventions, pp.303-317.

Slomka T., Kicinska-Swiderska A., Doktor, M., Joniec A. (2006) *The catalogue of geotouristic sites in Poland* (in Polish, English summary), Krakow, Poland: AGH.

UNESCO (2006) *Global Geoparks Network*, Paris: UNESCO, Division of Ecological and Earth Sciences.

Index